THE LITERATURE OF SATIRE

The Literature of Satire is an accessible but sophisticated and wide-ranging study of satire from the classics to the present in plays, novels, and the press as well as in verse. In it Charles Knight analyses the rhetorical problems created by satire's complex relations to its community, and examines how it exploits the genres it borrows. He argues that satire derives from an awareness of the differences between appearance, ideas, and discourse. Knight provides illuminating readings of such satirists familiar and unfamiliar as Horace, Lucian, Jonson, Molière, Swift, Pope, Byron, Flaubert, Ostrovsky, Kundera, and Rushdie. This broad-ranging examination sheds new light on the nature and functions of satire as a mode of writing, as well as on theoretical approaches to it. It will be of interest to scholars interested in literary theory as well as those specifically interested in satire.

CHARLES KNIGHT recently retired as a Professor at the University of Massachusetts Boston, of which he was one of the founding faculty. He is a specialist in eighteenth-century British literature; he has written *Joseph Addison and Richard Steele: A Reference Guide* (1994) and numerous articles for journals such as *Modern Language Review*, *Philological Quarterly*, *Modern Philology*, *Comparative Literature*, and *Eighteenth-Century Studies*.

THE LITERATURE
OF SATIRE

CHARLES A. KNIGHT

Emeritus Professor of English
University of Massachusetts Boston

 **CAMBRIDGE**
UNIVERSITY PRESS

PUBLISHED BY THE PRESS SYNDICATE OF THE UNIVERSITY OF CAMBRIDGE
The Pitt Building, Trumpington Street, Cambridge, United Kingdom

CAMBRIDGE UNIVERSITY PRESS
The Edinburgh Building, Cambridge, CB2 2RU, UK
40 West 20th Street, New York, NY 10011–4211, USA
477 Williamstown Road, Port Melbourne, VIC 3207, Australia
Ruiz de Alarcón 13, 28014 Madrid, Spain
Dock House, The Waterfront, Cape Town 8001, South Africa

http://www.cambridge.org

First published 2004

Printed in the United Kingdom at the University Press, Cambridge

Typeface Adobe Garamond 11/12.5 pt.   *System* LATEX 2$_\varepsilon$ [TB]

A catalogue record for this book is available from the British Library

Library of Congress Cataloguing in Publication data
Knight, Charles A.
The literature of satire / Charles A. Knight.
p.   cm.
Includes bibliographical references and index.
ISBN 0 521 83460 0
1. Satire – History and criticism.   I. Title.
PN6149.S2K48   2004
809.7 – dc21   2003055287

ISBN 0 521 83460 0 hardback

For Kathy

Contents

Acknowledgments

A book that has grown over a number of years quite naturally incurs a number of debts for which I now can only return my thanks. But one debt I cannot pay with thanks is to my late colleague Francis R. Hart, whose early support, intellectual and personal, enabled this project. A number of colleagues, fellow-scholars, friends, and where appropriate, relatives, read sections in their early stages, offered me advice about my plans as they developed, or have otherwise been of significant help: Andrew Boelcskevy, Neal Bruss, Robert Crossley, D. N. DeLuna, Linda Dittmar, Gillian Gane, Gerhard Gerhardi, Dustin Griffin, Phillip Harth, Susan Horton, J. Paul Hunter, Frederick Keener, Dudley Knight, Nathaniel Knight, R. J. Schork, Louise Z. Smith, and Howard D. Weinbrot. Dr. Linda Bree of Cambridge University Press has been a most helpful and responsive editor, the Press's anonymous readers have saved me from many solecisms and errors, and Audrey Cotterell, a sharp-eyed copy-editor, has caught a number of mistakes. None of the above is responsible for those that remain. I am indebted to the following libraries and their staffs: the Houghton and Widener libraries of Harvard University, the Bapst Library at Boston College, the Mugar Library at Boston University, the Healey Library at the University of Massachusetts Boston, the Boston Athenaeum, the Boston Public Library, the British Library, the Library of Congress, and the New York Public Library. The fact that I have written this book while teaching various courses on satire has generated complex relations between writing and teaching. I hope that the research and thinking that has gone into the book has benefitted my teaching, but I know that I have learned a great deal from many of my students, more than I can list. It is also true that writing the book has provided an outlet for ideas I could not develop in class and that teaching has supplied a forum for material I could not include in the book.

Earlier versions of sections of the book have been given as papers for the International Conference on the Enlightenment, the American Society for Eighteenth-Century Studies, the Eighteenth-Century Seminar at the

Harvard Humanities Center, and various colloquia of the English department at the University of Massachusetts Boston. Sections of chapter 1, now much revised and expanded, appeared in *Philological Quarterly* 69 (1990), 131–51, and *Comparative Literature* 44 (1992), 22–41. Part of chapter 2 appeared in *Eighteenth-Century Studies* 22 (1989), 489–511. I am grateful to the editors of these journals for permission to republish.

The love and support of my wife Kathy has been good-humored rather than satiric. Nonetheless, I dedicate this book on satire to her.

Introduction: the satiric frame of mind

Any attempt to account for satire in a general way is caught between two undesirable alternatives. A strong reading of satire is likely to produce sharp and stimulating definitions and distinctions that, if not actually fallacious, are reductive and incomplete. A general, conventional description is likely to be more various and open but also to seem familiar or superficial or disconnected. If the present study fails to steer a safe course between these hazards, it is more likely to become grounded on the shoals than wrecked on the rocks. Although it proposes a governing view of satire, encapsulated in the phrase "the satiric frame of mind," it is more concerned to uncover what satire does than to make authoritative statements about its essential nature. Its explorations begin with linguistic assumptions, though not technical ones, and tend to focus on the pragmatics of satire. Its scope is shamelessly broad: Archilochus to Zoshchenko implies the alpha and omega of the study, although I actually have nothing to say about either author. The selection of examples is based primarily on their relevance to my topics and their interest to me. But others will note relevant and canonic examples that I cannot include, and I could not make room for many satires and authors that I like. Thus I have little to say about *A Tale of a Tub*, although I recognize it as a central and almost defining satire, and I neglect a number of recent Russian satirists – Aksyonov, Zinoviev, Sokolov, and Aleshkovsky, among others – whose work strikes me as significant. I have not set out to cover a circumscribed body of satiric material. Given the indirection of satire, it seems appropriate to begin not by explaining what this book is about but by meditating on a useful emblem of satire – the Greek philosopher Democritus as represented in the seventeenth century by Diego Velásquez. He suggests the shape of the satiric frame of mind, and that shape in turn will suggest the shape of this study.

REPRESENTING DEMOCRITUS: THE SATIRIC FRAME OF MIND

Democritus as laughing philosopher, as polymath, and even as atomic theorist reflects salient characteristics of satire itself, and he has been called as a satiric witness by Juvenal, Burton, and Johnson, among others; the portrait of Democritus by Velásquez intensifies the satiric force of representation. The fact of representation and its non-verbal nature open a range of interpretive possibilities. The portrait, apparently from the painter's early years at court, is, like many of his earlier Seville paintings, almost entirely in brown.[1] It shows a black-haired, profusely mustached, large-nosed man smiling broadly and pointing with his left hand at a globe that sits on a table, along with several books. I have seen at least one reproduction of the painting entitled "The Geographer." The painting may not be a representation of Democritus; the name Democritus may be a representation of the painting. The subject of the painting may actually be one of the jesters or servants that Velásquez loved to paint. (The model appears in a similar painting, probably but not certainly by Velásquez, entitled "Court Jester with a Wineglass.") If the painting represents a geographer, the globe is literal, a tool of the geographer's trade. If it represents Democritus, human nature has been globalized. The representation of Democritus, or of a court jester pretending to be Democritus, changes the nature of the discourse and opens it to satire. (Viewers who are aware that the painting may not be read literally might be tempted to see it, for example, as a mockery of Spanish imperial ambitions.) The painting represented by the name "Democritus," characteristically in the style of Velásquez, thus represents a jester representing Democritus, who points to and laughs at a globe that at least represents humanity but may as well represent (among other targets the viewer might suggest) the folly of imperial ambition. The experience of looking at and interpreting the painting, with its multiple layers of representation, parallels the laughing interpretation of Democritus the painting's subject. The books on the table may indicate the sources of the philosopher's knowledge or may be inaccessible to the jester. Laughter may be the result of knowledge or of ignorance. The laughter of Democritus may suggest that naive viewers are part of the world he mocks or that sophisticated viewers are mockers themselves as well as objects of mockery. The painting is unusually and disturbingly intimate. The jester Democritus invites us with a smile to contemplate the globe at which he points. He shows us his geographic discovery that all the world is foolish. But he laughs directly at us.

There is a close relationship between Democritus the laughing philosopher and Democritus the atomic theorist. Physical reality, he contends, is not the world as we perceive it but rather atoms and their movement. What we see is not what is. The same is true of human behavior, his laughter implies. The skeptical but observant satirist recognizes that some people are evil, but all are foolish not only because they do foolish things but because they are unaware of their folly. They are errant in action but blind in perception. Hence they are incurable unless perception is changed. The effect of the Democritian satirist – the jester pointing his finger at the globe – is to correct perception. But the correction of perception is not effected by admonition – by the translation of behavior into abstract moral language – but by a form of representation so skewed as to allow recognition to take place and to force a new judgment on it, so that viewers recognize that they are what is represented and that what is foolish is them. We become both the subject and object of satire. Democritus as represented by Velásquez manipulates forms and images that engage perhaps unwary viewers and that multiply levels of meaning.

The satiric frame of mind, of which Democritus is an emblem, comprises complex and even paradoxical qualities. Like Democritus, the satirist is a skeptical and bemused observer. Like the jester portraying Democritus, he may be a trickster, an agent as well as an observer, proclaiming truths disguised as lies and directing the action to bring about the ends he has proclaimed (a pattern that will be a matter of major concern in my consideration of satiric performance in plays). As is the case with the portrait, these tricks may engage the ironies of reader or viewer involvement. The satirist is on one hand the dispassionate observer of humanity and, on the other, the irate attacker of particular individuals. His mode of both observation and attack is representation.

The qualities of satiric representation thus echo the paradoxes embodied by its emblematic figure. Satire takes the form of a specific attack, even when the real subject of the satire is not the object of attack. The element of play that usually marks the attack may make matters worse, insofar as, from the victim's point of view, being mocked may seem more distressing than merely being disagreed with, however strongly or publicly, or it may, to the audience, make the attack more tolerable by making it entertaining. The satirist operates not only by representing the satiric victim but by imitating a conventional genre. But satire also imitates what M. M. Bakhtin refers to as speech genres, the characteristic or conventional utterances developed in various spheres of communication, and it imitates these in ways that are rather different from their imitation in non-satiric literature.[2] When satire imitates speech genres, it characteristically makes them ironic, thus opening them to possibilities of meaning that are not usually noticed in ordinary usage. (William Gaddis's novel *JB* is a particularly rich instance of a lengthy work constructed almost entirely out of ironized speech genres. Josef Hašek's *The Good Soldier Švejk* consists largely of stories, speeches, and scenes where the speech genres are ironic in respect to the speaker or listener or the context: Švejk, for example, tells stories that are entertaining to the reader while maddening those to whom they are told.) Both literary genres and primary speech genres thus become both objects and instruments of satiric attack.

Satire is thus pre-generic. It is not a genre in itself but an exploiter of other genres. Nor is it quite a mode in the usual sense. In what I will come to call its Quixotic phase, satire is modal, and the identifying genre – the genre that provides readers with the richest set of signals as to how to read the work – is the novel. In contrast, Lucianic or Menippean fiction is satire that takes the form of a novel. As a pre-genre, satire is a mental position that needs to adopt a genre in order to express its ideas as representation. Satire, like Satan, as "a roaring lion, walketh about, seeking whom he may devour" (I Peter 5.8). It is a predisposition to find an appropriate object of attack that embodies its sense of human evil and folly and to utilize effectively a pre-existent form in order to represent that object in such a way as to make its objectionable qualities apparent. Its characteristic element of attack is often formal: the satirist means the attack but may also use the attack to imply further meaning. Satire's complex manipulations of forms and language in order to arrive at and present its negative representation establish the nature of its frame. Its skeptical attitude towards life, directed at historical examples, makes it a frame of mind.[3] Its character as a frame cannot be separated from its mental qualities because they are linked by perception. The satirist's manipulation of forms may enhance his perception of the object thus framed, but clearly that frame allows the reader to arrive at a parallel perception. Because this parallelism of perception lies at the heart of satiric exchange, a rhetorical approach is inescapable in studies of satire. Satire's often intense concern for historical problems is framed by its imaginative play; the relationship between history and imagination is paralleled by the relationship between perception and communication.

The satiric frame of mind can be located negatively as well. Outside that frame lie some traditional suppositions about satire that, to my mind, do not follow from my description. Primary among these are assertions about the intrinsically moral function of satire. The idea that satire is justified in its nastiness by its moral or didactic functions has run through the history of satiric theory from Casaubon and Dryden to Edward and Lillian Bloom. Dryden summarizes Casaubon: "Moral Doctrine, says he, and Urbanity, or well-manner'd Wit, are the two things which constitute the *Roman* Satire. But of the Two, that which is most Essential to this Poem, and is as it were the very Soul which animates it, is the scourging of Vice and Exhortation to Virtue."[4] Edward and Lillian Bloom take a milder position on the morality of satire: "What we suggest, rather, is the capacity of some satire to effect a gradual moral reawakening, a reaffirmation of positive social and individual values."[5] Wyndham Lewis articulates the opposite position: "It could perhaps be asserted, even, that the greatest satire *cannot* be moralistic at all: if for no other reason, because no mind of the first order, expressing itself in art, has ever itself been taken in, nor consented to take in others, by the crude injunctions of any purely moral code."[6] Of course, as Lewis himself admits, some excellent satire is moral, but many of the qualities revealed by satiric representation – ugliness, clumsiness, foolishness, bad taste, or stupidity – could not reasonably be thought of as immoral. In conventional terms, some satire would be considered decidedly immoral, designed to violate the norms of a moral code it regards as restrictive or wrong-headed. Some satire sees morality as hypocritical, or as a presumptuous effort to assert a social control to which the moralist has no right.

Satire, then, is independent of moral purpose. Its purpose, as I will maintain in discussing Horace's satiric performances, is perception rather than changed behavior, although change in behavior may well result from change in perception. Dustin Griffin appropriately argues that the functions of satire are inquiry and provocation rather than moral instruction and punishment.[7] If the notion that satire is intrinsically moralistic falls, so also does the criticism that satire fails to achieve its purposes because it does not change people's behavior (a criterion that is, of course, virtually impossible to measure). A further corollary that no longer seems tenable is the assertion that satire requires norms and is thus no longer possible in a culture which no longer accepts agreed-upon norms. Individual satirists and satires, acting either as speakers for their communities or as individuals seeking to castigate them for their betrayal of traditional values, may insist quite strongly on norms. But although satires may have norms, norms are not essential to satire, which may make judgments by internal shifts of perception that do not appeal to external values or by identifying the satiric object as ridiculous rather than immoral. Insofar as satire is moral at all, it tends to create its own values. But if it insists on such values, it must give them enough force to encourage readers to transfer them beyond the text. Because of its concern with the actualities of history, satire, more than most literary forms, exists both on the level of text, appreciable aesthetically in its own terms, and on the level of experience, engaged with its audience, whether by sharing the immediate situation of its readers or by arriving at a level of general significance that bridges the remoteness of history.

A further generic complication of satire is its relationship to a variety of analogous or overlapping forms. Satire's relationship to comedy will demand my attention in considering satiric plays (chapter 4), though I cannot pretend to establish a definitive distinction. But I will not undertake the task of distinguishing satire from irony, burlesque, caricature, lampoon, travesty, pasquinade, raillery, billingsgate, diatribe, invective, imitation, mimicry, parody, jokes, hoax, and spoof. Critics of satire might be tempted to see many of these forms as sub-genres within satire itself, as weapons by which satire wages its attacks. But many of them, perhaps all of them, have an independent status and emerged in the critical vocabulary independently of satire. Thus while I am making rather broad claims for satire, I do not want simply to establish satire as the governing genre of a large literary territory. Citizenship in that territory, it seems to me, does not require much proof, and its inhabitants come and go with the appropriateness of the occasion. But irony of perspective and the parody created by satiric borrowing seem central qualities of the satiric frame of mind. Irony corresponds to the dislodged perspective from which the subject of satire is perceived within the formal frame, and parody corresponds to the imitated or borrowed form of the frame itself.

One further quality of the satiric frame of mind needs to be noted, and that is its apparent gender exclusivity. Women, of course, are prominent enough groups within the satiric frame; their status as satiric victims, from Juvenal's sixth satire to the present, is familiar. The lineaments of the female satiric victim in the late seventeenth and eighteenth centuries have been traced by Felicity Nussbaum.[8] What makes satire more-or-less a masculine genre is not a gender exclusivity (satire and tragedy for men, comedy and lyric for women) as it is the fact that women as a gender were treated as an identifiable group, while men (as men all know) are merely people. Satire of men is thus satire of human nature, but satire of women is satire of a particular variety of people. I discuss satire of groups as an aspect of satiric nationalism (chapter 2), but not as an aspect of satiric gender, largely because Nussbaum has discussed gender so well. Nussbaum has little to say, however, about the relative silence of women as satirists. That men should treat women as a group distinct from general (that is, masculine) humanity is regrettable but not surprising. What demands more attention is why women did not respond in kind – why there is so little satire written by women, and why so little of that satire is written against men. The question is important in itself, but it also serves as a reminder of some salient features of satire.

There are two major elements that seem to discourage the emergence of satire written by women. Satire is not, on the whole, private and domestic. It tends to be concerned with public issues and with public examples of those issues. Thus in societies in which women are confined to the private sphere and in which writing of any sort by women is considered unusual or inappropriate, women's writing of satire seems virtually unthinkable. Moreover, satire is a transgressive genre, based on the socially objectionable element of attack, often personal attack. If it often requires male satirists to take a defensive, apologetic position, it places women, who assume a suspicious position even as writers, in a nearly untenable role. Thus it is not surprising that for most of western history, women have not been part of the main stream of satiric writers. Women who did write satire before the twentieth century, either did so privately or anonymously (Lady Mary Wortley Montagu), or were in other respects more-or-less notorious figures already (Aphra Behn, Delarivière Manley). Satire among women authors tends to take the form of a mode, so that women who wrote for the stage (as in the case of Behn's attack on the social and sexual pretensions of City merchants in *The Lucky Chance*) or who wrote socially significant novels (Burney, Edgeworth, Austen) could introduce satiric elements. Perhaps the most successful satire by a woman in the eighteenth century, Jane Collier's *An Essay on the Art of Ingeniously Tormenting* (1753), adopts the mock advice form of Swift's *Directions to Servants* to apply it, with several layers of irony, to anyone interested in stimulating domestic discomfort. Collier effectively applies ironic satire to private life, but most satire by women takes the form of satiric fiction.

Perhaps the most salient example of satire that addresses specifically the issue of gender from a feminist point of view is Charlotte Perkins Gilman's *Herland*, in which a young man writes what turns out to be a parody of a boy's adventure story recounting his journey with two friends to a hitherto unknown land of women. The land is utopian, and the satiric force not only derives from the contrast of "Herland" to the rest of us but from various misunderstandings by the young men. Satire in the twentieth century often takes the dominant form of fiction, where, as I will struggle to suggest in chapter 7 on satire and the novel, the genres overlap considerably. Such writers as Edith Wharton, Stella Gibbons, Muriel Spark, and Fay Weldon indicate the range of satiric fiction open to women. The emergence of women as reporters and columnists means that women assume a place as journalistic satirists. The emergence of women as recognized practitioners of a genre is followed by the emergence of women as satirists in that genre. The virtual absence of women as satirists before the twentieth century (and hence their absence from much of this study as well) seems an instance of the historical exclusion of women from authorship, from public activity, and from controversy.

THE SHAPE OF THIS STUDY

The form of my book follows the two dimensions I have suggested for the satiric frame of mind: ironic perspective on the historical subject and parodic borrowing of a literary form. The first half of the study deals with "satiric boundaries." The first chapter, on definitions of satire, somewhat prolongs the present introduction (thus violating a boundary) by considering the efforts of various definitions of satire – especially figurative ones – to mark off the boundaries of satire itself. But in the course of that exploration, the function of satire to make and protect boundaries is discovered. In the two chapters that follow, on satiric nationalism and satiric exile, boundaries become literal, and I try to determine satire's perspective on its historical subject by looking at the position of the satirist, in the case of nationalism, within large historical communities or, in the case of exile, excluded from them. In keeping with the historical focus of these chapters, the first looks at satire in relation to emergent nationalism in eighteenth-century France and England, and the second considers satiric exile in the last half of the twentieth century.

The second half of the study looks at "satiric forms," the relationship between pre-generic satire and the genres which it uses as its frames. I have used the most conservative delineation of genres – drama, poetry, novel, and journalistic prose – to identify some of the possible connections that I found interesting. The temptation of this approach is to use the pattern of classification and exemplification that I have found of limited value in other studies, and I think I have successfully avoided or disguised this method by concentrating on particular relationships between satire and its host and by reading exemplary texts in ways that allow me to build theory from interpretation. In discussing dramatic satire, or satiric performance, I pay little attention to contemporary performance theory that takes performances rather than texts as the subjects of critical scrutiny. I am particularly interested in tracing a dramatic pattern by which central characters, who may or may not be sympathetic, become satirists themselves by undertaking or staging a performance designed to expose the hypocrisies that otherwise dominate the play. In chapter 5 I extend the idea of satiric performance by seeing verse satires in the long eighteenth century (1660–1830) as a series of performances that were significantly modeled by Horace.

The concept of performance, as I see it, is a useful way of replacing the familiar satiric persona with a more flexible (and more historical) approach that accounts simultaneously for satiric sub-genres and satiric speakers. I develop this approach by pairing Horatian satires with eighteenth-century poems, usually not conscious imitations of Horace, that represent similar performances.

The relationship between satire and the novel, the subject of chapter 6, is difficult to sort out, in part because both genres are so broad and vaguely defined and in part because any connection between the two defies the distinction, which I find questionable in itself, between satire as an independent form and satire as a mode. Despite the difficulty of working out a stable notion of their relationship, the overlap between satire and the novel suggests a series of topics – the treatment of the "other" in novels and satire, the nature of Menippean satire, and the historical movement of satire into the novel in the eighteenth century and, in part, of the novel into satire in postmodernism. The function of satire outside the traditional genres of imaginative literature is the subject of my final chapters. Because satiric prose is such an extensive subject, I have limited my consideration to satiric treatment of the press by the press, and that limitation returns me to the pragmatic models I discuss in my second chapter. Examination of a relatively obscure political debate in the early eighteenth century (involving, among others, Swift, Steele, Defoe, and Manley) generates the notion that such satire operates not primarily by attacking the positions, behavior, and arguments of antagonists but by attacking their authority and capacity to communicate. That notion is both extended in significance and narrowed in scope by a consideration of attacks on the press by the Austrian satirist Karl Kraus. Kraus serves a further function for this study: as the great twentieth-century exemplar of the figure of the satirist, he brings it to a fitting conclusion.

Although the boundary I draw between boundaries and forms grows from my view of historical irony and formal imitation as essential constituents of satire, that boundary is permeable, and satires I consider under the category of forms frequently establish, violate, and play with boundaries both real and figurative. But this is inevitably the case in a kind of literature that is identifiable by both the drawing of boundaries and the imitation of forms. Whatever else may be accomplished by the critical movement through satiric boundaries and forms, I extend the scope of satire beyond the customary concentration on formal verse satire and Menippean satire by discussing novels, plays, and journalism. I have tried as well to incorporate a variety of figures absent from standard treatments of satire.

My understanding of satire, I thought, might be expanded by considering unfamiliar examples and seeing what conclusions I could draw from them, as I sought not merely to apply external theory to texts but to see what theoretical implications could be drawn from texts themselves. This approach, of course, has various limitations. In some cases obvious canonic satirists (Wyndham Lewis, for example) and canonic satires (*A Tale of a Tub*) go virtually unconsidered here, though their full consideration in other studies provides some consolation. Although I have tried to deal with Latin, French, and German texts in their original languages, the scope of my study exceeds the range of my linguistic abilities, and where I have had to rely only on translation, my discussion tends to shift to a somewhat higher level of generalization. The breadth of my study necessarily implies its incompleteness, but completeness seems illusory in describing a form as various and shifting as satire. Although the description is incomplete and tentative, it seeks to suggest a complex portrait of the satiric frame of mind.

PART I

Satiric boundaries

CHAPTER I

Imagination's Cerberus

SATIRIC DEFINITIONS

Cerberus is the three-headed dog who guards the gates of Hell – the bane of visitors from Hercules to Robert Graves. He has an ambivalence character- istic of dogs: he greets the dead who enter but seizes upon those who seek escape. This mixture of welcome and despair makes him a fitting emblem of satire, and the classical association of dogs with cynics allows him further levels of meaning. Whether as guard dog or yapping cynic, he retains the same powerful satiric function: his role is to protect the living from the dead. I am less concerned with his exactness as an image than with the pos- sibilities of an emblematic and Cerberean mode of defining satire. Satire, like Cerberus, functions to mark and defend boundaries. My object here is to see the ways in which it in turn may be bounded by definition.

Edward Rosenheim's definition of satire as an indirect attack on historical particulars, especially if one adds the characteristic feature of humor, is, with some adjustment, inclusive enough to serve as a working definition.[1] Nonetheless, some indirect attacks on historical particulars – Solzhenitsyn's *Cancer Ward* and *The First Circle*, for example – do not seem to be satires, and other works that have traditionally been considered satires may lack one or more of the terms that constitute Rosenheim's definition. Hence satires that suggest a general state of confusion or chaos, such as Nathaniel West's *The Day of the Locust*, may lack a particular target, since all particulars are governed by the broad assertion of chaos. The problems of inadequate inclusion may be partly resolved by looking at Rosenheim's definition as formal rather than essential. That is, as matter of form a satire may attack clear and specific historical material, but these formal characteristics may not be important to the work or its enduring satiric power. When satirists attack a clear and specific target, they may, of course, be primarily interested in displaying their virtuoso capacities to insult, but usually they attack for a commanding reason which they openly articulate or cunningly imply.

That reason, rather than the attack it provokes, becomes the real subject of the satire. The continuing significance of this general point and the pleasure provided by the virtuosity the satirist has displayed in attack are the reasons we continue to read satires long after their immediate target has been forgotten.

Satire's movement from attack to these larger targets reflects, then, the alternative notion of satire as an open and exploratory form, designed to pose questions and raise problems, suspicious of conventionally moralistic conclusions and those who pronounce them.[2] The combination of this skeptical suspicion (implying a certain distance from the object under consideration) and a sense of outrage sufficient to have prompted the satirist to write (implying a degree of emotional involvement) serve as dimensions for the satiric frame of mind that expresses itself through the formal characteristics of attack, indirection, and historicity. Seeing satire as a pre-generic form, as a frame of mind, does not locate it securely as an exclusive category allowing some works to be included and more left out. Satire's boundaries are opened by its adaptation of other forms, so that it is both pre-generic and modal. There are satiric novels (*The Way We Live Now, Little Dorrit*, and *Emma*), and there are novels that are satires (*Roderick Random, Bouvard et Pécuchet*, and *Decline and Fall*), but the distinctions between the two are approximate and subjective, depending in large part on how the generic energies of the text strike a particular reader in a particular reading. The question is not usually whether the identification is correct but whether it generates interesting ideas about the work identified or fruitfully extends an idea of satire and its functions. Satire asserts borders of various different kinds, to play with the elements on either side of those borders, and to use different territories as ways of adjusting perspective or distorting what is seen. But satire itself is defined by highly permeable borders. Its Cerberean functions might be set briefly in the context of genre itself and looked at through the lens of metaphor as an alternative mode of definition.

There seem two distinguishable but overlapping functions for generic definition. Defining genre is a way of explaining or exemplifying the content of literature, of mapping its territory. Genres are described and bounded according to the dominating features of their nature and their relationship to other genres. Satire archetypally becomes the "mythos of winter,"[3] but there are three other seasons as well and, in Frye's familiar classification, the archetypal co-exists with historical, ethical, and rhetorical approaches. The force of such classification lies less in the location of exclusive literary forms than in the suggestive power of its symbols. These operate on a different level when definition functions as a guide to the interpretation of individual texts rather than as a global configuration of literature. Genre offers preliminary and hypothetical signals of form and meaning. The function of genre to define prior expectations regarding an unread text may become more specific when the text is placed within sub-genres, when expectations become more sharply determined by early events in the text or redirected by later allusion. (When Milan Kundera asserts his interest in the satiric novels of Sterne and Diderot, we look in his works for characteristics that they share those not only with these writers but with others – Borges, for example, or Machado de Assis – who acknowledge a similar debt to Sterne.)[4] Without abandoning the notion that satire is pre-generic, one can assert that it functions as a genre in generating initial interpretive expectations.

But both genre and sub-genre tend to be replaced by the interpretive clues provided by a given text, which may distinguish itself from its apparent genre or may claim kinship with a variety of different, perhaps even conflicting genres. Genre may not disappear as an interpretive guide, but its force is weakened by the particular information that emerges from the text itself. That text may, in turn, expand or redefine the nature of the genre in which it appears. Genre may return even after the interpretive signals of a given text have replaced the signals of a particular form, becoming a way of explaining a text to those who have not read it and validating subjective readings of it. It remains one of the few ways of tagging and tracing literary species and of developing significant hypotheses about large elements of literature itself.[5] Although the less constrictive sense of genre as an early interpretive guide whose functions shift throughout the reading of a text avoids the rigidity that is perhaps inevitable in global projects of defining genres, a particular problem emerges in the case of loose, baggy genres, such as satire or the novel. Tight, rigid descriptions are inadequate to the variety and complexity of such forms, but loose, flexible descriptions tell us relatively little about the shape and content of the text we begin to read. My argument here is that the bind facing readers of broad genres may in part be avoided by thinking of genre in metaphoric terms and that satire especially benefits from such description. In particular, the etymological definitions of satire suggested by Diomedes are usefully metaphorical. Such a way of approaching the definition of genre is appropriate to the imaginative nature of literature and to the role of satire in embodying, articulating, and defending that imaginative discourse.

DEFINING AS METAPHOR

Diomedes was a fourth-century Latin grammarian, a seldom read author of a highly categorical, insistently organized, generally derivative, untranslated

discussion of the finer points of rhetoric and poetics which includes a definition of satire that I shall treat in a way perhaps inappropriate to his broader
(that is, more limited) intention.[6] I suspect that the suggestive nature of his
definition of satire derives from his lack of interest in a minor genre, and
that I may be undertaking a satiric treatment of an unserious definition.
Perhaps because his comments on satire are grounded in often unlikely and
unverifiable etymologies, he has been disregarded in most recent treatments
of satire. But because he postdates the body of classical satire, his alternative
definitions can be regarded as the theoretical summation of a completed
corpus which, in turn, exercised a particular influence on later satirists.
Hence the meanings to be gleaned from his definition may be apparent in
later satires, though the scope of the present discussion is primarily classical.

Diomedes, though not as strongly as Quintilian before him, notes the
particularly Roman nature of satire ("satura dicitur carmen apud Romanos"
["satire is the name of a verse composition amongst the Romans"]). His
identification of satire as Roman verse is narrow, but in other respects
his approach is broadly suggestive. He conjoins three distinguishable and
contrasting categories: satire may be old or new, definite or indefinite in
form, defamatory and carping in the manner of Greek Old Comedy or
miscellaneous in the manner of early Latin verse:

nunc quidem maledicum et ad carpenda hominum vitia archaeae comoediae char-
actere compositum, quale scripserunt Lucilius et Horatius et Persius, sed olim
carmen quod ex variis poematibus constabat satura vocabatur, quale scripserunt
Pacuvius et Ennius. [At present certainly it is defamatory and composed to carp
at human vices in the manner of the Old (Greek) Comedy; this type of *satura* was
written by Lucilius, Horace, and Persius. Previously however *satura* was the name
of a composition in verse consisting of miscellaneous poems, such as Pacuvius and
Ennius wrote.]

Diomedes goes on to list four rather different etymological explanations
of satire. He connects satire with satyrs (*satyroi*), with a dish of diverse
fruits (*lanx saturae*), with a sausage or stuffing (*farcimen*), and with an om-
nibus law (*lex per saturam*). Before examining these etymologies metaphorically, we must address the suspicion that such an approach imposes
anachronistic readings upon the material. In some cases self-consciously
anachronistic readings may be useful and appropriate, but here the relationship between what Diomedes may have understood by his etymologies and
my own figurative use of them is more complex – historically appropriate
in some respects, self-consciously anachronistic in others. The distinction
demands elaboration.

The *locus classicus* of philosophical etymology is the series supplied by Socrates in the *Cratylus*.[7] He has interposed between Cratylus, who argues that there is a natural connection between names and the things named, and Hermogenes, who asserts that the connection is conventional and even relative. Socrates argues against both positions, and his dialogue with each antagonist implies the presence of the other. He rejects both arguments; he shows that both, rather than being contradictory, are actually the same; he agrees in part with both but finds each so reductive as to miss the point which, with appropriate irony, he cannot claim to know himself. In his etymological display (391–422) his purposes are complex and in several senses duplicitous. Names of various classes (heroes, gods, elements, abstract qualities) are etymologically explored to reveal the hidden or original names that lie within. The comedy pits the literal mind of Hermogenes against the analogical bravura of Socrates, and it leads to the threat that etymology may only produce an infinite regression of names deriving from other names (422). Socrates' etymological exercise is itself a sign that has multiple ironic meanings in Plato's three-way dialogue: "the disclosure accomplished through the etymologies is immersed in the dramatic unfolding and is principally an illuminating by way of allusion and implication."[8] Plato's example reinforces the playful stance I seek to adopt towards Diomedes' etymologies of satire.

Diomedes is less likely to have developed his etymological interests from Plato than from Varro and Quintilian, among other rhetoricians.[9] Varro, from whom Diomedes may have derived much of his definition of satire,[10] devotes six books of *De Lingua Latina* to a general discussion of etymology (Books 2–4, lost) and to a treatment of the origin of individual words (Books 5–7). His concern is with the nature of change in language, with its patterns and with the various ways of explaining it. Some derivations are obvious to common people or, as in the case of poetic usage, to grammarians; changes in common usage are explicable in philosophical terms, but there is a further level which Varro describes in terms of religious mystery and which is approached not through certainty but through hypothesis (5.7–8). Quintilian notes that the suggestions of Varro and others are sometimes unsupported fancy, hardly worth serious consideration (1.6.34–38). He finds etymology a useful tool for interpretation (1.6.29) and helpful in distinguishing correct forms from barbarisms (1.6.30). But explanations of words are not always reasonable, and hence "perverseness of judgment leads to the most hideous absurdities" (1.6.32). These approaches to etymology are not concerned with relationships between languages. (For Socrates the discovery that a word is foreign puts an end to philosophical investigation.)

They are often playful exercises in fantasy. Isidore of Seville (*c.*560–636 AD) used etymology as a means of fixing his discussions of knowledge in general. His treatment of the etymologies themselves exploits artificial and circumstantial resemblances between words. As Henry Osborn Taylor commented some years ago, they reveal a "fantastic caprice" and "a mind steeped in allegorical interpretations": "this is not ignorance so much as fancy."[11]

But playfulness and fantasy are not meaningless. It is important to avoid a naive literalness in looking at such etymologies as these of Diomedes. The location of meaning through the identification of difference gives etymologies their metaphorical quality. The derivation of *satura* from *satyroi* is simply wrong, but the other definitions of Diomedes preserve the proper derivation of *satura* from *satur* (full). Bent, as he seems, on error, Diomedes particularizes his definitions by attaching *satura* to other terms – a dish, stuffing, a kind of law. This perverse specification makes his etymologies figurative rather than literal. But I do not seek merely to recover what he intended by defining through metaphorical connections; his etymologies invite his interpreters to explore the connections suggested, to look at them in light of examples, and to allow the possibilities of meaning to converge on the identification of genre. Metaphorical definitions of particular genres enact the metaphorical force of genre itself, which emerges from the same acts of locating, elaborating, exemplifying, and drawing together the various possibilities of meaning. Etymological equations of a word with its source (or sources) can thus be read as the figurative conjunction of vehicle with tenor, so that the essential question is not whether these etymologies are philologically correct but what they tell about the word being defined. I want to explore in detail each set of suggestive meanings implied by Diomedes' equations. The multiple origins that Diomedes sets forth confirm the multiplicity and the multigenerity of satire itself. They point to characteristics that are not only diverse in possible references to satiric texts but various in eliciting the personal values of satiric readers. Such metaphorical defining seems to conjoin the indeterminacy of texts with the instability of readers, without sacrificing the function of genre to signal useful guidelines for interpretation.

Satyroi

Satura autem dicta sive a Satyris, quod similiter in hoc carmine ridiculae res pudendaeque dicuntur, velut quae a Satyris proferuntur et fiunt. [Now *satura* is so called either from the Satyrs, because in this type of poem (i.e. *satura*) laughable and shameful things are related in the same way even as those recited and performed by the Satyrs.]

The connection of satire with satyrs is a literary mistake, popular in the Renaissance, when it was used to justify the rude, spirited, and defamatory character of satire.[12] Satyrs are woodland spirits – goatish, mischievous, and self-indulgent. They represent an alternative to humanity, a recombination of rational and animal qualities in which moral self-restraint has been replaced by unbridled hedonism. Subordinate to desire, intelligence is expressed not in reason but prankishness. To see satire in satyric terms drains it of conventional moral significance. In the world of satyrs, the preeminence of personal pleasure renders social morality irrelevant. Hence the treatment of satire as satyric explains or justifies its anti-social or even dangerous character. The nature and consequences of the *satura–satyroi* equation are apparent in the insults and dirty jokes of Martial and in the Saturnalia.

Martial did not regard his epigrams as satires (cf. Book XII, epigram 94), but they exemplify the primitive impulses of praise and blame, and the most memorable of them embody the satiric function of personal attack. Their form carries Horatian *brevitas* to its ultimate limit.[13] A poem as short as two lines must launch itself towards its victim (often through a well-placed vocative), must identify the fault of which that victim is guilty, and must condemn it in a witty way. In a flash the grammatical connections fall into place, and the acerbic dig both identifies and castigates the victim's failings. The metric and stylistic compression of the epigram intensifies its capacity to distort and insult. Its linguistic intensity formalizes the insult but gives it a privileged status, freed from the social restraints of conventional speech. By addressing its victim, the epigram contrasts to Lucilian satire, which rarely faces its victim directly, and hence it performs what we hardly can ourselves. However clever we may be, time, place, and the flash of wit seldom conjoin, as they do in Martial's contrived epigrams, and social rules hardly allow us to level such insults. Martial's virulent wit against a named victim allows us to witness destructive attacks beyond social rules and our own capacities. The epigram imitates a speech occasion we can rarely carry out, and it fulfills not the noblest but the most satyric aspects of our nature. In contemporary society its place is taken by the political cartoon, and the cartoonists seem to occupy the same protected position as the epigrammatist.

Although Menippean satire and similar works fashionably described as "Saturnalian" often possess a scatological glee like that of the epigram, they manifest an alternative reading of the satyric equation. Saturnalian satire is represented by a range of satire from Horace (*Satires* 2.3 and 2.7) through Seneca's *Apocolocyntosis* to the *Symposium* of Julian the Apostate.[14] Martial excuses the naughtiness of Book XI on the grounds that it was written for the

Saturnalia (Book XI, epigrams 2, 6, 15). Cronos in Lucian's *Saturnalia* has abandoned moral responsibility for merriment and equality. Saturnalian satire replaces the conventional by the natural. But that temporary replacement is complicated by identifying the conventional with the moral. On one hand the satiric insulter (like Martial) can indulge in direct condemnation that the false hierarchy of ordered society prevents. On the other hand, the reign of Cronos replaces moral judgment by the amoral self-indulgence of satyrs. If the satyric model seems to replace convention by unbridled license, thereby verifying the need for conventionality as a means of social control, it may also postulate a humane and affective force that the artifices of official culture cannot fully suppress. In both cases the derivation of *satura* from *satyroi* defines satire's power to articulate elements in our personal, public, and physical lives that cannot be expressed by conventional genres; it presents satire as a release from repression.[15]

Lanx saturae

Sive satura a lance quae referta variis multisque primitiis in sacro apud priscos dis inferebatur et a copia ac saturitate rei satura vocabatur. [Or it is called *satura* from a platter which was laden full with a large variety of first-fruits, and used to be offered to the gods in the cult of the ancients; and from the abundance and fullness of the dish it was called *satura*.]

Diomedes suggests that satire derives from a platter of diverse fruits offered to the gods. The derivation suggests the mixed and abundant nature of satire as a form (as in the mixture of poetry and prose that identifies Varronian satire as a particular type). The sacrificial offering of fruit suggests two distinct relationships between the natural and the divine. On one hand, natural objects may be symbolically united to the supernatural by a human offering that represents the spiritual motivation of the offerers. The literally impossible connection becomes possible by the intention of the sacrifice and by the priestly role of the sacrificers. The magic nature of the sacrifice underlines the wistfulness of a finite, tangible offering to the ethereal and infinite. But an alternative theology views the sacrifice as eminently possible because the natural is itself the generous product of supernatural blessing. The offering gratefully acknowledges that contingent relationship: the first fruits are offered to the gods from whom all fruits derive. Aspects of the ancient cult to which Diomedes refers reappear in the Christian view that the incarnation does not reject the natural things of this world but, by uniting the human to the divine, gives them transcendent meaning. This view, both pagan and incarnational, makes the natural an appropriate offering for the gods, and its propriety is heightened by the role of satire in purging natural impurities. The appearance of grotesques in the arches and buttresses of cathedrals locates the incarnational significance of satire.

In the contrasting eschatological tradition of *contemptus mundi*, which rejects the natural for the supernatural, the role of satire is not curative. The satire of Lucian and Swift implies the inadequacy of natural experience, even without articulating a religious alternative. The religious satirist accepts pessimism with an equanimity that derives from the knowledge that there is a truth elsewhere. The gift of fruit is an ironic gesture precisely because it cannot be accepted (or because the only acceptable sacrifice is Christ's). Early Christian interest in Juvenal (and Christians seem to have revived a satirist in whom Romans had little interest) seems appropriate: religion legitimates, indeed blesses, satire's worldly pessimism.[16] The incarnational and eschatological views imply opposing ideas of satire's functions: satire purges to realize the blessings of incarnation, or it reveals the radical disorders of a world that must be transcended.

The religious implications of sacrifice imply richer and more metaphorical connections that may be useful compared to the distinction between "angelic" and "diabolic" laughter made by Milan Kundera in *The Book of Laughter and Forgetting*.[17] The incarnational view may be identified with Kundera's description of angelic laughter, which, in his complex parable, is completely affirmative but imitative of the laughter of devils. In the angelic world satire has no place, for if everything is laughably holy, there is no need for satiric correction. The laughter of the incarnation subverts diabolic laughter by filling infernal gaps of meaning with the promise of angelic hope, but angelic laughter cannot be sustained – at least not by humans. Diabolic laughter is possible only in a secular culture, for if transcendent meaning is possible, then secular meaninglessness is untroubling. Just as angels are deluded by absolute meaning, devils are deluded by absolute meaninglessness, and satire, operating by exploring contrasts, is an exercise in the humanity of relativity.

The tension between incarnational and eschatological satire receives profound and brilliant play in the *Moriae Encomium* (Praise of Folly) of Desiderius Erasmus. Folly is both the deliverer of this mock encomium and its universal subject. Her speech follows traditional patterns of classical and medieval rhetoric.[18] She practices the intellectual methods of oratory, philosophy, theology, and textual interpretation that she castigates as foolish, creating a complex and satisfying network of logical fallacies. Preeminent among these fallacies is her habit of singling out particular features of the foolish activity that she identifies. Those features are then seen either as essential to such good activities as marriage, friendship, and social life in general or typical of such harmful ones as war, gambling, drinking. Folly's essential purpose might be foolishly described as cultural hegemony. She seeks to assert her true and universal divinity by fallaciously connecting all forms of human activity to herself. But the cost of her universality is her inconsistency, for she has to change her character to make it appropriate to the intellectual and behavioral territories she conquers.

That shift is characteristic of her rhetorical position as it is deployed over the structure of her oration, which moves from incarnational to eschato-logical satire. Critics agree that (after Folly's initial comic self-presentation) the structure of her speech falls into three sections. In the first and by far the longest part (to page 76 in the Miller translation) Folly considers the plight of ordinary folk and argues that she is the source of personal hap-piness and great actions.[19] Her position is a sympathetic one: human life would be unendurable without illusion, and folly thus allows us to survive. The position she assumes is thus a comic and pretentious equivalent to that of Christ. In this world of sin, she argues, it is Folly who redeems us, becoming the universal Goddess incarnate. Although Folly identifies some behavior as truly foolish, she argues that she, usually in the form of illusion, is a necessary condition for most of the relationships humans find essential. Her position is (ironically) a responsible one: she enables significant action, while the skepticism and pessimism of wisdom render action impossible. Having established this complex but relatively clear incarnational position, Folly reverses it in the next section of her speech. Here she argues that the wise and learned, her enemies in the first section, are also her worshipers, and they are joined by examples of secular and religious power. Folly's procedure at this point is Juvenalian, condemning directly, describing sub-classes of folly, and providing examples. Her pattern of attack on powerful people makes explicit the criteria hidden in her attack on the learned. If people in power (monarchs, popes, bishops) considered the actual duties of their offices, they would act out of a disciplined sense of public good. But fortunately for themselves, their folly lies in their lack of thought, and hence they engage in the typically foolish and essentially corrupt practices that Folly describes.

Folly seems to follow the same procedure as she begins the final section, which argues that she is supported by classical and religious authorities, including Christianity itself. Her citation of classical authorities amounts to the self-interested teasing of texts that she condemns in the learned, and her discussion of scriptural interpretations joins such text-teasing with far-fetched metaphorical explanations (124–27). But as she turns to Christianity itself, she shifts her position once again. Whatever primary satiric functions the middle of her speech has fulfilled, it is also a transition from her incarnational view to her final eschatological one, from her early claim that she is the incarnate Goddess to her final claim that she is the essence of Christianity: "the happiness which Christians strive for with such great effort is no more than a certain kind of madness and folly" (132), a folly that is the rejection of worldly considerations, *de contemptu mundi*. Unlike the worldly, "the pious strive with all their hearts to reach God himself, who is purest and simplest of all; this world takes second place, and even here they place most stress on what comes closest to him, namely the mind; they pay no attention to the body, they condemn and avoid money as so much trash" (134). Having reached this point, Folly foolishly and mysteriously breaks off; she has forgotten what she has said and hence can reach no conclusion.

But we readers, who pretend to wisdom, may be able to supply such a conclusion. Folly has been split between incarnational and eschatological satire. She redeems the world, she has claimed, by making action possible and life endurable. The powerful and learned, who ought to bear the responsibility for good action, are motivated instead by the folly of self-interest. But Christian piety rejects the world to concentrate on the purity and simplicity of God. It is not enough to argue that the final section "denies none of the perceptions embodied in the first two" and "essentially transvaluates both visions from its sure, eternal perspective."[20] Rejecting the secular temptation to see Christian wisdom as another illusion fostered by Folly, and the literary temptation to see it as a conventional palinode, we seem left with the final advice not to accept the usually innocent illusions that allow us to endure the world but rather to reject the world altogether. Does this last point, as Folly herself seems to suggest, represent the ultimate of Christian and Platonic mysticism, or is it the ultimate failure of human responsibility? To answer this question it is necessary to turn not to the absent conclusion but to the Preface.

The Praise of Folly is dedicated to Thomas More, and *Moriae Encomium* is also praise of More. W. David Kay describes More as "the ideal wise man who gives Erasmus' ambiguous title its special resonance"; Richard Sylvester asserts that "whatever Erasmus means by 'Folly' involves all that he understands and loves in Thomas More".[21] More is, as Erasmus points out, "far removed from the fact of folly" in his playfulness, intelligence, and gentleness (2). The question of how this mock oration can be in praise of More (beyond More's evident capacity to appreciate both its ironies and its purposes) coincides with the question of how Folly's shifting position can be interpreted, especially in light of her praise of Christian mysticism as the ultimate manifestation of Folly. Folly, as we have seen, makes three arguments: she is necessary to human action; she is characteristic of false learning and power; and she is manifested in the Christian rejection of the world. Her negative terms imply a positive one that is made up of the central elements of each argument. True wisdom consists of pious, learned, responsible action. This combination of the active and contemplative life, of the incarnational and the eschatological, is precisely the position occupied by More, who is praised because he is the human embodiment of the secret answer about which the text itself is silent.

Farcimen

Sive a quodam genere farciminis, quod multis rebus refertum saturam dicit Varro vocitatum. [Or (it is called *satura*) from some kind of stuffing which was crammed full with many ingredients and called *satura* according to the testimony of Varro.]

The equation of satura with *farcimen* (that is, with stuffing or sausage) stresses the function of satire as a mixture to be consumed by its reader.[22] In standing both for the feast as the satiric social occasion and for satire itself as the food, it seems the broadest equation proposed by Diomedes. Dustin Griffin notes that food in satire is traditionally considered "as a sign of festivity and as an index of character," but adds consideration of "the ambiguous character of the satirist's invitation to the feast, and the persistent associations among feasting, violence, and mortality."[23] In the *Satyricon* of Petronius, for example, food is virtually as important a topic as sex, and the work, especially in the "Cena Trimalchionis," its most extended and complex episode, explores the perversions of eating and the distortions of meaning that may accompany the corporate act of consumption.[24] Eating is a recurrent topic of satire: Horace recounts the dinner unsuccessfully provided by Nasidienus Rufus (*Satires* 2.8), Juvenal anticipates the humiliating repast of Virro (*Satire* 5; cf. Pliny, *Ep.* 2.6), and Lucian narrates a contentious wedding feast attended by philosophers (*Symposium*). Dining sets social conventions against the actual behavior of host and guest alike.[25] It offers occasions for private satiric performances rather than the public recitations that Juvenal deplores (*Satire* 1) and Horace avoids (*Satires* 1.4). The audience of satire, like guests at a dinner, is a circle of intimates, in whose presence readers may feel honored. The *satura–farcimen* equation and its rhetorical extension imply the equivalence of eating and interpreting.

Sausage is a literal metaphor: it is itself a stomach, the image of its own destiny. The *satura–farcimen* connection captures, among its other qualities, the mirror images of much satiric rhetoric. The act of consuming is self-consciously represented by the object we consume, and by eating it we transform the image into reality. Just as the stuffing of the sausage serves as model for the stuffing of the eater's stomach, the process of reading transforms the satiric representation of experience into the personal experience of those who read it. The stuffed sausage further suggests the intrusion of various and spicy substances into a flexible but limited form. The *satura–farcimen* equation, operating as metaphor, implies satire's self-conscious imitation and the threat that the form it imitates will ultimately prove inadequate to contain its message. The threat that the skin will burst and the contents pour out (the sausage as "banger") may provide a moral warning against overeating, but it also reflects the satiric rebellion of message against the confining characteristics of genre.

But François Rabelais, the preeminent theorist of eating and drinking as interpreting, introduces an alternative gustatory metaphor to embody the relationships of form to content, or language to meaning. His work is itself farced with the physical and social joys of eating and drinking, from the obstetrical consumption of tripe by Gargamelle to the concluding Oracle of the Holy Bottle. But in the "Prologue" to *Gargantua* he introduces his satire as an apparently barren bone which the wise and persistent dog cracks to arrive at the marrow within, and in the "Prologue" to *The Third Book* the tub of Diogenes becomes a cask of wine drunk by both author and reader.[26] Satiric meaning is profound, difficult to reach, at odds with its unprepossessing external appearance. The Rabelaisian program corrects the popular impression of satire as lively but superficial; the return of Cerberus the dog as cynical interpreter heightens the contrastive nature of the equation of satire with food. In Horatian and Petronian formulations the egocentricity of which both gluttony and bad manners are signs overrides the good will implied by dining and imposes on the proper expectations of guests. The more subtle Rabelaisian formulation sees self-indulgence as a paradoxical image of the search for truth. The satirist and the reader, joined by the conventions surrounding mutual consumption, may also be joined by their shared possession of hidden meaning.

Lex per Saturam

Alii autem dictam putant a lege satura, quae uno rogatu multa simul comprehendat, quod scilicet et satura carmine multa simul poemata comprehenduntur. [Others however think that it derives its name from a law, *satura*, which includes many provisions at once in a single bill, for it is evident that the verse composition *satura* also comprises many poems at once.]

Like the equation of satire with *farcimen*, that of satire to the *lex per saturam* indicates both a characteristic topic and a basic method.[27] Law is a natural satiric topic because, like the ritual of dining, it both embodies a quality of civilized society and is shaped by an artificial system that at times conflicts with actual behavior. But satire may complain more broadly about the problems of legal control, and the failures of law may imply the general collapse of social management, as in the case of Juvenal. The attack on law in *Satire* 13 takes the form of a traditional *consolatio*, but the loss of money, for which the victim is here consoled, seems a trivial satiric subject. Juvenal's friend Calvinus has lost the money that he entrusted to a friend who later swore he never received it. Juvenal urges Calvinus to take his losses without complaint rather than seeking legal redress. Juvenal's position seems inconsistent with the anger of his earlier satires, for the offense against Calvinus involves a breach of personal trust, a betrayal of friendship, and the violation of a sacred oath. The poem is anti-Saturnalian in comparing Calvinus' moral naiveté to the simplicity of the Golden Age, when dishonesty was a prodigy (lines 38–59). But in revealing that Calvinus' public folly lies not in his attachment to his money but in his expectation of honesty, the counsel to suppress indignation becomes an ironic pose that underscores the real sources of indignation. The indignant satirist poses as cynical consoler; it is as if Alceste, in Molière's *Misanthrope*, pretended to be Philinte.[28]

The court of law is an ideal location for the observant satirist because it gathers and concentrates the range of human evils within an institution of dubious utility: "humani generis mores tibi nosse volenti / sufficit una domus" ("If you want to find out the truth about human nature, it's all contained in one courtroom").[29] Juvenal asserts that other sources of moral justice are no more effective in achieving social order than is the law. Religion is no longer a sanction: the evil-doer is either an atheist or willing to risk divine displeasure for tangible rewards. The twinges of bad conscience are overridden by time and by human reversion to evil. As victim, Calvinus is helpless because law, religion, and conscience are ineffective, and he is foolish because he does not see his helplessness. If indignation is replaced by despair in the rhetoric of the poem, behind that rhetoric – even in the fact that the poem is written at all – satiric irony remains, however ineffectively, the last expression of vestigial values.

Although Juvenal implies that the moral outrage expressed by satire remains when such vehicles of social justice as the courts have failed, satire itself often parallels legal patterns of attack and defense: the satirist is a prosecutor, but he is also a defendant against the attacks of those he has offended, as are Horace in *Satires* 2.1 and Lucian in *Piscator* and *Bis Accusatus*.

Like Diomedes' other etymological metaphors, the equation of satire with law offers alternative possibilities, depending in this case on the nature of the distortion satire brings to the legal situation. Satire as a legal vehicle forces into the open arguments that might otherwise remain unexamined and subjects them to ostensibly unprejudiced analysis. Hence satirists may distort the courts positively by making them a disinterested forum for apology. But when satirists distort the courts negatively, the result is satire upon law itself, upon the impossibility of just social control in a world where the instruments of that control have themselves become corrupt. The legal metaphor thus provides alternative models for the defense of satire and for the satiric prosecution of evils beyond the reach of the law.[30]

LUCIAN: THE BOUNDARIES OF DISCOURSE

Diomedes' definition of satire substitutes the questionable authority of etymology for the constrictive authority of Aristotelian classification, much as Wittgenstein's application of family resemblances and strands of meaning allows a more open and indeterminate form of defining.[31] It pretends that causality is implied by metaphorical linguistic relationships. Once the temptation to accept that pretension is overcome, the connections embedded in etymology become variously suggestive, and the situation is opened more broadly still by alternatives whose range includes different but overlapping possibilities. The advantage of pseudo-etymological definitions is that they do not fix the interaction of defining and interpreting by setting static requirements for a rigid form; they suggest interpretive possibilities that are both clear and powerful. Diomedes' definitions are not only open but inconsistent. The religious view of *satura* as *lanx* suggests both the incarnational view that the natural is redeemed through satire and the eschatological position that satiric revelation of meaninglessness allows the perception of transcendent meaning. The Saturnalian view that satire allows anti-social behavior and makes the shameful laughable conflicts with the idea that satire, like law, is an agent of social control. The equation of *satura* with *lanx* sees food as offered to the gods, while its equation with *farcimen* sees food as enjoyed by its consumer. The proposal of diverse definitions, partly overlapping and partly conflicting, points to qualities of satire without seeking to encompass the genre as a whole. Diomedes' mode of defining implies that satire serves diverse and even conflicting ends simultaneously.

But the question raised by such diverse interpretations of Diomedes' etymological equations is whether, in effect, they point to any meaning in particular. If not, I have rescued Diomedes from deserved obscurity only to allow an excursion through various satiric occasions, and one may justly complain that the alleged value of metaphorical defining lies in its capacity to suggest possibilities without encompassing anything. Diomedes' definition may be saved from such objection by looking at the satiric functions that are common to its diverse suggestions and are embodied by its metaphorical way of defining. Its openness underlines satire's proclamation that the special value of literary thought is its distinction from other ways of thinking, especially the philosophical. Freed from Aristotelian categories, the metaphoric etymologies of Diomedes identify essential forces of satire itself and, despite his general rigidity, his definition of satire shares the literary program of the genre he defines. The nature and importance of that program seem most powerfully apparent in Lucian, whose satiric range reflects the breadth of Diomedes' equations.[32]

Lucian is notably perceived as an entertainer,[33] but the truth of that view gains seriousness in light of his criticism of rationality itself. The range of Lucian's satire suggests a persistent if not systematic treatment of intellectual discourses – philosophical and historical, rhetorical and sophist – as instances of the futility of human activity.[34] Fools may undertake an intellectual program for which they are unsuited (*Adversus Indoctum*), or the gullible may be deceived by the pretentious claims of the intellectual life (*Hermotimus*). We all know ourselves, Lucian seems to assert, to be motivated by self-interest, avarice, and love of fame. Intellectuals claim to be motivated by a pure love of truth, but the claim is pretentious on the face of it and is belied by the behavior of those who make it (*Symposium*). Hence philosophy is best represented by an auction (*Vitarum Auctio*), true histories are never written (*Vera Historia*), and rhetoric becomes the self-important display of trivia (*Rhetorum Praeceptor*). Beyond Lucian's paradoxical description of the philosopher as both eunuch and adulterer (*Eunuchus*) sits the richly endowed Chair of Philosophy for which he applies; his interest in the job ought to disqualify him.

Lucian's ironies extend beyond his belaboring of intellectuals; he raises questions that are as troubling as any. Are there genuine criteria for sincere and significant communication, or are human beings too manipulative and deceptive, too prone to illusion, for a relationship of trust to be established between an utterer and an audience? If we accept, even provisionally, the conditions apparently necessary for communication – that speakers mean what they say and that their meaning refers to a reality that is independent of their articulation – then we open ourselves to victimization by the deceitful talkers of Lucian's dialogues, and language becomes a vehicle for illusion.

Lucian's manipulations of the conversational situation are evident in the *Philopseudes*, which in several senses parodies Platonic dialogue. Its title is an inversion of the intellectuality it attacks: in place of the philosophers, the lovers of truth, it presents us with the lovers of falsity. Its narrative form is reminiscent of Plato's *Symposium*, but here the conversation suffers from the absence of Socrates. The assembled philosophers represent opinions so various that they may not share the assumptions about truth that are prerequisite to intelligible discussion. In the absence of such assumptions they seem to have agreed upon a principle of dialogue that is, perhaps, not unknown in academic circles. They have agreed to credit each other's dishonesty. (Indeed, if you agree to accept my fantasies here, I certainly must accept yours in return.) But Tychiades, the naive interlocutor, is unaware of this conversational postulate. He expects the philosophers, in accordance with their profession, to speak the truth; indeed, he comically insists on it. But each philosophical story is designed to test the agreement that no tale, no matter how tall, exceeds the height of credibility. As new philosophers enter, they too, however skeptical in their professional lives, play their role in the accumulation of dishonesties, and the game goes on until the story, familiar to us from Dukas and Disney, of the sorcerer's apprentice. The story itself, as the transformed broom unstoppably brings in buckets of water, seems emblematic of the intellectual situation. Once the magic of academic untruth has been worked, inundation is irreversible. But the honest seeker assumes a position similar to that of the magician who alone can return the broom to its usual inactivity. He can leave the scene to tell it to another; the philosophers are caught by the rising levels of dishonest discourse.

Taken as a whole, Lucian's satires make a frontal attack on the falsities of intellectual life. He typically imagines an ideal viewpoint from which human activity appears futile, and from which not even the feats of heroes can overcome the finality of death (e.g., *Charon*, *Icaromenippus*). If action is ultimately futile, systems of human belief, constructed to deny that futility, must be illusion or deceit. Faced by the realization that activity is fruitless, humans accept a justifying untruth. Lucian recognizes the need to believe and the apparent impossibility of belief. But he does not view this paradox as painful. If human activity is futile in the face of death, and if the pretense to knowledge is almost inherently questionable, true entertainment (as distinct from the pursuit of false goods) reemerges as Lucian's positive principle. All people are prone to illusion, but clearly some illusions are especially dangerous, injurious to the believer or to others. In face of the human need to believe and the impossibility of belief, Lucian asserts the importance of rejecting false belief, even at the risk of nothingness. But the risk

of nothingness is not unbearable. The need to believe can be filled by the
fantasy embodied in Lucian's satires. Fantasy admits its untruth, as Lucian
does in the Preface to *Vera Historia*. Because fantasy is the self-conscious
enjoyment of significant untruths, it both escapes from the delusions of
false belief and provides the vantage-point from which truth becomes apparent. Imagination breaks the limitations of disciplined thought, whose
inadequacies it exposes both by testing them against ordinary experience
and by asserting that experience becomes meaningful only when the clouds
of delusive reason are dispelled.

The satiric parody of more rigid genres, here exemplified by Lucian's
parody of Platonic dialogue to attack philosophers, parallels the satyric
release from constraining social conventions. The rigidity of a parodied
form often makes it a useful vehicle for the satiric revelation of incongruity;
a satiric but unparodied formal rigidity may establish the privileged nature
of the attack, as in the case of Martial. But rigidity conflicts with the anarchic
qualities implicit in the *satura–satyroi* equation; hence it in turn emerges
as the object of satiric attack. The parallel literary and moral impatience of
the satirist, illustrated by Juvenal's indignation at both the public recitation
of poetry and the ostentatious display of wealth (*Satire* 1), allows readers
to propose, extend, and enjoy connections between art and reality and
between the text and the self. Because both art and life become objects of
satiric judgment, satire combines the signals of other genres with its own
and serves as the self-appointed censor of art itself. Still more significantly, it
articulates the power of imagination in contradistinction to the traditional
forms of intellectual discourse that so often are its targets. Satire serves
as the Cerberus of art itself, guarding the kingdom of imagination from
the self-important pretensions of rational order and intellectual truth. Its
celebration of imagination explains the failure of many satires to propose
practical remedies for the evils they expose.

The traditional justification for satire's uncomfortable attacks lies in their
moral utility. Many satirists adopt the Juvenalian position, usually self-
serving, that they are defenders of real but neglected standards of moral
truth, though Juvenal himself sometimes located moral truth in a comic and
mythic past inhabited by virtuous but muscular matrons and their acorn-
belching husbands (*Satire* 6, lines 9–10). The moral pretenses of satire
enact the legal metaphor: satire operates effectively when legal institutions
themselves are corrupt, or the case-load is too heavy, or the faults are beneath
the seriousness of legal prosecution. But the *satura–satyroi* equation implies
the reverse situation – not where human evils are judged against the criteria
of moral law, but where the hypocrisies of moral law are revealed by actual

human behavior. Lucian's critique is more basic still: when the noise of intellectual discourse has been stilled by comic and ironic attack, silence remains, and when the voices of false discourse are no longer heard, genuine ethical statements become possible.

The satiric relationships between imagination and rationality, between art and life, join with other binary relationships. The satiric medley, however motley, implies contrastive pairs, both of substance and of form. Such pairs are implied by the double possibilities to be found in Diomedes' etymological metaphors (satire as a celebration of the unofficial or a warning of the need for official control; satire as incarnational redemption or eschatological rejection of the natural; satire as the pretentious dinner or the secret food of the initiates; satire as the agent of law or the attacker of legal institutions). Such binary contrasts may seem versions of the contrast between truth and falsity, but in the course of any given satire the nature of truth itself may become uncertain and confused. Satire often proposes apparently hard-edged contrasts to reveal the absurdity of human pretensions, but flaws and uncertainties appear in the contrasts themselves. The contrast between truth and falsity gives way at last to the opposition of doubt and certainty. What begins with Cerberus at the gates of Hell concludes on the brink of dubiety. Satire, like Diomedes' definition of it, proposes sets of alternatives at different or even inconsistent levels, thereby creating multiple possibilities for uncomfortable awareness and allowing imaginative truth to emerge from real uncertainty. The nature of such imaginative truth is manifested by the indirect, polysemous, and metaphorical nature of the genres through which it is perceived.

SATIRIC DISGUISING

The protean quality of satire is generally recognized.[35] It may explain the impossibility of defining satire or may itself define it. To grasp that defining quality with the intrepidity of Menelaos grasping Proteus may force the god to speak. Menelaos needed to learn from Proteus how to expiate the divine offense that had left him becalmed, but to do so, he required both disguise and the privileged information given to him by the god's daughter Eidothea. After he succeeded, unpleasantly dressed as a seal, in holding Proteus despite his transformations, to arrive at last at the god's true statements, virtually all he got, in the short run, was bad news (*Odyssey* 4.350–587). The image of Menelaos weeping for his brother is an instructive caution for readers of satire. Satire's power to reveal offenses and their remedies is elicited by the patience of readers in enduring its consciously adopted disguises and in penetrating its various generic and linguistic appearances. But it is only by persisting through the series of changes that one may seek to generalize about satire's identity.

Perceiving the identity of satire, if we are to be instructed by the myth, must begin with the process of disguising. A number of critics have noted the tendency of satire to parody or imitate other genres or literary models: "traditionally satire has always borrowed its ground-plan, parasitically and by ironic inversion, from other forms of ordered expression in art or in life."[36] James W. Nichols distinguishes between parody ("an imitation and alteration or distortion of the style or structure of an original for the purpose of criticizing it") and what he calls "pattern" ("any adaptation of an original for satiric purposes when the chief purpose is not parody"). Nichols goes on to distinguish between patterns that imitate specific literary works, those that imitate "originals found in a number of literary works," and those that are not literary at all.[37] The basic process which Nichols identifies as "pattern" is described by Leon Guilhamet as "transformation." For Guilhamet, satire is essentially "a borrower of forms", which it "de-forms" and transforms into "a new generic identity" by disruptive, fictive techniques.[38] Satire's imitative quality should be considered in light of the observation that genres are transmutations of speech acts into literary form: "In a society, the recurrence of certain discursive properties is institutionalized, and individual texts are produced and perceived in relation to the norm constituted by this codification. A genre, literary or otherwise, is nothing but this codification of discursive properties."[39] Close to the essence of satire as a genre is its powerful tendency to disguise as independent speech acts, whether formally recognized literary genres (as in mock epic), informal, sub-literary genres (the travel books imitated by *Gulliver's Travels*) or non-literary speech (the conversation in Horace's *Satires* or the correspondence in the *Epistles*).

The recognition that satire operates by imitating other genres or occasions of speech raises two issues. (1.) If satire can be identified by imitation, how can such imitation be distinguished from the mimesis characteristic of traditional genres? (2.) If, as Todorov asserts, genres are themselves a kind of speech act, what are the nature and consequences of satire's relation to speech? How is satiric imitation distinct from the imitation characteristic of literature as a whole? If linguistic imitation is a universal quality of satire, what are the satiric elements that it identifies in particular works? To investigate the generic distinctiveness of satire's linguistic imitation, I shall turn at first to the satiric nature of Aristophanic drama, and then to the distinction between satiric and poetic discourse, as adumbrated by

Horace and as developed by Lucian's treatment of Plato. These distinctions should allow some tentative conclusions about the relationship between mimesis and satiric imitation. The significance of satiric imitation, I shall argue, lies in its particular character as a speech occasion, describable in linguistic terms. The familiar model of communication set forth by Roman Jakobson may, like the advice of Eidothea to Menelaos, provide a strategy for encountering satire's protean nature. Jakobson's model engages both the triadic relationship of speaker, message, and audience and the linguistic functions of checking the contact of speaker and listener, explaining the code, and referring to external objects. The discrimination of satiric imitation from other kinds of mimesis and its description in terms of Jakobson's model for communication may reveal the prophetic identity that Menelaos discovered or may console us for the discovery that prophecy is the last disguise.

SATIRE AND THE IMITATION OF ACTION

"The objects the imitator represents are actions" (Aristotle, *Poetics* 2). In drama this imitation takes place through the personification of signs. The actor represents a character by using not only language but gesture and appearance. Dramatic imitation is thus distinct from other mimesis. The epic poet describes but does not impersonate the actions he imitates, even when a character's words are quoted directly; the epic describes a fixed past that is literally unrepresentable.[40] The personification of signs in drama seems to conflict with the strong self-consciousness of satiric imitation. For much non-dramatic satire, the presence of the satirist is a means of generic dislocation. The satiric speakers of Horace and Juvenal may be in part a fiction, as W. S. Anderson has noted,[41] but we tend to use those speakers as authorial images onto which we can project what we see as the author's intentions (or, when appropriate, from whose statements we distinguish those intentions). We can read irony in part because we are aware of an ironist, whose typical absence from plays yields the form of irony that we distinguish as "dramatic." The distinction between dramatic mimesis and satiric imitation is significantly clear in the satiric plays of Aristophanes. They are not merely imitation with the additional satiric feature of attack; their nature depends upon a self-conscious fantasy emerging from comic production, from the ritualistic treatment of plot, from formulaic structural patterns, and from the imitative pattern that P. Rau has described as "paratragodia."[42] In the fantasy world of Aristophanic comedy, the imitation of action is replaced by a formula in which an unlikely hero conceives an unlikely idea, persuades a chorus that it is practical, overcomes the hostility of antagonists, enacts it, and through it triumphs over a series of satiric victims.[43]

The fantasy of the plays lies in the improbability of the original idea. We agree to set aside our independent moral evaluation of that idea because the hero's conversion of the chorus stands for our own conversion, because it claims to solve a real problem, because, however fantastic, it touches and releases basic impulses in our own socially repressed nature, and because its fantasy defies normal moral judgment. (The idea of birds constructing a city to blockade heaven renders a bit pointless the objection that such a scheme is impious.) Our relationship to the play as audience gives the hero's fantastic scheme its thematic significance. Our willingness to withhold conventional judgments allows us to participate in the hero's individualistic triumph over authoritarian restraints. The simplistic fantasy releases us from the restraining complexity of actual experience.

The imposition of a subjective fantasy upon objective reality transforms the lowly protagonist into a triumphant hero. The hero's central encounter with the chorus enacts the conflict between aggressive individualism and the defensive community. Because the audience shares the civic problem from which the comic idea emerges, it takes a personal interest in the hero's triumph. At the same time, the play is a contestant in the dramatic festival, so that art conjoins with life when the victories of the hero and the playwright unite. Satiric imitation in Old Comedy creates a variety of contexts, allowing characters to assume multiple symbolic identities or to switch, with startling effect, from one identity to another, and these dislocations are often triggered by plays upon words.[44] The multiplication and shifting of levels allow each play to treat different topics simultaneously, but common to all is the instability of discourse itself, whether in philosophy, persuasive oratory, or poetic drama. The fantasy world of the hero replaces reality with its linguistic misrepresentation. The hero uses language to convince others that his metaphorical substitution is a real equation, and this persuasion parodies the political rhetoric of Athenian democracy. The linguistic replacement of reality by metaphor parallels the comic hero's disguises, and these have greatest force when poetry itself is the means of disguise (in *Acharnians*, *Thesmophoriazusae*, and *Frogs*). The complexity of Aristophanic language thus lies in its ingenuity of metaphor, in its attachment to the comic idea, in its overlapping of linguistic substitutions with the rhetorical experience of the audience, and in its parody of poetry's equation of words and experience. Aristophanes can function simultaneously in the worlds of civic reality and theatrical fantasy because imitation multiplies the possible levels of meaning. When Greek drama moves from a structure of imitated speech to a plot that imitates action, it moves from the satire of Aristophanes to the comedy of Menander.

In later plays (as in the "rehearsal" plays of the Restoration and eighteenth century) satiric disruption is achieved by reintroducing an absent author. In Jacobean plays the author may be replaced by a characterized satirist: Shakespeare's Timon is an archetypical figure of the misanthropic satirist;[45] Alvin Kernan describes Thersites (*Troilus and Cressida*) as "the most intense image of the satiric character in all Elizabethan literature";[46] John Peter sees Vendice (*The Revenger's Tragedy*) in the tradition of medieval complaint.[47] Such personification locates satire in the speech of dramatized satirists. Hence the Jacobean plays that seem most satiric are those which retain the strongest elements of the Aristophanic pattern. In *Volpone* and *The Alchemist* the disreputable hero undertakes a satiric idea requiring disguise, and he dupes a series of generalized characters in scenes that resemble the episodes of Old Comedy.[48] What Jonson adds to the formula is the victimization of the comic idea itself. Its satiric force derives from its ingenious engagement with the values of its dupes, and its exposure exposes the satiric hero as well. Jonson combines this modified Aristophanic pattern with the exploitation of particular jargons and general discursive models. The essential force of satiric plays, especially in Old Comedy, lies in the audience's recognition that the play's real subject is not the action it imitates. The satiric theater transforms this recognition and subsumes it within the play itself, so that both the text and the rhetoric of production point to the real subject outside the action. Its discourse becomes both the subject and instrument of attack. In an ultimate sense dramatic satire replaces the mimesis of action through discourse with the imitation of discourse through action.

SATIRE AND THE IMITATION OF LANGUAGE

The personal presence of the satirist in much non-dramatic satire is significant in various ways described below, but among them is his self-consciousness about satiric discourse. The distinctions Horace makes between poetic and satiric language in *Satire* 1.4 exemplify the force of this awareness. Horace sees his own satire as a variant on Lucilius, who followed the example of Old Comedy but changed the metrics ("mutatis tantum pedibus numerisque," line 7). Horace himself mockingly claims not to write poetry at all. The essence of poetic language is its forceful spirit and energy ("acer spiritus ac vis," line 46), and he quotes a poetic

passage that retains its force through its pretentious metaphor, even when
its words are rearranged. Horace's claim to improve Lucilius lies in his high
art, especially in an area of least importance to his bombastic quotation –
the arrangement of words in lines and sentences. Horace's point is that
satire need not seek the metaphoric force of poetic diction but may imitate ordinary language in ways essentially different from poetic discourse.
The elegance of Horace's satiric talk embodies his self-presentation as the
modest man of moral rectitude, but its art reinforces our sense that the
conversation is imitated – not spontaneous but constructed for complex
ends.

Horace's subtle efforts to separate the pretentious language of conventional poetry from the conversational constructions of his own Lucilian
satire gain clarity and force in light of Barbara Herrnstein Smith's distinction between natural and fictive utterances.[49] Natural discourse consists of
historical utterances, strongly lodged in an actual context from which they
derive meaning. Much written discourse (hence much literature) records
such natural discourse. Fictive discourse is not the record of natural utterance but its imitation, the creation of speech in imaginative literature.
"The distinction lies . . . in a set of conventions shared by poet and reader,
according to which certain identifiable linguistic structures are *taken* to
be not the verbal acts they resemble, but representations of such acts."[50]
Fictive utterance, unlike natural discourse, lacks meaningful contexts, and
its indeterminacy requires the reader to supply such contexts in ways that
respond to the text. Smith further distinguishes between poetry and fiction
by asserting that poems imitate speech while fictions imitate inscriptions
(such written records as biography and history). My problem with Smith's
distinctions is that they seem to place fictive utterance where I seek to put
satiric imitation. My claim, in extending Nichols, Stopp, Guilhamet, and
others, is that satire is essentially imitative and that it may imitate either
natural or poetic utterance. There are a number of small distinctions that
may allow satiric imitation and fictive discourse to share the same space,
but it seems economical and fruitful to point to a large one deriving from
the patriarch of mimetic theory. Book 10 of Plato's *Republic* sets forth the
familiar distinction among Ideas, their imitation in appearance, and the
imitation of appearance in art. Discourse seems to function as yet another
level of imitation: natural discourse imitates appearance; fictive discourse
imitates natural discourse. But satire, in this quasi-Platonic model, serves
as what might be called "meta-imitation." It imitates either appearance or
art in order to criticize; it deliberately distorts its model to expose it. While

imitating fictive discourse, it restores the context that fictive discourse excludes, and the restoration of context reveals the imitated discourse as not only fictive but unnatural.

The Platonic situation is made quite clear by Lucian's *Piscator*. Lucian (or his satiric alter ego) is mobbed by philosophers who are angered at his attacks, and his efforts to escape by quoting Homer and Euripides (an Aristophanic as well as Platonic touch) are unsuccessful.[51] Plato himself charges that the satirist has attacked philosophers in philosophical dialogues (*Piscator* itself is a dialogue, of course). The satirist answers by calling Philosophy herself as his judge (thus moving his imitation, benignly in this case, to legal discourse). He identifies himself as Parrhesiades (Free-speaker) and his vocation as exposing pretension. He has practiced this vocation out of love for Philosophy herself, whose image had been tarnished by the misrepresentations of her self-styled followers. Lucian thus provides an exact play on mimetic levels: the satirist uses Dialogue (imitates a mode of discourse) out of love for Philosophy (Idea) to reveal the falseness of philosophers (appearance). The program that Lucian establishes for satire is inherently a Platonic one. Loving but not knowing Truth, the satirist imitates discourse either to reveal its falseness or the falseness of appearances, thus preserving the integrity of Ideas. To shift Platonic metaphors, the satirist is the man who shouts "Shadows" in a crowded cave.

The mimetic situation which Lucian enacts for philosophy, philosophers, and philosophical discourse resembles the situation Smith describes for fictive discourse. Poetic discourse (the imitation of natural discourse) foregrounds figurative and oral connections in transmitting its message.[52] The imitation of inscriptive discourse in fiction, however, restrains the intensity of discourse found in poetry, so that the speech of fiction tends to be closer to that of natural utterances. As a result, satire, when it imitates either novelistic or natural utterances is more likely to uncover, as Lucian does in *Piscator*, the disjunction between appearance and reality. But when it imitates the fictive discourse of poetry, satire tends to reveal the disjunctions between the discourse it imitates and the familiar world of appearances. Satiric meta-imitation reveals the improprieties of other discourses in the Platonic hierarchy. Poetry imitates speech, in Smith's terms, to intensify discourse through figuration – to say what cannot be said; satire imitates both natural and fictive discourse to expose unreality or to reveal the problems of the discourse itself. Poetry claims a metaphoric force that satire usually discards, except in parody, to exploit the rhetorical possibilities of informal speech occasions.

SATIRE AND MIMESIS

The differences between satiric imitation in particular and generic mimesis in general should serve as a guide for interpretation. (Indeed, readers usually know that a given text is satiric and must be read with particular care.) My efforts to distinguish satiric imitation from the dramatic mimesis of action and the poetic (or fictive) mimesis of ordinary discourse seem to yield differentiae that can be usefully seen in terms of the meaning theory of H. P. Grice.[53] Grice argues that there is a contractual relationship between speakers and listeners, based on the listener's assumptions that the speaker's utterance will provide sufficient but not excessive information, that it will provide information believed to be true and supported by adequate evidence, that it will provide relevant information, and that it will do so clearly, unambiguously, concisely, and in an orderly manner. When there are obvious violations of this cooperative principle of communication – violations that the speaker might have been expected to recognize – the listener might assume that the speaker is incompetent or, for some reason, opting out of the communicative contract. But the speaker's violation may be an effort to communicate. Thus the following interpretive process seems to follow: readers recognize that a violation has taken place; they infer that the speaker is not opting out (speakers seldom do in literary works, or there would be no point in writing them); they infer that the speaker is aware of the violation and not merely making a mistake; they infer that the speaker, as they do, recognizes the specific and generic assumptions in effect (for example, that an argument should be directed against another position that people actually hold); they must then hypothesize plausible meanings that fit both the offensive utterance and the cooperative principle, and that seem relevant to the context.

Thus when Swift's arguer against abolishing Christianity apologizes for stating an unpopular position, the fact that no one actually proposed the position he attacks and that it certainly was not popular will lead us to hypothesize an explanation for the inconsistency, since we recognize that the first four assumptions must be true. When we check the notes, we realize from the context that Swift must be talking about the Test Act. But even if he is, his position still violates the principle of providing clear, concise, relevant, and not excessive information. Therefore, we recognize that he must be talking not only about the Test Act but more general beliefs and behaviors. Grice's model is incomplete in its exclusive concentration on a speaker's meaning, but its concern for what speakers must mean when their meaning must be different from what they say and its assertion that such meaning can be recovered from the speaker's violation of an implicit contract with the audience make it particularly useful in accounting for the meaning of a genre that is essentially transgressive. Three consequent principles serve to differentiate satiric imitation from ordinary mimesis.

(1.) In addition to what Grice refers to as maxims necessary to normal communication, literature and discourse generally involve conditions of politeness which may interdict certain kinds of statement (academic disputation, like debates in Parliament, may include attacks on an antagonist's competence but not honesty). Such conditions of politeness usually do not establish meaning, but they often establish generic features: the opening of a telephone conversation usually reveals the kind of conversation intended. In the case of satire, the ubiquity and intensity of attack, especially when the satirist is not justified by personal motives, violates the usual social prohibition against unmotivated assault, verbal or physical. The self-conscious satirist seeks to explain these assaults (as both Horace and Juvenal do), or he asserts that the substance of his attack or its value as entertainment justifies the anti-social act of attacking.

(2.) In a number of cases the imitative nature of satire is clearly indicated by the statements of the author (Lucian's *Vera Historia* and historical narrative), by the nature of the text (*Gulliver's Travels* and travel narratives), or by both. But the distance between the satiric text and its imitated sources may also be indicated by linguistic and formal disjunctions. Horace claims his satires are conversations, and their conversational elements are important clues to interpretation; but the artfulness of Horace's verse conflicts with conversational spontaneity. The awareness of such conflict may signal the presence of satire.

(3.) The audience of satire becomes aware that its subject lies significantly outside of the text itself. That subject may be another text or the other text may be imitated without providing a subject. Hence *I Samuel* is not the subject of *Absalom and Achitophel* but provides a dislocating source for imitation, and insofar as the subject of the poem is the Exclusion Crisis of 1680, it is independent of Dryden's text. In Old Comedy this awareness of an external subject takes place when the audience perceives the hero's comic fantasy as the response to an evident problem of the city itself.

These satiric signals are closely interrelated. An objectionable element of attack is the historicity of its victim: no reader objects when Micawber attacks Uriah Heep (though, of course, every reader agrees that the attack is deserved). The self-consciousness of imitation may motivate or establish the linguistic and formal disjunctions that identify the work as satiric. Because any particular signal may be present in a non-satiric work, the combination of signals is crucial in informing readers that they are confronted with a satiric text which must be understood as such.

The satiric signals provided by the justification of attack, by the consciousness of imitation, by linguistic or formal disjunctions, and by the extra-textuality of subject imply the distinctiveness of satire as a genre, despite its protean manifestations. Because satire both imitates genres and shares many of their distinctive features, it may appear either as a meta-genre or as what Alastair Fowler describes as mode.[54] The nature of satire, however, lies not only in its common generic signals but in its quasi-Platonic program. Satire imitates discourse (either ordinary language or what Smith calls "fictive discourse") to stress its inherent contradictions, to reveal the discrepancies between discourse and the appearances it claims to represent, or to unveil the conflicts between those appearances and the deeper reality that they in turn imitate. The prophetic power of Proteus correlates with the relentless nature of his disguises.

THE RHETORIC OF MIMESIS: THE BASIC TRIAD

Satire does not so much provide interpretive rules as thrust us into a communicative situation whose interactive nuances require us to behave in certain ways in order to understand. Though Roman Jakobson's familiar model of communication is schematically constructed for purposes rather different from the exploration of satire, it provides independent terms for describing satire's linguistic and imitative nature. It precisely locates a number of features that have already become apparent in distinguishing satiric imitation from mimesis, and it provides specific categories that characterize the functions of satire. Because it incorporates a range of functions, it allows the connections between satiric forms and functions to be more carefully articulated. In Jakobson's model, communication includes both a horizontal axis, consisting of the basic triad of addresser, message, and addressee, and a vertical axis, intersecting with the horizontal at the point of the message, that comprises the context within which the message takes place and to which it refers, the necessary contact between addresser and addressee, and the code in which the message is transmitted. But in given statements the role of any term may become dominant, and hence Jakobson recasts the model in terms of the functions fulfilled by such dominance. On the horizontal level, the position of the addresser is taken by the emotive function (expressive of the addresser's feelings), the position of the addressee by the conative function (seeking the addressee's reactions, as in

imperatives), the position of the message by the poetic function (embodying the self-referentiality of art). On the vertical axis, context is revealed by
the referential function; contact between addresser and addressee is checked
by the phatic function; the operations and even meaning of the code are
explained by the metalinguistic function.

The imitative and self-conscious nature of satire usually gives prominence to the vertical axis of Jakobson's model, but satiric self-consciousness
derives from particular problems within the basic triad. The triadic relationship of utterer, utterance, and listener subsumes a number of mutual
understandings necessary to adequate communication. These understandings include elements of propriety that seem violated by satire's tendency
to make attacks normally regarded as inappropriate or even unethical. In
satire the addressee and addresser must agree that the author's imaginative
attack and the reader's actual condemnation are justified by the values articulated or implied by the satire, or by the aesthetic qualities of the work.
The mutual nature of this understanding is crucial: satire that is merely
emotive – expressing the speaker's emotion without gaining the listener's
agreement – is unsuccessful as satire.

Satire's very nature imposes problems for the basic rhetorical triad.[55]
The attacking satirist seems arrogant, and his self-conscious manipulations
seek to control that arrogance so that his message becomes acceptable.
The problem hardly arises with satires that displace the function of attack
onto narrative or allegorical representations. When it does arise, the satirist
may admit his arrogance, thus seeking to compensate for negative pride
by positive frankness: "Yes, I am proud; I must be proud to see / Men not
afraid of God, afraid of me" (Pope, "Epilogue to the Satires: Dialogue II,"
lines 208–09). Alternatively, the satirist may create a counter image as the
humble writer of private rather than public verse: Horace extends that
image to the point of ironic self-attack (*Satires* 2.3 and 2.7). The satirist
may displace the arrogance of attack onto an externally represented satirist,
as in the cases of the satiric characters of Jacobean drama or of Swift's proud
Lemuel Gulliver. The most complex tactic for finessing the arrogance of
the satirist is Socratic irony, the satirist's pretense at unknowing. But the
pretense is justified for Socrates himself by the Delphic oracle's assertion
that he is the wisest of men (*Apology* 20–21). All of these maneuvers may
be seen as efforts to avoid or exploit the dangers posed by the arrogance of
attack.

The position of the audience may also be dangerous. Satire usually demands an audience that either agrees with the propriety of the attack or
will accept it for purposes of entertainment. But since the readers' willing

and even conspiratorial cooperation with the satirist implicates them in the guilt of attack, as perpetrators if not as victims, their position is often uncomfortable. If the discomfort derives from the readers' status as possible satiric victims, cooperation in attack may be a pretense that disguises guilt. A notoriously unstable discussion of audience–victim maneuvers occurs in "The Preface" to Swift's *Tale of a Tub*:

> But Satyr being levelled at all, is never resented for an offence by any, since every individual Person makes bold to understand it of others, and very wisely removes his particular Part of the Burthen upon the shoulders of the World, which are broad enough, and able to bear it . . . 'Tis but a *Ball* bandied to and fro, and every Man carries a *Racket* about him to strike it from himself among the rest of the Company.[56]

This passage is sometimes taken as an admission of satire's inefficiency, but it creates a double bind for the reader: to accept oneself as a satiric target is to admit one's guilt; to shift attack to the shoulders of the world is to reveal one's guilt, for individuals do not strike balls away that are not heading at themselves. Satiric audiences may take pleasure in the discomfort of satiric victims or may be victims themselves. But readers may assert that they are neither, and that Swift's double bind playfully proposes an overly literal relationship between "the reader" and the satire. Readers, after all, are more complicated and capable of assuming a variety of positions simultaneously, and identification itself may take various forms. Hence they may recognize themselves as satiric victims and yet (unless they are a named victim) take pleasure at the victim's implied discomfort, or they may retreat to the privileged role of readerly impartiality, although their resistance to the text may still lie in their awareness that their position as reader implies either guilty pleasure or victimization.

Readers may further resist the tendency of offensive attack to lead the satirist to tactics of irony and indirection, resulting in elaborate processes of interpretation or in confusion. But such difficulties and ambiguities are not limited to satire. They may derive as well from a doubleness in subject when attack engages and reveals a larger, more serious, and more urgent disorder of which the sinfulness of the satiric victim is only an instance. (Thus the subject of *MacFlecknoe* is bad writing and the commercialization of literature, of which Shadwell is a telling example.) Ideally, this deeper concern, the real subject behind the nominal object of attack, should justify the unpleasantness of the attack itself and may shift the reader's position from resisting the transgressive attack to interest in the subject it reveals. (There are, of course, numerous variations on this pattern of duplication, including the possibility that readers unoffended by the original attack may become offended when the satire's real target becomes apparent.)

Robert Scholes anticipates Smith's distinction between natural and fictive discourse by commenting that the written and imaginative nature of literary discourse doubles Jakobson's basic triad: the speaker may not be the actual author, the audience not the real listener.[57] In satire the speaker is often a pose allowing the author to escape responsibility for attack. Readers may assert a privileged role to avoid the double binds that would otherwise capture them. The meaning of the satire may, as in the case of *A Tale of a Tub*, differ from its literal message. Such duplicity shifts dominance in satire from the basic triad to literary self-consciousness.

Contact: the phatic function

Much satire, then, is based on a shared understanding between satirist and audience regarding the purposes and properties of attack; satire entertains, coerces, or argues the reader into accepting that understanding. But Jakobson's model is silent about the phatic function in written literature. It is apparent in performed works such as Old Comedy, where the correlation of heroic fantasies and civic problems parallels the actual presence of an audience and the judgment of its representatives on the dramatic contest. But in written literature, how is the reader to confirm that contact has been made and that satiric understanding is mutual? The image of the satirist is often intensely present in the satiric text and frequently addresses readers, both as general recipients of the message and as specific individuals, either real (as in the case of Horace's sudden shift to Maecenas as audience in *Satires* 1.3.64) or fictional (as in the woman instructed to reread Book 1, chapter xix of *Tristram Shandy*). The question is how the written text represents a contact with the real audience.

Occasionally the satirist shows an awareness of the real audience and of how it reads. At the end of Canto 1 of *Don Juan*, Byron begins a stanza with four conventional lines but concludes by insisting that they are not his but Southey's. He anticipates the reader's assumption that he has written the words on the page but denies it to prevent misreading and to shift Southey's lines from the level of sincerity to the level of parody. He implies that the reader has been foolish to interpret such banalities as his own, and he reaffirms his concern for the reader's good regard. But occasions where the reader is directed by the satirist's anticipation of misreading are rare. More frequently, the reader's position is incorporated into the text dramatically, as in the dialogue of some programmatic satires, or by the fictitious personification of the audience. Both means suggest that the satirist is aware of his rhetorical situation, and both supply the occasion for a phatic response, even if unheard by the author, by forcing readers to compare their own position to its representation in the text: "I" am unlike Trebatius (*Satires* 2.1) but his discomfort at Horace's attacks may articulate "mine." "I" am neither a woman nor an unsophisticated reader and therefore am not the "Madam" addressed by Tristram Shandy in Book i, chapter xx, but "I" too am puzzled by his assertion that his mother is not a Catholic. Contact takes place when readers confirm or renounce the satirist's representation of themselves. Satire, dependent on an understanding with its audience, may seek to verify its participation by a textual hypothesis.

Code: the metalingual function

Since satire characteristically imitates discourse, its subject is likely to be the disruptions of language itself. Its relation to the imitated utterances, however, is usually linguistic rather than metalingual. It distances its own language from the language it imitates: Byron renounces the borrowed language of Southey; the jargons of *The Alchemist* are perceptible as imitated and unnatural modes of discourse. But the relationship between social disorder and imitated language may require the satirist to provide a key for identifying the represented language and seeing its disorders. The key itself may be ironic: in Wagstaff's "Introduction to the Following Treatise," Swift offers a preface to *Polite Conversation* whose ironies imply critical rules for reading the "Dialogues."

In George Orwell's *Nineteen Eighty-Four* the parodied language of "Newspeak" co-exists with the discourse of realistic narrative. To clarify his satire, Orwell incorporates a series of metalinguistic keys within his text. Winston Smith's work in "Minitrue" and his talks with co-workers reveal the operations of Newspeak (e.g. Book i, chapter 5). Emmanuel Goldstein's "Theory and Practice of Oligarchic Collectivism" (Book ii, chapter 9), itself a parody of Trotsky, articulates the politics of "doublethink" whose vehicle of expression is Newspeak. Once Smith is imprisoned in "Miniluv," his interrogator O'Brien admits that he himself co-authored Goldstein's treatise, and he re-explains "Newspeak" as a means of absolute power over the minds and identities of individuals (Book iii, chapters 2–3). The "Appendix" to the novel is a straightforward (that is, ironic) description of "The Principles of Newspeak." The reader encounters a series of metalinguistic comments, each denying the authenticity of the previous one: Goldstein's treatise transforms Smith's consciousness of Newspeak;

O'Brien's admission deconstructs Goldstein; the "Appendix" implies the project's impossibility, thus rendering ironic O'Brien's dream of control. When satiric discourse represents the disturbances of culture, the metalinguistic function indicates how language embodies the underlying disorders. The fact that the code cannot be properly read without the key means that the parodied discourse embodies the social problems from which it derives. The metalinguistic function in satire implies the equivalence of meaninglessness and social disorder.

Context: the referential function

Satire's attention to metalinguistic and phatic functions largely derives from its concern to attack a target that is independent of the text itself. Satire's distinction from the genres it imitates lies in the presence of such historical attack, and referentiality is central because the identity of the satiric referent, its independence, and the transformation that occurs when satire may be said to textualize it are major elements of the satiric message. Satire straddles the historical world of experience and the imaginative world of Ideas and insists on the presence of both. We have seen in Old Comedy the satiric force that derives from the hero's fantastic response to a problem shared by the audience. That force is characteristic: satire makes an imaginative assertion about a historical topic. Hence it insists on the reality of that topic. The 1714 version of Pope's "Rape of the Lock" is prefaced by a dedication "To Mrs. Arabella Fermor" that explains in patronizing terms the "Machinery" of the poem, and that implies, by asserting that "the Character of *Belinda*, as it is now manag'd, resembles You in nothing but Beauty," that the poem is partly historical in its reference. The letter insinuates the historicity of the poem by proclaiming its "Fabulous" nature. Satire derives meaning from historical context much as natural discourse does. Swift's "Argument against Abolishing Christianity" may make sense outside of the context of the occasional-conformity debates, but that context supplies a reason for Swift's text and gives force to its arguments.[58] Similarly, "A Modest Proposal" seems in one sense more and in another less modest when the reader recognizes that the alternatives rejected by the proposer had actually been suggested by Swift. The context of *Absalom and Achitophel* is essential to the poem, which cannot be read as a history of King David's political and familial problems.

The referential function of satire implies an audience sufficiently informed of the context for the message to be comprehended. To disseminate this knowledge (as well as to perform the metalinguistic function), any of a variety of satiric "keys" may be provided – sometimes by the satirist, sometimes by an unscrupulous publisher (Curll, in the case of *A Tale of a Tub*); sometimes straightforwardly, but sometimes ironically. The ironic explanation of historical context sometimes seems anticipatory mockery of the scholarly apparatus needed to transmit the contextual meaning of satiric works to subsequent generations – as anyone can attest who has sorted through both Pope's annotations to *The Dunciad* and those of later editors.

The problem of contextual knowledge is complicated by the openness of satiric reference. Imaginative literature is relatively indeterminate; its contextual meaning is supplied by readers. Historical texts are determined insofar as their discourse refers to a meaningful context. Because satire insists on a duplication of discourses, readers may be uncertain whether a historical reference is predetermined or whether they are justified, given the assumptions governing a specific text, in postulating an identification. The interpretive rules themselves may change within a text. In *Gulliver's Travels* Flimnap (Book 1, chapter 3) may be Walpole, but Gulliver's Houyhnhnm master may not be Bolingbroke (though Swift owned a horse so named).[59] Phillip Harth has cogently argued that *Gulliver's Travels* cannot be read as a consistent political allegory in the mode of *Absalom and Achitophel*. In extending that view, F. P. Lock asserts an equally consistent rule against specific political identifications. J. A. Downie finds Lock's position constraining and unhistorical and argues that the *Travels* provides local allusions rather than general allegory.[60] The debate is not about context but about the relative force of historical and imaginative discourses for specific passages.

Sometimes the problem of referentiality can be reasoned out despite circumstances that point to a false conclusion. Any western reader is likely to view Zamyatin's *We* as anti-Soviet because it is a post-revolutionary attack on statist power, but George Orwell plausibly argued that its satiric message was inconsistent with the actual conditions of Russian life in 1923 and that its target was probably more general.[61] In cases less amenable to reason, traditions extrinsic to the text may supply interpretive keys. The tiger contemplated by the hero of Solzenitsyn's *Cancer Ward* has been confidently identified with Stalin because his eyes resembled those described by an old prisoner as belonging to another prisoner at Turukhansk, where (we know, but are not told in the text) Stalin was imprisoned in 1913.[62] But the identification of Stalinist politicians with characters in Bulgakov's *Master and Margarita* has no basis either in Orwellian common sense or in an insider's knowledge.[63] The reader's uncertainty regarding context, though sometimes born of ignorance, is sometimes the result of a shifting between imaginative and historical discourses necessitated by difficulties in the context. When things cannot be said in ordinary language, they may be said in fictive discourse, and the repression requiring such transformation is itself satirized. The referential function is dominant in satire because satire attacks real offenders; it reveals disorders of the discourse that it imitates or disorders in the world to which that discourse refers. But the dominance of context in the kingdom of imagination creates political and textual disorders of its own. The problems of satiric contextuality may be created by the reader's factual ignorance, by unconcern for the historical issues, by the dated and transitory nature of historical reference, or by the unstable relationship between ordinary and fictive discourse that results from satire's simultaneous imitation of literary models and historical appearance. Or they derive from a suppression of discourse that itself becomes a satiric target.

A significant problem for the referential function of satire is raised by Michael McKeon's consideration of the cultural crisis that satire signals in the early eighteenth century.[64] Even if we skirt the positivistic implications of referentiality and agree that we can identify a historical world to which satire refers, a problem in the relationship between politics and literature (and hence between satire and its subject) arises, McKeon suggests, if we look beyond simple referentiality to interaction. He sees literature in general and satire in particular as trapped by its recognition that the political reform it identifies as needed will not (can not, as society is presently constituted) come about. Hence the satirist issues a call for reform that he is well aware will be fruitless, or he retreats into a self-consuming irony. The frustration of literature in its desire to act upon the world (like the frustration of Pygmalion before his statue) marks the separation of literature from political reality. If one thinks of politics as social behavior (more specifically governmental behavior) within a given historical context, McKeon is right in seeing it as unresponsive to literature. But if satire cannot work directly on events, it can affect the minds of those who act. The real crisis therefore lies in the gap between the urgency with which the satirist articulates the problem and the slow indirection with which readers can respond. Satire addresses the crisis McKeon describes by shifting from specific political action to general political consciousness and by transposing the burden of frustration from the satirist to the reader. It cultivates the will to resist and enables the power to say no.

SATIRIC IDEAS

Genres may be distinguished, Jakobson predicts, by the dominance of functions in his six-term model.[65] In satire that dominance begins with the relationship of a satiric text to its context. Satire's imitation of speech occasions, whether oral conversations or literary texts or other satires, is directed at contextual subjects; it makes imaginative assertions about historical topics. This procedure implies a conflict between fictive and natural discourse; further, it takes place through personal attack on actual people, invoking social disapproval of rude behavior and requiring a validly overriding purpose or a self-conscious explanation. Self-consciousness about the imitation of discourse and (on occasion) about the distinction between imitated discourse and the natural language of satire requires attention to the metalingual function. Satire's need to implicate its readers as allies in the attack or as its victims implies attention to the phatic function, which can be realized in written discourse through a fictional audience with which real readers can compare responses. The referential function is dominant within a pattern of functions emphasizing the historical and imaginative duplicity of satiric discourse.

Satire's imitation of conventional speech occasions implies problems we recognize from our own experience of speech. Language – both at the level of syntax and at the level of conversational exchanges – sets forth structures that may be too stable and confining for changes in intention or for the instabilities of meaning itself. Hence utterances such as this very sentence may be overstatements necessitated by the hearer's expectation of a strong enough signal to be comprehended as distinct meaning. In conversation listeners can demand a stronger, more definite statement or may correct an ill-advised one. Genres similarly may possess conventional meanings or may yield their true meaning only when challenged. Satiric imitation challenges both genre and language. Its insistence on historicity proclaims the actuality of experience and the inadequacies of generic and linguistic codes to represent it. Its insistence on imagination mocks the thoughtlessness of experience in relation to the reality conceived by the mind.

Satire's imitation of other genres self-consciously preserves their alterity, thus differing from novelistic parody that "squeezes out some genres and incorporates others into its own peculiar structure, reformulating and re-accentuating them."[66] The reader distinguishes satiric discourse from the generic discourse it has adopted. But the relationship of imitative levels is dialectic on two counts. On one level the individual work struggles to impose its autonomous shape on the template of genre. While readers begin by interpreting the work in terms of generic anticipations, they continue by interpreting it in light of the signals the work itself has provided, sometimes in contrast to the generic model. On a second level, Jacques Derrida is correct in his playful proclamation that "genres are not to be mixed," correct both in the statement and in abandoning it.[67] Within a given work, especially a satiric work, genres struggle to proclaim their preeminence as definite, to banish the usurper to the lesser status of mode. *Don Quixote*, however satiric, is a novel because its generic dislocations continue to return it to the status of fiction. (Fiction, like home, is difficult to escape and tends to manufacture and tolerate its own disharmonies.) But the satiric quality of *Don Quixote*'s dislocations, its dialectic struggles for generic supremacy, necessitate a dazzling array of self-definitions. Even in modal form satiric imitation may instigate generic struggles with salutary and clarifying effect.

According to the Platonic model adopted and enacted by Lucian in his satiric self-defense, satire, the meta-imitation, imitates the forms of appearance or the discourses of art in order to reveal inherent disorders within the discourse or to expose the relative disharmonies between discourse and appearance or between appearance and reality. In undertaking these motley and protean disguises, satire claims to act in the name of Ideas, before which all imitations pale. The Platonic model is only metaphorically useful because it assumes an ontology that lodges reality firmly in Ideas. Both genre and language itself are more unstable than this Platonic location implies. But satiric imitation remains even if its Platonic defining terms are perceived as metaphors that distinguish relative rather than absolute relationships. Because of satire's imaginative as well as historical force, it replicates and criticizes discourse in the name of Ideas located in imagination.

CHAPTER 2

Satiric nationalism

SATIRE AND HISTORY

This chapter and the one that follows try to look at one aspect of the relationship between satire and history by considering how satire expresses and questions nationalism and how nations are seen from the perspective of the satiric exile. The present chapter looks at images of nations in France and England between 1650 and 1760, a period during which, through different historical processes, nationalism was being defined in both countries. The next chapter, on exile, where the very topic renders national identification problematic, looks at satiric novels written since the 1960s. Nationalism and exile are complex metaphors suggesting relative historical positions. Their metaphorical quality creates a flow between the psychological condition of individuals and political conditions of states. Nations may then be seen as metaphors of inclusion. Nations conceive of themselves in relation to other nations; they are bounded or defined in relation to Others. Satiric nationalists write, however critically, as members of a group calling itself a community. For the exile, however, this connection is broken, so that exiles, cut off from the state, must redefine a personal relationship to the culture that state once embodied. Satiric nationalism and satiric exile explore the relationship between the position of the observer and the historical reality of the material observed.

In questioning that relationship, satiric nationalism and satiric exile embody satire's traditional concern for historical particulars. Although its enduring value derives from its capacity to suggest the connections of historical moments to larger issues, satire remains rooted in the experience of history. The generalities of satire are implicit in particular events, inescapably tied to those events but at uneasy tension with them. Like all literature satire reflects its culture, but it seeks to establish a distance from it and to reveal its false elements. Satire both explores and reflects the gaps and contradictions of its culture; it is both critic and representative of those contradictions.

It attacks ideologies but cannot escape them or avoid the implicit expression of alternatives that may exist only within the text. It may subvert the ideologies it seems to express.

Satire's historicity profits from its fictional perspective, for the construction of an imagined speaker opens various ways by which satire can seem to interpret its historical context independently. Rather than becoming trapped by the Gordian knot of intertwined variables, satirists can cut it by looking to a fictional realm where they can control both the process of seeing and the objects regarded. The indirection of satire thus arises from the complexity of the interpretive situation it seeks to address: if matters were clear, there would be little reason to express them indirectly. A result of this uneasy relationship is that satire's historical complexities are signaled by its formal complexities. The construction of satiric frames becomes a means of avoiding the traps implied by the uncomfortable fact that neither language itself nor the vocabulary of literary forms can fully escape the limitations of the culture they seek to attack.

Satire's double relation to history may be further complicated by the imagined position of its speakers in a pattern that can be represented by a general and approximate model. The real (historical) author, responding to a particular set of circumstances that embody general problems or principles (or a real author fortuitously finding general principles represented by a particular set of circumstances), constructs analogous but fictional conditions described by a fictional observer (who may or may not be a constructed version of the original author). Readers must resist the temptation to see such fictional observers – Gulliver, Candide, Usbek, and Kinbot – as realistic, for the discovery of meaning may be a product of that resistance. Meaning emerges when readers see fictitious observers as constructs undertaken to identify and analyze problems and to warn of their dangerous consequences; readers can then postulate the plausible or likely intentions of a real author behind the fictional text.

The location of the speaker in relation to the historical material observed is thus a crucial factor in how satire implies meaning. Meaning might emerge within the distance between the imagined speaker and the material; at least that distance allows the satiric object to be implicitly evaluated. At the heart of the issue is the question of how, amid the uncertainties of observation and the fallibility of the observer's report, satirists and readers can make serious judgments. The issue may not be one of shared values but of shared recognitions. The point of exercising these double manipulations (manipulated targets, manipulated observers) may be to make the reader aware that the historical reality behind the speaker's representation constitutes an offense, which readers may recognize by the offensive nature of the satire. The satirist needs not only to depict an evil but, by manipulating perspectives, to establish the values by which it is seen as evil. If the satirist's manipulations are successful, the perceived evil need only be relative – the product of tricks of perception rather than of values that are universal or confidently shared by the historical author and readers. But the perception of even a relative evil is a positive good. The satiric text will have done what it can, and it will be up to the readers to consider that perception in terms of the world they experience.

Exile and nationalism are alternative ways of looking at material that is defined by its identification with a nation (that is, a group of people within a demarcated territory, governed by a central state, and possessing a common culture and common social and economic institutions). Because the scope of the nation is both focused and general, and because the nation exists as both historical actuality and ideological construct, it becomes an ideal frame for satiric observation, and the targets of attack are on one hand the bounding and threatening Other, and, on the other, the nation itself and the principles and practices associated with it. Satiric nationalism looks at a nation from the critical or sympathetic position of a member of that nation. Satiric exile looks at both the nation that had been the exile's home and the nation in which the exile now lives from the position of an outsider. The satirist may exercise a role as the voice of social responsibility, speaking on behalf of a communal consensus and excoriating those who have made themselves enemies of the people. This role as spokesperson for the voice of the community was played by the satirist in primitive societies.[1] But in the case of satiric nationalism, this role is characteristically directed outside of the nation. The image of the guilty Other who represents the sins of the people is shifted from the scapegoat driven into the desert and becomes the image of another nation, another people. The work of satiric nationalism is to explore, sharpen, and complicate the image of the Other, or, more disturbingly, to see the satirist's own country as if it, in turn, were the Other.

The satiric exile, in contrast, stands outside of the nation. The exile is the satirist as outcast, the transgressive attacker, the despoiler of social harmony, the sower of discord and suspicion, the unwelcome observer who sees more about us than we perceive ourselves. Unlike the satiric nationalist, whose multiple perspective is an exercise of the imagination, the exile is forced to double vision by his exclusion from the country he had, with whatever ambivalence, thought of as home and by his arrival in a nation he cannot help perceive as alien. This coerced vision gives a personal tone to the exile's satiric exploration of both nations. The dual countries of satiric nationalism and satiric exile parallel the dual location of the author as a historical person writing about historical particulars and as an imagined observer writing about imagined countries. The present chapter examines the nature of what is seen by authors who are located within national boundaries but look at images of other countries or imagine their own country as alien, observed by travelers rooted in the culture of a foreign land. The following chapter, on exile, looks at alternative countries from the vantage point of writers who are outcasts from one and strangers in the other.

SATIRE AND NATIONALISM

Thinkers on nationalism have shown, despite their sophistication, some uncertainty in defining.[2] They have concerned themselves with the ontology and etiology of nations, with what a nation is, and when nationalism came into being, both for individual nations and as a world-dominating ideology. The question of the nature of nations was notably asked by Ernest Renan in his 1882 lecture "Qu'est-ce qu'une nation?", but he dismisses the traditional answers. He rejects "race, language, material interest, religious affinities, geography, and military necessity" as determinants of nationality, to see it instead as consisting of two elements: "One is the possession in common of a rich legacy of memories; the other is present-day consent, the desire to live together, the will to perpetuate the value of the heritage that one has received in an undivided form."[3] It is that "present-day consent," an implied choice of nation, that the equation of *natio* with *natus* seems to withhold. Renan's skepticism about definitions of nations is extended by E. J. Hobsbawm, who finds objective definitions faulty because the criteria are vague and exceptions can always be found, and who sees subjective definitions as tautological.[4]

Renan's emphasis on a common heritage and the desire to preserve its value, a desire that usually takes political form, leads to the view of nationalism as a set of conditions that prompts a group's awareness of both its cultural and its political union – or, more sharply, that justifies its political claims on the grounds of its culture. In his important 1983 study of nationalism, Ernest Gellner defines it as "primarily a political principle, which holds that the political and the national unit should be congruent."[5] His posthumously published rethinking of nationalism describes it, more elegantly, as "a political principle which maintains that similarity of culture is the basic social bond."[6] Anthony D. Smith defines nationalism as "an ideological movement, for the attainment and maintenance of self-government and independence on behalf of a group, some of whose members conceive it to constitute an actual or potential 'nation' like others."[7] For both thinkers political and cultural nationalism coincide, but they coincide in different ways. For Gellner nationalism is primarily a principle regarding the politics of culture. Smith, who is interested in the links between nationalism and ethnicity, sees it as ideology.

Although objective factors of nation formation remain important, the focus of nationalism does seem subjective: nationalism is the consciousness of being a nation. Although such a subjective description is unavoidably circular, its objective factors point to the dangers of false consciousness: the ethnic identification of a "people" without the political and economic structures required for a nation. A difficulty of defining nationalism lies in the need to identify what is universal in both the demand for nationhood and the behavior of existing (self-styled) nations. Benedict Anderson's notable definition points towards that universality: he defines the nation as "an imagined political community – and imagined as both inherently limited and sovereign." He goes on to discuss his defining terms. "Communities are to be distinguished not by their falseness/genuineness, but by the style in which they are imagined." Nations are limited by "finite, if elastic boundaries, beyond which lie other nations." They are sovereign "because the term was born in an age in which Enlightenment and Revolution were destroying the legitimacy of the divinely-ordained, hierarchical dynastic realm," and communities because "the nation is always conceived as a deep, horizontal comradeship."[8] Anderson's definition can be restated along the lines of Anselm's description of God: a nation is the largest practical imagined community. As an imagined community it has the characteristics described by Anderson, who distinguishes between an imagined community and an imaginary one. The idea that the community is practical as well as imagined limits both its size and its imagined nature. The practicality of the nation is both external – limited, as Anderson notes, by the territorial and economic competition of other nations – and internal – limited by the capacity of the state to exercise control over its people and to exert ideological dominance over its culture. The development of nationalism thus depends not only on the concept of citizenship but on the development of effective political infrastructures that tie citizens to the nation as a whole. It also depends on technologies that allow the exercise of what Louis Althusser calls the ideological state apparatus.[9] Ideological state apparatuses – religious, educational, family, legal, political, trade-union, communications, and cultural – operate semi-autonomously to create a common culture or to remind citizens of its importance, so that they will accept their responsibilities to the state. In Althusser's terms, "the individual *is interpellated as a (free) subject in order that he shall submit freely to the commandments of the Subject, i.e. in order that he shall (freely) accept his subjection.*" For Althusser the primary ideological state apparatus is education,[10] but Anderson sees the emergence of the print media (and their electronic successors) as a major factor in the building of national ideologies.[11]

What emerges in the definition, therefore, is the convergence of a number of variables in the building of nations; these variables generate one another and support each other while, at the same time, remaining independent.

(1.) Government coincides with a relatively stable territory, perceived as a natural unit.

(2.) That government reflects the interests of the country as a whole (or of a dominant elite) rather than those of a personal monarch (such as Louis XIV).[12]

(3.) The yoking of government, territory, and economy is supported by national language and religion and by a sense of ethnic identity.[13]

(4.) National identity is heightened by distinguishing one's own state from others, a distinction justifying national rivalries, international alliances, and colonial expansion.[14]

(5.) The territorial definition of the nation gives particular weight to property: one feels a member of the nation because one owns a part of it. The nation functions as a territorial collective of the properties owned by its members, and, until relatively recently, the right to vote was derived from ownership of property.

(6.) The nation is responsible for the production of currency and hence for monetary policy.

(7.) Because trade and colonialism require state support, and because the expenses of war and government require heavy funding, nationalism is essentially economic as well as political. (A major question for developed seventeenth- and eighteenth-century nations was how to finance government itself.)

(8.) The nation becomes an ideological center, controlling education and emerging as the central subject of history.

(9.) Nationalist ideology ultimately asserts that loyalty to the state is primary, transcending and subsuming individual loyalties (as in the claim that the state has the right to conscript citizens as soldiers).

The importance given to these factors differs among theoreticians, in part because nationalism explains two quite different phenomena: the shift in consciousness and political organization among developed states of

Western Europe between 1600 and 1900, and the emergence of newly independent political units among underdeveloped states since 1850. Nationalism claims that corporate values are superior to individual ones, that loyalty to the state may be more important than loyalty to personal commitments. Hence it gives the state an ultimate secular moral authority, both as the agent of law and as the embodiment of communal interests. The philosophical and moral stature of national ideologies ranges from the noble to the execrable, and satire functions to evaluate the moral force of national claims.

The question of when states on one hand and ethnic groups on the other became nations is connected to the question of what a nation is, and it is complicated by the multiple variables that constitute nationality. It is, moreover, a question of concern to a project that proposes to look at the representation of nations in eighteenth-century satire. One can reasonably ask whether eighteenth-century satire represents nations that do not actually exist. My argument here is that satire both represents nations and constructs them, at a point of transition between the state and the nation, in two different countries, one of which (Britain) became a nation at the end of the seventeenth century, the other (France) at the end of the eighteenth.

A broad series of dates can be identified to mark the nationalization of England. The Battle of Bosworth Field in 1485, followed by Henry Tudor's marriage to Elizabeth of York, not only ended the Wars of the Roses but ended the power of feudal magnates relative to that of the monarchy. Liah Greenfeld dates the inception of English nationalism in the 1530s, when separation from Rome inaugurated not only a state-centered religion but a shift in the nature of the nobility. "By the 1530s the idea of service to the nation had entered, or at any rate was entering, the discourse, as was the concept of England as a separate entity, and as a polity which was not simply a royal patrimony, but a commonwealth."[15] English resistance to the Spanish Armada of 1588, especially the mobilization of civilians, inspired by the Queen's famous speech at Tilbury, is arguably another national moment. The execution of Charles I was justified by Milton on the grounds "that the power of Kings and Magistrates is nothing else, but what is only derivative, transferr'd and committed to them in trust from the People, to the Common good of them all, in whom power yet remaines fundamentally, and cannot be taken from them, without a violation of thir natural birthright."[16] Milton's position that power inheres ultimately in the people as a whole, although a minority view at the time, articulated a nationalist ideology. The revolution of 1688 revisited the relative power of Parliament and the monarch. The accession of William III, even as co-monarch with his English wife, raised the question of the foreign monarch for the first time, essentially, since William the Conqueror. If national identity is embodied by the monarch, a foreign monarch creates an uneasy relationship between dynasty and ethnicity. If national identity is embodied in the people as a whole, the ethnic identity of the monarch seems to matter less. The ease with which the Elector of Hanover ascended the throne in 1714, despite a residual British Jacobitism that occasionally broke into violence during the following generation, suggests not only the importance of religion but also the degree to which the nation's sense of itself was independent of the King. The period between 1688 and 1714 saw the emergence of a number of nationalist factors: the settlement of 1688–89 increased the relative power of Parliament and royal ministers who were its members; political parties developed; the Bank of England was founded as a means of financing King William's wars; Parliament established the Protestant succession; England and Scotland united; England's colonial power substantially increased; new plays tended to reflect middle-class rather than aristocratic values; the first daily newspapers and the first literary periodicals were published; coffee-house society flourished; and political events, both national and international, became matters of public curiosity. The elements of Althusser's "ideological state apparatus" had fallen into place.

Linda Colley, like Gerald Newman, sees antagonism to the French as an important element in the emergence of English nationalism, but her scope is broader than his. While he is concerned with the causes of English nationalism, she is concerned with the operations of British nationalism – the distinct appeal to Scottish, Welsh, and eventually Irish people to see themselves as citizens of the same nation. She sees the appeal to a union based on citizenship as addressed not only to the various ethnicities of Britain but to various classes as well, especially to workers and to women. Although she canvasses multiple factors in the development of British nationalism and understands the importance of rhetoric in creating an "imagined" nation in Anderson's sense, she sees Protestantism as "at the core of British national identity."[17] This emphasis puts her at odds with modernist theorists who see nationalism as the product of industrialization, commercial competition, the economic effects of war, and uneven economic development. But it is consistent with her central concern for how "a sense of British national identity was forged" (1), since appeals to national identity are seldom economic and usually seek to elicit national loyalty by invoking the highest authority. Colley shares with most writers on nationalism a sense that it requires the convergence of diverse factors and presents an ideology addressed to a diverse audience.

This convergence of factors is similarly a major theme of Howard Weinbrot's massive study of eighteenth-century British literary nationalism.[18] Much of the study is composed of his sensitive readings of particular texts, but these readings are governed by his thesis that the defining accomplishment of literary Britain was its incorporation of cultural influences from a variety of sources. He corrects the descriptions of eighteenth-century literature as "neo-classical" and "Augustan," to see instead a literature drawing its identity from diverse cultures, including the Celtic north and Jewish tradition. Weinbrot's argument is consciously paradoxical: the strength of British culture lay in its foreign borrowings and its amalgamated nature, but Britain remained an intensely xenophobic nation. Although the degree to which nations establish their identity in distinct contrast to other nations is sharply recognized by literary historians such as Weinbrot and by historians such as Colley and Newman, it seems underemphasized by theorists of nationalism. But Josep Llobera notes that states appear "in the context of other emerging, sovereign states," and theorists such as Tom Nairn who are particularly interested in the economic characteristics of development emphasize the importance of uneven economic development on an international scale.[19] In a sense nationality is bestowed from without as much as it is developed from within, and national status is confirmed when other nations recognize that a state has become a nation. The imagined nation becomes real when it is imagined by others as well as by itself. Thus the deployment of satiric images of other nations serves a double function. By setting the satirist's nation in the context of other nations, it reinforces an exalted sense of nationhood, but by representing even distorted images of the other, satirized nation, it verifies its identity as well.

Satire plays several minor roles in the development of nations. It is part of the print culture that disseminates a broad ideology capable of stimulating the loyalty of a variety of citizens, and its essential function to attack makes it an ideal vehicle for defining and distorting other nations. Benedict Anderson discusses the force of print in replacing Latin with the vernacular, in building the image of an ancient national culture, and in fostering homogeneity of dialect and hence communication among linguistically different speakers.[20] The growth of a literate public allows the discovery of commonality, and reading itself becomes an experience shared among that public. Satire, as a form that ranges from high art to low buffoonery, addresses a broad spectrum of the population. National feeling takes on positive and negative modes in satire: the characteristics of one's nation are celebrated, while those of others are mocked. The mockery intensifies the celebration; the celebration motivates the mockery. Satire's characteristic function to attack and its concern for historical particulars engage it closely with the ideology of nationalism and involve it in the print culture by which that ideology is promulgated. The satirist asserts membership in a nation and looks on the distorted but revealing images of other nations, or it looks at its nation as identified by imaginary outsiders. This double nationalistic perspective, however, is echoed by a deeper doubling. Satire evaluates the validity of the nationalist claims it assists in asserting. As satire proclaims the ideology of nationalism, it calls the project of nationalism into question. The boundaries it defines become permeable.

SATIRE AND PROPAGANDA

Simple nationalistic satire stresses the distinction of one's own country from others by exaggerating their negative qualities. The use of local stereotypes to represent what the satirist claims as large cultural threats has a long (if not distinguished) history. The most familiar classical example is Juvenal's description of Greeks as fast-tongued rhetoricians, effeminate actors, shameless flatterers, sexual virtuosi, blackmailers, and spies.[21] For Juvenal the image of Greeks allowed him to fix a nexus of dangerous artificialities. In transferring Juvenal's Rome to modern England, Samuel Johnson had no trouble projecting similar qualities onto the French:

> No gainful Trade their Industry can 'scape,
> They sing, they dance, clean Shoes, or cure a Clap;
> All Sciences a fasting Monsieur knows,
> And bid him go the Hell, to Hell he goes.[22]

But despite his legendary antipathy to Scots, Johnson's *Journey to the Western Islands of Scotland* rejects simple nationalism to perceive the universality of human nature. Insistent upon accurate observation, he shuns the conscious overgeneralization of satire. "Novelty and ignorance must always be reciprocal, and I cannot but be conscious that my thoughts on national manners, are the thoughts of one who has seen but little."[23] Juvenal's image of Egypt in *Satire* 15 treats Rome's relationship to foreigners quite differently from his earlier attack on Greeks. Juvenal records a riot that apparently took place in 127 AD and resulted in the eating of one rioter by the aggressors from a rival town. This Egyptian cannibalism is contrasted to universal Graeco-Roman civility. The foreign nation is culturally distinct from the satiric norm by virtue of its barbaric religion, and that distinction is intensified by the extreme contrast between the decent values of the satirist and his audience and the revolting cannibalism of the satiric target. In *Satire* 15 Juvenal does not, as in *Satire* 3, conveniently use foreigners as a way of talking about his own society; instead he explores a terrible and alien extreme of human nature.[24]

Such local stereotypes as Juvenal's urban Greeks and uncivilized Egyptians existed long before the emergence of modern states. But when national identification is culturally important, the satirist can project onto other nations the qualities of his own. The French of such eighteenth-century English writers as Addison, Arbuthnot, and Johnson, like the Greeks of Juvenal, become threatening precisely because they represent characteristics of one's own culture. Satire defines these unwelcome qualities as the contagion of foreign influence and transfers them to the alien nation, whose very nationhood suggests differences of history, politics, language, and belief. The Dutch in Book III of *Gulliver's Travels* are emblematic of mercantile values, but in attacking the Dutch, Swift attacks English merchant activity as well. Simple satiric nationalism allows one nation to look critically at itself in the guise of another.

Juvenal's Egyptians are judged barbaric by the shared standards of civilization. The depiction of their cannibalism resembles the modern propagandistic use of national images to justify warfare on grounds that the enemy is guilty of atrocities a civilized people must avenge with violence.[25] These warfare stereotypes are distinguished from Swift's Dutch or Johnson's French by their claim to represent literal truths about the enemy. Because they seek to encourage public support for retaliatory acts of war, they lack satire's humor and its self-conscious play with pre-existent images. The stereotypes of satiric nationalism often imply the satirist's recognition that they are falsehoods shared by the culture; his proclamation that they are truths verified by the facts he records thus has a comic or paradoxical character. The effect of propaganda's dark images depends upon their skill in enlisting the fears of their audience; they cannot function, as satiric nationalism often does, to criticize the internal politics and values of their own country. Simple satiric nationalism manipulates gross images, complicating them and rendering them ambiguous. Propagandistic images lack the complicating elements of artistic self-consciousness and rhetorical play. They have no moral ambivalence: guilt is not admitted but is projected onto the enemy. For satire the stereotypes of simple nationalism are a language from which it creates a text; for propaganda that language is itself the text.

The nature of simple satiric nationalism is apparent in graphic satire, where national stereotypes are displayed in their most conventional and accessible form. The conventionality of such stereotypes in literature is exemplified by the stock epithets for countries and peoples listed in such rhetoric books as the *Gradus ad Parnassum* (1687),[26] but they form a familiar satiric language whose literary uses create a number of interpretive pleasures. Unsurprisingly, a major stereotype of England was its xenophobia. In English prints, Scots appear as "filthy bloodthirsty brutes, destitute of civilization" – clannish and sycophantic.[27] The Spanish are seen as proud, lazy, and obstinate – guilty of the atrocities of the Inquisition, the atrocities of colonization, and such personal atrocities as the removal of Captain Jenkins's ear.[28] But the major targets of English satire were England's most serious rivals, the French and the Dutch.

The Dutch were closest to the English in their religion, their democratic pursuit of knowledge, and their mercantile culture. But they are viewed as dull accountants and avaricious merchants. They are proud, covetous, low republicans – drunken, dishonest, and exploitative.[29] The three naval wars of the seventeenth century stimulated satiric poems which, though directed at diverse English targets, joined in attacking Dutch vices. When Holland's major politician became England's King, his foes used negative Dutch stereotypes to attack his policies, his advisors, or himself, while their answerers were silent about such images.[30] After Holland became an ally, its satiric shortcomings returned in Swift's *Conduct of the Allies* to justify England's pursuit of its own interests.[31] One's allies are appropriate satiric targets, especially when the alliance masks significant economic competition. English attacks on France seemed based on conflicts of culture, values, and beliefs. The French were Catholic in religion and absolute in politics, and the person of Louis XIV embodied French cultural pretensions and political mismanagement. The French provided contrasting images of an effeminate aristocracy and a deprived peasantry: dandified and foppish lords were set against poor, ignorant, and hungry commoners, in rags and wooden shoes.[32] The contrast of wealth and poverty ran through a range of attacks on French manners, economics, and politics, and reflected the ambivalence of the English aristocrats who aped their customs.

William Hogarth's *The Gate of Calais, or O! the Roast Beef of Old England*,
roughly coincident with the Treaty of Aix-la-Chapelle in 1748,[33] is both an
instance of English xenophobia and an illustration of how complex graphic
images could become when handled with dexterity. The picture is organized around the gate itself (built by the English, and the only object in the
picture receiving direct sun), through which one sees a religious procession
and before which a servant carries a hunk of British beef, in contrast to
a pot of French soup. Around the beef are grouped stereotypical images
of a fat friar and a starving soldier; at the left a painter, Hogarth himself, sketches oblivious of the hand about to arrest him – the image of
arbitrary French tyranny. (Hogarth in fact was arrested in precisely those
circumstances, prompting the questionable line of defense that he was not
a spy but a satirist.) The central images are in turn framed by a prosce-
nium arch, before which huddle a ragged woman and a Scot who has fled
to France from the Jacobite defeat. These figures are in turn framed by
the edges of the picture itself. Hogarth's sequence of inner frames or satiric
boundaries emphasizes the inferiority of French to English life. The various
stereotypes and graphic distortions are mixed with realistic and personal
observations to clarify the nature of the primary satiric target: if the French
are hungry, superstitious, and the victims of political tyranny, then France
itself is responsible. The connections of politics and religion, of food and
economics, sharpened by the picture's repeated framing, move the attack
from particular institutions to the level of national character. Through
the manipulation of simple stereotypes, the nation becomes a general
target that gives force and direction to a variety of specific attacks and
allows the viewer to observe multiple connections among satiric vehicles and
objects.

SIMPLE SATIRIC NATIONALISM: MANIPULATED IMAGES

Literary instances of simple satiric nationalism, like graphic ones, exploit
pre-existing stereotypes of nations. As in Hogarth's *Gate of Calais*, they may
manipulate those images in complex ways to multiply the satiric targets.
Andrew Marvell's *Character of Holland* (1652), an important influence upon
later anti-Dutch satires by Marvell and others, has the simplicity of satiric
prints; it is "an educated ecphrasis of the anti-Dutch political broadsides."[34]
Marvell arranges various negative images around the dominant feature of
Holland as what he nastily calls "this undigested Vomit of the Sea" (line 7).
The sea plays "Leap-frog ore their Steeples" (line 24); it suggests the equation
of "pickled *Herring*" with "pickled *Heeren*" (line 34); Dutch religion derives

from the fact that "Th' *Apostles* were so many Fishermen" (line 58). Verbal play with the oceanic imagery "reveals Holland as the sea's unwanted residue and the Dutch as 'anxious,' materialistic, and wholly preoccupied with the accumulation of what after all is no more than dirt."[35] The waves of sea imagery connect the opening character of the Dutch to the concluding celebration of English naval victory. In his analysis of the poem Suvir Kaul points out that "in key passages Holland functions as a sort of perverse mirror in which we can trace the contours of economic, political, and religious issues important to English self-conception."[36]

Daniel Defoe's *The True-Born Englishman* finds that national stereotypes, however negative, imply qualities that may be absent from one's own country. The poem begins by charting such familiar patterns as Spanish pride, Italian lust, German drunkenness, and French passion (lines 82–144). But the English, combining the characteristics of many invaders, lack the identifying mark of simple nationalism, unless it is their instability of values, politics, and loyalties. Simple national stereotypes contrast to Defoe's analysis of the contradictions of English character (lines 429–876). The presence of such stereotypes is the manifestation of national shortcomings; their absence implies the lack of nationhood. There is no such thing as a "true-born Englishman." Defoe's paradoxical play of stereotypes underlines a lack of national purpose that can be remedied only by the unity of public action and values. As Kaul points out, Defoe reverses the image of English colonial expansion by depicting the country as "the virgin land raped by the violence of competing conquerors."[37]

In John Arbuthnot's *The History of John Bull*, rather a collecting point for national stereotypes, the animalistic features of Lewis Baboon (Louis XIV), Nic. Frog (the Dutchman) and John Bull himself are given little subtlety but provide a basis for the allusive ingenuity with which the events of war and international activity are shifted to equivalent matters of law and domestic commerce. John Bull's faithless first wife stands for the Whig ministry, his helpful second wife for the Tories. His lawyer Hocus represents the Duke of Marlborough; Don Diego Dismallo is the Earl of Nottingham (called "Dismal" by satirists such as Swift). John Bull's mother is the Church of England; his sister Peg is Scotland, and her husband Jack its Kirk. Jack is, of course, borrowed from Swift, but Arbuthnot richly extends his allusions to the literature of political controversy.[38] Arbuthnot's political allegory, though occasionally inconsistent and frequently changing in form, is worked out with a detailed significance. Simple satiric nationalism gives an allegorical clarity throughout the separate pamphlets that compose the work.

While Marvell exploits the linguistic means by which traditional stereo-types of the Dutch can be attached to his central metaphor, Defoe estab-lishes simple stereotypes in order to contrast them to the paradox of England as a nation without national identity, and Arbuthnot builds his political allegory with detailed narrative ingenuity. These examples of simple nation-alistic satire share an elaborate manipulation of existing images to organize witty responses to particular historical exigencies. The very simplicity of the images contributes to their manifold satiric uses; the conjunction of imaginative constructs with detailed historical fact verifies the metonymic truth, or the political utility, of the stereotypes themselves.

COMPLEX SATIRIC NATIONALISM: MANIPULATED OBSERVERS

A complex satiric nationalism, or implicit anti-nationalism, is exemplified by the foreign observation characteristic of philosophical and satiric fiction in the Enlightenment.[39] It typically explores the relative claims of national cultures as they come into uneasy conflict with universal and rational prin-ciples. The traveler encounters a new culture, alien to him but familiar to us, and his efforts to interpret it lead him logically to principles and values, or alternatively to problems and uncertainties, that both cultures share. Foreigners may see as shocking eccentricities our long-standing habits or our unexamined assumptions.

The danger that such satire may offend the powerful by charging that the familiar is unreasonable makes the imaginative indirection provided by a patently fictional foreignness especially prudent. Montesquieu excuses his attacks on Catholicism by pointing ambiguously to the ignorance of his Persians: "et, s'ils trouvent quelquefois nos dogmes singuliers, cette sin-gularité est toujours marquée au coin de la parfaite ignorance des liaisons qu'il y a entre ces dogmes et nos autres vérités" ("And if they sometimes find our dogmas odd, the oddity is always characterized by their total ignorance of the way in which these dogmas are linked with our other truths") ("Quelques Réflexions").[40] Montesquieu's explanation may well make his satire more intense rather than less. The connection of "dogme" to "vérité" suggests that dogmas are fictions serving the convenience of questionable truths. Just as (I will argue) nationalism in *Lettres persanes* stands between the individual and universal human nature, complexly linked to both, "dogme" stands between truth and illusion. Montesquieu's prudent indirection attacks constrictive local culture but also questions claims of universality and the standards by which satiric targets may be judged.

The major English heir of *Lettres persanes* is *The Citizen of the World*, which significantly appeared during the Seven Years War. As an Irishman, Oliver Goldsmith projects his alienation from England onto Lien Chi Altangi, the fictional Chinese observer. Goldsmith exploits the intricacies of foreign observation to delineate the nature of general human sympathy. His Chinese persona is occasionally the object of English scorn or misapprehension ("some fancy me no Chinese, because I am formed more like a man than a monster" [Letter xxxiii]),[41] but he is critical of English nationalism and nationalism in general. In Letter iv he mocks English pride in the concept of "liberty," and in the next he considers the xenophobia of English periodicals. Letter xvii attributes the Seven Years War to "one side's desiring to wear greater quantities of *furs* than the other," but he later praises English kindness towards French prisoners: "National benevolence prevailed over national animosity" (Letter xxiii). His disapproval of the war with France extends to war in general (Letter lxxxv). He asserts that "true politeness" is universal but "ceremonies" are local (Letter xxxix). He is repeatedly interested in the interconnections among luxury, wealth, and knowledge (e.g., Letter lxxxii). Like Montesquieu's Persians he is struck by variations in law and in the treatment of women, and his survey of nations leads him to attribute their decline to "the natural revolution of things" (Letter lxiii). He concludes by resolving to continue his travels: "the world being but one city to me, I dont much care in which of the streets, I happen to reside" (Letter cxxiii). His consideration of English life engages specific stereotypes but uses them to detach his perspective from local culture and to assert a larger humanity by virtue of which local variations, perceived through the clarifying experience of travel, can be explained and evaluated.[42] In Hogarth's *Gate of Calais* satiric images transfer their force to the nation as a generalized target. Goldsmith's movement towards the general transforms particularities; the observation of cultural eccentricities produces a cosmopolitanism that, in turn, asserts its superiority over the narrow views and odd behaviors that brought it into being. Universal wisdom is paradoxically achieved through local knowledge.

Voltaire's satire similarly observes images of the local to question national differences. The social and intellectual accomplishments of the English become, in *Lettres philosophiques*, criteria by which French limitations can be attacked, but French sophistication becomes the basis for judging the crudities of the English. At times the contrasts are doubly ironic, as when, at the opening of Letter 23, Voltaire praises French "établissements en faveur des beaux-arts," only to contrast English rewards of artistic merit, most powerfully in the relative treatments of Mrs. Oldfield and Mlle. Lecouvreur.

The opening conversation between the elaborately polite Voltaire and the self-assured Quaker is a model for Voltaire's intercultural ironies.[43] The contrast stresses the force of the nation in determining the intellectual possibilities of individuals: Voltaire and the Quaker are what they are in part because of where they have been.

Voltaire's manipulation of perspective in *Candide* is still more elaborate. The naive satiric victim travels through nations characterized by injustices practiced in the names of civic virtue and religious pride. The vanity of the Westphalians is an extension of their personal self-satisfaction. (It seems appropriate that Voltaire located his pompous Count in the place that not only served as a major battleground of the Seven Years War but gave its name to the 1648 treaty delineating the shape of European nations.) The King of the Bulgares and the King of the Abares mutually exercise the atrocities of war and duly celebrate their Te Deums of victory (ch. 3). The wise men of Lisbon respond to the earthquake with a splendid *auto da fé* (ch. 6). The Jesuits make war on the Spanish and Portuguese kings in Paraguay but are their confessors in Europe (ch. 14). The Dutch in Surinam mangle their slaves as the price we pay for sugar (ch. 19). The French, as described by Martin, are occupied in making love, spreading scandal, and talking nonsense (ch. 21). For Goldsmith's Chinaman the Seven Years' War is fought for furs, but for Martin it is fought for snow, and the English kill their leaders "pour encourager les autres" (ch. 23). The result of these local follies is the reader's sense that absurdity is universal; for nations either cannot perceive the cruelties to which their pretensions lead, or, perceiving them, believe them to be justified.

But the evils associated with nationalism are not merely the result of ignorance; they are, to a degree, structured into the constitution of nations. The differences between the Bulgares and the Abares, between Catholics and Protestants, between Christians and Moslems, mark the otherness that defines nations and that drives their irrational behavior. The utopia of Eldorado, standing at the center of the satire, began as an escape from an external threat, but, having found an inaccessible refuge, its inhabitants no longer fear outsiders. Eldorado, like other utopias, is an anti-nation. Like Houyhnhnmland, it is satiric because it represents an impossible dream.[44] In the end the central characters, by virtue of their exclusion from the false paradise of Thunder-ten-tronckh, have lost their nationality, and hence they witness and suffer the injustices of the lands they have visited. Hardly innocent victims themselves, their lack of national identity parallels their freedom from the quests for money and power that are characteristics of both national and individual competition. Because they are denationalized and hence disconnected if not disinterested observers (contributing therefore to the complex tone of the satire), they are finally capable of forming a semi-autonomous and anti-national community. Although their *jardin* is threatened by the unstable politics of Turkey, it remains viable not only because Candide and his friends have agreed to work but because they do so with no expectation of significant wealth. The renunciation that allows the characters a precarious shelter at the end of *Candide* only reinforces its attack on the nations, real and figurative, through which they have passed to reach that final but not conclusive position. Nationalism is a position that exempts nations from common morality, but their blind behavior writes large the evils of individual human nature. Voltaire's characters may be fictional marionettes, but his nations, alas, are historically real. If individuals must learn to cultivate their own gardens, nations must learn humility about their claims to moral superiority. But individuals may relinquish their pretensions, and the defining characteristic of nationhood is the arrogance of nations. Nations allow Voltaire to extend his satire beyond the easy target of Leibnizian optimism and to verify his pessimism by a wide survey of the intractable evil of human societies.[45]

GULLIVER'S IMAGINED COMMUNITIES

If nations did not exist, satirists would have to invent them. Because national pretensions comprise a variety of vague qualities, they become powerful satiric targets and useful focal points for the convergence of connections the reader might make among satiric targets. This is true not only for the strangely real nations of Voltaire but for the familiarly fictional nations of Swift. Few readers over the age of eleven would see the subject of *Gulliver's Travels* as the actual countries visited by its hero or claim that the story is really about Lilliput, Brobdingnag, Laputa, and Houyhnhnmland. But that is, in a sense, the argument I am making here. Its original title was *Travels into Several Remote Nations of the World*, and the popular change of title to *Gulliver's Travels* seems to shift readings away from the nations observed to Gulliver as character and observer. Since my concern here is with nations, I want to follow the interpretive implications of the original title rather than to provide a comprehensive reading of *Gulliver's Travels*. It can certainly be seen as a satire both on England and on human nature. One might argue that the first two books emphasize political satire, that the last book, in which Gulliver speaks more often of European Yahoos than of English ones, universalizes Swift's subject, and that Book III, beginning with a satire on England's colonial exploitation of Ireland and ending with the disturbing description of the Struldbruggs, serves as a transition to the general subject. "Nation" is the intermediate term between specific politics and general human nature, and Swift uses it to explore connections and to manipulate levels of meaning. *Travels into Several Remote Nations of the World* is the great proto-nationalist satire on nationality.

Gulliver is, of course, an Englishman and writes throughout from that perspective. In Lilliput he is comically unaware that he is the observer of a political allegory, and in Brobdingnag he is doubly unaware that his own jingoism as a little person replicates the jingoism he had condemned in the Lilliputians and that the recent history of Brobdingnag reflects that of England. For most of the *Travels*, he follows complexly the pattern of simple nationalism in locating himself within a particular nationalist ideology and looking at other (remote) nations. But in this case the other nations he sees are fictional ones. Their connection with historical nations lies in the specific analogies that Swift suggests and in the typology of nationhood that he presents.[46]

Swift does not seem interested in such theoretical issues of nationalism as the sources of political power, and the qualifications for enfranchisement. But he is concerned with whether government acts on behalf of the country as a whole, the same art "of instructing Princes to know their true Interest, by placing it on the same Foundation with that of their People" that Gulliver found so chimerical on his visit to Lagado (III.6).[47] Swift's satire mixes clear contrasts with relative and subjective perceptions. The government of Brobdingnag, though significantly lacking political parties, is as monarchical as that of Lilliput but, unlike Lilliput, acts in the interests of the people as a whole. That contrast in political principle underlies the relative situation of the tiny Lilliputians, the normative (Gulliver-sized) English, and the huge Brobdingnags. The Brobdingnag King dismisses the pretensions of Gulliver even more strongly than Gulliver (or his readers) had those of the Lilliputians, but there is relatively little difference between the three countries – or, more precisely, Lilliput and Brobdingnag resemble each other insofar as they resemble England. In a sense Gulliver is right when he attributes the Brobdingnag King's antipathy to the English to his "*narrow Principles* and *short Views*" (II.vii), for if the King had visited Lilliput, he would have ranked Gulliver's countrymen as only the second most "pernicious Race of little odious Vermin" (II.vi). The relative position of the countries is a matter of time as well as size. Gulliver attributes Lilliput's failure to live by its original principles to "the most scandalous Corruptions into which these People are fallen by the degenerate Nature of Man" (I.vi). But the politics of Brobdingnag has improved since the civil wars of several generations ago: "For, in the Course of many Ages they have been troubled with the same Disease, to which the whole Race of Mankind is Subject; the Nobility often contending for Power, the People for Liberty, and the King for absolute Dominion" (ii.vii). The superiority of the Brobdingnagians does not derive from their size or innate nature but from decisions based on national values. England, with a similar history and the same disease, could have reached the same point if it had acted from the same values. The English are not actually odious vermin; they just behave that way.

Gulliver's Travels pursues a variety of satiric targets simultaneously, and this is certainly true of Book iii, where Swift's satiric treatment of national models is complicated by his treatment of human knowledge. Dividing knowledge into science (the synchronic study of structures) and history (the diachronic study of behavior), Swift sends Gulliver to Laputa, which practices false deduction, and to Balnibarbi, which applies false induction.[48] Gulliver travels to Glubbdubdrib, where the magic invocation of the past reveals the corruption of public history; he travels to Luggnagg, where the Struldbruggs exemplify the degeneration of private history. The problem is to connect the description of nations in Book iii to its analysis of knowledge. The practical incompetence of Laputa contrasts to its obsession with power. Its deductive approach, even to the measurement of clothing, results in complete ineptitude, and its array of abstract misfits, flappers, and adulterous wives, fleshes out the impression that the Laputans not only have the wrong idea but insist in imposing that idea universally. They are intensely political ("perpetually enquiring into publick Affairs, giving their Judgments in Matters of State; and passionately disputing every Inch of a Party Opinion," iii.ii), not only, as Gulliver claims, because of their misdirected curiosity but because their self-enclosed mode of reasoning does not allow debates to be resolved by appeal to external factors. Laputan power is simply territorial and technological: by virtue of their magnetic suspension over Balnibarbi and their capacity within limits to control their position, Laputans are able to exert an almost literal oppression on their colony. But, in a shift from economic to scientific energies, the magnetism that enables this power depends on the colonized nation. Politically the relation between Laputa and Balnibarbi represents English colonial dominance over Ireland, and the mildly successful rebellion of Lagado parallels Swift's campaign against William Wood's copper half-pence. In part, then, the disconnect between the Laputans' intellectual confusion and their colonial power underlines the arbitrary nature of that power. But ideology is also connected with colonialism in its insistence on imposing false principles of behavior and belief on resisting subjects.

When Gulliver arrives at Lagado, the capital of Balnibarbi, the results of this imposition can be seen on the ground, so to speak. The false deduction of Laputa is transformed in the colonial sphere into the false induction of Balnibarbi and the Academy of Lagado. The isolation of Lord Munodi shows that national illusions render right-minded individualism impossible. The point that Swift drives home here, as in so many other places, is that imagined ideas have real consequences, for the land of Balnibarbi has been wasted by bad agriculture. The obverse of a self-enclosed deduction that refuses to ground its premises in experience is an induction that does not subject its hypotheses to the scrutiny of common sense. Whether inductive or deductive (or a combination of the two) reason is a tool whose intrinsic flaws require that it be guided by common human experience.

When Gulliver travels from Lagado to Glubbdubdrib, he shifts from science to history, and the government of nations shifts from false reason to superstitious magic. The magicians of Glubbdubdrib summon past sights and spirits, from whom Gulliver learns lessons that have nationalistic implications. Nationalism is based on the myth that public events have public causes, a myth that Swift earlier punctuated in the "Digression on Madness" in *A Tale of a Tub* (1704). Gulliver's magic view of the past is unfiltered by historical accounts, which are written by winners and based on what historians and their patrons want readers to see in the past. There is a parallel problem with how the past is read, and the texts of the past are misinterpreted by later generations. The falsity of writing is equaled by the falsity of behavior. In the past the celebration of virtue produced virtuous people; now the pretension to virtue insufficiently conceals the corruption of the vicious. Seeing the past in a clear and unfiltered way, Gulliver understands that history is driven not by public and apparent causes but by unknown motives, secret causes, and backroom scandals left out of historical accounts, and he sees that the path to historic success is dishonesty and pandering to vice.

But the force of relentless change governs all understanding of history. Even science, as Aristotle explains to Gulliver (iii.viii), is the product of paradigmatic shifts. Time is the measurement of change, and change is entropic, a process of loss and corruption. Hence the present, as Gulliver observes, is inferior to the past. This equation of time to corruption is one of Gulliver's central discoveries, and it correlates closely with nationalist theory. Nations, as Renan pointed out, require "the possession in common of a rich legacy of memories," but the falsification of the past is of equal importance: "Forgetting, I would even go so far as to say historical error, is a crucial factor in the creation of a nation, which is why progress in historical studies often constitutes a danger for [the principle of] nationalism."[49] Benedict Anderson points out that the replacement of a concept of simultaneous time by a concept of sequential time allows the nation to be imagined: "The idea of a sociological organism moving calendrically through homogenous, empty time is a precise analogue of the idea of a nation, which is also conceived as a solid community moving down (or up) history."[50] The process of imagining a nation is, then, a process of imagining a past significantly connected to the present. Gulliver emerges from Glubbdubdrib with two rather different nationalist principles regarding time and history: nations rewrite their pasts – recent or remote – in order to represent the outcome that serves the interests of those in power; but all history is a process of corruption.

It is perhaps because of the force of corruption that Gulliver, when he visits Luggnagg and learns of the Struldbruggs, embraces human immortality as a way of transcending history. The advantage of being a Struldbrugg, from Gulliver's naive perspective, lies in the ability of ancient memory to check the slide of history into modern mediocrity. But he discovers that Struldbruggs, growing continually older, unredeemed by death, are the most accursed of humans, the bodily manifestation of the absolute corruption of time.[51] This revelation humiliates Gulliver even more deeply than the practice of licking the dust by which he has been admitted to the royal presence. But dust-licking identifies the corruption of absolute power, which is marked by a capacity to humiliate others, just as access to power is characterized by a willingness to endure such humiliation. Because access to power is closely tied, for Europeans, to access to money, Swift's exploration of the relationship of nationalism to knowledge concludes with Dutch willingness to trample on the cross in order to gain access to Japanese trade. It is not true, we learn by the end of Book III, that knowledge is power; what is true is that power is knowledge.

The false nations of Book III contrast to the utopian realm of Book IV. In one sense Houyhnhnmland, like El Dorado, is not a nation at all, for it is not defined by borders with other nations. But the Houyhnhnms have a significant and inimical Other, in this case an internal one. The Yahoos, regarded as a distinct species, humanoid rather than equine, represent the irrational bestiality that the Houyhnhnms reject. Houyhnhnms have several myths of Yahoo origins: two of them "appeared together upon a Mountain; whether produced by the Heat of the Sun upon corrupted Mud and Slime, or from the Ooze and Froth of the Sea was never known"; alternatively, that the original pair "had been driven thither over the Sea; that coming to Land, and being forsaken by their Companions, they retired to the

Mountains, and degenerating by Degrees, became in Process of Time, much more savage than those of their own Species in the Country from whence these two Originals came" (IV.ix). Either Yahoos are a species unique to Houyhnhnmland, or they are a decadent version of humanity, a product of the degenerative process described in Book III. Gulliver is initially repelled by the Yahoos but is led by the Houyhnhnms to identify himself as one. The Houyhnhnms are initially confused by Gulliver's clothes (thus literalizing the saying that clothes maketh the man), but they ought to be equally confused that Gulliver has a language (as the Yahoos do not) and can learn one, as he does theirs. So far as I know, no one has argued that the Yahoos are the real heroes of Book IV, but virtually every other interpretive position seems to have been covered. From the present limited perspective of Houyhnhnm nationhood, the major question is what the Houyhnhnm utopia implies about the nature of nations.

In the real world ideal nations do not exist, and Houyhnhnmland is therefore a satiric exemplum rather than a social or political model. For Swift, there is no ideal because everything exists in time, and the product of time is corruption. Although Houyhnhnms are and remain much better than European Yahoos, they are not immune to change, and that change takes place through their encounter with Gulliver. He informs them not only of the perversion of reason but of the existence of an external Other (and hence that Houyhnhnmland too is a nation). His identity as a reasonable, cleanly user of language blurs the boundary between Houyhnhnm and Yahoo on which Houyhnhnm culture depends. Though European colonialism would be impractical in Houyhnhnmland (IV, xii), the chance that Yahoos might turn rebellious by the misinstruction of reason warns the Houyhnhnms that they too have interests to protect – which they do, in the manner of nations, by exiling Gulliver (IV, x). European nations cannot equal Houyhnhnmland because, among European Yahoos, reason without authority cannot serve as the basis for government. Before the arrival of Gulliver, the Houyhnhnms, ideal but also funny, arrogant, and naive, were prelapsarian. They knew no evil (or thought they did), and nationalism is the product of sin. Gulliver may be the serpent in their midst.

Swift has moved from his satiric consideration of remote nations to his pessimistic revelation of human nature by treating the individual as a nation. The human individual is composed of Yahoo-like lust, greed, and desire for dominance but also by the capacity for Houyhnhnm-like reason, and that reason (like the Houyhnhnms) must decide whether to allow itself to be corrupted by the Yahoos of passion, to exterminate the brutes, or to control them, making passion the slave to reason. Swift seems in Book IV to arrive at a conclusion rather different from the one he reached at the end of Book II. The experience of the Brobdingnags suggested that a strong government acting on behalf of the country could balance the interests of monarch, nobility, and people. That hopeful possibility seems quite remote if human nature and the corruption of reason are as evil as Book IV suggests. The difference between Books II and IV leaves readers with more than merely an interpretive decision. If there is a possibility of even a temporary balance of competing interests, they must, as nations and as individuals, test that possibility through action.

"I have ever hated all Nations," Swift wrote to Pope, shortly after completing *Gulliver's Travels*, adding that he hated mankind in general.[52] The problem with nations is that, although they have differentiating national characters, they are units embodying mankind in general. They eliminate individual qualities and act on behalf of a baser aggregate. Such corporate action would be worthy if, as in the case of the Brobdingnags and Houyhnhnms, it were undertaken in the interests of the common good. But nations act on behalf of dominant interests instead. The process of degradation that Gulliver sees as the unavoidable effect of time is the movement away from the good of the community to the advantage of the powerful within it. Gulliver's imagined nations are, of course, a satiric fiction. But they correspond to actuality and become, for Swift and for his readers, a way of perceiving the evil that really exists.

THE COMPLEXITY OF MONTESQUIEU'S *LETTRES PERSANES*

Though it seems unlikely that Swift read *Lettres persanes* (1721) before writing *Gulliver's Travels*, the publication of both books within a few years marks a complex satiric moment resembling the close publications of *Candide* and *Rasselas*. Voltaire surely read Montesquieu, and Goldsmith self-consciously uses his topics. As in the later works, the perplexities of *Lettres persanes* derive from foreign observers, but Montesquieu complicates his perspective by using two significantly different observers.[53] Rica, the livelier but less complicated Persian, reports French political and social absurdities and comes to see the world with a cynical, if superficial, aplomb. It may be that "challenge and response in a new culture end happily for Rica in integration of personality,"[54] but his lack of commitment and intellectuality suggests a happiness achieved by minimizing risks. Tired of seeming an oddity in Paris, he early on (Letter 30) adopts Parisian dress, only to find that he has become a non-entity ("j'entrai tout à coup dans un néant affreux" ["all at once I fell into a terrible state of non-existence"]). In the same letter his protestations that he is Persian are answered by the question how can one be Persian ("Comment peut-on être Persan?"). His witty investigation of French appearances is prompted in part by his personal experience of the power of dress in determining identity. Nationality, he discovers, is literally and metaphorically a matter of costume. Usbek's combination of philosophical depth and personal naiveté makes him an object of unstable irony. He struggles to distinguish between the local and the universal but suffers a destructive incapacity to surmount his own cultural limitations. Rica inconsistently accepts a culture whose follies he reports; Usbek inconsistently practices one whose cruelties conflict with the values he has discovered. Their judgments may be set before us not for our agreement but for our disinterested consideration.

But disinterested consideration may in turn be an interpretive fallacy, allowing the illusion that we readers are not targets of Rica's satire or sharers of Usbek's practices. Usbek, as the more complex character, presents more substantial problems. Rather than defining a character such as Usbek as "other" (the subject of disinterested consideration), satiric nationalism penetrates the boundaries between otherness and selfhood, but without asserting that the connection derives from universal principles. Readers tend to see Usbek as an Enlightenment *philosophe* or as an oriental despot, thus replicating in interpretation the nationalisms of the text. But those who see him as a *philosophe* tend to neglect the horrors of the seraglio or to regard it as a regrettable lapse.[55] Those who see the harem sequence as Montesquieu's essential story of sexual, personal, and political despotism tend to disregard the wisdom Usbek shows in the course of his quest for knowledge.[56] Usbek does not succeed in his search for universal truths because truths, as the manipulation of cultural perspectives implies, are relative, but his search is important. Usbek's harem does indeed represent the nature of despotism, but to see him simply as a despot is to close off the disturbing possibility that he is everyman as well.

Usbek asks whether reason is adequate for understanding behavior, both personal and social.[57] Early in his journey, he writes a Mullah about the conflict of rational and religious principles, but the answer condemns any intellectual activity contrary to faith and obedience (Letters 17 and 18). He sees the emotional nature of individuals (Letter 33) but tries to account for society rationally; in Letter 35 he hopes that religious differences will give way to "un jour où l'Eternel ne verra sur la terre que des vrais Croyants" ("a day . . . when the Eternal will see only true believers on the earth"). Governments, he argues in Letter 80, can be evaluated by a universal principle that applies despite local differences ("le plus parfait est celui qui va à son but à moins de frais" ["the most perfect is the one which attains its purpose with the least trouble"]), like Thoreau's dictum that "that government is best which governs least." Justice is "un rapport de convenance, qui se trouve réellement entre deux choses; ce rapport est toujours le même, quelque être qui le considère, soit que ce soit Dieu, soit que ce soit un ange, ou enfin que ce soit un homme" ("a relation of suitability, which actually exists between two things. This relationship is always the same, by whatever being it is perceived, whether by God, by an angel, or finally by a man") (Letter 83). The laws of legislators are mutable; the laws of science and philosophy have the eternal but abstract validity of mathematical formulae.

But rational discernment of universal laws is complicated by the relativism of knowledge. The conflict of French and Persian customs parallels the conflict of Christian and Moslem beliefs, and neither national nor religious claims fare well in the encounter. Usbek adumbrates the distinction of *L'Esprit des lois* among republican, despotic, and monarchic governments, and his views on moderate and cruel governments (Letter 80) resemble the familiar distinction between nationalism and *étatisme*. He listens to a Frenchman describe "la gloire" in terms similar to the appeals of nationalism: "Mais le sanctuaire de l'honneur, de la réputation et de la vertu, semble être établi dans les républiques et dans les pays où l'on peut prononcer le mot de *Patrie* . . . Tout homme est capable de faire du bien à un homme; mais c'est ressembler aux dieux que de contribuer au bonheur d'une société entière" ("But it seems that the sanctuary of honour, reputation, and virtue is to be found in republics, and the lands where men can speak of 'my country' . . . Everybody is capable of doing good to one man, but it is godlike to contribute to the happiness of an entire society") (Letter 89). But "cette passion générale que la nation française a pour la gloire" ("this passion for glory that the French nation has in general") (Letter 90) is absurdly manifested in dueling. Not even glory retains a stable meaning: the citizen's self-respect becomes the nobleman's *amour propre*; national altruism becomes a selfish quest for personal honor. Such shifts subvert the meaning of Usbek's major terms. As social thinker, he is concerned with freedom and moderation, but he is the tyrannical master of his harem.

Much of the complexity of *Lettres persanes* derives from the disorienting intersection of binary contrasts achieved by the manipulation of foreign observers and the cultures they observe: the rational is set against the emotional, the temporal against the eternal, the local against the universal, the personal against the social, *moeurs* against *lois*, behavior against belief, subjective knowledge against universal opinion. Usbek's travels are undertaken as a journey to knowledge (though that purpose is questioned by the revelation in Letter 8 that his quest is a pretext for escaping his enemies), but his enlightenment and our own are threatened by the likelihood that neither individual knowledge nor corporate wisdom can control the instabilities of so many conflicting and exclusive variables. Such binary oppositions are further confused by the passage of time: the Troglodytes move from revolution to aggressive individualism, and from an altruistic community to a national monarchy; individuals are similarly trapped by time.[58]

The dislocating force of Montesquieu's binary conflicts is particularly significant in the recurrent issues of sexuality and the treatment of women. The early letters from Usbek's concubines may tempt voyeuristic readers to identify with Usbek, the supposed sexual hero, but long before the appearance of heroism has given way to despotism and finally to the destruction of the harem, moral judgment will have replaced sexual fantasy. Sexual desire is both universal and personal, but the customs governing the lives of women are local. The differentiation of these local customs is simultaneous with the harem's close enactment of the political principles Usbek discovers from the observation of European governments. The relationship among Usbek (the absent monarch), the eunuchs (his ministers or regents) and his wives (perhaps the nobility) also parallels the relationship between the pope, priests, and the faithful.[59] These relationships are based on a sequence of falsities behind falsities. Despite the early sensuous letters to Usbek from Zachi (3) and Fatmé (7), the blandishments of the wives are enforced performance motivated at best by pride. But Usbek, in his turn admits that he does not love them: "Ce n'est pas, Nessir, que je les aime: je me trouve à cet régard dans une insensibilité qui ne me laisse point de désirs" ("It is not, Nessir, that I love them. I find that my insensibility in that respect leaves me without desire") (Letter 6). Roxane's attractive modesty turns out to be Usbek's misinterpretation of her loathing for him (Letters 26, 161). Usbek's desperation at his inability to control his harem at such a distance leads him to give his eunuchs harsh orders that, when carried out, seem a more sadistic profanation of his wives than the infidelity he sought to prevent. Although he has become a philosophical moderate, Usbek is a despotic figure in the context of the harem, in part because he is caught in a cultural institution in which he no longer believes, and in part because power magnifies the inconsistencies of human nature. (Usbek describes the inconsistencies of Louis XIV in Letter 37.)[60]

Many issues in the harem letters, in Rica's reports on French society, and in Usbek's quest for knowledge reappear in Usbek's reflections on the worldwide decline in population.[61] Some causes are international:

plagues, venereal disease, and the loss of resources, but depopulation is also caused by the national sexualities that organize Usbek's analysis. Moslem seraglios place the procreative burden on a few underproductive fathers. In Christian Europe the interdiction of divorce holds couples in loveless, sex-less, and childless marriage, and clerical celibacy reduces the supply of potential parents. Primogeniture discourages childbearing beyond the first son. For primitive peoples hunting and gathering require a sparse popula-tion. Slavery depletes Africa without increasing the colonies, which in turn weaken their mother country. The convergence of local practices on the universal phenomenon of depopulation shows the sensitive but irresolute differentiation of Montesquieu's text. The variety of nationalistic causes im-plies that multiple solutions are unlikely, even if they have in common the freeing of restrictive attitudes. Universality may be linked to understanding, but behavior is constrained by the local.

The unresolved gap between knowledge and action apparent in Usbek's discussion of population is reproduced within his own character. His movement towards a sophisticated, liberal, and tolerant understanding seems admirable.[62] But his Persian identity distances us from him, just as it keeps him from seeing the French as they see themselves. Nationalism sug-gests, in *Lettres persanes* as it does in *Candide*, that an intermediate culture stands between human individuality and the comprehension of universal human nature. On one hand, national culture, in law, politics, religion, and sexuality, shapes individual character in ways that individuals may not recognize or cannot overcome. On the other hand, national culture makes claims for temporal and local principles that rival and even obscure the claims of general human nature; hence Usbek's effort to perceive the universal is implicitly revolutionary (an unwitting parallel to the revolution of Roxane), even though he remains unaware of limitations implicit in his own Persian nationalism. The effect of complex satiric nationalism is to introduce a powerful new lens between the individual and the universal, so as to transform the telescope focused on truth into a kaleidoscope of paradoxes.

Montesquieu's claim that the work is held together by "une chaîne secrète et, en quelque façon, inconnue" has been the subject of much discussion.[63] Such readings underline major aspects of the novel but do not seem fully satisfactory in balancing the thematic nexus of philosophy, politics, and morality against the formal elements of epistolary fiction to which it is tied by a chain that is both binding and secret. Montesquieu's claims may frame a screen on which readers may project particular interpretations. The satiric nationalism of *Lettres persanes* does not pin down this elusive image, but it gathers the various combinations that it proposes. Montesquieu significantly chooses a chain to identify a work whose topic is liberty. The intellectual instabilities of its national perspectives (a chain in intellectual and structural senses) are also manifested in a rhetorical chain that ties readers to the text. We cannot dismiss the observations of the Persians because we are repeatedly if not consistently struck by their truth; we cannot, much as we wish, regard them merely as alien, for on a number of levels, figurative as well as literal, we perceive their kinship with ourselves. Our sympathetic but distant attachment to the text makes us feel the binding force of an unknown chain. The connections of philosophy, religion, and politics, of thematic structures and epistolary form, are held together by rhetorical, affective relationships between readers and the text. But such connections are paradoxical: chains connect but also bind. We perceive the nature of freedom by understanding how we are not free. The national chain binding us within a circumscribed culture seems both necessary and false, imposed by arbitrary authority rather than by natural truth. Beneath that chain lies the truer link of human sympathies, could we but see it. But perceiving it is the feeling act of the free, as the subversion and rebellion within the harem insist; the reality of social institutions is constraint.

By observing Usbek, the fallible observer of our own false behavior, we become aware of our unreliability both as subjects of *Lettres persanes* and as its readers. Our own uncertainties echo the ironic instability of the observers, distanced from them, as we are, by their foreignness and from the text by its apparent randomness. As topics emerge and recur, they engage a series of contrasts, sometimes paralleling each other, sometimes indicating contrasts within contrasts. These contrasts create confusion, but although perception seems unpredictable, our understanding of its process is revealing. In perceiving the forces that shape our attitudes and behavior, we become aware of our limitations. The novel's social and political satire, its fictive rendering of character and plot, and its unresolvable philosophical search for universal truths beneath the diversity of experience, are embodied in the narrow nationalisms of both Persians and Parisians. Such nationalisms embody qualities that we cannot, perhaps must not, reject, but their distortions require a complex, questioning understanding.

SATIRIC SUBVERSION

Complex satiric nationalism creates such understanding by allowing unstable, ironic, or victimized perceivers to look at the foreignness of familiar society. Simple satiric nationalism, in contrast, begins with old images and shows the unusual ways they may be true. Its stereotypes feature the wit of the satirist, the relationship of national prejudices to historical facts, or the faults of the home rather than the foreign nation. Complex satire destabilizes its subject by questioning communal values and loyalties. It may, with Goldsmith's *Citizen of the World*, assert the priority of the universal over the local. It may contrast local cultures to emphasize their faults, as in *Lettres philosophiques*; or, as *Candide* and *Gulliver's Travels* do, it may survey mankind from Westphalia to Peru in order to generalize on particular disgusts. But *Lettres persanes* asserts the inevitability of national culture at the same moment that it questions its values and warns of its dangers. The ambiguities of nationalism are illustrated by its movement from the Enlightenment to the French Revolution. Enlightenment figures could question the absurdity of national pretensions, or an expatriate from Geneva, living in Paris, could write instructions to Poland and Corsica on forming a nation. But such efforts may conclude that nationhood itself is universal, that local loyalties derive from universal values. The exact nature of those principles, whether shared language, communal memory, political authority, or economic interest, is itself the issue that theorists debate in defining the meaning of nationalism. But the resultant demands of the state lie in areas which satire may identify as uncertain or untrustworthy.

Satire, like other forms of literature, may be useful during the transition to nationalism because it can coordinate and even transcend the interests of diverse social groups.[64] But the relatively free press in England, the printing of French books in Holland, and the literary underground of France were difficult to control, and the ease of satiric production (at its simplest, scribbling an anonymous libel) served diversity rather than control. Neither simple nor complex satiric nationalism is a reliable support for national ideology. Arbuthnot's *History of John Bull* reduces the politics of nations to the domestic and legal manipulations of ordinary citizens, and in personalizing the pretensions of nations, it subverts their claim to a moral authority above that of individuals. Mockery of nations finally questions the claims of nationhood: it may assert the priority of universal over local values; it may expose the shortcomings of contrasted nations; it may insinuate that the culture of peoples is created by individual consciousness; and it may recognize the inevitability of nationhood while exposing its limitations.

Historically the effect of Enlightenment internationalism may have been the emergence of secular nationalism in the next century. By yoking the satire of other nations to the mockery of religion, satiric nationalism fostered the secular ideology that justified the power of the state. The claim that reason and nature give priority to the universality of human experience returned as a romantic, revolutionary argument that nations were universally needed to embody the cultural identity of particular peoples, and this argument transposed religion, education, and military service to the realm of state enforcement.[65] But satire often possesses an anarchic force that may undercut the principles that nationalism establishes. It is too unstable to be a reliable tool of national ideology, and nations do well (or ill) to use the darker weapons of propaganda. Satire exploits the nation's double image. On one hand, nations reflect the human sympathies that bind communities together. It is no accident that the nation's most powerful and recurrent analogy is the family. On the other hand, nations are imagined communities – artificial constructs, political abstractions whose claims to loyalty are paradoxically personal and moral. Satire plays these natural and artificial images against each other; it scrutinizes national claims by shifting the levels on which they are regarded or by revealing the poses of political self-interest masquerading as morality. By calling into question the certainty of knowledge itself, it subverts the authority of the state that claims to know and calls its citizens, at whatever cost, to serve that knowledge.

The major issues of nationalism and its cognate terms remain unreconcilable not only because of the large number of variables that make them up, the tensions between universal and local patterns, and the exigencies of particular times and places, but also because of the ambivalence that people feel about their own nations and nations in general. Because they remain unresolved, the issues of nationalism leave citizens with questions of how nations determine the identity of their citizens and how individuals define their nation. Nationalism shifts from a generally definable state of affairs to a process of identifying changing relationships. Satire plays a useful role in this process by providing sharp but complex modes of presentation and distinction. Satiric nations operate on a double level of imagination. They are imagined as communities, and satire both exploits and questions the images of which they are made. But reimagined within the satiric text, the nation reveals to the satirist's gaze the interconnections of social manners and political behavior, of cultural particulars and of general wisdom. The nation thus becomes both a political structure and a literary one.

CHAPTER 3

Satiric exile

The nationalistic satirist writes as a member of his country, whether he likes it or not. He may define it as a community – perhaps even a real one – and use its values to attack the Other. He may project its values (aggressive economic individualism, for example) onto other countries (such as Holland) to attack local values by pretending to attack foreign ones. He may imagine exotic foreign observers whose astonished reaction defamiliarizes the familiar and brings it under critical scrutiny. Such a strategy reflects the dual nationality that many of us possess – a literal citizenship within a political nation and a metaphorical allegiance to Israel, Rome, or the Republic of Letters. The metaphorical citizenship of the world may subvert political nationalism, but it does not deny it. The satiric exile is in quite a different position – distinct from other exiles by being a satirist and from other satirists by being an exile. The satiric nationalist exploits his nationality for the purposes of his satire; his country literally defines the scope of his satire. The satiric exile, in contrast, is displaced; he is both *from* a country and *in* a country, but he is not *of* a country. The isolated position of exiles differs from that of refugees, immigrants, and expatriates by virtue of its enforced political nature.

Satiric exiles differ from satiric expatriates (for example) by the political focus of their satire and by the intensity of their forlorn hope for return. They remain attracted by their native country but are trapped apart from it by the disjunction between the country and its government. Return does not depend on their will but on the government that has exiled them. But because governments are not conterminous with countries, a change may call the exile back. Indeed, for the exile it may seem the only way of return. Hence exile has a particular political force. Because of that political force, exile is essentially historical, deriving its character from the political factors producing it; the exile of Ovid from Rome was different from that of Dante from Florence. It is not clear that Ovid's exile was political; Dante's clearly was. Ovid was banished to the barbarous outskirts of empire, where he died; Dante traveled through Europe and declined to return to Florence under less-than-honorable conditions. Exiles may be, like Ovid, isolated individuals, or, like Brecht, part of a political diaspora.[1] But they share a sense of essential estrangement.

Exiles are cut off from their roots, their land, their past. They generally do not have armies or states, although they are often in search of them. Exiles feel, therefore, an urgent need to reconstitute their broken lives, usually by choosing to see themselves as part of a triumphant ideology or a restored people. The crucial thing is that a state of exile free from this triumphant ideology – designed to reassemble an exile's broken history into a new whole – is virtually unbearable, and virtually impossible in today's world.[2]

Satiric exiles use this displacement as a complex means of manipulating perspectives on their native country, their adopted country, and humanity itself. They begin with the evident discomfort that exile has caused them. Exile becomes an extreme manifestation of personal alienation, but it is political alienation as well. The fact that two countries, two cultures, two languages are involved internalizes a comparative point of view that raises the personal and political concerns of the satiric exile to a more general level, so that the flawed alternatives of the countries between which the exile is caught reemerge as paradoxes of the human situation. But the famous doubleness of exile vision is clouded by this separation and alienation. On one hand, what the exile can say about the country of origin is limited by the fallibility of memory; the replacement of observation by memory is a defining characteristic of exile. On the other hand, the exile's perception of the adopted country is skewed by its strangeness or by the exile's refusal to relinquish the culture he has been forced to leave. The movement from one culture to another may limit the exile's capacity to perceive and evaluate a variety of matters, from foodstuffs through politeness rules to language itself, and the exile's audience may have a corresponding problem. Emil Draitser, himself a satirist in exile, acutely notes that distance from the cultural details that satire requires is a serious difficulty when the satirist's audience is incapable of recognizing their cultural significance.[3] Thus the double vision of exile creates a double uncertainty, and the satiric exile, whose *métier* depends on acuity of vision, may recreate both old and new worlds in the medium of fiction.

The satiric exile often begins with the personal pain of separation; non-satiric exiles may remain trapped by that personal pain and the unfulfillable longing to return, so that they never move to the cultural and political analysis that makes exile satiric. Such was the case of Ovid, the classical embodiment of the exile. The technical distinction between a *recusatio* (who, like Ovid, was allowed to retain his property, although banished from Rome) and an exile (who lost his property) does not seem relevant to Ovid's exile experience. He consistently refers to himself as an exile. His art is both a cause of his banishment and the medium of its expression. His last books of poetry (*Tristia* and *Epistulae ex Pontis*) deal exclusively with his exile. He complains about his hardships on the frontier, but the heart of his concern is his banishment from the center of culture. By an ironic twist, the changes depicted in his *Metamorphoses* are now represented by his exile. He has lost his poetic vocation except in writing about the exile that has caused that loss. He creates surrogate selves who remain in Rome. He still has friends to whom he can write and who can express their support. His wife has stayed to protect his property and to seek his recall (*Tristia* 1. iii. 87–88). His poems now take the physical place of the poet in Rome (*Tristia* 1.i.15, 57–58; 3.i) and preserve his identity in the land to which he cannot return.

At the heart of Ovid's complaints about his exile is silence. His exile was partly the result of his early amorous poems, which offended the moral standards that Augustus sought to elevate and enforce. But Ovid alludes to another reason which he does not specify; indeed, to specify it would be to repeat his offense. He thus cannot discuss the injustice of his exile because he cannot reveal its cause.[4] The emperor whom he offended was the man who exiled him and the only man who can reverse his sentence. Ovid's physical exile in Tomis is the outward sign of the legal and political bind in which he is trapped. The subjects of his exile poems are the outward signs of a reality that must remain unspoken. Reality is also hard to perceive in his description of Pontus, which goes beyond exaggeration to outright fiction. The conflict between his account of perpetual frosts and the data on climate supplied by the Romanian Tourist Board led A. D. Fitton Brown to speculate that Ovid had not been to Tomis at all.[5] Jo-Marie Claassen argues that Ovid uses largely fictional geography and literary stereotypes to create a world of exilic myth.[6] The reality of his exile lies not in its geographic or ethnographic accuracy but in the intensity of its pain. Its mythic land contrasts to the inescapable empire within which he remains.

Although Ovid's inability to articulate the radical cause of his exile traps him as fully as exile does itself, satiric exiles, in contrast, may be quite articulate about the political causes of their displacement, their political and cultural distance from their adopted country, and the difficulties of transferring from one national culture to another. Thus while they remain distinct from other kinds of expatriates, they share most of the problems of those who move from one country to another. Consequently, satiric exile may be seen as a particular kind of cross-cultural literature. The characteristics of satiric exiles can be conveniently listed.

(1.) Exiles are hopelessly severed from their country of origin. Although they may begin with the hope that their absence is temporary, they may come to feel that return is politically impossible, or that, if they could return, they would find that the country they had left now exists only in their minds, and they, rather than those who live there, are its only citizens. Exiles acquire the permanent status of temporary residence.

(2.) The exile is caught by a struggle between the personal experience of exile from the home country and the preconceptions that have been manufactured by the ideologies of the new country. In addition to other adjustments of migration, exiles must assert or discover their identity in the face of stereotypes and must correct the stereotypes they bring with them. The interplay of stereotypes and realities becomes both a problem and a technique for the exiled writer.

(3.) Even exiles who have been forced to leave their native country may nonetheless feel some guilt at leaving, and that sense is intensified by the hardships and deaths of those left behind – spouses and children, family and friends. But they may also fear that they have not succeeded in escaping the past they have left. They cannot disconnect their new identity from the causes that drove them from their country. Hence they fear the hidden messenger or secret assassin who tracks them from the past to the present.

(4.) Because the native country is both a land from which they have been estranged and a part of their own selves, they may be unwilling to adopt the country where they now live, either because they perceive its citizens as barbarians, as Ovid did the Getae, or because their identity belongs to what they have left behind.

(5.) In light of their imagined destiny to return, the time they spend in exile seems wasted but endless, measured against a return that always recedes into the future. The irrecoverable past is disconnected from the present, sundered by the fact of exile itself. But time exists simultaneously in both countries, and experiences seem simultaneously to touch the past and the present. The exile speaks to the future, but his primary concern is the past: "It's not that he wants to be young again; he simply does not want tomorrow to arrive, because he knows that it may edit what he beholds."[7]

(6.) Exiles may associate with other exiles or emigrés from their native country, perpetuating a sub-culture that concentrates on events in the native land, that produces publications in the native language, and that forms an independent (often cash) economy. Such sub-cultures may reinforce the temporary and provisional nature of the individual exile's experience, but they ultimately solidify into a ghetto culture on the fringes of mainstream or national culture. Because that sub-culture consists of successive waves of immigrants, its exact nature changes over time. Such changes may mean, however, that the exile finds in the emigré sub-culture precisely the attitudes he sought to escape in exile. The emigré audience may be the community to whom and against whom he writes.

(7.) Exiles, like other immigrants, are faced with a difficult decision regarding language. In hopes of return, they may reject the new language, or they may seek to learn it quickly, or unusually they may, like Nabokov, be multilingual before becoming exiles. More unusually still, they may, like Conrad, find in the new language their capacity to speak in a liberated voice. But even linguistically able exiles are likely to feel that only their native tongue can adequately express their essential identity and communicate what they truly have to say.

(8.) The problem of exile subsumes all others. Personal or social difficulties that existed before the exile now become problems of exile itself. Exile becomes a metaphor for other losses – for the loss of youth, for lost love, for the death of parents, for the irrecoverability of the past, for personal failure. Thus exile cannot be sharply defined; the metaphor blurs at the edges, creating figurative images whose emotional impact echoes the loss of one's country.

(9.) But its multiplicity of focus and its capacity to stand for other human conditions transform exile into art. The doubleness of vision, the isolated individuality of the artist, and the indeterminate figurations of literature make the language of art particularly appropriate to the articulations of exile. But exile is also an appropriate location of the artist, so that twentieth-century writers from Mansfield, Joyce, Pound, and Eliot to Brecht, Broch, Mann, and Musil, whether political exiles or not, have written self-consciously as people who have been displaced (or chosen displacement) from their original homes. Exile becomes, as Michael Seidel describes it, "a symptomatic metaphor for the state of the narrative imagination."[8] The fragmented, uncertain qualities of the exile's memories and of the past's fictional nature produce the discontinuities and uncertainties of postmodernism.

(10.) Exile thus stands for liminality of all sorts. The borders between countries, between ideologies, turn, extend, or duplicate to become the
borders between genders, between generations, between sexual ori-
entations, between literacy and ignorance, between fact and fiction.
Other borders are marked by writing itself. The book that may bring
a sign of its absent author to the country he has left also demarcates
the ideas and experience it records from all the world not included in
its pages.

(11.) The status of the book itself as exile becomes all the more pronounced
when its message is a satiric one of rejection. Because satiric exiles begin
with anger and pain, they can hardly be dispassionate when these are
projected onto the political and cultural analysis that articulates the
nature of their exile. But that passionate analysis is not likely to be
readily accepted either by the native country or the adopted one,
and thus the satire itself becomes an exile. Satirists may confront
their alienation by directing their anger defiantly at the audience, or
they may elaborate the fiction by which it is articulated, so that the
reader's game of decoding becomes more immediate than the force
of the anger. Or satirists may bypass the nationalistic nature of their
audience by insisting that its members locate themselves not as citizens
of the countries they attack but as denationalized human beings whose
sympathies they enlist.

(12.) Exile may have its positive side as well. The exile may take on the
nationality of his new country, effectively rejecting the desirability of
return. He may, like Nabokov and Kundera, shift to the language of
the new country. Or he may, like Rushdie, rejoice in exile's doubleness
of vision, seeing it as a more-than-adequate compensation for the loss
of the home country. His satire may reflect that transition from one
country to another, it may remain self-consciously captured in the
moment of exilic tension, when the gravitational pulls of home and
host countries are approximately equal, or it may recreate that moment
in order to make the exilic tension a satiric one as well.

Traps and paradoxes are inescapable in satiric exile. Exile itself involves
a three-part relationship of the exile, the lost homeland, and the difficult
new culture. To these facts of exile, satire adds the intention of attack, the
various and unstable locations of the target of that attack, and the equally
uncertain source of the values that justify it. Because exile further stands
for a series of losses (personal, cultural and political, belonging to the exile
and to the countries left and gained) the ubiquity of loss renders satiric
exile artistically fruitful and personally disturbing.

The complexities of satiric exile correspond to familiar characteristics of postmodernism: its paradoxes, its indeterminate discourses, its formal fragmentation, its skepticism of unified meaning. To explore satiric exile, I will look at three texts written since 1960. Charles Kinbote, the narrator of Vladimir Nabokov's *Pale Fire*, imagines himself an exile but is a more troubling one than he imagines. Milan Kundera wrote *The Book of Laughter and Forgetting* shortly after he himself left Czechoslovakia; he exploits the multiple topics made possible by exile to analyze public history and private experience in eastern and western Europe. Salman Rushdie, in *Shame*, self-consciously adopts the position of an exile, but Pakistan, the country of which he writes, had never quite been his homeland: he left Bombay to be educated in England, where he remained when his family moved to Pakistan against his will. Hence he left one homeland only to have another supplied in its place. Taken together the three works present a range of countries, issues, narrative modes, fictional structures, and satiric models. The pattern of satiric exile involves a three-part movement, beginning with the anger and pain of the satiric exile, moving outward to an analysis of the political and cultural conditions in both the home and host countries that have produced this distress, and carrying the analysis further, to see exile as emblematic of the human condition. The application of this model thus involves a consideration of the troubled voices of the exiles (or their surrogates), the false or fictitious orders by which they seek to analyze the experience of exile, the troubled lands from which they have come or in which they now find themselves, and the unstable world of which those nations are a part.

THE DISLOCATED VOICES

The voice of the exile is dislocated in three ways: it is cut off from the home country, it is strange in the host country, and it is distant from the reader. That dislocation is exemplified with considerable complexity by Vladimir Nabokov's *Pale Fire*. Charles Kinbote, its mad annotator and exiled figure, is cut off from an unrecoverable past and experiences a shift of values that disorients his adopted country. He is misperceived in his adopted country, and those misperceptions lead to disguises by which he compensates for the identity left in the past. Preeminent among those disguises is the novel in which he appears. *Pale Fire* is both satire and novel. It fulfills, with a self-conscious literalness, Barbara Herrnstein Smith's description of the novel as an imitation of an inscription.[9] Here the imitation destabilizes the inscription (the text of Shade's poem), the act of inscribing (its composition, as described by Kinbote), and the process of deciphering (the extensive and unreliable annotation that Kinbote attaches to the poem). The book consists of a poem of 999 lines by John Shade, preceded by a "Foreword" in which Kinbote, the editor, explains, with significant omissions, how he came to edit the poem. The poem is followed by a lengthy commentary that intermittently tells three stories: (1.) the story of the composition of the poem as Kinbote, Shade's neighbor, partly witnesses and partly reconstructs it; (2.) the story of Charles Xavier Vseslav, the last King of Zembla, who fled his country in disguise and now teaches at an American university in the person of Kinbote himself; (3.) the story of Jacob Gradus, whom Kinbote identifies as a Zemblan assassin who seeks to kill the exiled King but kills Shade instead. (Readers conclude that he is an escaped madman who wants to kill the judge who sentenced him, whose house Kinbote has rented.)

The novel is, in significant ways, an imitation of Nabokov's own texts. Nabokov wrote it while he was correcting his heavily annotated edition of Pushkin's *Eugene Onegin* (1964), and, along with *Lolita* and *Pnin*, it comes between the rewriting in Russian of his memoir *Conclusive Evidence* and its revision as *Speak Memory*. But it becomes the fictional antithesis of his own work by combining disparate forms. In effect, Nabokov has Kinbote, his agent, superimpose a "fictional memoir" onto the text of Shade's poem. Kinbote had wanted the poem to be an epic of his own fictionalized life, as told to Shade, but the poem is an autobiography of Shade himself, which Kinbote editorially reinterprets to replace the poem he had hoped for. His efforts parody the worst excesses of readerly subjectivity, but Shade's poem effectively resists this revenge on the text. As the "plot" unfolds in the commentary, the reader becomes quickly aware that Kinbote claims to be "Charles the Beloved," the gay King of an irrecoverable northern land. But further levels are added to the fictionality of Kinbote's story, and further doubts emerge that destabilize one's understanding of what *Pale Fire* is as a fictive text. Is Kinbote really Kinbote, or merely the mad disguise of still another figure? At the end of the commentary he suggests further future manifestations, including Nabokov himself ("on another campus, as an old, happy, heterosexual Russian, a writer in exile, sans fame, sans future, sans audience, sans anything but his art.")[10] In notes prepared for a 1962 interview Nabokov wondered if any reader would recognize that the narrator is actually a Russian professor named V. Botkin and that he commits suicide before completing the index.[11] The possibilities are thrown open by the fact that the disguiser has disguised himself as a disguiser. The structure of narrative disguises in the novel resembles a more elaborate puzzle than the *matryoshka* it seems to be. The Index, which refers not to pages but to lines of Shade's poem, contains no reference following its entry on "Zembla, a distant northern land" (just as there is no final line in Shade's poem). Botkin's suicide is consistent with the unhappy personality of Kinbote, who thus seems a disguise rather than a fiction. Beyond these disguises, critics have suggested that Shade, like the commentary on his poem, is a creation of Kinbote,[12] or that Kinbote is a creation of Shade.[13] There is an interpretive fork created in part by Nabokov's proclivity to pose problems. One direction moves towards the deciphering of riddles, towards which the text provides an oversupply of hints; the other moves towards the discernment of significance. I have not been convinced that suggestions concerning the riddles always bring with them an increased significance. They seem intriguing but not finally soluble.

The disguise of voices in *Pale Fire* is analogous to the force of exile in its dislocations. Shade's voice – ruminative, conversational, and informal – plays against the artful couplets of his poem, producing a tension that, on one hand, defines the aesthetic limitation of his verse and, on the other, supplies his concluding view of "the verse of galaxies divine / Which I suspect is an iambic line" ("Pale Fire," lines 975–76). Kinbote poses as an exiled monarch in disguise. He, or his alter ego Botkin, is clearly an exile. But his double disguise suggests his homosexuality, thus resulting in an ambiguity when, late in the novel, Shade tells him that "I think I guessed your secret long ago" (288). Martine Hennard points to the closeness of exile and disguise: "The exile must indeed redefine, and to some extent invent, an identity in order to make sense of his translated self."[14]

The novel manifests mirror-like reflections both between the poem and the commentary and between the paradoxically overlapping and contrasting characters of the two authors. "The name Zembla is a corruption not of the Russian *zemlya* [land]," Kinbote tells an antagonist, "but of Semblerland, a land of reflections, of 'resemblers.'" "Resemblances," Shade responds, "are the shadows of differences. Different people see different similarities and similar differences" (265), a phrase that might well be a motto for reading the novel. The instability of Kinbote's character and the apparent solidity of Shade's point back to the creator whose intelligence and art is capable of creating both, to Nabokov himself. Nabokov the exile, by creating Kinbote the exile, has made a fiction whose confusions nonetheless enable the reader to work beyond the text, not in the egoistic direction of Kinbote's efforts to impose his own self on Shade's poem, but towards the creator's power to hold in a creative balance the countervailing forces implied by exile – the pull of a madly fictional past against the harsh reality of the present.

One form of such creative balance is the capacity of the exile to see from both sides of the boundary. That doubleness of perspective is particularly evident in *The Book of Laughter and Forgetting*, where it is established by the way in which Kundera treats himself. There is a sense in which Kundera's novel is an exercise in autobiography, in which the author's commentary and confessions imply his presence in the novel's topics and even characters. Kundera writes himself into the book as witness and sharer in the history of Czechoslovakia and as an exile looking at it from a distance both of miles and years. He tells us of his own place in the circle of Communist ideology and power and of his fall from that circle.[15] His fall moves him into a condition of internal exile, from which the only recourse is the obsolescence or eventual disappearance of the circle itself, a situation almost achieved by the spring of 1968, only to be ended by the Russian invasion. Thereafter, the dominant metaphor becomes not exclusion but erasure, the rewriting of history by the elimination of the public identity of its participants and ultimately of historians themselves.

The metaphor of erasure is combined with that of falling when Kundera feels a sudden desire to rape an admirable woman who had helped him and been discovered:

It may be that the insane desire to rape R. was merely a desperate effort to grab at something in the midst of falling. Because ever since they expelled me from the ring dance, I have not stopped falling, I am still falling, and all they have done now is push me once again to make me fall still farther, still deeper, farther and farther from my country into the deserted space of a world where the fearsome laughter of the angels rings out, drowning all my words with its jangle. (106)

Kundera's literal urge to rape R. seems to correlate with the state's intention to rape her figuratively. At the time of their encounter, her efforts in publishing an astrology column he has ghost-written have cost her job and may create serious dangers. Kundera is physically stimulated by her physical fear. The scene makes him realize that he cannot remain in his country without endangering his friends. He flees to western France, from which he looks back at the events of Part Five (where he appears himself in the poets' club as the character Boccaccio) from "the great distance of two-thousand kilometers" and a gap of eight years. As M. N. Banerjee points out, "distance creates an inner intensity that abolishes the borderline between the fantastic and the real, muddles time."[16]

Kundera's flight into exile and the banning of his books in Czechoslovakia created for him the exile's problem of language. Nabokov himself was multilingual (as well as being the ingenious inventor of Zemblan), but his central character betrays significantly comic lapses in language, from his inability to understand the significance of "Chapman's Homer" for the game of baseball to his inability to find the title of Shade's poem ("Pale Fire") in his English translation of a Zemblan translation of Shakespeare's *Timon of Athens*. Despite his English education, Salman Rushdie's narrator sees English as the language of colonizers, whose shamelessness forces him to write "shame" as *sharam*: "No, I must write it in its original form, not in this peculiar language tainted by wrong concepts and the accumulated detritus of its owners' unrepented past, this Angrezi in which I am forced to write, and so for ever alter what is written."[17] Rushdie's use of *sharam* for "shame" may be a tactic he learned from *The Book of Laughter and Forgetting*, where Kundera uses the Czech term *litost* for a similar humiliating quality. For Kundera the problem of translation was intensified by the fact that the language in which his novel was written is not the language in which it is read. Kundera's now-famous concern for the status of his translations exemplifies the linguistic problems of the writer in exile. He has more-or-less disowned the original English translations of his Czech novels. Since he now writes in French, the new English translations use his revised French translations rather than his original Czech as their source. Kundera's shift from a Czech to a French identity (he is now a French citizen) parallels Nabokov's shift from a Russian identity to an American one. Kundera's anxiety to control translations exemplifies interrelated problems of the exiled writer: the problem of language and audience, the problem of disjunctions in time, and the problem of transformed identity.[18] Because Kundera is, in effect, writing for translation, the novel becomes an exercise in definition: *litost* ("a state of torment created by the sudden sight of one's own misery" [167]), the laughter and forgetting of the title, and the political and sexual meanings of "borders" in Part Seven. But the terms defining these terms are in turn subjected to definition, so that the book establishes a counterpoint of intersecting words (as, for example, in Kundera's description of musical tonality in political terms [244–47]).

One response to the problem of translation is for Kundera (exercising Jakobson's phatic function) to create a bilingual audience who is, at the same time, his central character: "it is a novel about Tamina, and whenever Tamina goes offstage, it is a novel for Tamina. She is its principal character and its principal audience, and all the other stories are variations on her own story and meet with her life as in a mirror" (227). She is the novel's prime representative of the situation of exile; her name is partly derived from the Czech word (*tam*) for "over there."[19] The sympathy that both author and reader feel for her predicament links us in ways that are central to the ineluctable problem of meaning towards which the novel moves. But the distance between Tamina and authors lies in "the difference be-tween human being and writer" (146). Writers, from Goethe to Kundera, personify the egotism in which "a man turns into a universe," and each universe struggles with others to impose its uniqueness. But the situation is intensified by what Kundera refers to as "graphomania," the universal desire to impose one's subjective universe on external reality, a trait echo-ing the politicians' desire to rewrite history in terms of ideological order. The danger of graphomania is that meaning disappears in the cacophony of self-centered pronouncements. The multiplicity of exile, apparent in the diverse and overlapping themes, images, and characters of *The Book of Laughter and Forgetting*, is evident as well in the multiple ways in which the author is self-consciously present in the text – as narrator and commentator, as confessed self, as represented self, and as akin to the characters he has created. The double vision of the exile who sees his country from within muddles Kinbote but allows Kundera to achieve the dimension of depth.

Salman Rushdie quotes Kundera, whom he describes as "the exiled Czech writer," on the relationship between names and cultural identity: "A name means continuity with a past and people without a past are people without a name" (*Book of Laughter and Forgetting*, trs. Heim, 157, quoted in *Shame*, 88). Rushdie therefore gives his "fairyland" the name "Peccavistan," after the outrageous pun of victorious colonists: "'Peccavi': *I have Sind*" (*Shame*, 88). But in Kundera, to extend the intertextuality, the comment on names refers to Kafka's sense of the lack of continuity and memory in Prague, and, by extension, in modern life. Rushdie's quotation of Kundera points to a far more significant common theme – the notion of the palimpsest, or the rewriting of history in the interest of the present. For Rushdie Pakistan is precisely such a palimpsest. Its name is an artificial acronym concocted in England,

a word born in exile which then went East, was borne-across or trans-lated, and imposed itself on history; a returning migrant, settling down on partitioned land, forming a palimpsest on the past . . . To build Pakistan it was necessary to cover up Indian history, to deny that Indian centuries lay just beneath the surface of Pakistani Standard Time. (87)

The imposition hides or rewrites the past and substitutes new languages and people. In a sense, then, Pakistan is itself a fictional country, made up by emigrants, and *Shame* is thus a fairy tale about a fiction. But the parallelism of these imposed fictions complicates interpretation. As we are concerned with Rushdie's narrative self-consciousness, we are analogously concerned with the fiction that is Pakistan itself, and the unfolding of the novel's events into a perverse order that is both historical and artistic returns us to the relationship between the controlling mind of the narrator and the randomness of history, a relationship distinctly different from Kundera's contrast of writers to human beings. The fictions of the author enable us to perceive the randomness of history as cruel. The equivalent image in *The Book of Laughter and Forgetting* is that of the airbrush that removes Clementis from the picture of the balcony declaration of Czech Communism, leaving only the hat which he had kindly placed on the head of Klement Gottwald: "We want to be masters of the future only for the power to change the past. We fight for access to the labs where we can retouch photos and rewrite biographies and history" (30–31).

While Kundera creates, in the character of Tamina, an imagined audience with whom both author and audience share sympathies, Rushdie creates a fictional anti-self in the character of Omar Khayyam Shakil, the overweight, sensual, shameless observer of the events of the novel.[20] Just as Rushdie is caught between two countries, Shakil is caught between two families, having moved from debauchery with Iskander Harappa to marriage with the daughter of Raza Hyder. He is named after the Persian poet who became more popular in a distorted translation than in his native land. Translation, the shift in language, values, and meaning, becomes another image of exile. ("I too," Rushdie tells us, "am a translated man. I have been *borne across*. It is generally believed that something is always lost in translation; I cling to the notion – and use, in evidence, the success of Fitzgerald-Khayyam – that something can also be gained" [29].)

Rushdie spoke of the depressing nature of the first draft of *Shame* and his revision to combine its morbidity with comedy.[21] It is tempting to associate that revision with the appearance of *The Book of Laughter and Forgetting* in 1980 (*Shame* was published in 1983), for *Shame* shares its mixture of distance and closeness, comedy and violence, history and autobiography, irony and sincerity. The conscious fantasies of both novels imply a world that cannot be analyzed directly (and Rushdie's rejection of realism is ironically explicit [69–71]), but the novelists rush to overt authorial statements that seem too urgent for indirection. The result is a paradox of writing in *Shame* that contrasts to the simple egocentrism expressed in Kundera's concept of "graphomania." Rushdie, the colonized author writing in the tongue of the colonizers, complains that the modern history of the former colony is an imposition of present-day lies on the reality of the past. But in order to make that complaint, he must turn history into his own imposing fairy tale. The resultant dislocation produces the exile's double vision:

"what from one point of view seems to be an opportunity for change and moral transformation is from another a process of cultural dispossession and degradation."[22] The off-centering of the *soi-disant* exiled narrator and palimpsest homeland of Pakistan – the constructed country beneath which there is a reality denied by the fact of construction – combine to create what Samir Dayal describes as a "deliberate exploration of liminality" that "blurs normal categories, dismantles conventional definitions and boundaries of nationness and belonging, deconstructs simple divisions of masculine and feminine, and thematizes subjectivity as *enigma*."[23] In both *Shame* and *The Book of Laughter and Forgetting*, the historical situation cries out for direct description, but the compromises of satiric exile – especially the creation of a fiction to express an analysis that political reality would not permit – allow only irony.

The fictional narrator of *Pale Fire* extends alienation into a madness that mocks the acts of reading by imposing completely subjective constructs onto the text he has been trusted to interpret. But his dazzling correspondences and inconsistencies lead us back to the wizardry of the author himself. The duplicity of perspective that, in *Pale Fire*, creates a series of games for the puzzlement of readers allows Milan Kundera to achieve a dimension of depth that is manifested by the ubiquity with which the author projects himself into his text. That ubiquity and that act of projection are adopted by Salman Rushdie to fit the circumstances of postcolonial history, but the harshness of that history gives *Shame* a sharper satiric edge than that of *The Book of Laughter and Forgetting*. In all three works the narrative mode has become unstable, but such instability does not imply an equal instability of meaning. The possibility of meaning lies in the fictional structures by which the narrators seek a stable order to replace the double disorder that dislocates them.

THE FALSE ORDERS

The complexities of the exile's three-dimensional view lead to the construction of parallel fictions. These serve two functions. Unlike history, of which exiles perceive themselves the victims, fictional constructs allow the exile to take control, to shape reality, and to explore the possibilities of meaning. The constructed form also allows the exile to reconstruct the political and cultural dynamics that produced the state of exile, to transform history into satire, and thereby to justify the negative judgment implied by voluntary exile or to denounce the condemnation imposed by a forced one. The orders thus constructed are false in two senses: they reveal the political and cultural lies that produced the satiric exile, but they are themselves necessarily unreal. A closed order may arrive at a determined meaning that is of little value when the exile seeks to retranslate it into the ambiguities and confusion of exile itself. An open structure allows a rich array of connections and polysemous meanings, but these reproduce the instabilities of exile. In either case, the imposition of a necessarily false order parallels the essential separations that define exile. In addition to their intermediate position between the country they have left and the country they have gained, exiles are caught between the historic lands and the fictional realm, the Zembla or Tomis they have constructed.

The creation of an alternative order that moves from history to art carries with it an intertextuality that both anchors the alternative order in the realm of literature and provides familiar and intermediate terms to assist the exiles as their own commentary translates the language of their constructs into the language of history. In *Pale Fire* intertextuality appears not only as Shade and Kinbote refer to real or imagined texts but also as Kinbote's commentary parodies the process of reading. *Pale Fire* presents itself as an edition with the usual apparatus of a preface, text, commentary, and index. But soon into the preface the reader recognizes that the editor is highly eccentric and that the edition as a whole is a hoax. The preface ends with the astonishing assertion that since Shade's poem is a "skittish" and "reticent" autobiography it has no human reality apart from Kinbote's extensive commentary. Despite the jarring nature of the preface, we are used to the editorial convention that privileges the edited work as a "text" and relegates the accompanying apparatus to the status of commentary or non-text. But Kinbote's commentary itself is a text whose relation to the poem it annotates is both symbiotic and parasitic. The transformations that convert the edition into a novel establish alternative possibilities of reading that are signaled by the diverse genres that jockey for preeminence.

The generic location of *Pale Fire* is as nebulous as the identity of Kinbote. But although it is in some senses unsatiric, it is self-consciously comparable to such satires as Pope's *Dunciad*, Swift's *Tale of a Tub*, and Sterne's *Tristram Shandy*, and it raises central questions about satire. Insofar as it resembles Nabokov's own autobiography and his commentary on Pushkin, it replicates the imitative and parodic functions of satire, and it is satiric as well in the mixed nature of its form (including its combination of prose and verse). It is a stunning manifestation of the role of literature in exploring the boundaries of selfhood and of the role of satire in monitoring the boundaries of art. But it also raises a problem about the nature, even the possibility, of satire in modern times. Exile is a powerful modern image not only because tyranny, war, and colonialism have caused such ambiguity about what one's country means, but because the loss of one's country is so often an image of the loss of certainty itself, the place where one could understand the language, culture, and values by which one leads one's life. Lacking such certainty, the satiric exile cannot assume that the strange new land possesses the shared values which (some critics claim) make satiric attack communicable and justifiable. Thus the dominant mode of satire shifts to fiction, which can imagine those values whose absence seems to rob satirists of their calling. The importance of *Pale Fire* lies in the comedy, seriousness, and self-consciousness with which it explores the possibility of values in the process of creation.

The crux of *Pale Fire*'s ambiguous vacillations between poem and commentary, novel and satire, parody and self-parody, lies in the problem of pinning down its fictional nature. The center of uncertainty does not lie between Shade and Kinbote so much as between Nabokov and his reader. The slyness of creating a disguiser who disguises as a disguiser lies in its effacement of the boundaries between narrator's fictions and character's fictions. Is Zembla, whatever its etymology, a "real" country? It may be Kinbote's creation (or Botkin's or Shade's), but it is certainly Nabokov's, and Nabokov has created other lands (Paduk's nameless country in *Bend Sinister*, the Terra and Anti-Terra of *Ada*) whose quasi-reality we accept as part of the fiction. But we remain uncertain whether Zembla is only the author's creation or the creation of his character as well. The reader's uncertainties about the fictional nature of the central characters parallel uncertainties about the possibility of design in random events or of meaning in linguistic correspondences. The dislodged reader seeking to account for the strangeness of Nabokov's Zemblan text resembles the exile cut off from the past culture that defined his life.

At first glance the two central characters of *Pale Fire* seem as dissimilar as possible, differentiated by significant points of contact. Shade is a poet; Kinbote, although clearly imaginative, is not. Shade is married to his childhood sweetheart, whom he still loves; Kinbote is gay, with many partners, but essentially lonely. Shade teaches at a university in his home town; Kinbote, even if not the exiled monarch of Zembla, is certainly an exile. Shade is an honored member of his community; Kinbote is regarded as unpleasantly eccentric and perhaps mad. Kinbote is obsessed with Shade to the point of voyeurism; Shade seems to have a tolerantly affectionate attitude towards Kinbote. Yet their unequal and surprising friendship is in many respects at the heart of the novel: "the fireside poet and exiled romancer join forces against debunkers and blatant literalists."[24]

A central event of Shade's poem is the suicide of his sensitive, over-weight, and unhappy daughter Hazel. The intersection of her death with the trivial actions of her waiting parents is perhaps the poem's most moving section, and serves as the catalyst for Shade's inconclusive investigations of the afterlife. He has difficulty in accepting the painful fact that his love for Hazel could not compensate for her loneliness, and her death has torn him from the object of his love. But Kinbote too identifies with Hazel. Shade describes her mirroring of words: "She twisted words: pot, top, / Spider, redips. And 'powder' was 'red wop'" (lines 347–48). Kinbote's commentary underlines the connection between Hazel's linguistic gaming and himself: "One of the examples her father gives is odd. I am quite sure it was I who one day, when we were discussing 'mirror words,' observed (and I recall the poet's expression of stupefaction) that 'spider' in reverse is 'redips,' and 'T.S. Eliot,' 'toilest.' But then it is true that Hazel Shade resembled me in certain respects" (193). More than in her propensity for perverse word games, she resembles Kinbote in her alienation and her lone-liness, and the pain of her suicide may contribute to the compassionate understanding with which Shade regards his eccentricities. Shade describes Kinbote's monarchist fantasies when he tells a woman that mad "is the wrong word . . . One should not apply it to a person who deliberately peels off a drab and unhappy past and replaces it with a brilliant invention. That's merely turning over a new leaf with the left hand" (238). Kinbote's disguises are a benign equivalent of Hazel's suicide, and Shade's friendship may derive from his lost love. The writing of his poem is, for Shade, an ad-mission of the failure of his love to rescue his daughter from despair. Insofar as the exile is a surrogate for the alienated girl, his telling of the Zembla story to the poet may have inspired Shade's poem in ways that he cannot comprehend.[25]

But there are other senses as well in which Kinbote cannot comprehend Shade's poem. It manifests the poet's struggle to make sense of life by making sense of his own life. An agnostic, Shade finds life meaningful primarily through the mediation of art:

> I feel I understand
> Existence, or at least a minute part
> Of my existence, only through my art,
> In terms of combinational delight;
> And if my private universe scans right,
> So does the verse of galaxies divine
> Which I suspect is an iambic line.
>
> (lines 970–76)

In contrast, exile has wrested Kinbote's life out of one context that has no meaning into another. The vacancy of the past requires him to supply it by fantasy. Whether he is Kinbote, Botkin, or King Charles, disguise is the inevitable result of his exile. Since his own identity lacks solidity, he finds the existence of an independent, teleological meaning essential, and hence he is intensely religious – nearly offended at Shade's doubts. For Shade "combinational delight" is a function of the artist that may (or may not) be replicated in the universe at large; for Kinbote it is a series of occurrences whose coincidence is providential. The coherence of Shade's life and imagination gives him the strength to doubt; the incoherence and mysteries of Kinbote's disguises and fantasies require belief. Shade and Kinbote are both transformers of perception, but the transformations of the artist have the last word precisely because Kinbote is the disguiser disguised within the creation of Nabokov, the artist and the hero of his art.

In *Pale Fire* Nabokov moves a considerable distance in complexity beyond his treatments of exile in *The Gift* and *Pnin*. Here the former country and the exile's personal past appear as ineluctable products of the imagination. Zembla and New Wye act as mirrors, but the characters looking into those mirrors are doubled as well, the imagined and imagining Kinbote and Shade. Each functions as an autonomous figure and as the mirror image of the other (reversed, as in mirrors). Both poem and commentary abound in mirror images, as virtually every critic has noted.[26] The mirroring seems endless, but the image seen in the mirror is different from the self that observes it. To look in the mirror is both to see oneself and to represent what one is not. It is the false (mirrored) azure that slays the waxwing in the second line of Shade's poem, the line that significantly would not be mirrored if, in Kinbote's doubtful conjecture, the poem is meant to end with a repetition of the first line. (Kinbote's commentary itself begins with the first line of the poem, and thus, if one reads it immediately on finishing the poem, it competes the rhyme.) But there is a true azure that is the bird's natural habitat. Kinbote, the exile, must create a self to replace the past he has lost by exile and must imagine a habitat appropriate to his eccentric personality. Shade, the tolerant native, uses his own past and habitat as sources of genuine creation. Exile thus functions as the source and symbol of the destabilization of both the self and its literary (mirrored) expression. Kinbote, however unconvincing he may be as a Zemblan king or editor of poetry, is a fully convincing representation of such exile. He has a loneliness and paranoia that await a Gradus from the personal and collective past of the homeland to penetrate the disguise of exile with fatal effect. He is cut off from the values that justify his identity, and he is marginal in the land he has adopted. Exile leads to disguise, and the images of memory and imagination become indistinguishable. (Shade himself suffers the same phenomenon in the unconsciousness following his heart attack, when the white fountain that he sees becomes interpretable "only by whoever dwelt / In the strange world where I was a mere stray" [lines 718–19]). Verification becomes impossible, and trust is doubtful, at the cost of credibility.

What makes Shade conventionally superior to Kinbote is not merely that one is a poet and the other a fallacious commentator but that one is able to face cosmic doubt and personal failure by transforming it into art, while the other seeks to efface that transformation by overlaying it with fictions designed to disguise his own identity. But because we have come to see these fictions themselves as text, as artful products of Nabokov's imagination, we are able to retrieve Shade's poem and to perceive possibilities of its connection to its commentary that are not limited by the madness of the commentator. The peculiar structure of *Pale Fire* – even the difficulty of turning back and forth between the poem and its annotations – makes a linear reading of the work impossible. This release from linearity renders the maze-like structure of the work comprehensible. To experience a maze in linear terms is to become trapped and bewildered by its false turns and dead-ends. Freed from its linear confinement, and reading it from the outside, one can, with sufficient patience, comprehend its structure and trace a path from the center to the exit. The position of exiles as outcasts and outsiders makes possible the liberating vision of their works and of the non-linear structures by which they are perceived.

Salman Rushdie casts his outsider's fairy tale in the form of compelling symmetries. Timothy Brennan notes the ubiquity of the number three in the novel:

Omar's three mothers with their "trio of manservants" lived in a town which witnessed a triple murder, and encountered Raza's three grandmothers who had three brothers. The story is about three families (Shakil, Hyder, Harappa), three countries (England, India, Pakistan), three religions (Islam, Zoroastrianism, Hinduism) and three capitals (Quetta, Karachi, Islamabad). The familiar significance of the number "three" in religious and folkloric texts is not the point; rather, it is the monstrous exaggeration with which it is carried out – another signal that the genre is the message.[27]

The number three is particularly significant in its grouping of the novel's central characters, and it underlines the inevitability that is a central force in the novel. The novel is ordered around three triads of characters – a triad of fathers, a triad of mothers, and a triad of daughters. The narrator is placed in a position of an exile from the historical Pakistan, and the incessant nature of his triadic structure expresses his need to use an exile's artificial structure – the fairy tale he tells us he is creating – to see and express the disorders of his homeland.

One might describe *Shame* as a tragedy *manquée*, an *agon* of national and cosmic conditions, witnessed by a third actor. Because the *agon* has signifi-cance without meaning, it falls short of tragedy and is more appropriate to the parody and satire with which Rushdie treats it.[28] Iskander Harappa, the Bhutto figure, is brilliant, alternately charming and vexing, dissolute until he begins his political career, and thoroughly secular; Raza Hyder, the Zia figure, is brutal and stupid, puritanical and jealous, and a hardline Muslim fundamentalist. Isky sees Raza as insignificant, and thus puts him in control of the army. "'He will be my man. And with such a compromised leader the Army can't get too strong.' This single error proved to be the undoing of the ablest statesman who ever ruled that country which had been so tragically misfortunate, so accursed, in its heads of state" (181). The third character, the witness to the events of the novel and the stand-in for the author within the fantasy itself, is Omar Khayyam Shakil, the son of one of three rebellious sisters (neither he nor the reader knows which) who live in a fortress of isolation after the death of their unsympathetic father. Shakil is raised in that fortress, which Rushdie describes as both labyrinth and jungle. Shakil leaves his mothers to become both a doctor and a physically indulgent man. He is connected to Isky as a partner in his debaucheries and to Raza by marrying his retarded and magical daughter, whom he had treated as his most unusual patient. Husband and wife embody the extremes of shamelessness and shame.

The masculine triad of the novel is paralleled by a triad of their wives, who are the products and victims of the repression of women. Isky Harappa's wife Rani spends most of the novel isolated in his country house, to which she is initially relegated by the sexual affairs of her husband, and where she is later imprisoned after his death. There she weaves eighteen shawls depicting "The Shamelessness of Iskander the Great." Bilquis Hyder is also connected with clothing. When her father's cinema is exploded at the partition of India and Pakistan, because, in a spirit of tolerance, he shows films offensive to both Muslims and Hindus, her clothes are blasted from her, and she is eventually clothed by Raza Hyder, who falls in love with her and marries her. At the end of the novel, close to its final apocalypse, she helps her husband escape the collapse of his tyranny by disguising him and Shakil in shawls and veils. But between these two acts of clothing she fails to produce a son for Raza but rather a daughter (Sufiya Zinobia, the incarnation of her mother's shame, and everyone else's), who is followed by a probably illegitimate sister, Naveed ("Good News"). Bilquis gradually breaks down and withdraws behind veils of her own. The triad of wives leads in turn to the triad of daughters, with Sufiya as the common figure in the two groups. Naveed produces children in arithmetical progression and hangs herself when she becomes pregnant after giving birth to twenty-seven. Arjumand Harappa ("the Virgin Ironpants") is the sterile answer to such fecundity. She rejects men, except for her devotion to her father, whom she follows into power after the death of Raza. (Since it was published in 1983, before the death of General Zia in a plane crash and the rise of Benazir Bhutto, the novel creates a fiction that came true.)

As both wife and daughter, Sufiya Zinobia ("Shame") is the common figure of both female triads and the central figure of the novel. The most vividly imaginary of its characters, she can be associated with three fairy-tale or mythological figures: she inverts the beauty and the beast of the story, since she is a beauty inclosing a beast; critics have also identified her with the Goddess Kali[29] and with "'Chudale,' – the bogey woman who eats children."[30] But Rushdie tells us that she is an amalgam of three historical figures: a Pakistani girl in London killed by her father because of his shame at her suspected sexual relations with a white man; a girl beaten and humiliated on a subway whom Rushdie imagines avenging herself on her attackers; and a boy found burning in a parking lot, apparently self-ignited spontaneously. Sufiya Zinobia is the embodiment of shame. When her father rejects her at her birth because she is not a boy, she blushes. Brain fever that she catches before she is two retards her mental growth, so that by the time she is in her late twenties she still has a mental age of nine.

She acts out the shame felt by members of her family. After her mother expresses disgust at the turkey farm of a neighbor, she tears the heads off 218 turkeys and disembowels them. When her enraged mother attacks her torn hair with scissors, her shame turns on itself and breaks out into a fever that brings her to the hospital of Shakil, an eminent immunologist. When her sister, at the last minute, breaks off her engagement to marry another man, she viciously attacks him. On learning that her husband, with whom she has never had sexual relations, is unfaithful with her *ayah*, she entices four young men into sex and tears their heads off as she did the turkeys. When her father and husband discover her extraordinary power, they confine her, drugged and fettered, in the attic, but, after Raza deposes Isky and gains control of the government himself, she escapes and begins a series of rampages that ends her father's power and leads at last to her murder of her husband and her spontaneous self-immolation.

At one point Rushdie lists some of the reasons for shame. "Shameful things are done: lies, loose living, disrespect for one's elders, failure to love one's national flag, incorrect voting at elections, over-eating, extramarital sex, autobiographical novels, cheating at cards, maltreatment of womenfolk, examination failures, smuggling, throwing one's wicket away at the crucial point of a Test Match; and they are done *shamelessly*" (122). The list is a motley one, both conventional and subjective. A shameful act is anything that an individual believes to be morally wrong (or socially embarrassing) but does anyway; or it is anything condemned by an authoritative social group. It may be generated from within or imposed from without, but when it is externally imposed it runs the risk of perpetuating injustice. (Rushdie offers further examples: "Tell a lie, sleep with a white boy, get born the wrong sex.") Innocent acts socially construed as shameful lead to the emotion of shame; truly shameful acts are done without shame. From the counterposition of convention and subjectivity, Rushdie implies a third but unspoken criterion, not merely subjective or conventional, by which some acts (treason, murder, betrayal) can be absolutely described as shameful, but whose perpetrators feel no shame. The fiction that creates Sufiya Zinobia's character is that she absorbs the unfelt shame that surrounds her, that it transforms her into a beast and, in turn, transforms shame into violence. She thus internalizes the unending triadic cycle that spins the characters of the novel and their nation: violence leads to repression; repression to shame; shame to violence.

After the marriage of Omar Khayyam Shakil and Sufiya Zenobia, Rushdie pauses to note that the transformations of the novel have surprised even its author.

I had thought, before I began, that what I had on my hands was an almost excessively masculine tale, a saga of sexual rivalry, ambition, power, patronage, betrayal, death, revenge. But the women seem to have taken over; they marched in from the peripheries of the story to demand the inclusion of their own tragedies, histories and comedies, obliging me to couch my narrative in all manner of sinuous complexities, to see my "male" plot refracted, so to speak, through the prisms of its reverse and "female" side. (173)

The connection between the stories of the two sexes, which, as he realizes, "are the same story, after all," lies in the nature and effects of repression: a society that is repressive in its treatment of women is repressive in other forms. The stories of the men and the women are the same because sexual and political repression are inseparable.

But the nature of that complementary relation does not quite lie, as Stephanie Moss has argued, in an allegorical structure by which the women represent the historical sequence acted out by the men.[31] Nor is it quite true to say that Rushdie offers no alternatives for women except passivity and violence, although these are the only alternatives present in the satiric fantasy of the novel.[32] Rushdie adds that some women cannot be crushed by the system and are stronger than men. But "their chains, nevertheless, are no fictions" (173). Women, as Rushdie has explained, are part of the same repressive cycle as men, but they are a different part.[33] The triad of men represents the interconnection of sexual dominance, personal ambition, and political corruption; the women – mothers and daughters – are mostly cut off from political power, but they represent cultural conventions, imprecisely defined but powerful nonetheless, of which shame is a principal manifestation. The shame represented by the women connects the personal and the political because it embodies the cultural conventions that underlie and motivate both individual behavior and public action.

For Aijaz Ahmad, women in *Shame* are its only depicted victims, powerless to resist their victimization successfully, and several implications follow from this victimization. The pattern implies the futility of resistance to arbitrary political power. Moreover, this bleak picture is treated as comedy, resulting in a novelistic cartoon. The deterministic character of this cartoon is intensified by treating Sufiya Zinobia's shame as physiological (resulting from a brain disease) rather than psychological and political. The cartoon-like quality is also manifested in the novel's satiric oversimplification. Pakistan is the novel's satiric target, but the plot is limited to a few elite families. Neither the victimization of the people themselves nor their resources as potential agents of resistance are represented. This lack of representation intensifies the sense of inevitability about events and eliminates hope of political action.[34] Aijaz Ahmad's case, written from a Marxist perspective, rests in part on two kinds of overliteral reading. The transposition of historical figures into a comic and demeaning world of fantasy is a characteristic of Menippean satire.[35] In satires such as *Shame* and *Candide*, which may be its closest model, where history collides with fantasy and comic exaggeration, the satirist's anger plays against his narrative disengagement, creating the tone of satiric exile. The exile is cut off from the "country" satirized and hence displays a sense of pessimism that may be reinforced by the apparently helpless condition of the country itself. The satiric exile thus develops a nostalgia for the unrepresentable. By virtue of his position as exile and by virtue of the country about which he writes, the positive alternative cannot be represented, although it can be imagined. Ahmad complains of the absence of that which is implicitly longed for. Kathryn

Hume suggests that Rushdie implies two responses to the plight of the decentered hero in the face of tyranny – to write history and to act locally. But the second alternative, she notes, does not become apparent until *The Satanic Verses*.[36] In *Shame* the narrator becomes the anti-tyrannic hero by virtue of the fact that his exile allows him to write his novel. A second kind of overliteral reading sees elements of plot as representations rather than as signs. Had Rushdie been writing a realistic novel, the physiological inevitability of Sufiya Zinobia's disorder would have been a problem. But the fantasy and comic overexaggeration of satire push readers outside of the text of the novel, transforming them into potential actors.

I have seen *Shame* as organized by a triad of triads: three husbands, three wives, and three daughters, with one of the daughters also one of the wives. The triadic structure thus serves as a useful clue to the structures of meaning in the novel. The three triads specify its family character, whose significance becomes more ominous by being extended over generations. The force of history lies in its inescapable quality, in the fact that the evils of one generation engender those of the next. The ironic optimism and real pessimism of the apocalyptic ending lie in Rushdie's proclamation (257) that the ending of dictatorships and the culture that sustains them can only be achieved in fairy tales. The inescapable force of history is figured by the transformation of Sufiya Zinobia, the child of shame, into a beast of prey, but it is implied by other transformations as well. Structurally, the political career undertaken by Isky Harappa transforms the novel from family chronicle to political satire and darkens its black comedy to the point of apocalypse. This linear movement intensifies the novel's sense of paranoid destiny. Two forms of inevitability are at work. Near the end Rushdie announces that "my dictator will be toppled by goblinish, faery means" (257). The fantasy of liberation is an escape from the somber inevitability of history. "Tell me," the diplomatic wife of a diplomat asks Rushdie, "why don't people in Pakistan get rid of Zia in, you know, the usual way" (29). As Rushdie asserts, in defense of his fantastic conclusion, "*you* try and get rid of a dictator some time" (257). But if fantasy escapes from history, it is also trapped by its own inner logic and its own moral forces, which lead the novel to its apocalyptic conclusion. An apparent counterforce multiplies a profusion of images rather than restricting and determining them. As images proliferate, they carry similar meanings and are linked by their symmetries to the chain of inevitability driving the novel. But the inevitability of structure is misleading, for history is the product of human choices and open to change. By presenting an alienated world, Rushdie reinforces "the impression that politics dehumanizes human beings" and makes them monstrous.[37] History's movement to apocalypse is the fictional evidence of the satirist's moral despair and the helplessness of his exile.

The mixture of autobiography with fiction, the tension between history and fantasy, the diffusion of images that combine and fragment significance, are all as characteristic of *The Book of Laughter and Forgetting* as they are of *Shame*, and the talkative nature of Rushdie's narrator may derive from the garrulity of Kundera's. But, in contrast to *Shame's* inexorable movement to catastrophe, these elements remain remarkably open, exploratory, and suggestive in Kundera's novel. For both works exile marks not only the separation between countries but also the divisions among the genres that make them up. Kundera explains that "this book is a novel in the form of variations. The various parts follow each other like the various stages of a voyage leading into the interior of a theme, the interior of a thought, the interior of a single, unique situation, the understanding of which recedes from my sight into the distance" (*The Book of Laughter and Forgetting*, 227). Kundera had in mind Beethoven's Opus 111 piano sonata, whose variations preoccupied his father in the months before his death. But he stands the variation form on its head; instead of beginning with the clear enunciation of the single theme, his variations move towards but never articulate their single underlying statement. *The Book of Laughter and Forgetting* comprises seven parts, each containing several elements, and each overlapping with other parts. Parts One and Four have the same title ("Lost Letters"), as do Parts Three and Six ("The Angels"). Parts Four and Six are about Tamina, thus linking One, Three, Four, and Six. Parts Two, Five, and Seven are primarily about sexuality, a topic of other sections as well, and Kundera's discussion of "graphomania" in Part Four is related to his treatment of the egocentric poets in Part Five who argue with Boccaccio (Kundera) about the romanticization of women. Kundera's distinction between the laughter of angels and of devils in Part Three recurs throughout the novel. The result is a network of themes that allows significance to be switched from one topic to another, creating the essential polysemy that defines the novel's openness. But a primary link in the novel, as in most of Kundera's Czech work, is between politics and sexuality, and this topical linkage holds together the structure of the novel.

Virtually every part includes multiple elements, but these settle into fairly predictable generic patterns. Each chapter contains fictional elements ranging from realism to fantasy. Most also contain essayistic treatments of major topics, discussions of history, and autobiographical elements. The mixture of genres, with its implicit mixture of narrative and history, is one of the major devices of disruption in *The Book of Laughter and Forgetting*: "by disrupting the seamless effects of narration, Kundera wakens his readers from the 'spell' cast by art and confronts them with the burden of history."[38] Herbert Eagle stresses the dominance of the essay in the novel but also the importance of autobiography. Rather than simply using privileged characters who reflect the position of the author, "Kundera thrusts the entire process into the open by paralleling with the fictional stories other stories taken from his own life which use his own name and embody the same paradigms."[39] The distribution of major genres can be represented in tabular form:

Fiction	Essay/History	Autobiography
1. Mirek and Zdena	Clementis's hat; sketch of post-war Czech history	Kundera as supporter of early post-war Marxist realism
2. Karel, his mother, Marketa, and Eva	The mother's disregard of the Russian invasion and confusion about celebrating the First Republic	
3. Michelle, Gabrielle, Madame Raphael; Sarah	Divine and satanic laughter; circle dancing and Paul Eluard	Kundera's fall; his column on astrology; his desire to rape R.; his decision to leave Czechoslovakia
4. Tamina, her dead husband, her need for her lost diaries, her exile	Graphomania; the author's imposition of a private world on his audience.	Kundera as author and exile
5. The student and Krystina; the poets	The nature of *litost*; the poets discuss sexuality; the power of poetry	Kundera as Boccaccio
6. Tamina and the Children's Island	Time and forgetting; variation form; the novel as variations on or for Tamina; the hierarchy of musical keys; twelve-tone democracy; "the stupidity of music"	The death of Kundera's father; President Husak as Honorary Pioneer; children as the future
7. Jan's sexual and political encounters	Blackbirds; sexuality as the underside of history; the sexual and political meaning of borders	Kundera as exile

But *The Book of Laughter and Forgetting*, like *Shame*, may also be seen as an arrangement of contrasting pairs that become ambiguous when subjects on one side of the contrast reappear on the other. Lars Kleberg identifies such "paradigmatic" pairs as including "memory/oblivion, life/death, childhood/maturity, lust/boredom, language/silence, ring dance/ostracism, insular life/journey."[40] The uncertainty of these pairs, their significant overlapping, and the ambiguity caused by their shifting terms, make them particularly evocative and join them to the exile theme of east and west.

In addition to the overlapping of parts and of themes, the characters overlap with each other and are connected to Kundera himself. Thus Tamina, like Kundera, is an exile seeking to recover the past, but she is conspicuously compared to Kundera's father, whose historical death parallels her own in the novel's most fantastic tale. She is connected with Mirek of Part One by yet another dominant theme, the importance of memory and the rewriting of history. Such rewriting is ubiquitous: the novel begins with the story of Clementis being airbrushed out of a nationalistic picture, leaving only his hat behind, a rewriting that is the product of the urge for universal meaning; it ends with a paunchy, middle-aged, naked man lecturing to an equally naked audience on "the idea that Western civilization is going to perish" (312), a rewriting that is meaningless. Total meaning and total meaninglessness both require the rewriting of history, since neither provides an adequate account of experience. But rewriting is personal as well as political. Mirek, in the first story, asserts that "the struggle of man against power is the struggle of memory against forgetting" (4), and hence he keeps careful records of meetings and correspondence. But he wants to retrieve the letters that document the past love he now remembers with shame: "Mirek rewrote history just like the Communist Party, like all political parties, like all peoples, like mankind" (30).

Tamina, on the other hand, cares nothing about public history but struggles to hold on to the memory of her dead husband (also named Mirek). Hence she wants to get the diaries she has left in Czechoslovakia, for they can unlock her memory of her past life. But she refuses to return to Czechoslovakia because, like Clementis, her husband has been officially erased from history. To return, she feels, is to cooperate with his betrayers, perhaps to betray him herself. Her escape from exile turns to fantasy and brings her to the Children's Island (Czechoslovakia too is depicted as a land of children), where, indeed, she does forget him. Both are sympathetic characters, but both are trapped by the contradictions they seek to achieve: if Mirek seeks to retain public history, he must be willing to accept the failures of his personal past as well; if Tamina is to retain her memory of her husband,

she must encounter the history of which he was a part. The fact that
Mirek has the same name as Tamina's husband is not accidental. In a
sense Mirek in Part One and Tamina of Parts Four and Six are mated: they
are internal and external exiles, and for both the means of controlling the
past is the possession of private documents. Mirek's efforts to retrieve his
letters are compared to a novelist's revision of a manuscript; Tamina's purely
personal concern for her lost diaries is contrasted to the urge of individuals
to transmute their lives into novels. Mirek and Tamina represent complementary masculine and feminine responses to the problem of recollecting
and rewriting a victimizing past.

But they are also different in ways that are central to the moral shape of the
novel. Mirek's efforts to retrieve his letters are fruitless and arrogant. Unlike
Tamina's victimization and passivity, his desire to bring his past under
his own control evidences the assertiveness of selfhood, the self-conscious
exhibitionism that runs through the satiric targets of the novel, from the
sufferers of *litost*, through the various sexual adventurers and pretentious
politicians, to the sexless nudists of the last scene. What trivializes politics
and, at the same time, makes it attractive is its capacity not only to validate
the individual self but also to extend that asserted self by means of an
illusory common bond. But the overrepresented self, whether written out
in absolutist states and universal novels or displayed at Barbara's orgies or the
nudists' beach, betrays or even annihilates the inner self that writes poems or
plays Beethoven or deeply loves. The distinction between political ostracism
and personal despair threatens to collapse because of the centripetal force
of exile as a metaphor; the terms reverse themselves – personal ostracism
and political despair – creating that particularly distant voice that can
speak only by constructing an artificial land. The distance of that voice
and the artificiality of that fiction are ways in which the exile avoids the
abandonment of the self. To avoid the self-pity that entrapped Ovid or
the helplessness that engulfed Tamina, the exile must become satiric. Ann
Stewart Caldwell points out that Kundera "seeks to achieve what he terms an
'anti-poetic posture' based on a distrust of one's own feelings and sensations
and even a distrust of the feelings and sensations of others."[41]

Pale Fire, *Shame*, and *The Book of Laughter and Forgetting* sit on the
boundaries of fiction. If the novel is a country bounded by such other
countries as history, personal essays, autobiography, philosophical and political discourse, fairy tales, subjective fantasies, and even poetry, the works
of satiric exile transgress these borders in significant and often disquieting
ways. In doing so, they exemplify the concept of satire as a combination
of discrete forms. But this satiric form also exemplifies the problems of

exile that are both its subject and its essential condition. The trap of exile is different in these different works, but they share the fact of entrapment and the need to escape that trap by the creation of alternative structures within which complex and otherwise imperceptible truths can be articulated.

THE TROUBLED LANDS

The satiric exile is not only caught between the home and host nation but by the problems of articulating the identity of the homeland. For exiles the homeland may be subjective – the home to which they cannot return, the family, friends, language, and culture they have lost. For satiric exiles, history challenges that subjective view, and satire requires an exercise in national definition. Pakistan, as Rushdie reports, was a synthetic country given a conglomerate name by the British, created in a postcolonial settlement that, as it turned out, settled little, and then split into separate parts. Czechoslovakia was formed as a republic at the end of the Austro-Hungarian empire, invaded by the Germans, liberated by the Russians, restored as a republic under Soviet influence, and, in 1968, invaded by the Russians. When he wrote *The Book of Laughter and Forgetting*, Kundera looked upon Czechoslovakia as a small nation invaded and controlled by its larger neighbors, and in danger of losing its language to German on one hand or Russian on the other. But Czechoslovakia itself turned out to be an unstable and synthetic state, eventually (like Pakistan) splintering into two separate countries. Ann Jefferson sees the "double vision" of exile as "equally ingrained in Czech culture as a whole."[42] The complex and shifting identity of the homeland corresponds to the multiple perspectives of the satiric exile, whose task becomes the discovery of cultural and political forces that control or transcend historical change.

Satiric exile, like other kinds of satire, is definable in terms of its indirect attack on historical particularities. Its indirection is apparent in the fictional constructs that it imposes on history, but it is concerned with specific problems of history itself, which it sees from the vantage-point of exile, an enforced application of multiple perspectives producing, as we have seen, both confusion and depth. The actuality of these historical problems is literally embodied in the figure of the exiled writer, so that authorship is an echo of the problem it addresses. (Kundera dissects books to reveal the dominant and repressive ego of the author; Nabokov annotates them to show the imposing ego of the reader.) The oversupply of authorship, the graphomania of western culture, becomes an ironic inversion of the suppression of Kundera's books in Czechoslovakia. *Shame* is allowable only as fantasy; a realistic novel about Pakistan would be impossible: "By now, if I had been writing a book of this nature, it would have done me no good to protest that I was writing universally, not only about Pakistan" (70).

But it is fair to ask what Rushdie means by claiming to be writing universally, or whether the claim is merely the satirist's pose to avoid responsibility for his personal and historical criticism. The particularity of exile itself, the artificiality of the constructs by which it is articulated, and the distant, ironic voice of the author all raise problems for readers who can identify neither with the causes of exile nor with the ironic voice of the exiled author. It is easy enough to feel sympathy for Tamina and anger against Pakistan, but such feelings are merely sentimental exercises unless they are bolstered by broad principles that give them meaning. Where, in the troubled lands that satiric exile takes as its topics are the concerns that extend beyond borders? Are authors and readers both trapped by the duality of a fact–fiction dichotomy demarcating the separate lands and languages across which significant communication is impossible? If specific history is the penultimate concern of satiric exile, what is its ultimate one? These questions are most clearly focused in *Shame* and *The Book of Laughter and Forgetting*, which discuss the issues of lands and borders explicitly.

Feroza Jussawalla has suggested that western readers of *Shame* may not understand the actuality of some of its apparently fantastic material.[43] For example, the dormitory of women at the house of the matriarchal Bariamma, to which husbands sneak by night for their matrimonial rights, may be seen by westerners as a fantasy but is recognized by Pakistanis as an exaggeration of what Rushdie describes as "the old village way" (74). This difficulty marks satiric borders, for some meaning cannot be transferred from the text of one country to the readers of another. To write a book that is about Pakistan is therefore, in some respects, to write a book that cannot be fully comprehended by westerners. At the same time, however, the historicity of the major issues is obvious enough, and Rushdie's intrusive narrator reiterates the recognizable importance of details in his novel. The fantasies of the story keep reverting to the truth. In a 1983 interview Rushdie suggested that western readers of *Shame* should see the complicity of the west in perpetuating their own democracies at the expense of eastern liberties.[44] But beyond the west's share of responsibility for the political tragedy of Pakistan, the novel traces a commonality in the breakdown of personal and political values. The mode of presentation suggests a broad characterization of modern public life. In the same interview Rushdie describes the fantasy of his satire as a kind of realism:

If you look at Reagan's America or Thatcher's Britain, it seems to me that it is self-evidently true, that what you have is very low-grade people, second-rate clowns playing out what are in fact tragic plots . . . And it seemed to me that what one should do is to write a story which in its shape is tragic, because there's no doubt that what is happening in Pakistan is a tragedy, it's a tragedy on a national scale. So it was correct to write a story whose form was tragic, but then to write it with all the language of comedy and farce you could muster, because that was what the people merited, and that would be the way of creating a description of the world as it really was. ("Interview," 15)

Such farce is enabled by a double dislocation in the relation between author and subject. The author writes as an exile, distant from the land he satirizes and contemptuous of it; but he also writes of a seceded land, cut off from history by the illusions that create the present.

Rushdie finds a juncture of the personal and public in the theme of shame. If shame is a universal quality, it is also an ambivalent one, and its ambivalence seems a trap. The lack of shame implies the lack of moral judgment. But shame itself evokes revenge, the perpetuation of the injustices that gave it birth. When the moral response replicates the injustice to which it responds, the reason why dictators are hard to get rid of becomes quite evident. As well as being ambiguous, shame is also the product of an ironic inversion. It is victims who feel shame; the bullies are shameless. The inescapability of historic destiny, made so painfully clear in *Shame* by the oppressive symmetries of its structure, parallels the central theme by which one is either guilty and shameless or innocent and shameful.

The universality of *Shame* lies in the reader's recognition of historical reality as the product of the exiled imagination. The dichotomy between Pakistani reality and Rushdie's fairy tale, proclaimed so disingenuously at the outset, collapses because history is as bad as nightmares and because the fantasy itself enacts deeper truths than history does. ("The reader is guided through a fantasy so closely aligned to history that he finds himself constantly confusing the two, only to have the narrator interfere to show that the reality is stranger and worse than the fantasy.")[45] The fact–fiction duality transforms into a triad in which the third term is satire, which mediates between the abstract truth of fantasy and the specific experience of history. The universality of absurdity may be pessimistic, but it transforms absurdity into meaning. By recognizing that meaning, readers may be forced to take responsibility for their own shame.

Rushdie, therefore, sees one element of shamelessness as an unwillingness to assume responsibility. But for Kundera responsibility is complicated by the fact that it takes different forms in Czechoslovakia and western

Europe. In Czechoslovakia responsibility is tainted with Kafkaesque guilt and, more specifically, with the writing down of secrets or dissent that may in turn become evidence of disloyalty. To be responsible is thus to be held responsible, and the reaction to such danger is a land without responsibility – a children's island. The problem of progressives in the west, such as the cartoon-like Clevis family in Part Seven, is that they do not see values in personal terms but in terms of political formulas and abstractions that distance them from responsibility. Here, as elsewhere, the appearance of the same term on either side of the border reveals ironic dislocations. The problem of responsibility, the juncture between the personal and the political, lies in the connections among sexuality, the problem of meaning, and the idea of borders.

The Book of Laughter and Forgetting reaches its climax in Part Six, in which Kundera's efforts to help his dying father are contrasted to official platitudes as Czech President Huzak is named an honorary Pioneer, and in which Tamina, ferried to the fantasy island inhabited only by a Pioneer-like camp of children, loses her memories, her sense of identity, indeed everything but her will to live, and finally drowns in an impossible effort to escape. It is this fruitless effort to recross, to escape the final conjunction of meaninglessness and total meaning represented by the children around her, that leads to the final section of the novel, entitled "Borders."

Jan, the central figure of Part Seven, like Tomas in *The Unbearable Lightness of Being*, is a sexually active man. But unlike Tomas, who returns to internal exile in Prague, Jan plans to go to America to pursue his (unspecified) career. His relations to Edwige, a thoughtful woman for whom sexuality is "merely a sign, merely a symbolic act, that confirms friendship" (*The Book of Laughter and Forgetting*, 212), are contrasted to his relations to other women, especially a girl from a sports store for whom sex is a mechanical process for producing orgasms. Jan participates in three incidents illustrative of the absurdity of society on the border. At the burial of a beloved optimist, a bowler hat comically falls into the grave ("as if Passer, with his indomitable vitality and optimism, was trying to stick his head out," 303), creating inexpressible problems for the mourners, who can neither laugh at the hat nor grieve for their friend. At an orgy staged and managed by his acquaintance Barbara, for whom sexual arrangements should be executed without love, Jan bursts out laughing and is sent away: "'Don't think you can pull on me what happened at Passer's funeral!'" Barbara tells him (308). Jan and Edwige go to an island, echoing the Children's Island where Tamina dies, inhabited by nudists who believe that they have shed the restrictions of western civilization along with their clothes. But nature has only rendered sexuality superfluous.

The border, with its suggestions of differences between past and present, between homeland and land of exile, between man and woman, between meaning and meaninglessness, is the most complex of Kundera's images, compressing a variety of judgments. The border is where life is most vivid but also most dangerous. Kundera identifies internationalism with meaninglessness, although he is equally aware of the vacuities cultivated within nations or imposed by invasion. Like other satirists, Kundera proposes sets of sharply opposite terms that seek to occupy the same space; life is most appropriately on the border because neither contrasting term by itself is adequate to the complexity of the human situation. (Hence most of the unsympathetic characters of *The Book of Laughter and Forgetting* become unsympathetic precisely at the moment when they become reductive in their manipulation of others.) Exile, the determined crossing of a border, stands for Kundera's pessimism about history. It represents the collapse of justifying values characteristic of the postmodern condition. The false alternative is the conspicuous proclamation of selfhood – not where one has an identity to proclaim, but where one wishes to assert the possession of an identity, however illusory. *Litost*, the sense of the miserable nature of one's self, is the recognition that the illusion of identity is inadequate. One becomes exiled from one's self.

This personal pessimism thus parallels Kundera's historical pessimism, where the real country becomes perverted by the politics of artificial personal exhibition, so that the individuals actually on the balcony at the proclamation of Communist Czechoslovakia are replaced by the figures in the altered photograph, just as the individual self is replaced by the image one projects to hide the void where (no) one really lives. These images of political and personal exile cross and recross in Kundera's novel, as the transformations of the nation force its inhabitants to flight, confine them to jails or to silence, or impose a childish culture, and as the transformations of individuals deprive them of the depth of their homelands and leave them to loneliness or to meaningless personal relations. The borders that define the states of exile in *The Book of Laughter and Forgetting* are shifting but real: once crossed they may become uncrossable. They serve as extreme examples of the liminality characteristic of the postmodern condition. Personal identity and political community stand on opposite sides of such a border. Art and experience are separated by another. Crossing such borders – the act of flight or the position of exile – effects transformations. Political issues are transformed to personal anger. The fall of the state prefigures the disintegration of the individual. Meaning becomes meaningless. The experience of exile, of looking backward over borders, destabilizes knowledge, and memory becomes indistinguishable from illusion.

The multiplication of historical particulars as objects of satiric attack produces satiric generalizations. The tentative, polysemous quality of the generalizations possible to satiric exile derives from the multiplicity of corresponding details, topics, and characters that are governed by inexorable symmetries in *Shame* and by the web of overlapping identities in *The Book of Laughter and Forgetting*. The antinomy of shame and shamelessness becomes universal in Rushdie's novel; for Kundera the ubiquity of meaninglessness is created by the parallel forces of political repression and vacuous personal assertion. But these negative universals imply an opposite in the assertion of personal responsibility that ties the flawed and exiled self to significant commonalities. Cut off from the nation, the imagined community in which the exile is born, and finding no place in the land to which the exile has arrived, the satirist creates from the negations of exile itself a community of readers.

The problem of exiles is not merely the injustice of the land from which they have escaped or out of which they have been driven. It is the eternal irresolution of exile itself, for either there is no real escape, or the act of flight stands the problem on its head, so that it appears in inverted form – tyranny's repression replaced by the irresponsibility of freedom. Exile carries the metaphoric weight of all sorts of boundaries, as well as intermediate points – no-man's lands, places of transition, temporary resting places – between opposing states of being: between men and women, between the past and the present, between what is lost and what is recovered, between what is hoped for and what is achieved, between cultures and sub-cultures, between experience and art, history and fantasy, reason and madness. These boundaries exist in the external world but they are internalized as well, becoming both psychological and political.

The problem of exiles lies in their dislocation between two countries, between past and present, between a nostalgia for meaning and a fear of meaninglessness. Each country is caught between real human community and rigid order (or, alternatively, the vacancy produced by the collapse of order). The exile uses the double vision created by dislocation to perceive the contradictions of both old and new countries. As the exile is dislocated from a country, the reader is alienated from the exile's text. The reader's efforts to interpret that text – to reassemble the discontinuities purposefully left by the exiled author – become analogous to the exile's problem of interpreting countries. The position of exiles means that they embody the universal dehumanization of politics (the repression of tyranny, the irresponsibility of democracy); the text is the human testament of that inhumanity. But that dehumanization is a historic fact rather than a structural necessity. Satiric exile reveals the universality of disorders that can be changed, even if, at the same time, it shows the flaws inherent in the human condition. Without abandoning the pessimism that grows from experience, the complexities of satiric exile provide ways of looking beyond the surface of history to suggest the hidden or repressed values that affirm dissent and proclaim the urgency of change.

PART II

Satiric forms

CHAPTER 4

Satire as performance

The element that makes plays satiric is the nature of the performance they contain. Plays, of course, are performed, and their appearance before a public becomes the object of critical scrutiny in performance theory. Satire does not flow from the performance of a play but from the performance within it. My concern, therefore, is not with the substitution of performance for text but with satiric performance as represented by the text. A brief distinction of three levels of satiric performance should define such internal performances. (1.) At a primary level of satiric performance, language itself, as is generally agreed, is performative. Certain uses of language are classifiable as speech acts which function, as J. L. Austin long ago suggested, to do things. But simply to make a statement is to perform an act, to interpellate the auditor and to seek a response. Insofar as performance implies a distance from actuality, language is performance because words never completely represent what their speaker intends, even if, as we cannot, we could assume that they are accurately heard by a listener. The distances between signifiers and what they signify, between what speakers mean and what they say, and between what is said and what is understood, become both subjects and vehicles of satire. (2.) Language is uttered by characters who may have both personalities and social roles. Characters perform in those social roles, however strongly the roles also reflect their personalities. In some cases characters may be identified merely by their social role ("Messenger"). Because similar roles may be performed by other personalities, roles are independent of the specific individual. Satire analyzes and exploits the generalities implicit in the relationship between individual actors and the social roles they perform, and such analysis becomes the secondary level of satiric performance. (3.) At a tertiary level a character in the play may duplicate the performances by staging a plot intended to reveal the hidden personalities of other characters, their untrue language, or their inappropriate social roles. Such characters take on the role of the satirist or become the satirist's agent, and their chief function is to make public the guilt of significant offenders. The central characters in Aristophanes often play this performative role, and the comic idea (withholding sex, building a city of birds, retrieving Euripides from the dead) becomes the revelatory plot. The tertiary level becomes theatrical because the satiric performance by a character echoes the theatrical performance of the satirist, calling attention to the performative nature of the play itself. Tertiary-level performance may change or underscore the importance of the other two levels, making them subjects and devices of satiric contemplation. The question for analyzing satire, for observing satiric analysis, is how, in various kinds of plays and in various historical contexts, this underscoring takes place. In the chapter that follows, I will look at satiric performances in verse plays by Jonson and Molière, in the realistic drama of Ostrovsky, and in the epic or dialectic theater of Brecht.

THE ALCHEMIST

Ben Jonson's *The Alchemist* is pervasively performative. It adopts the standard Aristophanic pattern in which an unofficial hero, a marginal member of society, undertakes an illegitimate and metaphoric plot by virtue of which he will not only triumph personally but perversely correct the central social problem that regular, non-comedic society has been unable to solve.[1] Other Aristophanic patterns occur as well: in both *The Alchemist* and *The Birds*, the plot is concocted by two heroes, and in both cases the initially dominant hero, Euelpedes or Subtle, is replaced by his more aggressive and successful cohort, Pisthetairos or Face. In *The Alchemist* a fairly close approximation of the Aristophanic *agon* is the debate between Subtle and Surly regarding the legitimacy of alchemy (II.iii), in which Mammon acts as the third party who witnesses the debate. One of the central tests of the play is whether Jonson will be able to reconcile the perverse pattern of Aristophanic comedy with the moral and didactic tradition of Renaissance comedy.[2]

Even more strongly than the plays of Aristophanes, *The Alchemist* is located in a specific time and place. It takes place on November 1, 1610, beginning at about 9:00 a.m. and ending in the early afternoon.[3] The play's unity of time serves its satiric purpose by equating the temporal experience of witnessing the play with the action of the play itself. That equation is furthered by the probable identity of place as well. Blackfriars is the location of Lovewit's house, the scene of the action of the play, but it was also the site of the theater at which the play was probably first performed (as well as being the residence of Jonson and occupied by a number of

Puritans, one of the play's major satiric targets). At Blackfriars the worlds of actuality and theatricality coincide. "The house in Blackfriars is capable of being whatever people most want it to be: it is a shell within which their fantasies may be projected, a sounding-board for the imagination."[4] Lovewit is absent because of his fears of the plague, which, earlier in 1610, had closed the theaters. If indeed the play was performed at Blackfriars theater on or near November 1, the presence of the audience in the theater would prefigure Lovewit's return at the end of the plague. In any case, the closeness of the world of the audience to the world of the play is indicated clearly enough in the Prologue:

> Our scene is London, 'cause we would make known,
> No country's mirth is better than our own.
> No clime breeds better matter for your whore,
> Bawd, squire, impostor, many persons more,
> Whose manners, now called humors, feed the stage,
> And which have still been subject for the rage
> Or spleen of comic writers.[5]

Nor do we need to attend the play in person to be involved in complexities of illusion, fantasy, and actuality. In his prefatory comments "To the Reader," which appeared in the quarto but not the folio edition of *The Alchemist*, Jonson distinguishes between "an understander," who is more than merely a reader, and "a pretender," who is warned that "thou wert never more fair in the way to be cozened than in this age in poetry, especially in plays" (20). He goes on to describe his fellow playwrights in terms not unlike those one might use to describe the alchemists of his play. Whether attending a performance at Blackfriars or reading the quarto, Jonson's audience needs to work out the relationships among actuality and imagination, and that challenge may parallel Jonson's task of reconciling moralistic and Aristophanic tendencies in his play.

In *The Alchemist*, the central plot is undertaken by three conspirators – Subtle the false alchemist, Face the go-between, pander, and factotum, and Dol Common the prostitute – who use the pretense of alchemy as a metaphor that, in one way or another, deceives a series of gulls: Dapper the feckless clerk seeks to become a successful gambler and man-about-town by following the advice of his alleged aunt, the Queen of the Faeries; Drugger the industrious tobacconist seeks to set up his shop on astrological principles and serves as an unwitting agent of the conspirators; Sir Epicure Mammon, the most grandiose of gulls, seeks wealth to buy both limitless pleasures and charitable extravagance, but through an alchemical process that depends (or so Subtle tells him) on his purity; the Anabaptists Tribulation and Ananias want money for their congregation, and in their cause alchemy becomes coining, a capital crime they see as justified by its religious purposes; Kastril the country heir wants to be a London roaring boy and thus to master the conventions of disorder. All seek power, and to achieve it they need the personal transformation promised by alchemy. But the conspirators direct this interest in power and self-aggrandizement into specific purposes that can be achieved through the devices they promise. We are partially sympathetic to the alchemists because their devices unmask the false values that allow the gulling to take place. The conspirators become satirists, and deception seems a proper outcome for the misplaced values of their victims.

The sequence of plots is complicated by the emergence of doubles to the alchemists, so that the second level of performance, that of social roles, operates for disguising cons as well as for deceived gulls. Surly, the dubious gambler, is the double of Face and, like Face, disguises himself in an effort to unmask the alchemists, but he becomes the victim of his own disguise. Pliant, the rich and beautiful widow, is the double of Dol, and plays the role intended for Dol (who is occupied with Mammon) as the object of Surly's passion. Like Dol, her identity is determined by her sexual attractions, for the sake of which men project their illusions onto her, hence giving her a satirically appropriate disguise, for sexuality parallels alchemy insofar as it involves the projection of aggressive desire. The names of the women imply their roles in response to this projected identity: Dame Pliant is pliant; Dol Common is a common prostitute who changes her identity like a doll, depending on how she is dressed.[6] Subtle and Face are attracted to Pliant, but each succeeds in the plot by his capacity to renounce her – Subtle in order to allow her to take Dol's place, Face to marry her to Lovewit. She is irrevocably stupid and wants to be deceived: she does not recognize the mendacity of Subtle and Face even after Surly points it out to her. If she is ignorant enough to mistake Surly for a Spaniard, she mistakes Lovewit in a Spaniard's costume for Surly in one. Lovewit emerges at the end as the substitute for Subtle, who has in fact been defeated already by the superior bluster of Face. Instead of Subtle stealing off with the wealth given to him for alchemical purposes, it goes to Lovewit, who now replaces Subtle as Face's partner. In place of the proto-Hobbesian world of the initial argument between Subtle and Face and the contractual democracy urged by Dol Common, the play ends in an appropriately hierarchical order. Lovewit and Face can cooperate because Lovewit is the property-holder and master, Face the servant. The apparently orderly triumvirate of master–wife–servant replaces that of contesting knaves. The triumph of the rascal

Face ironically and ambiguously solves the problem of aggressive economic individualism by replacing it with a traditional hierarchy.

As this plot of plots develops, the experienced playgoer frames alternative expectations as to how matters will turn out, and each expectation carries its own satiric implications. Each, in effect, represents, an alternative potential performance. (1.) Early in the play Dol (1.1, 7–9) worries that the neighbors will hear the quarrel between Subtle and Face. The alchemical scheme is based not only on performance but on secrecy, and discovery by the neighbors, the revelation of falsehood to the judging community, will bring the plot to an end. As she makes this threat, she may well point in the direction of the audience, for in a sense we are the neighbors, and our perception of the play is our eavesdropping on the suspicious house. (2.) The argument and the threat that the neighbors will overhear point to the possibility – indeed the likelihood – that the conspirators will self-destruct, that their internal disunion will prove more powerful than their capacity to deceive. "Will you undo yourselves with civil war?" Dol asks (1.1, 82). The plans of evil, after all, are built on conflicting aggressions and on deception, and hence they contain, one might think, the ingredients of their own destruction. (3.) The likely form of evil's overreaching may be the multiplicity, complexity, and confusion of plots, which threaten to exceed the power of the trickster to control them. If the conspirators do not devour each other, they may be devoured by the conflicting forces they have set in motion. If evil does not destroy itself, it will be destroyed by its illusion that it can control, even for a few hours, the forces it seeks to harness. The plots are based on the desire for money and the desire for sexuality, and these desires may come into conflict. (4.) The conspirators (we suspect) will be detected and revealed by the counterplot of Surly. Either Surly will be successful in uncovering the alchemical hoax by means of disguise, and the play will end in a personal triumph for him, or he will invoke the appropriate authorities, and the ending will be a triumph for social order. (5.) We are aware from early in the first scene that Lovewit may return, and our expectation is likely to be that such a return will bring normality and the appropriate punishment of the plotters. (6.) These alternatives have depended upon the moral myth that evil will not triumph (at least in plays) because it destroys itself, because its nature is inevitably revealed, or because normative moral forces are summoned to judge and punish. But the Aristophanic plot suggests that evil will comically triumph, that two wrongs will not make a right but will substitute for it in a world where right does not triumph anyway. The satiric point of the Aristophanic pattern may be that its deviant schemes are the only ones that can succeed where ordinary morality has failed. In a world of falsehood, only performance triumphs. The final alternative is that the plotters will be successful, at least within the limited time-frame they have set for their activities (and the author has set for the play).

What makes *The Alchemist* so startling is that the viewer is not forced to choose among these alternative performances, for all of them are realized by the play but not in the way we anticipated. The neighbors do gather to complain to Lovewit about the strange events in his house, but they get them wrong and are outfaced by Jeremy's assertion that they have been deceived (5.2, 31–32). The conspirators do turn against each other, but the plan of Subtle and Dol to leave with the money is thwarted by Face's revelation that Lovewit and the authorities have arrived. The triumph of Jeremy-Face has, at the end, been effected by his restored connection with Lovewit. Surly does indeed uncover the plot, but his efforts to bring the villains to justice and to attain Pliant are saliently unsuccessful. On two occasions he has been trapped by his disguise – when Subtle and Face pour insults on him to which he cannot respond because he pretends to know no English (4.3) and when his Spanish costume opens him to the attacks of Kastril and the Puritans (4.7). Moreover, his revelation to Pliant goes for nought because of her stupidity and her willingness to be deceived. The excessive complexity of the plotting goes beyond Subtle's control but ultimately proves to Face's advantage, for it allows him to feed one plot into another – to use Kastril and the Puritans to expel Surly and to use Drugger to fetch the parson who marries Pliant to Lovewit. The return of Lovewit has not restored conventional morality, for he is as interested in money and sexuality as anyone else in the play, but, unlike the others, succeeds in achieving what he wants because he actually is the owner of the house and the master of Jeremy. The role of Jeremy the butler becomes another disguise by which Face manipulates others, and as long as he can use the disguise to further Lovewit's ends, he is in no danger. The tricksters thus triumph almost as they do in Aristophanes, but the trio of tricksters has shifted from Subtle, Face, and Dol to Lovewit, Face, and Pliant.

As the neighbors gather and complain at the beginning of Act 5, we recognize that we, like them, have drawn erroneous conclusions from what we have overheard at Lovewit's house. When Face addresses us in the final lines of the play, reinforcing the identification of the play with the con game and the actors with the characters, we may intuit that our failure to predict the appropriate ending from among the choices available to us, our failure, in effect, to detect the deceptions of the play, places us distinctly among its gulls. But the play's fulfillment of so many possibilities of plot has been unusually satisfying, and, like the gulls, we really want to be deceived. The difference is that we have self-consciously indulged in a deception, knowing it to be a deception. The conspirators may have concocted more plots than they are able to control, but Jonson has mastered his plots, and thus he emerges as the extraordinary alchemist, demonstrating the superior but acknowledged trickery of art to the deceptive foolery of the tricksters. Deception is intrinsic to the idea of performance. The transformed selves that the gulls seek to perform and the performances that Subtle sets them to effect that transformation are distinct from each other and from the inadequacies of the characters' actual personalities. The resemblances heightened by the significant overlapping and parallelism of character, speech, and action often mark the differences among the similarities. R. L. Smallwood correctly asserts that "the Blackfriars of the play and the Blackfriars in which Jonson's theatre stood are inseparable," but further distinction is necessary.[7] The audience is aware of the space between Lovewit's house in Blackfriars and Blackfriars Theater, and therefore it remains in an ironic, complex, and judgmental position. It is aware of disguises that characters cannot detect (Surly as the Spaniard, Face as Lungs), but it is deceived into predicting outcomes based on familiar patterns of plot and meaning, only to have those outcomes withdrawn but returned in shapes that have been artistically (one might say alchemically) transformed.

The play itself represents further performances directed and enacted by Subtle, Face, and Dol both in order to gain money for their "venter tripartite" and to win the contest as to which "shall shark best" (1.1, 135, 160). For the audience these plots are interesting both as entertainments and as satiric devices that reveal, trap, and punish social offenders. Hence the audience's interest in these performances differs from that of the characters: the gulls seek to transform their dreams into actual power, the conspirators seek to maximize their profit, and the audience seeks both to be entertained and to work out the psychological forces that underlie the behavior of gulls and cons both. The test of the gulls is activated by their desire to perform. As audience members have noted, each of them comes to Subtle in order to become something he or she is not already. The characters may, as Alvin Kernan suggests, seek by alchemical means to move to a higher level in the hierarchical order,[8] but their desire alternatively reflects a monstrous self-interest that replaces social order with the drive to self-fulfillment. In any case, Kernan is surely correct in describing the characters as "satiric portraits of Renaissance aspiration, of the belief that man can make anything he will of himself and of his world, that he can storm heaven and become one with the gods, or make of earth a new paradise."[9] But this transformation is accompanied by a performance of rather a different sort. On one hand, Subtle becomes something of a father-confessor to the gulls: in order to enable him to realize their desires, they need to tell him what they are, and this revelation, of course, supplies him with the secret information on which his scams are based. On the other hand, Subtle, as a practitioner of alchemy, requires the conformity of the gulls with certain rules of behavior supposedly requisite to his art. The gulls must perform according to these rules, which place Dapper in the privy for Act 4, and result in the comic contortions of Mammon, who fantasizes lavish sexual lust while claiming that his interest in gold is purely eleemosynary. The transformative relationship between the old self and the new self is thus paralleled by, but different from, a performative relationship between the real self and the pretended self.

The primary of these performances by both gull and con is, of course, language, and the play is an anthology of social dialects rendered by striking characters. As Kernan observes, the ultimate "stone" of Jonson's fools is language, and the plays themselves become a "vast Babel."[10] The alchemical language of Subtle is the language of mystification – perhaps as incomprehensible to its original audience as to modern ones. Hence the fact that Subtle's alchemical language is not gibberish but a faithful representation of alchemy is a joke at our expense, since it is still incomprehensible to us. Its faithfulness is crucial to the functioning of alchemy as a metaphor for the basic process of transformation through performance. At the heart of the alchemical metaphor is the conjunction of chemical and moral processes. The purification of base metal into gold reenacts the Mass which transforms bread and wine into the saving body and blood of Christ: the purification of metal through alchemy represents the purification of the soul. Hence Subtle insists that the user of the stone be free from sin, a requirement that leads to the ruinous explosion when Mammon seeks to seduce Dol in her linguistic disguise as a mad follower of Broughton. Of course, Subtle is a fake and a non-believer. But from a Christian position, the irony is that the alchemical position, although it is blasphemous in arrogating to itself the redemptive power of God, is, in a sense, correct in its premise that the instruments of power in the world do no good unless they are wielded by good people for good purposes. (The rarity of people with that nature and those motives – indeed, their complete absence from the play – is a major satiric point.) Subtle's alchemical language is thus in several senses meaningless, but it is in another sense a counter-parody – the apparently meaningless language conceals a truth, in contrast to the parodic language of Dol and the gulls that merely reveals hypocrisy or meaninglessness.

Beyond the play's representation of various social discourses, the fact that the play is written in poetry intensifies it as a satiric performance. Paul Goodman describes the linguistic accomplishment of the play itself as "the particular Jonsonian mixture of base speech and Marlovian high rhetoric."[11] Unlike *Epicoene* and *Bartholomew Fair*, which are set in London and written in prose, and unlike *Volpone*, which is written in verse but set in exotic Venice, *The Alchemist* takes place in familiar London. The play's verse gives a mock-heroic character to the comedy, underlining the grandiose aspirations of its characters and supporting the metaphoric quality of the language, running from the initial flyting of Subtle and Face through the poetic flights of Mammon's erotic fancy, the scriptural discourse of Ananias and Tribulation, the Spanish of the disguised Surly, and the Broughtonian mythologies of Dol, to the matter-of-fact verse of Lovewit.

At the secondary level, that of social roles, performance in *The Alchemist* equates duplication with duplicity. The performance of Surly as Spaniard is outperformed by Face; when Lovewit returns, we learn that he too is a performer, and he wins Pliant by adopting the costume Surly had already introduced. At the end the performative nature of the play is reinforced by the duality of Face as actor and the actor as Face. Performance is replicated in the parallel nature of the characters. We have seen the replacement of the initial triad of Subtle, Face, and Dol by the final one of Lovewit, Face, and Pliant. The dual characters of Mammon and Surly resemble the pairing of Tribulation and Ananias, and both pairs parallel Subtle and Face or Dol and Pliant. Performance is manifested in disguise, self-assertion, trickery and deception, language, and the enactment of the play itself. If performance is pervasive in *The Alchemist*, the problem is to determine what that performance means, and how it serves the satire of the play.

The elaborate self-presentations of the characters capture and display the central satiric topics. The distance between the play as performed and the audience reinforces the distance between the satirized self-presentation of the characters and their actual intentions, motives, and identities. But those self-presentations are achieved by the characters' manipulations of social conventions and social expectations. The characters thus present to the audience both the weaknesses of their natures – the deficiencies that require the transformations that they seek, the products of society or the typical characteristics of social "estates" – and the false and pretentious conventions and attitudes they seek to emulate.[12] The satiric performance of self-presentation doubles the vehicles of satiric attack by including both the actual and intended natures of the self – the performing self and the role to be performed. But, in *The Alchemist*, there is a further level of satiric attack: alchemy, the means by which the characters seek to transform their flawed selves to their pretended selves, is certainly a central satiric object, and, far from being a dated target, it stands for any effort to change the real nature of things by the mendacious or unreal use of language and any effort to effect a spiritual change by mechanical means. Subtle has no laboratory, he conducts no experiments, and the attraction of his schemes lies in the enticements of his verbal manipulation.

The play itself differs from the performances of its characters, and Face's final speech equating the audience with the gulls is a joke – partly true and partly metaphorical. Its truth lies both in the likelihood that we are watching characters whose selfish desires resemble our own, even if they take a different form, and in the resemblances, of which Jonson has warned us in his advice "To the Reader," between the deceptions portrayed on the stage and the deceptions of the theater itself. Peter Womack stresses the connections between Lovewit's house and Blackfriars theater: "Like the 'grand balcon' in Genet's play, Face and Subtle's establishment is a brothel which is also a house of illusions: a place where fantastic, phoney images of gratification and power are tailored to the outrageous desires nursed by the paying customers. Also like Genet's, Jonson's house of illusions is a scandalous reflection on, and of, the theater in which it's exhibited."[13] We are aware observers who see the artificialities of the characters, but we may be temporarily deluded by the possibilities of the play as it is performed. We see ourselves as different from the play's gulls, but the more we see their behavior as illustrative of general illusions, the more we may wonder if we too are guilty parties.

Our sense of uncertainty seems connected with the infamous lack of judgment at the end of the play. When Lovewit arrives in Act 5, he turns out to be similar to the criminals he replaces, and his ultimate victory is dependent not on his higher moral stature but on his rights of ownership. He deserves his victory only because of his toleration of Face and his skill in dismissing the gulls. We are likely to be ambivalent about the conspirators themselves. Such ambiguities and the duplication of characters make the point that arrogance and illusion are basic if not universal characteristics, but they also force the audience to make distinctions – for example, between our sympathy for characters and the moral judgments we make on them. Our capacity to make such distinctions is what differentiates us from rogues and gulls alike and what marks the gap between the play that is performed and the performances it records.

The multiple performances of *The Alchemist*, with its overlapping correspondences, leading to and including the production of the play at

Blackfriars Theater, satirically assure maximum publicity for the guilt of characters and audience alike. The characters seek to fulfill the selfish desires of their fantasies, and that fulfillment would require them to perform roles devised by Subtle that comment ironically on those desires. Subtle's enticements invoke impressive linguistic performances on his part and those of his fellow conspirators. When Lovewit returns, he too becomes a performer in a script written for him by Jeremy-Face. But in addition to the multiple performances of the characters, we are aware that they are actors performing in a play whose deceptions are devised by Jonson. Peter Womack distinguishes sharply the discourse of the characters from those of the actors and the author ("the theatrical world is the site of a fraught conversation between three speakers – the writer, the dramatis personae, and the actor").[14] We are aware that the characters themselves are pawns in a contest between the actors and the author as to "who shall shark best." Because of the gap between stage and pit, we distinguish ourselves from fools and knaves alike, and naively may adopt a position of superiority. But insofar as we are deceived by the possibilities of false outcomes and morals, we are fools; insofar as the evils of selfishness, avarice, and lust may be motives for our own performances, we are knaves. But in recognizing our complicity and in rejecting the active practice of deception, we can still distinguish ourselves from the characters. We most resemble them in that we, like the gulls, must perform a rite of transformation. That rite is our experience of the play itself, and in requiring us to undergo it, Jonson is most like the alchemists. But his characters do not change, and he has devoted his play to the task of changing us. He reconciles the inverted world of Aristophanic theatre (the inverted world that never reverts) with the upright world of moral comedy by lodging his most important moral not in the play but in the experience of the play. He has overlapped as fully as seems possible the tertiary, secondary, and primary performative levels of theatricality, social roles, and discourse, and amid the resulting confusion he has insisted that we make the distinctions necessary to judgment.

LE TARTUFFE AND LE MISANTHROPE

The layering of performances produces gaps that may be exploited to attack the social institutions, ideas, values, and practices that these gaps reveal. Such gaps are apparent in Molière's *Tartuffe*, whose satiric quality is evidenced clearly enough by the *querelle du Tartuffe* that delayed its performance and forced it through several versions before its public staging in 1669.[15] Michael Spingler has argued that in *Tartuffe* Molière developed the theater "into a self-conscious instrument of ironic political and social commentary," especially to criticize society's "excessive reliance upon performance as a means of self-authentication."[16] Tartuffe, the center of satiric attack, is an apparently unsuccessful performer in comparison to the ingenious Subtle; he fools only Orgon and Mme. Pernelle, his mother. But these offer him a degree of devotion and even sacrifice that certainly rivals the gold of Jonson's gulls. The other members of Orgon's household, who are fully aware of the dangers presented by Tartuffe, fall into two groups. The *raisonneurs* comprise Orgon's young wife Elmire, her brother Cléante, and the servant Dorine. Dorine taunts Orgon unavailingly, but Cléante's rational and conventional speeches on behalf of moderation are hardly more successful. The weight of persuasion falls on Elmire, who is partially successful through performance rather than reasoned discourse. The second group consists of the younger generation, whose inheritance is figuratively and, at last, literally threatened by Tartuffe: Damis and Mariane, Orgon's son and daughter by his first marriage, and Mariane's fiancé Valère.

The featured performance is that of Tartuffe, and his immediate audience is Orgon. The members of the household form another, unappreciative, audience, and we form still another. Further audiences are implied by the play, including people outside the family unit who, we are aware, may hold Tartuffe in esteem, religious people who practice their faith more sincerely than he, and, ultimately, authorities who perceive him as a criminal. Tartuffe's performance prompts performances by Orgon, who plans to break Mariane's engagement to Valère in order to marry her to Tartuffe, and who later will disinherit Damis. The performative nature of these actions lies in an unnaturalness that defines itself in Orgon's mind as religiosity and as an appropriate response to a man of unusual piety and integrity. Lionel Gossman argues that Orgon uses Tartuffe in order to solidify and extend his own power over his family, and he traces the political implications of that possibility.[17] But an actor might project the opposite pattern. Rather than seeking to gain power through Tartuffe, Orgon may seek to relinquish responsibility. He is willing to hand Tartuffe his daughter, his secrets, his property, and almost his wife. Decisions become merely a matter of conforming to the will of Tartuffe. If Tartuffe can be seen as an embodiment of religion, or of a certain kind of religion, the significance of his appeal to Orgon becomes apparent. Religion offers an external guide to life, and, rather than leading the life of reason, pallidly represented by Cléante, one merely needs to follow a pattern supplied by belief. That Tartuffe proves signally unworthy of Orgon's trust is, of course, unfortunate, but even if he were worthy, the problems he presents to Orgon's family in the first two acts would remain more-or-less the same. His unworthiness, however, shows the difficulty of the position adopted by Orgon. The complete faith Orgon reposes in Tartuffe requires a certainty that cannot be found in human affairs. The danger of religion as presented in the play lies in the fact that it is performed by human beings who are unreliable, fallible, or false. Orgon's fanaticism isolates him from common sense and encloses him in an illusion that seems nearly impregnable. Elmire's performances, involving her responses to Tartuffe's seductive advances, provide breaches in this prison that ordinary discourse cannot.

In the first instance, Elmire has, according to Dorine, sent for Tartuffe to explore his attitude towards his projected marriage with Mariane. His expression of passion for Elmire seems a reversal of his previous performance, for if his religion is hypocrisy, his sexual passion may not be. Alternatively, his passion may itself be yet another pose in his repertoire, and his real concern is the power he can command over others. In either case, he connects his sexual passion to his religious professions through the familiar Platonic rationale:

> Et je n'ai pu vous voir, parfaite créature,
> Sans admirer en vous l'auteur de la nature.
> Et d'une ardente amour sentir mon coeur atteint,
> Au plus beau des portraits où lui-même il s'est peint.
>
> [How could I look on you, O flawless creature,
> And not adore the Author of all Nature,
> Feeling a love both passionate and pure
> For you, his triumph of self-portraiture?]
>
> (3.3.941–44)[18]

Having conquered Orgon through the pretense of religion, he seeks to conquer Elmire through the pretense of love. She allows Tartuffe's seductions to continue to the point at which she can broach the marriage of Valère and Mariane, the secret object of her forbearance. But at that point the hot-headed Damis, the secret audience, bursts forth from the *petit cabinet*, promising to expose Tartuffe to Orgon. His rash effort to denounce Tartuffe replaces Elmire's subtle performance with a crude and ineffective directness that leads to his disinheritance.

The secret audience of Elmire's second performance is Orgon, concealed beneath the table and hidden by the tablecloth. Elmire encourages Tartuffe to resume his wooing in an effort to convince her husband that Damis's accusations were correct. Having concealed Orgon and left his intervention, prompted only by a cough, up to him, Elmire momentarily seems to lack complete control of the scene. Orgon's behavior has been so unreliable that it is just possible that he will not save her. He has sacrificed his son to Tartuffe and plans to sacrifice his daughter, raising the question whether he will sacrifice his wife, a question that becomes more pressing as he continues not to appear. Having seen *The Alchemist*, we may fear that she, like Surly, will be trapped by her costume. But we trust that Molière the author (who acted Orgon) will not allow her to grant her full favors to Tartuffe on stage. More significantly, we know that she knows that Orgon is beneath the table, and she is engaged in a double performance. Her pretense of love to Tartuffe is a performance for Orgon, whom she wishes to restore to his proper role as husband and head of the family by leaving to him the decision to save her. Her goal is to replace Tartuffe in Orgon's affection, even as Tartuffe seeks to replace Orgon in hers. We are aware, even when her situation and Tartuffe's passion grow urgent, that she need only ask Tartuffe to look beneath the table, as she eventually asks him to look in the hall. Her prolongation of the scene is part of her game with her exasperating husband, but she remains in control of the situation. There is an earlier fear that Tartuffe himself may detect her, for he seems initially suspicious. He cleverly turns his skepticism into a demand for full proof. That demand supplies the evidence that Elmire wanted her husband to hear. But the words that bring Orgon from beneath his table are not crude advances to Elmire but a characterization of Orgon himself:

> Qu'est-il besoin pour lui du soin que vous prenez?
> C'est un homme, entre nous, à mener par le nez;
> De tous nos entretiens il est pour faire gloire,
> Et je l'ai mis au point de voir tout sans rien croire.
>
> [Why worry about the man? Each day he grows
> More gullible; one can lead him by the nose.
> To find us here would fill him with delight,
> And if he saw the worst, he'd doubt his sight.]
>   (4.5.1523–26)

If Orgon has erred in his excessive trust of Tartuffe, Tartuffe has been excessive in his trust of Elmire. Here is a statement that is, in a sense, more harmful to Tartuffe than being caught in the act, for it allows no recovery. It denies the possibility of denial.

Elmire's essential mistake, despite the brilliance and control of her performance, is her assumption that Orgon is ultimately the head of the family, and that his knowledge of Tartuffe's treachery will bring his deceptions to an end. But in that assumption she is, alas, mistaken. Tartuffe's reaction to each performance is significant and successful. He counters the first, the accusation of Damis, by pretending to admit his miserable nature – if anything by overstating it. The fact that his confession seems to be an over-statement marks it as a performance, and the fact that it turns out to be literally true is an irony of which the audience is not yet fully aware. The overstatement is a sign of false confession, but Orgon misinterprets it as the sign of a humility that renders false the accusation of Damis. Tartuffe responds to Elmire's second performance quite differently. Orgon orders him out of the house, but Tartuffe now owns the house, which Orgon has deeded to him, and orders Orgon out. Orgon has given him the secret box of a friend who took the losing side in the Fronde, and Tartuffe goes to turn him in. The revelation of Tartuffe's mendacity has been complete, but the penalty for complete revelation is complete revelation: the extent and consequences of Orgon's trust are now all too clear.

The relationship between Tartuffe and Orgon is the same contrast be-tween knave and gull that stands at the center of *The Alchemist*. The per-formances of the knave set in motion those of the gull, but the foolishness of the gull cannot be revealed by advisors whose interests, as in the case of Orgon's family, lie in ending the folly. The gull can only be disenchanted by the knave himself, and the words of disenchantment can only be forced by a superior performance – in this case Elmire's. The gifts that have put Orgon in Tartuffe's power are unknown to the audience until the end of Act 4, but they are consistent with the folly of Orgon's infatuation. Having emerged to save his wife, Orgon now appears to have sacrificed himself and his family. The intervention of the wise, all-seeing monarch is necessary to prevent the usurpation of secular order by religious hypocrisy, a usurpation of interest to the King, even if monarchs are seldom concerned with the ruin of individual households. In Molière's symmetrical comedy, Tartuffe has made the same mistake as Elmire in mislocating the center of power. As long as the comic sphere remains domestic, his deceptions retain their extraordinary force, but when he interferes with the legal rights of prop-erty and inheritance and asserts his alleged rights through civil authority, he moves into an arena of legal and, ultimately, monarchical scrutiny, the arena in which his criminality cannot be concealed. The actual unlikelihood of royal intervention does not make it ironic at the expense of the King but rather, in a play that satirizes knaves and fools, shows that the extremes of knavery and folly allow no ordinary solution. The extraordinary nature of the solution here underlines the force of the play as satire and marks the play as a theatrical performance, in which Molière acknowledges his own debt to the intervention of Louis XIV for the production of this very play.

The initial hostility of religious forces that necessitated the King's inter-vention for the production of *Tartuffe* clearly indicates that it was originally perceived as a satire, directed against specific religious institutions and practices and therefore dangerous to society. But the specific satiric targets – the Jansenists, the Jesuits, or *La Compagnie du Saint-Sacrement* – are not easy to identify, and there seems to be enough satire in the play to offend them all. James F. Gaines describes *Tartuffe* as "a veritable fruit salad of religious doctrines."[19] *Le Tartuffe* may be a case in which a satire has turned into comedy with the passing of the historical circumstances of its early performances. But false religiosity remains, and there is still the danger of becoming, as Dorine puts it, *tartuffiée*. The overt satire of hypocrisy was perhaps as far as Molière could go in his historical circumstances. The play had enough difficulty at that. But the implications of the play go still further. Religion may serve as a distorting cover for human weakness. The performances of knaves still set off the performances of gulls. *Tartuffe* functions through the temporary separation of knowledge and power. The skillful counter-performances of Elmire lead to knowledge but, having relinquished his identity into the hands of Tartuffe, Orgon lacks the power to save himself. The combination of knowledge and power lies only with the King, or it lies nowhere. The message of the play may indeed be a dour one – the mistake of Orgon is a naive trust based on specious faith. But by enacting the performance that engenders knowledge, Elmire, without being a satirist herself, has played the satiric role.

If *Le Tartuffe* lacks a fully dramatized satirist, *Le Misanthrope* supplies an abundance of them. In addition to Molière, the controlling satirist, the role of satirist is shared, in significantly different ways, by Alceste, Philinte, Arsinoé, and Célimène. Alceste, the misanthrope-in-love who gives the title to the play, is infatuated with coquettish Célimène, who entertains her admirers with devastating verbal portraits of their absent friends. Arsinoé, the contrasting prude, whose dour views in some respects echo those of Alceste, is herself interested in Alceste, and her vengeance against Célimène supplies much of the motive for the events that lead to the coquette's ultimate embarrassment. The rational and worldly Philinte seeks to restrain the impulses of his friend Alceste. The play provides a sequence of conversations between pairs of satirists, combined with larger groupings, in which the positions of the different satirists play off against each other and against the behavior of the satiric targets. The first of these duologues, between Alceste and Philinte, defines the most important of the contrasting satiric positions and raises perhaps the play's central issue.

Alceste berates Philinte for his insincere flattery of a worthless man, but Philinte contends that his behavior is simple politeness. It is this politeness, however, that Alceste finds objectionable, since superficial but general friendliness means that real friendship becomes indistinguishable. The prevalence of this insincere behavior sours Alceste on the human race in general:

> Mes yeux sont trop blessés, et la cour et la ville
> Ne m'offrent rien qu'objets à m'échauffer la bile:
> J'entre en une humeur noire, et un chagrin profond,
> Quand je vois vivre entre eux les hommes comme ils font;
> Je ne trouve partout que lâche flatterie,
> Qu'injustice, intérêt, trahison, fourberie;
> Je n'y puis plus tenir, j'enrage, et mon dessein
> Est de rompre en visière à tout le genre humain.
>
> [All are corrupt; there's nothing to be seen
> In court or town but aggravates my spleen.
> I fall into deep gloom and melancholy
> When I survey this scene of human folly,
> Finding on every hand base flattery,
> Injustice, fraud, self-interest, treachery. . .
> Ah, it's too much; mankind has grown so base,
> I mean to break with the whole human race.] (1.1.89–96)

Philinte's response to this righteous indignation is both tolerant and cynical, the toleration growing from the cynicism. To be angered by human folly is to be blind to human nature:

> Oui, je vois ces défauts dont votre âme murmure
> Comme vices unis à l'humaine nature;
> Et mon esprit enfin n'est pas plus offensé
> De voir un homme fourbe, injuste, intéressé,
> Que de voir des vautours affamés de carnage,
> Des singes malfaisants, et des loups pleins de rage.
>
> [Why, no. Those faults of which you so complain
> Are part of human nature, I maintain,
> And it's no more a matter of disgust
> That men are knavish, selfish and unjust,
> Than that the vulture dines upon the dead,
> And wolves are furious, and apes ill-bred.]
> (1.i.173–78)

Alceste's initial position might nonetheless be described as optimistic, or at least humanistic. He feels that he can hold people responsible for their foolishness because they are rational creatures with the capacity to act otherwise. Philinte's toleration, in contrast, is based on his belief that the qualities for which Alceste seeks to hold his fellow-humans accountable are

inevitable, beyond human control, and therefore beyond accountability, to
be endured rather than to be corrected. Because Philinte sees correction
as impossible, it is tempting to see him less as a satirist than as a member
of the satiric audience. To put the matter paradigmatically (but paradigms
are what Molière's misanthropic conversations offer), satirists assume the
position of Alceste in order to produce an audience of Philintes. They
condemn mankind universally with a shrill voice of absolutism, but their
audience cannot follow them to the position of isolation that their satiric
misanthropy implies, any more than Célimène, at the end of the play, can
follow Alceste. For Alceste the responsibility of the satirist is to speak sincerely, and the satirist's purpose is to correct and reform the behavior of
society. For Philinte, the purpose of the satirist is to remind the audience
that humanity everywhere is "fourbe, injuste, intéressé," but to insist therefore upon a tolerant conformity rather than an absolutist singularity. In
addition to defining the play's primary set of satiric positions, the first act
addresses, at least implicitly, a central social problem represented in the
play. After a period of civil war, religious conflict, and dynastic uncertainty,
France in 1666 needed a period of civil peace. It needed, in short, the moderate, restrained behavior embodied by Philinte and Eliante. The Court
of Marshalls, to which Oronte appeals on behalf of the sonnet abused by
Alceste, is a royal effort to minimize dueling by resolving divisive issues. As
Jules Brody suggests, "the opposition to Alceste . . . builds on a need and
a willingness to safeguard the benefits of civilization, despite its attendant
discontents."[20] The conflicts of the play raise a larger political question:
should society be structured to assure its own survival by encouraging social
conformity and avoiding serious conflict, or should it promote and protect
basic moral positions, regardless of the divisions to which they may lead?

The satiric confrontation between the coquette Célimène and the prude
Arsinoé takes place at the center of the play (3.4). Arsinoé uses the privilege gained by the retired and virtuous position she has assumed to tell
Célimène that others are gossiping about the easy access she allows to men
and about the questionable virtue it implies. Célimène, in response, tells
Arsinoé about her own reputation for hypocritical prudery. Arsinoé's attack is hardly satiric, for its only indirection lies in attributing to others
the barbs with which Arsinoé herself wishes to wound. Célimène, on the
other hand, puts her attack on Arsinoé in the form of a parody that doubles
the pain she wishes to inflict: she hypocritically parodies the hypocritical advice of the prude whom she accuses of hypocrisy. Arsinoé's satire
derives, if hypocritically, from a pseudo-Jansenist view of the universality
of human evil and the consequent need for intrusive moral instruction;

Célimène sees satire as the sharp exposure of social pretension, of which she, as the charming figure to whom so many men pretend, is a privileged observer. Her satire becomes the means of entertaining her admirers and assuring the superiority of her *salon* to the society around it. Its attraction lies less in its moral instruction than in the acuity and wit of her descriptions.[21]

She roundly defeats her rival in the scene, but her character raises problems in the relationship between language and behavior. Her verbal triumph inspires Arsinoé to show Alceste a letter by Célimène, purportedly written to another lover. Verbal manipulation, in which Célimène excels, has a limited capacity to control the manipulation of reality by other people. When Alceste confronts Célimène about the letter in 4.3, it has almost hopelessly been taken out of context. It is neither addressed nor signed, although she admits that she wrote it. It might be, as Arsinoé told Alceste, written to his hated rival Oronte. When Célimène admits that it was, she is unclearly ironic, and her admission does not confirm the fact. It may have been an unfinished draft intended, as Richard E. Goodkin has argued, for Alceste himself.[22] Célimène startles Alceste by suggesting that it was written to a woman rather than a man. Its lack of an address is appropriate to her coquettish character, since any suitor can project himself or his rival as the addressee. It might have been sent to anyone – or possibly to everyone. The letter perfectly represents the lack of context that is characteristic of Célimène's speech, and each of her admirers seeks to supply that context by envisioning himself as the person loved, a vision that she encourages in them all.

In Act 5 the wonderfully superficial *marquis* Acaste and Clitandre produce letters written to each in which Célimène attacks the other, as well as further suitors, notably including Alceste, who is present. Since the *marquis* had brought the letters to Arsinoé, who encouraged them to confront Célimène publicly, the scene is another performance directed by the prude. But since Acaste and Clitandre encouraged and applauded Célimène's satire of others in Act 2, they can hardly object to being victims here. But her efforts to encourage each to think himself beloved and the others scorned separates signifiers from the signified and renders her language incredible. Alceste's final proposal that she retire with him in the rural desert to which he intends to flee seems a test designed to cut through her now-notorious verbal manipulation, to replace language with behavior.

Alceste and Célimène are the final satirists in confrontation, and their incompatibility involves both the satiric implications of their language and the personal motives that drive their speech. The problem of satiric language, for Célimène, lies in the conflict between satiric attack and the desire to seem universally desirable, and this incongruity, mirroring Alceste's hope to be admired for his sincerity in rejecting others, undercuts the reliability of both her satire and her protestations of affection. In Act 5 she becomes the satiric victim rather than the satirizer, and her expressions of affection follow the discredited pattern of preferring one by condemning the others: "J'ai des autres ici méprisé le courroux," she tells Alceste, "Mais je tombe d'accord de mon crime envers vous" ("The anger of those others I could despise; My guilt toward you I sadly recognize") (5, final scene, 1741–42). In Célimène's case, communication has virtually become impossible because her language has lost the certainty necessary to make meaning. But certainty is precisely what Alceste needs. His satire implies a moral absolutism that justifies the intensity of his judgments and almost justifies their self-serving personal nature. If he cannot authorize his judgments by reference to an external standard, his condemnation of Oronte's sonnet indeed becomes an effort to put down a rival lover rather than a reluctant exercise in literary criticism. The problem with such absolute judgments lies in the unlikelihood, perhaps impossibility, of certainty. The dramatic manifestation of Alceste's quest for a certainty that justifies his self-cast role as sincere satirist is his love for Célimène, and the play concludes with their paradoxical relationship: if her satiric position renders certainty impossible because language has become unstable, his satiric position requires precisely such certainty.

Behind the imperfect satirists of the play, of course, stands Molière. He can assume the position of the perfect satirist because he is disguised. He was literally disguised as Alceste, the role that he acted at the first performance. But he is also the author whose identity is not directly involved in the satiric statements of the play. Therefore it is not appropriate for the audience to interpret his satire merely or primarily as the manifestation of his personal desires or deficiencies, precisely the interpretation to which Alceste is liable. The fact that his satire cannot be explained away so easily gives it greater authority and supports his great satiric portraits of Acaste, Clitandre, and Oronte, of Arsinoé, and of Célimène. But the audience is also aware that offstage there is a world that is satiric or worse. The fact that Alceste has been found faulty by the Marshalls is due perhaps as much to his obstinate behavior as to Oronte's vanity, but the existence of a court to deal with foolish quarrels that might otherwise result in duels is itself an indication of the falsity and superficiality of society. Philinte never disagrees with Alceste's claim that he is right in his law suit but argues that law cases are not decided by the rightness of the cause but by personal contact and corruption. The positions of courtly eminence claimed by the vacuous *marquis* and promised to Alceste by Arsinoé (whose assertion that the court does not recognize the merit of Alceste is another satiric comment on artificiality of court life) extend the satire of Molière's play. By the beginning of Act 4, when Alceste's jealousy, fueled by the letter that Arsinoé has given him, starts to take its toll directly, the events of the play seem to have shown the plausibility of his dim view of humanity.

The one character of the play who is neither satirist nor satiric victim is Eliante. She admires Alceste but accepts the hand of Philinte. Although she is a proponent of plain speaking and urges Célimène to tell her lovers what is on her mind (5.3.1660–63), her long Lucretian speech in 2.4 (her only long speech in the play) recognizes the value of illusions that turn the beloved's faults into beauties. Her consent to marry Philinte is more than a comedic convenience that allows someone to marry in this otherwise dour play. She joins with Philinte in performing the final reconciling gesture of the play. Alceste gives them a blessing that is profoundly consistent with his beliefs throughout the play – that the integrity of their relationship will bring them a happiness that is not fortuitous but deserved. But for himself, integrity requires isolation.

> Puissiez-vous, pour goûter de vrais contentements,
> L'un pour l'autre à jamais garder ces sentiments!
> Trahi de toutes parts, accablé d'injustices,
> Je vais sortir d'un gouffre où triomphent les vices,
> Et chercher sur la terre un endroit écarté
> Où d'être homme d'honneur on ait la liberté.

> [May you be true to all you now profess,
> And so deserve unending happiness.
> Meanwhile, betrayed and wronged in everything,
> I'll flee this bitter world where vice is king,
> And seek some spot unpeopled and apart
> Where I'll be free to have an honest heart.]
> (5, final scene, 1801–6)

But if Alceste leaves the play (as here he does) with a contrast between the sincerely loving couple and the unhappy isolated individual, Philinte still insists on reconciling him to society. He asks Eliante to join him in retrieving Alceste:

> Allons, Madame, allons employer toute chose,
> Pour rompre le dessein que son coeur se propose.

> [Come, Madame, let's do everything we can
> To change the mind of this unhappy man.]
> (5, final scene, 1807–8)

The play began with Alceste's jealousy not of Célimène but of Philinte, with his complaint that Philinte's casual compliments of everyone left his feelings for anyone in doubt (precisely the complaint that he and the other suitors had about Célimène). But Alceste is as superficial in seeking the manifestation of friendship in conventional compliments as he accuses Philinte of being when he makes such compliments. Philinte's concluding resolution to try every means to reverse the plan proposed by Alceste's wounded heart seems at first ridiculous, yet another effort to force a man of integrity into a position of compromise. But if Alceste asked at the outset how friendship can be determined in false discourse, the answer lies in Philinte's expression of personal loyalty and concern. One hopes that the famous empty stage at the conclusion of the play will not remain empty long.

The character of Alceste and how to regard it is the famous crux of *Le Misanthrope*. His insistence on integrity seems at odds with his demands for attention and even singularity and with his choice of a coquette as his beloved. As most critics and directors now agree, he is a comic character. But from Visé onwards, and in a variety of productions, audiences have found sympathetic qualities ranging from the likeable to the heroic.[23] His argument with Philinte, his criticism of Oronte's sonnet, his accusation that Acaste and Clitandre have prompted Célimène's scandalous and satiric portraits have been seen not as the frank statements of an *honnête homme* but as retaliations against rivals. Certainly, after Arsinoé has shown him Célimène's letter, he seems to have lost his emotional control. The main contrast is between his condemnation of society and insistence on integrity on one hand and his emotional instability on the other. But the paradox of the play does not lie only in the contradictions of Alceste's character. There is a parallel satiric paradox as well. Society is indeed vain, false, and selfish, as the other characters of the play clearly show. But for a satirist to say as much seems to manifest the weaknesses of his own character; the public utterance of a blanket condemnation seems a statement of one's own superiority and a demand for attention. Alceste and Gulliver seem brothers in misanthropy. His case thus shows the value of the hidden satirist, whose social analysis cannot be dismissed as personal disorder. In *Le Misanthrope* that satirist is the brilliant actor who hides his face behind the mask of the foolish Alceste and becomes thereby the ultimate satiric performer.

My use of comic plays by Jonson and Molière to exemplify the performative nature of satiric drama requires a glance at the generic relationship between satire and comedy. Distinguishing between comedy and satire, either on a broad generic level or, more modestly, in relation to particular plays or groups of plays, is complicated by the fact that both are definable only in terms of a number of independent variables. Both function as genres and as modes, and both can arguably be established as pre-generic bodies of literature, rooted in archetypal attitudes towards human life. One can speak of the comic spirit as easily as one can of the satiric frame of mind. The area where satire and comedy overlap becomes a battleground for theorists of one genre or another, where each seeks to limit the ground available to the other genre. Thus George Meredith speaks of the satirist as "a moral agent, often a social scavenger, working on a storage of bile," while defenders of satire might be tempted to see comedy as perpetuating the socially useful untruth that life is not only good but resolvable into a happy ending.[24]

Satire works on comedy much as it works on other forms that it borrows, and the overlapping of generic markers is a manifestation of its parasitic nature. Comedy ends happily – even, in its purest instances, with a sense that the world of the play has, if temporarily, reached a resolution that leaves nothing significantly lacking. A look at the endings of the three plays by Jonson and Molière reveals the disconcerting elements produced when satire takes over the comic form. Comedy traditionally ends in marriages; *The Alchemist* ends with the marriage of Lovewit and Pliant, *Le Misanthrope* with the expected marriage of Philinte and Eliante, and *Tartuffe* with the restoration of the family, instanced by the forthcoming marriage of Mariane and Valère. But the ending of *Le Misanthrope*, with the isolation of its hero and the humiliation of its heroine, is hardly celebratory, despite the marriage of important secondary characters. Lovewit's marriage to Pliant is partly a manifestation of power, partly a result of good luck, and partly the triumph of machination and lust. It is ironic rather than comic. The ending of *Tartuffe* takes place thanks to the unexpected involvement of the King himself, and the instability of Orgon's character does not predict a harmonious future. When consciousness of the untruthful but entertaining nature of comic optimism is emphasized, as seems the case in *Tartuffe*, comedy moves in the direction of satire. The happy endings of *The Alchemist* and *Tartuffe* climax a series of surprises that undercut the audience's sense of the predictability of human nature. The unhappy ending of *Le Misanthrope*, in contrast, relentlessly fulfills the expectations generated by the plot, though it denies the resolution promised by the genre. When satire adopts the form of comedy, the usual characteristics of the host are rendered problematic by the parasite.

The classical nature of *The Alchemist*, *Le Tartuffe*, and *Le Misanthrope* – their exemplary status as comedies – may lie in the language in which their self-conscious performances take place. In particular, all three plays are written in verse, that of Molière still more distant from ordinary language by its rhyme. All three represent and even parody distinct discourses in dramatic conflict – so that, for example, the hypocritical piety and moralistic lecturing of Mme. Pernelle in the first scene of *Tartuffe* contrast to the discourse of the other members of the Orgon household.[25] In *The Alchemist* the heightened language of poetry frames the exaggerated discourse both of the most discursive gulls – Sir Epicure Mammon and the Puritans – and of the verbally resourceful cons. The use of verse serves not only to define unordinary discourses but to distance the audience from the proclamations of the characters, rendering Alceste, for example, the object of analytic scrutiny, even if, at the same time, the substance of what he says seems not only sympathetic but, at the outset, modest.

The combination of diverse exaggerated discourses and a marked differentiation between what is said by the characters and what is heard by the audience becomes a means by which performative comedy presents characteristically satiric themes and approaches. The world perceived by the satirist and revealed by the play consists largely of knaves and fools. Such knaves as Subtle and Face, Tartuffe and Arsinoé, are set off against Mammon, Wholesome, Orgon, and virtually all of the other characters of *Le Misanthrope*. (One characteristic of Alceste's misanthropy may be that he mistakes fools for knaves.) Satirists themselves may be among the knaves but not among the fools. Genuinely sympathetic characters are rare in satiric comedies. The interactions among satirists, knaves, and fools set off the series of performances that gives the play its satiric pattern. These performances stimulate and encompass the variety of discourses in conflict and are heightened by the poetic discourse of the play itself. Significant as this pattern may be, it should not be mistaken for the substance of the satire itself. Characters, after all, are not merely knaves and fools but often typify social orders and classes, and the discourses of performance are not only personal but common to social groups and reflective of shared values and interests. Thus the knavery and foolishness of the characters performing within the performance of the play carries much of the force of the attack, whose satiric nature is identified by the presence of a surrogate satirist, by the exaggeration of language beyond meaning, and by the falsity and artificiality inherent in the double performance. Once this satiric pattern has been identified in the classic comedy of Jonson and Molière, we need to ask whether it has at least a rough equivalent in dramatic satire that is more realistic, that is not heightened by poetry, and that is not as strongly marked in its genre. A satiric source that meets these criteria is the drama of the nineteenth-century Russian playwright Alexander Nikolayevich Ostrovsky.

OSTROVSKY

While Jonson and Molière need no introduction to educated English-speaking readers, the same is not the case with Ostrovsky. While his plays are a staple of Russian theater, they are only occasionally performed in the west. His father was a wealthy lawyer, and after Ostrovsky dropped out of the university, he worked for several years as a clerk in Moscow courts, where he became familiar with the manners and values of a range of people, especially in the emerging merchant class.[26] His early plays grew out of this interest, but they were censored, earning him a lecture from the government on the importance of allowing virtue to triumph, and leading to dismissal from his court job.[27] He served for a period as quasi-editor of the journal *Moskvitianin* and figured among the intellectuals associated with it.[28] But he soon became a full-time playwright, eventually writing over fifty plays. His most famous early play, *The Storm* (*Groza*, 1859), was given its atmospheric exactness in part by several trips he made to the Middle Volga region, during which he made extensive notes on language and customs.[29] His interest in ethnography is reflected in his use of social dialects (a feature that is impossible to render in English but also distances him somewhat from modern Russian audiences), and his plays are filled with proverbs, songs, and other folk elements.[30] Not only did he develop the realistic speech and action of Russian drama, but he was an important figure in the development of Russian theater as well, especially the Maly Theater, where many of his plays were first performed. He organized the Society of Dramatic Authors and Composers (1874), argued persistently for the training of actors, and became director of repertory for the Moscow Imperial Theater in the last year of his life (1886). He was an immediate predecessor not only of Chekhov but of Stanislavsky.[31] As a satirist he uses the generic breakdown of tragedy and comedy to show the breakdown of traditional classes of Russian society.[32]

This clouding of genres can particularly be seen in the reappearance of parallel characters and patterns of action in both serious and comic plays. At the center of the pattern, especially in the early plays, is the *samodur* or petty tyrant (literally "self-deceiver") – a businessman or landowner, male or female, whose oppressive influence extends over both workers and, especially, family. Sometimes the *samodur*'s illusion of power and control is easily demolished. The pattern in which an inveterate schemer is defeated by a surprising but still more unscrupulous antagonist is repeated in Ostrovsky's plays. Because Ostrovsky concentrates on ruthless and unreasonable power exercised in a domestic sphere, the instrument of that power is usually marriage, and its victim is usually a young woman. In *A Protegée of the Mistress* ([The Ward] *Vospitannitsa*, 1859) Madame Ulanbekov, an elderly owner of nearly 2000 serfs, takes attractive peasant women as wards, gives them a genteel education, and marries them off at will.[33] When one of them, Nadya, falls in love with Mme. Ulanbekov's son, the old woman plans to marry her to a drunken and abusive government clerk. The play ends before it is clear whether Nadya allows herself to be married or commits suicide. Much the same pattern occurs in *The Forest* (*Les*, 1871), a more complex and sophisticated play, in which the heroine tries to commit suicide but is rescued by the kindly actor Neschastlivtsev.[34] In *The Storm*, the heroine Katerina is victimized by her mother-in-law, just as her weak lover Boris is victimized by his uncle. Here the heroine, who guiltily confesses her illicit affair, does commit suicide. Ostrovsky's female tyrants usually hide behind and speak through the authority of highly conservative social and religious values, and the female victim is surrounded by weak, ineffective males. At times the pattern occurs when the social and economic forces are not manifested in an unsympathetic tyrant but nonetheless operate powerfully on the heroine. Marya, the poor but attractive heroine of Ostrovsky's early play *The Poor Bride* (*Bednaia nevesta*, 1852), is surrounded by three weak suitors.[35] She ultimately marries an uncouth government official because he is the only available man who can supply her mother with the means of financial survival. As the play progresses, and Marya's options close, she shifts from being a superficial girl to becoming a strong and even radiant woman. In *Without a Dowry* (*Bespridannitsa*, 1878) Larisa, one of Ostrovsky's most sympathetic women, is destroyed by her choice between marriage to an awkward and pretentious man she does not love and life as a roué's kept mistress.[36] Sometimes the victimized women are rescued by benevolent men, but what Ostrovsky's young, victimized women have in common, whether rescued or not, is a vulnerability that is powerless in the face of economic pressure and rigid conventional morals. Such women represent a combination of deep feeling and instinctive morality that contrasts to the hypocritical piety and calculated self-interest that surrounds them. Although not satiric characters they perform the satiric functions of revealing the evil of the others and of embodying the criteria for evaluating them. They gives a satiric focus to the plays by dramatizing the effects of repression. Ostrovsky's early and sympathetic critic Nikolay Dobrolyubov published an article in 1859 entitled "The Dark Kingdom" (Temnoe tsarstvo), in which he delineated the world of domestic tyranny and economic exploitation revealed in Ostrovsky's early plays. After the first performance of *The Storm* later that same year, he published a subsequent article, "A Ray of Light in the Dark Kingdom" (Luch sveta v temnom tsarstve), in which he sees Katerina as a free-spirited character who reacts strongly but tragically against the certainty of being engulfed in the world of darkness around her.[37] Dobrolyubov's reading of Katerina seems to simplify her character by neglecting the degree to which she has internalized the values against which she reacts and by overstating the rebelliousness of a decidedly passive figure. But his approach emphasized, perhaps in the mind of Ostrovsky himself, the satiric contrast between the dark world of petty tyranny and repressive values and the bright if flickering light of some of the women it victimizes.

Ostrovsky extends and complicates this contrast between the satirized world and the sympathetic woman by setting it in the context of a similar contrast between knaves and fools. "Wolves and Sheep," observes Lynyayev, the feckless *raisonneur* in the play of that title (*Volki i ovtsy*; 1875): "The wolves devour the sheep and the sheep not only allow themselves to be devoured, but seem to like it!"[38] Lynyayev, despite his perspicacity, belongs with the sheep, more through lack of will than lack of intelligence. He tries to save his country neighbor, the young widow Kupavina, from the illegal and unscrupulous machinations of Murzavetzkaya. But Kupavina is actually saved, if that is the term, by the aggressive Berkutov, who has an estate in the area and seems equally interested in Kupavina and in the land she has inherited from her husband. Lynyayev, in turn, is caught by Glafira, a young niece of Murzavetzkaya, who is anxious to find a husband to support her fashionable tastes. Wolves exercise their lupine nature by undertaking performances, directed, on behalf of the sheep and in their own interests, against less skilled, more evil performers. The ironic truth of Lynyayev's observation about wolves and sheep is that the wolves may be nice people, needed to protect the sheep and instrumental in securing their happiness.

Most of the satiric elements of Ostrovsky's plays come together in *Even a Wise Man Stumbles* (*Na vsiakogo mudretsa dovol'no prostoty*, 1868), perhaps his most popular play in the west.[39] What is missing among Ostrovsky's satirical arsenal is the sensitive but victimized young woman, since Mary, the ingénue here, is conventional and superficial. But, to compensate for this loss, the play features a characterized satirist, in fact a professional satirist. Glumov, poor but dishonest, decides to give up his career as the writer of satiric squibs in order to practice his well-honed cynicism and irony in real life by becoming a toady. (His name in Russian suggests that he is a mocker.) Since effective toadyism requires both skillful performance and complete suppression of his contempt for the people he deals with, he records his actual thoughts and feelings in a secret diary. He is aided in his search for position by his unscrupulous mother. His quest engages him with a series of richly satiric characters. His projects fall directly into the areas of politics and romance, and the two are connected by his pompous uncle Mamayev, who functions in the play as a male *samodur*; his personal absurdity contrasts comically with his sense of self-importance. But people whose major pleasure is contemplating themselves are perhaps the easiest to please, and Glumov immediately finds the secret of doing so.

Mamayev introduces Glumov to Krutitzky, an elderly conservative, traditionally played as a bumbling general.[40] Glumov pretends to sympathize with his distaste for the present order and its social mobility, and Krutitzky quickly commissions him to ghostwrite a tract explaining his views in the appropriate formal language. But Mamayev's wife introduces Glumov to the rising young liberal Gorodulin, who similarly commissions tracts and speeches. The ultimate plan is for Glumov to write for Gorodulin an answer to the tract he has already written for Krutitzky. For Glumov the ultimate political principle is getting ahead, but his contradictory efforts to do so are certain to clash in the future. Glumov's game of performance is more important than the end it achieves.

Uncle Mamayev is equally instrumental in Glumov's romantic performances, and these involve conflicts that turn out to be more disastrous than his political contradictions. Mamayev is married to a younger woman whose name (Cleopatra) perfectly indicates her character. To keep any young Antony from appearing, he suggests that Glumov become his wife's friend and companion. But Cleopatra does indeed see Glumov as an Antony, and here, as everywhere else, he is glad to play a part. Their mutual declarations of passion are probably sincere on neither side. Glumov's other romantic performance finds him engaged to Mary, the niece and heir of Turussina, a rich widow who, after an apparently lively youth that included an affair with Krutitzky, has become a model of pretentious piety. She has separated Mary from her previous suitor, a friend of Glumov, on the grounds of his freethinking, but Mary, who is primarily concerned with finding a husband and having a good time, does not seem unduly upset. After Mamayev, Krutitzky, and Gorodulin all recommend Glumov as a possible husband for Mary, he is greeted as a prodigy. Although he succeeds in becoming engaged to Mary, his affairs unravel when the jealous Cleopatra learns of the engagement and discovers the secret diary in which he has recorded his satiric impressions of each of the characters. She is happy to reveal its contents to the others, in a scene directly reminiscent of the reading of Célimène's letters by Acaste and Clitandre. But Glumov has resources that

Célimène did not. If he is not an honest man, he tells them, they are all complicit in his dishonesty. "You all need me, gentlemen. You can't live without me. If it's not me, then it will be someone else like me" (Act 5, p. 91). The others reluctantly agree that he might be restored to favor, since the alternative is their exposure.

What makes *Even a Wise Man Stumbles* such a satisfying satire is not only the way it unites so many satiric modalities – the satirized satirist, the ubiquity of performance, the parody of discourse, the prevalence of pretension, and the interplay of knaves and fools (especially the casting of the fools as would-be knaves) – but the way its plot assembles such an effective range of social attack. This assembly is heightened by the grouping of contrastive pairs. The merchant *samodur* Mamayev pairs with the hypocritically pious widow Turussina; Krutitzky, the blustering defender of autocracy, contrasts to Gorodulin, the slimy middle-class liberal on the rise; the vacuously virginal Mary to the oversexed Cleopatra. Glumov is paired on one hand with Kurchayev, whom he seeks to replace as Mary's lover, and, on the other, with Golutvin, who seeks to replace him as gossip columnist and newspaper satirist. All three exemplify the callow young man hovering on the margins of society and waiting the opportunity to enter it by marriage, position, or influence. The play achieves a satiric solidity closely resembling that of *The Alchemist*, in which the satirical con man parodies and produces the performances of representative gulls who think that they are using the figure by whom they are abused. In both plays the con man enters into a variety of plots which, the audience must be convinced, he cannot successfully pull off simultaneously. In both plays the revelation takes place with surprising consequences, for it provides the con man occasion for a further performance that allows his final triumph. Both plays leave us admiring the skill and audacity of the satiric con man within the play and the qualities of the satirist outside it.

Ostrovsky extends his satiric vocabulary in other plays. In *Easy Money* (*Beshenye dengi*), self-consciously an imitation of *The Taming of the Shrew*, Glumov reappears as a social hanger-on who eventually acts as companion and presumed heir to a rich old woman.[41] Vassilkov is an aggressive provincial entrepreneur who has some money, expects to make more, and may pretend to more than he has. Lydia is the daughter of an aristocratic civil servant who has ruined his estate and gone in exile for official peculations. It is important that she marry wealthily if she is to keep up her spendthrift Moscow life, but, like Marya in *The Poor Bride*, she is surrounded by useless men who, despite their attraction to her, are unable to fill the gap between her income and her expenses. As Telyatev, the most honest and articulate of the false suitors, tells Lydia, all of them live on a combination of charm and debt: "Only recently I understood why your money and my money was easy money. It was because we did not earn it ourselves. Money which you earn by hard work is sensible money. It keeps still" (Act 5, p. 175). Thus instructed, Lydia returns to Vassilkov, but it is clear that she has not changed her ways, and it is not clear that his grinding avarice represents a morally superior position. (His character seems reminiscent of Stolz in Goncharov's *Oblomov*, published twelve years earlier [1859].) The marriage of Lydia and Vassilkov gives us the union of wasteful charm with charmless gain. If Lydia and Vassilkov are performers who are not to be believed, Ostrovsky provides much solider performances in his plays about the the-ater. His actresses, Negina in *Talents and Admirers* (*Talenti i poklonniki*) and Kruchinina in *More Sinned Against than Sinning* (*Bez viny vinovatye*), are stronger than the victimized women of the earlier plays, in part be-cause they stand outside of the money-marriage nexus and in part because their artistic stature correlates with their magnitude of spirit. The satiric paradox of Ostrovsky's theatricality, implied quite clearly by the character of Neschastlivtsev in *The Forest*, is that the professional role of actors as performers gives them a sincerity denied to the *poseurs* around them.

Ostrovsky's vocabulary of satiric performances is directed at a social analysis that began with his treatment of the Russian merchant class that lived "across the river" in Moscow, that continues through such plays as *The Storm*, *The Forest*, *An Ardent Heart* (*Goriachee seròtse*), and *Without a Dowry* that are based on Ostrovsky's ethnography of provincial village life, and that leads to the socially broader plays of his middle and later period, such as *Even a Wise Man Stumbles* and *Easy Money*. Their analysis concen-trates on a lust for power manifested in a personal dominance over people who are dependent on the petty tyrant, either through traditional social hierarchies or through the power of money – family members, servants, employees, and social subordinates. It is also evident in the naked greed that overrides both individuals and affective relationships. The power inherent in traditional social arrangements and the power of money are themselves in conflict, and the satiric treatment of both sources of power renders the plays ambivalent. The position of *samodur*s may be reinforced by appeals to traditional values that they claim to uphold, and this is particularly the pattern with women, whose authority is neither patriarchal nor economic. This pretense to traditional values provides one level of performance, but Ostrovsky is also interested in the functions of performance in situations of class movement or class conflict. Examples of characters who pretend to a social status they do not possess or cannot afford abound in Ostrovsky's plays. Beneath these performances the social world of Ostrovsky's Russia is exposed as crude, crass, or hollow.

The basic pattern of domestic power in Ostrovsky's plays lacks the inevitability that usually characterizes traditional tragedy and comedy. We do not know whether the pattern of power will ever be broken, whether the heroine will be rescued or will rescue herself or will be destroyed. Similar plays with similar patterns have contrasting endings. Larisa in *Without a Dowry* rejects life as a kept mistress but is killed by her feckless fiancé, a death that, in her despair, she welcomes. Negina, in *Talents and Admirers*, rejects her poor but scholarly fiancé to become a kept mistress. The interworkings of Ostrovsky's dramatic pattern become more important than its generic markings. What becomes most strongly marked is the function of the domestic scene as a microcosm for broader social forces whose conflicts or contradictions become the ultimate source of the dramatic tension. By representing the intersection of threatening social forces as the performances that characters undertake, either as the means suggested by their personal aggression or as the social roles forced upon them by society, Ostrovsky replaces the distance between audience and stage with a social realism that underscores the performances of the characters and, through them, the falseness of society itself.

BRECHT

The function of satiric performance to engage sharp social analysis is manifested in perhaps the most important modern craftsman of satiric drama and its most articulate theorist, Bertolt Brecht. One of the difficulties in approaching Brecht as a theorist lies in the persistent evolution of his theoretical statements. This pattern of evolution reflects the function of his theory to articulate practice. Thus a term associated with Brecht is "epic theater," a term and practices which he derived from Piscator and others.[42] Brecht used the term in a short 1927 essay, "The Epic Theatre and its Difficulties," where he states that "the essential point of the epic theatre is perhaps that it appeals less to the feelings than to the spectator's reason. Instead of sharing an experience the spectator comes to grips with things."[43] As a term it signals Brecht's antagonism to the "dramatic" theater of Aristotle and Stanislavsky; for Brecht the function of epic theater lay in its presentation of a story rather than in character. ("Everything hangs on the 'story'; it is the heart of the theatrical performance. For it is what happens *between* people that provides them with all the material they can discuss, criticize, alter.")[44] He later found the term epic "too slight and too vague for the kind of theatre intended," and in "A Short Organum" and later appendices he suggested other terms – "theatre of the scientific age" (which he also found too narrow) and "dialectical theatre."[45]

Although Brecht shifted his terms for what is usually translated into English as the alienation effect (he first used *Entfremdung* but shifted to *Verfremdung*), his sense of the term is precise: "A representation that alienates is one which allows us to recognize its subject, but at the same time makes it unfamiliar."[46] The effect of alienation or distancing is to make the essential representation of the theater thematic. "Oil, inflation, war, social struggles, the family, religion, wheat, the meat market, all became subjects of theatrical representation."[47] Brecht saw the play as distant from the audience, which, rather than empathizing with the characters, subjected them, their roles, and their interactions to analysis or saw them as representing issues that were not circumscribed by the illusory world of the play. Brecht emphasized, therefore, the self-conscious theatricality of action. This emphasis recognized the independent roles of the designer, the composer, and the actors, so that the presentation of the play presents as well a number of distinct comments on it. The function of the actor lies in representing that character rather than pretending to be the character, in presenting not only what the character is but the actor's judgment about the character. Helene Weigel commented on this function in her most famous role: "How, for example, am I as Courage at the end of the play, when my business dealings have cost me the last of my children, to deliver the sentence: 'I have to get back to my business,' if I am *not* personally shattered by the fact that this person I am playing does not possess the capacity to learn."[48]

This emphasis on theatricality stresses the performative character of social roles. Brecht's theory, especially in its early versions, derives from his attack on bourgeois ideas of individuality that, in his view, had been effaced by modern science, by urbanization, by the organization of labor, and by militarism.[49] But Brecht did not see individual identity as an unquestioned good and therefore as a criterion by which the forces destroying it could be satirized. The forces into which the individual is subsumed may indeed be dehumanizing and destructive, as they are in the case of Nazism, but they may be collective, progressive, and positive, as in the case of socialism. In either case, individuals, in Brecht's plays, tend to disappear into their roles. Performance, at the secondary level, becomes transformation. Two plays that particularly manifest the absorption of individuality into social roles are *Mann ist Mann* and *Der Gute Mensch von Sezuan*.

Performance is closely correlated with transformation in *Mann ist Mann*.[50] The play takes place in a fantastic and Kiplingesque India that is the locus of British imperialism.[51] Therefore its context is the imposition of an artificial and external order on the indigenous culture (about which Brecht is as vague as he is about the geography). Imperialism's claim to impose order is of course false, as illustrated in scene 2, when four soldiers rob a pagoda. Soldiers are both perpetrators and victims of the imperial order they represent. The army identifies them less as individuals than as groups, and therefore, since Jeraiah Jip has disappeared as a result of the robbery (he eventually becomes a god in the pagoda), the loss of one of the four presents a problem for the remaining three, a problem they solve by creating a fourth. The raw material for this replacement is Galy Gay, an Irish porter, described by one of the soldiers when they see him as "a man who can't say no" (scene 3). He has gone to buy a fish, is swept up by the soldiers, with the help of the canteen owner Leokadja Begbick, and is transformed into a human fighting machine by a performative process of ritual death and rebirth. It is not quite the case that man equals man, since Gay must be transformed to take on the role of Jip. But although humans are subjectively individual, they are functionally identical. The point is not that individuality does not exist but that it does not matter. Gay's transformation manifests the process of satiric exaggeration by which equation becomes identity. Widow Begbick, who serves both as agent and chorus, delivers an Aristophanic parabasis that makes Brecht's meaning clear:

> Herr Bertolt Brecht behauptet: Mann ist Mann.
> Und das ist etwas, was jeder behaupten kann.
> Aber Herr Bertolt Brecht beweist auch dann
> Dass man mit einem Menschen beliebig viel machen kann. . .
> Herr Bertolt Brecht hofft, Sie werden den Boden, auf dem Sie stehen
> Wie Schnee unter Ihren Füssen vergehen sehen
> Und werden schon merken bei dem Packer Galy Gay
> Dass das Leben auf Erden gefährlich sei.

> [Herr Bertolt Brecht maintains man equals man
> – A view that has been around since time began.
> But then Herr Brecht points out how far one can
> Manoeuvre and manipulate that man. . .
> Herr Brecht hopes you'll feel the ground on which you stand
> Slither between your toes like shifting sand
> So that the case of Galy Gay the porter makes you aware
> Life on this earth is a hazardous affair.   ("Interlude" following Scene 8)

Gay responds to this functionality by internalizing the military values it is his function to serve. In taking on Jip's function, he seems to take on his personality as well, shifting from a passive and conventional character to an aggressive and self-centered one. At the end of the 1954 version, Gay is told that the fortress he has destroyed sheltered seven thousand refugees. "But what is that to me?" he responds. "The one cry and the other cry." Man, after all, is man. Gay is thus distinguishable from Švejk, the character from Hašek's novel, much favored and adapted by Brecht, whose efforts to conform to command mask his own internal resistance and expose the foolishness of the commands. Gay's ritual transformation is accompanied by mythic characters. Charles Fairchild (known as "Bloody Five") is as bloodthirsty a sergeant as Kipling might have created, but in private life he is a highly sensual man. He reacts to his transformation into civilian status by castrating himself, an act of transformation and dehumanization that parallels the changes of Gay, who ultimately replaces him as the army's best soldier.[52] Leokadia Begbick, the proprietress of the canteen that moves to accompany the troops, reappears as the same character in *Aufstieg und Fall der Stadt Mahagonny* and anticipates Mother Courage. She is the mother figure of capitalism. (She has three daughters in the 1926 version.) Brecht commented, in his notes to the 1937 edition, on the parallel changes: "The four transformations were clearly distinguished from one another (transformation of Jeraiah Jip into a God; transformation of Sergeant Fairchild into a civilian; transformation of the canteen into an empty space; transformation of the porter Galy Gay into a soldier)."[53]

The performance of Gay as Jip can be read in a variety of ways. (1.) Gay becomes Jip – perhaps even a more ideal soldier than Jip – a successful participant in the collective process by virtue of his imposed collective identity. The other soldiers function as Communist comrades who transform a meaningless man into one with meaning (albeit functional).[54] (2.) Rather than being transformed to a hero, Gay is exploited and dehumanized; his transformation is the process of Nazification that threatened Germany at the time of the play's famous 1931 production, in which Brecht directed Peter Lorre as Galy Gay.

The ambiguous transformations of the play are paralleled in other works by Brecht. One of his first poems was "Legende vom toten Soldaten" (Legend of the Dead Soldier), in which a soldier who dies in 1918 but before the war is over is dug up, is dressed up and marched through the streets with colors painted on his shrouds and a priest swinging incense to cover the smell. Brecht's school-play *Der Jasager*, first performed in 1930, the year before Brecht's revision of *Mann ist Mann* for the 1931 production, concerned a schoolboy who, conforming to an ancient tradition, consented to his own death rather than impeding his classmates' trip across the mountains to get medicine for his mother. The play was welcomed on the right because its theme of individual sacrifice for the good of the whole suited Nazis as well as it did Communists. But when the play was performed in schools, students questioned the boy's acceptance of tradition, and Brecht rewrote the play as *Der Neinsager*. Instead of accepting tradition, the boy insists on the importance of questioning it. The uncertainties of Brecht's plays have at least two functions: as in the case of the boy who says no, they raise questions and doubts which pose threats to those in authority (a pattern made clear in *Leben des Galilei*), and they become a means by which Brecht attaches a quasi-allegorical significance to the narrative of his plays. Underlying the ambiguity of *Mann ist Mann* is its recognition of the power of the collective over the individual. The direction of that power is a matter of politics, rather than of a morality based on the illusion of individual agency.

Another character who, like Galy Gay, cannot say no, is Shen Teh in *Der gute Mensch von Sezuan*.[55] She begins the play as a prostitute, but that is only the first of several performative levels that she must play. In the Prologue, Wang the water carrier encounters three gods. They must find a good person if the world is to continue as it is. At the outset we are caught in a satiric paradox. The world as it is should not continue, and, we suspect, the gods may be at fault; thus the discovery of the good person who will save the world (as it is) seems a means by which they can shirk their responsibility. As is often the case with satire, the real alternative – neither to save nor destroy the world but to change it – is not articulated. Criteria for the good person are modest – to provide free lodging for the gods. Shen Teh, whom Wang describes as a person who cannot say no, fulfills that role; being a good person seems an extension of her role as prostitute. The gods leave her a substantial reward, with which she purchases a tobacco shop, thereby substituting one form of performance (capitalism) for another (prostitution). The question for the play becomes whether a good person can also be a capitalist. The short answer is no, for good people act on behalf of others, bad in the interests of themselves. Shen Teh's charities leave her open to exploitation by those who impose on her generosity. Her solution is to invent an alternative self whose capacity to say no can protect her from the ruinous consequences of being a good person.

As with the transformation of Galy Gay, the emergence of Shui Ta raises a significant ambiguity. Is Shui Ta merely an artificial construct created by Shen Teh because she seems to have no alternative? (The character is actually invented by an elderly couple to fend off a carpenter who wants payment for the shelves he has built for Shen Teh's shop. When Shen Teh animates the role of her invented cousin, Shui Ta's first action is to evict the family that invented him.) Or are Shui Ta and Shen Teh, played by the same actress, alternative forces in the same person? John Willett comments on the danger of overfeminizing and oversentimentalizing the role of Shen Teh in the theater, but he notes that productions have not used a male actor to play both parts, a solution that would heighten the androgyny of the role and seems appropriate to the play's descent from No-plays, where the roles of women were traditionally performed by men.[56] If Shen Teh acts the role of Shui Ta, much as the actress performs Shen Teh, the performance may imply that human beings are essentially good and corrupted by the roles in which they are cast by others and by necessity, or that the evils of society merely perpetuate the evils of humans themselves, or that human beings have no natural character that is unperformed outside of a defining social context.

As the play goes on, the split characters become more exaggerated. Shui Ta, with the help of the barber Shu Fu, who wants and expects to marry Shen Teh, converts the tobacco shop into a factory that helps but exploits the poor of the district. Shen Teh falls in love with Yang Sun, a would-be pilot, and becomes pregnant. Sun is another case of the Brechtian divided character. He is the lover for whom Shen Teh would sacrifice herself; Shui Ta hires him as the foreman who drives his workers. Shui Ta knows him to be crass and self-centered; Shen Teh loves him nonetheless. The inconsistent gender roles of the play exploit what Brecht sees as basic contradictions of the human condition, ultimately represented by Shen Teh's pregnancy. (Her maternal instinct is to protect her child at whatever moral cost, and her two roles converge through the agency of the unborn child.) Despite the uncertain implications of the central character's ambiguous gender, the paradox with which the play ends is clear enough. Even if people can be naturally good, they naturally live within human societies that do not allow goodness to survive in the struggles for self-assertion, survival, and capitalist domination. Therefore, the role of the good person, the *gute Mensch*, can only be a role performed for the benefit of the gods.[57] At the end, the gods refuse to admit that the goodness of Shen Teh is compromised by the existence of Shui Ta. "Only be good," they tell her, "and all will be well" (scene 10). In the Epilogue, an actor apologizes for the lack of a satisfactory ending, which now must be the responsibility of the audience.

Many of Brecht's major plays fall naturally into definable categories – plays with exotic settings (the imaginary India of *Mann ist Mann*, the imaginary America of *Mahagonny*, *Im Dickert der Städte*, and *Der heilige Johanna der Schlachthöfe*), plays with strong historical settings (*Mutter Courage*, *Leben des Galilei*), operas, *Lehrstücke*, parables for the theater (*Der gute*

Mensch, Kaukasische Krederkreis) – all of which emphasize narrative, distance from the immediate experience of the audience, and implicit (often explicit) political analysis. The force of Brecht's satiric theater rests to a large degree on the self-consciousness of its presentation. Brecht's satiric performances represent the social determination of performance at the secondary level (social roles) by emphasizing performance on the tertiary level (self-conscious dramatization). In doing so, he eliminates the mediating functions of art, the reconciliation of contradictions by defeat (tragedy) or by celebration (comedy), in order to transfer that function from the play to the audience. Having seen the play, the audience must now change life.

In looking at satiric performances in the theater, I have distinguished between primary (linguistic), secondary (social), and tertiary (theatrical) levels of performance. At the primary level, speech is often representational and therefore the gap between the signifier and the signified may be seen as performative. The difference between what is said and what is meant is a primary source of dramatic tension, of satiric dislocation, and of irony; this is more evidently the case when the observing audience is aware that the speaker is deceiving the listener. But speech also becomes a significant element of satiric performance when, as is most clear with the gulls of *The Alchemist* and the provincials of Ostrovsky, satire parodies discourse. The secondary level of satiric performance, representation of the otherness of social roles, defines both the social nature of individual characters and the significance of their interaction. The conflict among characters becomes a conflict of social forces, so that the domestic scene represents the political, and such issues as marriage or inheritance become the nexus of conflicting social forces. The performance of social roles foregrounds the drama of contradiction, and the play therefore becomes a narrative (an "epic," in Brecht's terms) that analyzes social contradictions and their consequences. Because the staginess of plays is virtually inescapable, and because satire thrives on its self-conscious nature, the representation of performances undertaken by characters, the tertiary or theatrical level of performance, is of central importance. The acting of acting itself becomes judgmental, but the performances thus acted are not fully resolved, and the audience is left with the problem of interpreting, and thus in some sense resolving, that irresolution. The interpretation of unresolved satiric performances in a real sense repeats the Aristophanic pattern of lodging its real subjects beyond the stage itself. The real subject of satiric performance is its audience, and the act of interpretation thus becomes political.

CHAPTER 5

Horatian performances

POETIC PERFORMANCES

In mimetic drama, the performance of social roles is particularly important to satire of the social contexts represented in the play. The implicitly negative nature of social roles in satire is clarified by the self-conscious nature of the performances through which they are presented. In satiric poetry, self-consciousness intensifies language. Language, of course, may be intensified by being metrical and "poetic" (that is, charged with conventions, perceived as poetic, often by way of parody). But it may also be self-consciously performative in two other ways that help define its satiric character. (1.) The language does not mean exactly what it says, and this obvious otherness of meaning signals that it is a performance enabling the language to become ironic, not merely a statement but a vehicle for commentary. (2.) The fact that the satire is being written at all calls attention to the possibility of a problem, external to the text, that the satire seeks to redress.

A further element of satiric drama is the distance it creates between the author and the message conveyed by performance. By placing the message in the mouth of a character, the satirist shields himself both from its unpleasantness and from the unpleasant fact that he is writing it, thereby retaining the force of the message without taking responsibility for it. Molière plays the role of Alceste – perhaps knowing that Alceste plays the role of Molière. When satire moves off the stage, the dramatic mask is retained, and the devices by which the satirist distances himself from his message create, for critics, the problem of identifying who is writing – the persistent problem of the persona.[1] The issue of the persona arises with particular intensity for satire because satirists may want to distinguish themselves from the unpleasant messages they deliver. Reading the speaker of the first two books of Juvenal's *Satires* as a persona, for example, distinguishes the historical Juvenal from the ranting poet.[2] Robert Elliott argues that by reading the speaker of Pope's "Epistle to Dr. Arbuthnot" as a persona rather than as Pope, despite the personal and historical references that seem to identify him, we prevent Pope from lying in his claim to have avoided literary conflict.[3] But, and the example of Pope seems particularly appropriate here, one characteristic of satire is its historical rootedness. If we exculpate the poet by inventing a mediating figure or mask, what prevents us from performing a similar exercise on the satiric target? Although satiric attack is often entertaining, there seems little point in a literary construct (the persona) attacking a fictional victim he has constructed.

The battle between critics who read texts as the statements, however ironic, of historical authors and those who read them as the statements of personae is waged in studies of both ancient and modern literature. Roland Barthes claims that the author is replaced by a "scriptor" who "is born simultaneously with the text, is in no way equipped with a being preceding or exceeding the writing, is not the subject with the book as predicate."[4] Michel Foucault similarly asserts that "the mark of the writer is reduced to nothing more than the singularity of his absence."[5] In two essays published in the mid-sixties, William S. Anderson applied to Juvenal the satiric persona described by Alvin Kernan in *The Cankered Muse* (1959).[6] Gilbert Highet, the biographer of Juvenal against whose literal readings Anderson's argument was directed, responded that the inconsistencies Anderson found in the persona of Juvenal's first satire might as easily be inconsistencies in Juvenal himself. He argued that "the theory distinguishing author from 'satirist' has not yet, as far as I know, been applied to the Sermones of Horace," and that a theory that was valid for Juvenal should be valid for his predecessors as well.[7] But in the thirty years since Highet's article appeared, persona theory has been abundantly applied to Horace. Kirk Freudenburg, for example, maintains that Horace's satires derive from a tradition of rhetorical role-playing and "that the diatribe satires are completely detached from the true spirit and intent of the ethical treatises that they imitate. They are, in fact, a burlesque of Greek popular philosophy."[8] Hence their speaker is not the able Horace but a bumbling persona. David Armstrong, on the other hand, claims that *Satires* 1.3, rather than a parody of philosophical ineptness, is "one of the most beautiful poems of friendship ever written."[9] Ellen Oliensis avoids a sharp distinction between Horace and his persona, but sees him as presenting a face that shifts from poem to poem and even line to line. She sees the Horace of Book II as mounting "a brilliantly entertaining but nonetheless devastating satirical attack on the poet of *Satires* 1."[10] Although I am not convinced by Freudenburg's characterization of the ineptness of Horace's diatribist or by Oliensis's discovery that Book II of the *Satires* attacks

Book 1, their general approach seems a useful response to the problem of identifying satiric speakers. What is needed is a theoretical explanation that will allow authors to take responsibility for their moral analysis irresponsibly, that will distance them from the offensive antagonisms of satiric attack but will preserve the concerns from which it flows.[11] Satiric poems are performances undertaken by historical authors. Their force and nature are evident in characteristic and influential performances of Horace and in analogous Horatian performances in the long eighteenth century. Such performances need to be distinguished from Horatian imitation, a topic that has been well canvassed by other critics.[12] Indeed, later Horatian performers may have been unaware that they were adopting a role that Horace himself had played. Five kinds of performance by Horace are of particular interest both in themselves and in their eighteenth-century repetitions: (1.) the ambiguous mediating speaker, (2.) the Saturnalian reversal, (3.) the shifting satiric scene, (4.) the mock-heroic parody, and (5.) the shifting satiric voice. These five stances include authorial self-presentation, dramatic representation, two characteristic problems of the anarchic satiric landscape (its subordination of hierarchy and its lack of self-control), and its parody of unfortunately outdated values as represented in literature.

The kinds of satiric performances modeled by Horace become, in effect, sub-genres of satire, located within satire itself but distinct from the imitated or parodied genres that satire typically uses. Once an author such as Horace has performed, that performance separates from the author, becoming reproducible not only in the sense that the poem may be recited, modified, elaborated upon, translated, or imitated by another but also in the sense that the structures, gestures, tones, procedures, and rules that mark the performance are available to others. Because performances are modeled rather than driven by rules, performance is a more open critical instrument than either genre or persona, not limited either by formal constraints or by the psychology of character. Performance functions as an intermediate term, touching upon genre and author, performances and performers. The repeatability allowed by the separation of performance from performer and the relative independence of performance from either literary form or philosophical meaning imply that performance is functional, and that the critical issue is identifying what performances do.

THE MEDIATING SPEAKER

A mediating speaker does not pose, as do the shifting satiric speakers I will later discuss, as the actual author but is not clearly an ironic speaker, such as Damasippus of *Satires* 2.3 or Burns's holy Willie. The mediating speaker may function as a transparent but not uncolored screen, who passes on the satiric information or good advice more-or-less straightforwardly. This is the situation in several of the even-numbered satires of Horace's second book (in contrast to the ironic dialogues in the odd-numbered satires). Ofellus, the virtuous peasant of *Satires* 2.2, and Cervius, who tells about the mice in *Satires* 2.6, are presented straightforwardly, regardless of whether we want to read them that way. Catius, the culinary student of *Satires* 2.4, is a mindless disciple, and the force of the satire is heightened by his failure to recognize the triviality of what he describes, indeed by his insistence on seeing the trivial as glorious. Fundanius, the comic poet and narrator of *Satire* 2.8, recognizes that the dinner given by Nasidienus Rufus is comic, but he does not recognize that the behavior of Maecenas and the other guests may also be subject to satiric scrutiny. Mediating speakers may be figures of some confusion or doubt, but primarily they reproduce the uncertainties of their subject, embodying the problems and confusions explored in the poem rather than merely commenting on them.

Such, I think, is the situation of Artemiza in Rochester's *Artemiza to Chloe*. Rochester's poem presents the misogynism of Juvenal's Sixth Satire from the point of view of a woman functioning as a Horatian mediating speaker.[13] The tension between its horrific material and its suavely ironic speaker encapsulates the problems explored by the poem and seems (perhaps misleadingly) to throw the weight of interpretation onto an understanding of Artemiza herself. Artemiza has been variously interpreted. At the negative end of the spectrum, Howard Weinbrot, perhaps blaming the messenger, sees her as corrupted by the material she narrates and thus as shifting from a reluctant poetess to an eager conniver of gossip and scandal, "an agent for the propagation of infamy."[14] At the positive extreme, Carole Fabricant identifies Artemiza with Rochester himself, David Farley-Hills finds the poem triumphant "because she has made a coherent account of the chaos she describes," and Marianne Thormählen argues that she is an effective ironist both in her observation of the town and her reflections on herself.[15]

Artemiza begins the poem by distancing herself from the masculine medium of verse and, still more sharply, from the feminine practice of love. She speaks as one who has suffered a romantic disappointment, but there is no direct evidence that she has, for her lament is not for the loss of a lover but for the loss of love itself, "That Cordiall dropp Heav'n in our cup has throwne, / To make the nauseous draught of Life goe down" (44–45).[16] Artemiza argues that the trickery and hypocrisy that have corrupted love have been chiefly practiced by women, and, to exemplify the point, she produces the character and monologue of the Fine Lady, who carries on for most of the rest of the poem. The Fine Lady argues that love depends on the arts and illusions that women can practice on men, and that fools therefore are preferable to men of wit, whose insistence on seeing things as they are makes them restless and dissatisfied. She, in turn, exemplifies her argument by telling the story of Corinna, a woman of the town who was betrayed and defamed by a man of wit and who, after much suffering, was able to ensnare a country fool, whom she eventually poisoned. Corinna, of course, exemplifies Artemiza's point as strongly as she does that of the Fine Lady, and such double exemplification is a repeated characteristic of the poem. At the end, Artemiza is confused by the Fine Lady and what she has said: "some graynes of Sense / Still mixt with Volleys of Impertinence" (256–57).

Women are betrayers of love because, like the Fine Lady, they sacrifice mutuality for dominance in the game of sexual politics; men are unworthy objects of love because they are either fools or dangerous men of wit whose knowledge destroys love. (The Fine Lady's ideal man is the monkey she caresses in the middle of her monologue.) Artemiza is, like the reader, more radically confused by the paradoxical nature of her material, and at the heart of those paradoxes is the real predicament: life is made bearable only by true love, "the most gen'rous Passion of the mynde" (40), but such love is impossible. The generosity of love is dangerous because it exposes the self to betrayal and loss; it is replaced by the vicious game of self-interest and sexual dominance. If the ideal man is a monkey, the ultimate woman is a murderer. Artemiza is confused because she is caught in a trap, the same trap, in fact, that imprisons the man of wit – indeed, the witty Rochester who impersonates her: she like Eve and he like Adam have tasted the tree of the knowledge of good and evil. Immobilized by perception, she can only record and report further stories, "As true, as Heaven, more infamous, then Hell" (263). Artemiza may have written an ordered poem about confusion, but she has not brought order to chaos, for confusion remains confusion still. She is a stunning speaker not because she is a model character (though she is a model of perception and honesty) but because she functions both ironically and transparently as a mediating speaker who transmits, without false resolution, the paradoxes and contradictions of the human condition. The mediating speaker embodies the problems and confusions explored in the poem rather than merely commenting on them.

The performance of the mediating speaker opens the performance of the words. The speaker's text no longer operates primarily as a message from a real utterer to an audience but becomes an object of scrutiny itself. The purpose of the author's performance is less to convey a message than to convey another performer. The mediating speaker therefore may present material about which the author is uncertain or wishes to make the reader uncertain. That uncertainty is achieved by a disparity of value between the performer and the text performed. A likeable performer may utter a text in which the subject is disgusting. An unlikeable performer may articulate values with which we agree. An ironic disparity may exist between the performing speaker and the message of the text, as when the war-maimed soldier of Burns's "Love and Liberty" celebrates military values. The ironic nature of the text may itself be uncertain, since we do not know whether it was or was not intended either by the performer or the author. Hence readers may see Artemiza as villainess or heroine. But because she functions as a translucent lens, the evils of the world she describes are clear in either case. The mediating speaker detaches the author from the text, even if, as in the case of Horace's speakers, we are given insufficient information to see that speaker as an independent character. The uncertainties of perception raised by a mediating speaker whose character is not a useful guide to the reading or even identification of irony render sharply the problems of the subject itself.

THE SATURNALIAN SPEAKER

Two of Horace's satires (2.3 and 2.7) take place on the Saturnalia and involve dialogues in which roles are reversed. Saturnalia represents the temporary return of the Golden Age of Saturn, a period of feast and carnival, carefully defined as a holiday season. It is marked not only by general festivity but by the temporary disappearance of the social hierarchy, by the reversal of established roles and relationships, and by the tolerance or even celebration of transgression. Slaves could confront their masters; the powerless could replace the powerful.[17] Hence Horace's slave Davus, in *Satires* 2.7, uses the occasion to berate Horace for being a slave himself. But the governing characteristic of Saturnalia is its strict temporal limitation, its perceptible difference from ordinary life. In *Satires* 2.3 Horace, during the Saturnalia, has retired to the country, where he encounters an unwelcome guest in Damasippus, a failed businessman and Stoic convert, who begins by berating him for his literary sloth. Horace, the satirist, has become the satiric victim, and Damasippus, an exemplary satiric victim, has become the satirist. But the reversals extend even further. Damasippus, whose garrulity is one of his characteristics available for satire, goes on at considerable

length. Most of his discourse, which makes up most of Horace's longest
satire, consists of a speech by Stertinius, his Stoic teacher, a speech that
Damasippus, the good disciple, has learned by heart. Horace's antipathy to
Stoics is clear enough from *Satires* 1.3, but the speech of Stertinius resembles
Horace's own diatribes. It is constructed in similar ways, moving between
example and precept, targeting the same human failings, and making comparable points. Thus Horace seems victimized by both direct attack and
by self-parody. But one difference defines the invalidity of the diatribe of
Stertinius and affirms the validity of Horace's satire. Stertinius argues that
all but the wise Stoic are mad, precisely the kind of satiric universal that
Horace has studiously avoided. Moreover, Damasippus has memorized the
speech not as an appropriate satiric guide to moral behavior but as a means
of personal retaliation:

> haec mihi Stertinius, sapientum octavus, amico
> arma dedit, posthac ne compellarer inultus.
> dixerit insanum qui me totidem audiet atque
> respicere ignoto discet pendentia tergo.   (lines 296–99)

[Those are the weapons Stertinius, the eighth wise man, supplied
for his friend, so that if abused I'll always be able to retaliate.
The man who calls me a lunatic will get just as many brickbats
in return – which will help to remind him that he lives in a glass house.][18]

Horace claims that his own satire is driven by moral outrage rather than
personal revenge. Damasippus is neatly caught in the Stoic paradox of his
own recitation: his nasty and self-serving assertion that others will be told
of faults they cannot see is, of course, a fault that he cannot see. If Horace
remains abused but still standing at the end of the poem, it is because his
proximate and remote antagonists have destroyed themselves and because,
within the principle that all men are mad, Damasippus is madder than he.
But Horace is not only standing, he has composed the poem he retired to
write at the outset.

The nature and limits of the Saturnalian metaphor are explored in the
most Saturnalian of British poems – Robert Burns's "Love and Liberty. A
Cantata."[19] (Burns is curiously neglected in the history of satire, whether
because his dialect poses problems for busy modern readers, or because
he seems most familiar in the apparently antithetical genre of the lyric,
or because he wrote relatively few satires. But he connects self-consciously
with both the Scottish satiric tradition represented by Robert Fergusson
and the English tradition represented by Pope; his satires attack Scottish

religion in particular and British politics in general.) Apparently based on Burns's actual observation of beggars at Poosy Nancie's low-class tavern in Mauchline, where it is set, "Love and Liberty" is decidedly literary and relentlessly Saturnalian. In mock-heroic imitation of a cantata, it consists of beggar songs interspersed with connecting "recitativo" passages in contrasting rhythm. But they contrast as well in language: the songs by beggars are in a relatively accessible dialect (the final one in English), the poet's recitativos in Scots. The songs and their links form a plot. From among the gathering of beggars, a former soldier rises to celebrate his military exploits, even though they have literally cost him an arm and a leg. He is appropriately followed by his girlfriend, who sings of her life as a follower of soldiers. The next woman announces herself as the "widow" of a highwayman hanged for his gallant but otherwise unsuccessful life of crime. A tiny fiddler tries to comfort her, but he turns out to be less attractive than a brawny tinker who succeeds where the fiddler failed. To resolve matters happily, the bard of the beggars, who is accompanied by several women, lends one of them to the fiddler for the evening. It is the bard, the hero of the piece, who articulates its final moral:

> A fig for those by law protected!
> *Liberty*'s a glorious feast!
> Courts for cowards were erected,
> Churches built to please the priest.
> (lines 306–09)

The Saturnalian occasion of the poem could hardly be more pronounced. It takes place, as did the Saturnalia, in late fall or early winter ("When lyart leaves bestrew the yird . . . When hailstanes drive wi' bitter skyte" [1,4]). It is enclosed in a tavern; the characters are all drunk. Although they are ragged enough already, they conclude by pawning whatever clothes they have left "to quench their lowan drouth" (265). Each performs to the applause of the others, but each performance reveals the sorrows and desperations of their situations. The reader is invited into a world where convention no longer reigns, where spontaneous lust, affection, violence, thirst, and generosity replace the niceties of social behavior. The running theme, beginning with the soldier, ending with the bard, and propelled by the energy of the recitativos, is that the human spirit is capable of finding joy in the most dire of circumstances. But that spirit is the product of alcohol and delusion. "Liberty" is the glorious feast – the Saturnalia – for which we long, but its context is the reality that renders liberty self-destructive.[20]

In a correction to Bakhtin's view of the saturnalian and carnival, Michael André Bernstein argues that the inverted, liberating, and spontaneous values of the Saturnalia were not only limited in time but darker in character than often supposed.[21] Saturn was not, after all, a faultless or happy god, and it may not have been a bad thing that Jupiter deposed him. The world turned upside down turns out to be the same world as when upright. When Davus the slave takes on the role of satirist, he shows that he is still a slave; when Damasippus the fool takes on the role of wise man, he manifests his folly. Saturnalian performance explores the limits of performance itself: when our roles are changed, we are still stuck with who we are. The upside-down world of the Saturnalia leaves us with the human predicament. The Saturnalian satires of Horace and Burns are narrated by speakers who represent the real author (Horace in his cottage, Burns at Poosie Nancie's) but who present, within the satire, alternative speakers (Damasippus and the beggars) whose assumption of a dominant role reveals their fallibility. Saturnalian satire, like carnival itself, is a performance, and its performance reveals who we are, both as we become the victims of the internal speakers and as they become the victims of the satirist.

THE SHIFTING SCENE

Uncertainty within satires may be represented by a shifting satiric scene. The speaker remains the same, but that sameness emphasizes the changes that have occurred in the location that the speaker witnesses. Such changes may be geographical, as they are in Horace's *Satires* 1.5, or they may be temporal, as in the case of Andrew Marvell's *Last Instructions to a Painter*. In either case, the hapless satirist seems out of control, for the flow of events and the organization of the poem are dictated by the progress of a journey or by historical causes on which he can only comment. The shifting satiric scene thus places the satirist, and perhaps the reader as well, in a situation of considerable discomfort. The reason for remaining in that situation – for taking the trip or recording the events, for writing the satire or reading it – must have considerable urgency, and that urgency must be felt as a force from the world that is satirized.

Towards the end of *Satires* 1.5, Horace describes a wet dream.

> hic ego mendacem stultissimus usque puellam
> ad mediam noctem exspecto: somnus tamen aufert
> intentum Veneri; tum immundo somnia visu
> nocturnam vestem maculant ventremque supinam.
>
> (lines 82–85)

[Here, like an utter fool, I stayed awake till midnight
waiting for a girl who broke her promise. Sleep in the end
overtook me, still keyed up for sex. Then scenes from a dirty
dream spattered my nightshirt and stomach as I lay on my back.]

This embarrassing detail not only reveals Horace's messy humanity and his willingness to make himself the fool of his own satire (even if by borrowing from Lucilius) but also exemplifies his situation as the woebegone but good-humored traveler.[22] From the outset he has been plagued by bad eyes, lazy boatmen, noisy frogs at night, biting mosquitos, bad food, worse water, a stove catching fire, a smoky villa, and gods who do not perform miracles. But the lines in which he records his wet dream are elegant, with their intricately woven consonant sounds. Their style sets off their content, and the contrast that is true of this passage is true of the poem as a whole.

At the outset, we have no clue as to where Horace is going or why. His purpose becomes apparent when, in lines 27–28, we learn that he and his companion will be joined by Maecenas and Cocceius, who are serving as envoys for Octavian, and we find that they are traveling with Fonteius Capito, a friend of Antony. The primary (non-poetic) members of the party are underway to conduct negotiations among the triumvirs. The year is 37 BC, and their destination is Tarentum, although the poem ends at Brundisium (Brindisi). Soon after (line 40), Virgil joins them, with his friends Plotius and Varius. The poem thus becomes the record of a journey of friends, and the effect of friendship in smoothing disastrous incidents parallels the effect of Horace's language in turning humble events into art. But *Satires* 1.5 is literary in other ways than the companionship of Virgil and Horace. A similar journey had been recorded in a long poem (*Iter Siculum*) by Lucilius, which survives only in fragments. Horace had, in *Satires* 1.4, complained about the verbosity of Lucilius, and although *Satires* 1.5 is not a direct parody of Lucilius, it practices a pyrotechnical conciseness in contrast to his garrulity. The poem thus seems to have at least three levels of contrast. The hardships of the journey contrast to the warmth and charm of the interactions among friends; the concise artfulness of Horace's poetic language contrasts to the homely nature of the events he records; the self-conscious literary imitation contrasts to the personal material of the poem.

It is not surprising that critics have not agreed about what this tour de force finally signifies. For Niall Rudd, it is an artful instance of boisterous humor.[23] Emily Gowers similarly finds it entertaining but "a poem that stops short of its full potential and turns out to have been a shaggy dog story."[24] P. M. W. Tennant argues that the poem is designed to enhance Horace's standing with Maecenas.[25] The poem has elements of all of these readings: it is broadly entertaining, but it has, as Gowers points out, an element of frustration; it is modeled on Lucilius; and it seems designed to please Maecenas. From the time Maecenas and his cohort join the party, the poem becomes urgent, as the trip's political purpose becomes apparent. The urgency seems expressed by the conciseness of the poem: although the journey itself is leisurely, the poem moves with stunning speed. The three contrasts that I have seen as organizing the poem – the hardships of the journey contrasting to the friendship of the travelers, the artful language to the crude material, and literary imitation to personal experience – point to the larger contrast between significant events and the ordinary people who undertake them. Accomplishments such as a successful treaty are all the more to be valued because they emerge from a world where so much goes comically wrong, as it does on Horace's travels. Failure to appreciate the universality of imperfection results in the pretenses Horace satirizes throughout the poem. There is a further level that, depending on one's attitude towards the obvious, seems either deeper or more superficial: Horace's journey is, in effect, the journey of life, and against its hardships – irritating or laughable – Horace places companionship, a sense of purpose, however hidden, and the grace of art.

If Horace's poem is a modest celebration of temporary success, Marvell's *The Last Instructions to a Painter* loudly mourns a significant military failure. Horatian conciseness seems to give way to elaborate verbosity. Like *Satires* 1.5, *The Last Instructions to a Painter* (1667) is an imitation of an earlier poem, in this case Edmund Waller's *Instructions to a Painter* (1666), But the parody had been more direct in the earlier *Second Advice to a Painter* (1666), which covered the same material as Waller's panegyric.[26] *The Last Instructions* begins by alluding to *The Second and Third Advices*, and its parody is less important than the painterly characteristics needed to complete the portrait of "Lady State," the task of the present sitting.[27] Critics disagree over whether the poem that follows is random and disorganized or consciously shaped.[28] Horace moves through space, Marvell through time; the poem concerns the political affairs between September 1666 and August 1667, at the center of which lies the Dutch naval raid up the Thames that destroyed much of the English fleet moored at Chatham. It considers the responsibilities for this military disaster and its consequences, but it has, like Horace's, a hidden agenda that becomes evident only after one has first perceived its apparently random surface.

The composition of the portrait of State begins with three characters – Henry Jermyn, Earl of St. Albans; Anne Hyde, Duchess of York; and Barbara Villiers, Countess of Castlemaine. They are presented in terms of sexual perversions and imply the betrayal of the state by self-directed passions. They introduce the central metaphor that equates the physical body with the body politic, sexual perversion with political disorder.[29] The poem turns to a Parliamentary debate on the Court proposal for a monstrous excise tax, and the description of Court and country leaders resembles the epic naming of heroes and the naming of places in *Satires* 1.5; the brief descriptions practice a Horatian conciseness. Marvell apparently combines several Parliamentary debates into a single dramatic session whose plot involves the Court's attempts to sneak the general excise through a poorly attended House in the early morning. But the excise is successfully opposed by a small but growing number of country members, and a combination of taxes is substituted.

With Parliament now prorogued, the courtiers in general and Clarendon in particular lull themselves into a dream of peace with the Dutch by disregarding evidence of preparations for a naval invasion. Despite England's last-minute desperation measures (the provision of an army to fight a navy), the Dutch admiral de Ruyter sails up the Thames in a striking (and much-discussed) passage of sexual pastoral. The Dutch break the chain that protected the English fleet at Chatham, capture the ironically named *Royal Charles* (the ship that brought back the King in 1660), and burn several other ships. This destruction is surrounded by a series of hopeless actions – Sir Edward Spragge deserts the fort of Sheerness as undefendable; Monck watches helplessly from shore as the Dutch destroy the fleet; Sir Thomas Daniel flees his ship, in contrast to Archibald Douglas, a Scot who is burned to death in the poem's most celebrated passage. Douglas (though he was in fact married) is presented as a virginal figure, unlike the sexual misadventurers of the rest of the poem, and his death is the result of his loyalty, in contrast to the treachery and cowardice of the others.

> Like a glad Lover, the fierce Flames he meets,
> And tries his first embraces in their Sheets.
> His shape exact, which the bright flames infold,
> Like the Sun's Statue stands of burnish'd Gold.
> (lines 677–80)[30]

The Dutch threaten London, but the Thames is blocked by sunken merchant ships, and the Dutch retreat to its mouth.

The government unconvincingly tries to lodge blame on Peter Pett, a Commissioner of the Navy, largely, Marvell implies, because his name fits so many rhyme words. A peace is quickly cobbled up, and parliament prorogued. The poem concludes with King Charles receiving two visions. The first is a "sudden Shape with Virgins face" (line 892), who is bound, gagged, and blindfolded. He at first thinks of her visit as sexual, but as he reaches for her, she disappears, and he concludes that she must be England or Peace. The second vision is of his ancestors Henri IV of France and Charles I of England – the first assassinated, the second executed. What they reveal to him is unclear, but their presence indicates that his survival depends on his conduct in office. At any rate, Charles suddenly (and properly) decides to remove Clarendon, for his father tells him "that who does cut his Purse will cut his Throat" (line 938). The envoy "To the King" is complex. Satire is compared to a telescope that reveals the spots on the sun, and the sun–king analogy is stressed throughout, but the sun (according to Marvell's astronomy) can "hurl off" the spots, just as the King can cast off his blemishing courtiers. The fiction that the King can do no wrong but his courtiers can wrong him is manipulated so that the failure of the courtiers seems a metaphor for the failures of the King.

The structure of the poem moves between portraits and scenes, between the narrative of present history and quasi-heroic set-pieces, between time and stillness. (Horace also suggests motion by depicting isolated moments.) These shifts emphasize the contrasts between sexuality and purity, treachery and loyalty, past and present, and painting and poetry. The paradox of representing linear time (the poet's mode) within the painter's static image is the structural paradox of the poem itself. The poem is propelled by the mistakes and disasters of time that force politicians into fruitless reaction. But the poet too is required to react, to shift his voice and mode to account for the onslaught of events. His situation differs from that of the shifting speaker of Horace's diatribes, whose changes involve deliberate manipulation of perspective. Here the rush of history threatens the speaker's control, which repeatedly reestablishes itself through its metaphorical (painterly) understanding of the significance of events. But the poet struggles to catch up, to find the voice responsive to the disorder he describes. The contrast between the impossibility of painting the sequence of time and the poet's instructions on painting it mirrors the contrast between historical disorder and poetic order.

Marvell is not merely the satirist of the poem, and therefore his accomplishment in wresting poetic order out of political chaos is not fully satisfactory. He is himself a Member of Parliament and a participant in the portrait of Lady State that his poem creates. As John M. Wallace argues, Marvell hopes that the constitutional issues raised by the poem are resolved by a cooperative relationship between the King and Parliament, so that in actuality as well as in theory "the Country is the King" (line 974).[31] The secret alternative that lurks behind *The Last Instructions* is another civil war, just as the threat of war between Antony and Octavian is the hidden threat of *Satires* 1.5. But the path to constitutional cooperation rests with the King, who can achieve it by choosing advisors whose independence of wealth and judgment reflects that of the country faction. Hence both satirist and painter must leave the creation of reality to Charles:

> *Painter* adieu, how will our Arts agree;
> Poetick Picture, Painted Poetry.
> But this great work is for our *Monarch* fit,
> And henceforth *Charles* only to *Charles* shall sit.
> His Master-hand the Ancients shall out-do
> Himself the *Poet* and the *Painter* too.
>
> (lines 943–48)

Beneath the specific events and details of the poem lurks the constitutional question unresolved by the Restoration, the question of how power and responsibility are distributed within the nation. Who is responsible for funding the government, for paying the unpaid sailors, for repairing the damaged ships? Who is responsible for administrating the policies under which money of the state is spent? Who actually fights (a question that raises the traditional abhorrence of a standing army)? Who takes final responsibility? The possibility that the King will dismiss Clarendon and appoint representative and independent advisors is the most immediate resolution, but the poem and the events it records reveal that the constitutional issues remain unresolved.

Satires 1.5 and *The Last Instructions to a Painter* share contrasting senses of movement and conciseness that serve as defining features of both poems. Both are partly modeled on earlier poems, whose politics or poetics they correct without direct parody. Both depict shifting scenes and struggle significantly to deal with those shifts in an orderly poem. Their purposes are, in a sense, quite different: Horace seeks to give the impression that all is well with the triumvirs, and in consequence he writes a poem of elegant and classical understatement; Marvell wants to reveal disorders and writes a poem of baroque exaggeration. But behind that difference is a fear that remains hidden from the surface of the poems. The problems that Horace conceals and Marvell records threaten a more serious civil disaster. For Horace the tensions between Antony and Octavian threaten that the triumvirate will break down, renewing the civil war that followed the assassination of Caesar some seven years earlier. For Marvell there is the possibility that Charles, separated from his country by his courtiers, will repeat the errors of his father and suffer his fate. The capture of the *Royal Charles* by the Dutch (and perhaps the heroic fate of Douglas as well) suggest that the Dutch invasion parallels the Civil War, an idea reinforced by the appearance of the assassinated monarchs to Charles. The shifting of the satiric scene manifests the troubled nature of the political situation. The problem of the satirist is to make that disorder pleasing and even orderly, and in doing so to model the possibilities of political order. The poet's efforts to control the constant motion of the shifting scene, though doubtful of success, parallel equally dubious political attempts to channel the torrent of history. Because the shifting scene is performed rather than merely described, it becomes the subject as well as vehicle of meaning. Behind the theatrical setting lies a further reality perhaps unmentioned in the performance itself but evident in the fact that it is undertaken at all. The threat of civil war that might return the confusion of the present to the anarchy of the past is signaled by the struggles embedded in the performance, especially the satirist's struggle to control his material. In both poems significance is supplied by shadowy threats in the historical context.

The performing poet is both a formal author and a perplexed human being who struggles to respond to the exigencies of his time. The inversions of the Saturnalian occasion are in turn inverted by the performing satirist, who restores slave, fool, and beggars to their original nature. The replacement of love by self-interest is articulated directly by Artemiza but verified by its emergence as the only available subject for her observation and reinforced by the fact that she is a cross-dressed performance of the satirist himself (a cross-dressing that equates the antithetical frustrations of crass women and heartless men of wit). Satiric performance generates meaning, shifting it from what the language says to how it is enacted.

THE MOCK-HEROIC

The mock-heroic overlaps significantly with the two performances we have just considered. Like Saturnalian satire, it involves an inversion of tradition; like the shifting satiric scene, it generates meaning by comparisons that are complexly encapsulated in simultaneity. Satiric subjects exist simultaneously in the tawdry present and in a heroic past whose values are invoked by poetic language and allusion but are otherwise notable for their absence. The satirist's performance is his ironic equation of past and present to produce this ubiquitous doubling. The positive half of that doubling consists of the values and behaviors that are conventionally identified with the epic. Because that doubleness sets the ancient and heroic against the modern and insubstantial, the mock-heroic is particularly useful to the historical concerns of satire. It stands for and within a spectrum of analogous contrasts whose positive terms either are associated with the heroic to begin with or become associated with it by virtue of their function in the contrasts.[32] It is important that mock-heroic doubleness be maintained, so that the conflict of ancient and modern values remains at the center. Hence a work that merely trivializes the epic – such as the quasi-Homeric *Batrachomyomachia*, which records in epic style a deadly combat between mice and frogs – can hardly be thought of as mock-heroic satire.

Since the positive material of the contrasts is publicly associated with the epic, and since the epic is a poem about communal values, the contrast between the heroic and the modern often sets the private (selfish) against the public (communal). Insofar as epic values are still maintained by the culture in which the mock-epic is produced, that culture becomes the target of its satire. Most members of a culture claim to believe in its nominal heroic values and associate them with such terms as "western civilization." The point of the mock-heroic is that those values have actually been abandoned. Although they retain a vestigial force in the belief system, the actual behavior of individuals, institutions, and culture is governed by an ideology that cannot be reconciled with them. The importance of that vestigial belief in a lost ideology cannot be overstated, since significant criticism can hardly be made on the basis of values long forgotten. The doubleness of the mock-heroic form thus reflects a historical situation where what a culture claims to believe contradicts how it actually operates, and it is therefore no accident that the mock-heroic flourished in the late seventeenth and early eighteenth centuries, when an ideology of economic individualism was replacing an aristocratic ideology. The mock-heroic mourns the loss of irrecoverable past values, and that mourning that gives serious tone to its comedy.

But, as Claude Rawson has pointed out, the contrast between past and present may be clouded by the satirist's ambivalence towards the heroic past and, in particular, towards the barbaric violence with which its heroism is associated. Hence Swift avoids the mock-heroic, except in *The Battle of the Books*, where it is "flattened by the prose-medium and by an interposed dimension of mock-journalese." Pope's translations of Homer moderate and civilize the force of his violence, but that force and hostility are released in the displaced and perverted form of the mock-heroic, whose ironies could both direct the attack and shield the positive values of civilization from his perhaps uncontrollable military energy.[33] After decades of violent civil conflict, Horace may have felt a similar ambivalence about the heroic past. Such ambivalence becomes more complicated because the mock-heroic intensifies both sides of the past–present contrast. The heroic past may seem more glorious even in its absence; the unheroic present is trivialized to the point of monstrosity. The mock-heroic transfers as well as intensifies, so that the heroic is trivialized by the modern and the monstrous is glorified by the heroic.

Horace is not the first writer to spring to mind as a mock-heroic performer, and the role seems somewhat inconsistent with the poet of the *Carmen Saeculare* or Book 4 of the *Odes*. But several of his satires have mock-heroic features and introduce characteristics that will reappear, much amplified, in Pope's *Dunciad*. The mock-heroic performance of Horace's *Satires* 2.5 enacts a post-Homeric conversation between Ulysses and Tiresias. In Book 11 of the *Odyssey*, Odysseus, following the instructions of Circe, goes to the world of the dead, where he has a crucial conversation with Tiresias on the steps he needs to take to return to Ithaca, and Tiresias tells him of his future life. In Horace's version Ulysses asks a question not found in Homer: how can he recover his lost property? (In fact, the further question Odysseus does ask in the *Odyssey* is about the shade of his mother, so from the outset Horace seems to have replaced familial values by economic ones.) The answer of Tiresias is in effect an advice manual on the means of success in modern life – fortune-hunting, conning, and pimping. In contemporary Rome, the cash nexus has replaced, indeed destroyed, traditional values. Familial inheritance, a central theme of the *Odyssey*, is replaced by an inheritance based on flattery and deception. Throughout Horace's poem Ulysses, who functions as a heroic figure in contrast to the modern figure of Tiresias, complains that the advice on how to behave at Ithaca is inconsistent with his behavior at Troy. The advice itself might have been written without its Homeric setting, but its heroic context supplies values that make it particularly comic and satiric.[34] In the absence of a narrator Tiresias, as the prophet of the new economic man, is allowed to speak for himself, becoming both Homeric and Horatian, and articulating his own condemnation. But we are aware of his dual status through our knowledge that this is neither Homeric nor an advice manual but a performance by the satirist. Our awareness of the quasi-absent performer of the mock-heroic renders the poem's theatrics ironic.

The modern mock-heroic – anticipated in Horace by *Satires* 1.7, fully realized in Dryden's *MacFlecknoe* and Pope's *Dunciad*, and recollected in Eliot's *The Waste Land* – eliminates ancient actors, at least as performers on the epic stage, only to return them through analogy and allusion. It describes modern life in terms of the language and conventions of classical epic, whose unarticulated values condemn the present, at the same time as the present, by its distance from those values, shows the impossibility of recovering them. Narrative consciousness here is important in delineating the ambiguous relationship between the past and the present. The narrator distinguishes himself from modern (wasteland) activity by virtue of his knowledge of past values. The narrator is feckless, however, because it is no longer possible to practice those values. The part–present contrast yields to the frustrating contrast between knowing and doing. Things are not quite so bad in Horace's *Satires* 1.7.

Satires 1.7 is generally thought to be a lesser poem, perhaps an unsuccessful one. Its brief but elevated gesturing concludes in an obvious pun. Rudd complains that "after all the fanfare and skirmishing the knock-out punch comes as an anticlimax, and having paid for a ringside seat we feel like demanding our money back," but Fraenkel finds the poem "refined."[35] In form and substance it is basically a joke, but its mock-heroic characteristics are useful in illustrating the multiple levels opened by the form. The basic pattern of the story, which Horace describes as well-known, is judicial, involving two adversaries, a judge, and an audience. P. Rupilius Rex, a Roman proscribed by the triumvirate, has a lawsuit with Persius, a wealthy local (the poem is set in Asia Minor), half-Roman and half-Greek. Persius states his side of the case with wit or foolishness enough to amuse the onlookers, but Rex responds with a torrent of abuse that leads Persius to suggest to the judge – Brutus himself, for whom removing kings is a family tradition – that he get rid of this one (Rex). The two antagonists are introduced in triply mock-heroic terms: the passion of their antagonism, we are told, resembles that of Achilles (corresponding to the half-Greek Persius) and Hector (corresponding to the Roman Rex); they are contrasted to Glaucon and Diomedes, the Trojan and Greek heroes who, in *Iliad* 6, refuse to fight each other because of their friendship; they are as well matched as two well-known Roman gladiators who succeeded in killing each other simultaneously. The Homeric comparison links heroic wars to modern squabbles.

The terrible pun connects this literary mock-heroic to a historical one. The judge rather than the litigants is most seriously mock-heroic. The suggestion that Brutus, by virtue of familial and personal experience, is

well equipped to deal with "Rex/rex," in turn involves a mock-heroic conjunction of Brutus the assassin with his ancestor Brutus the patriot (who
defeated but did not kill Tarquinus). The family connection, the poem
seems to imply, is no more than a pun. But there is a mock-heroic level to
the pun as well, for in the era of Brutus the assassin there is no "rex" but
only "Rupilius Rex." Killing Caesar thus seems a mock-heroic act, since it
applied a pre-Republican terminology (rex) and perhaps outdated values
to a modern situation. Brutus becomes a mock-heroic figure embedded in
the confusion of the pun.[36] The connection of Brutus to his ancestor was a
commonplace of Republican propaganda, which asserted that both acted
to free Rome from the tyranny of kingship. The poem denigrates that claim
by reintroducing it in a context already established as coarse, trivial, and
mock-heroic, so that the claim of propaganda is seen, like the equation of
the two squabbling litigants to Homeric heroes, as a pretension that would
be ridiculous if it had not unleashed a civil war. The pun itself, trivial and
obvious, is the poem's final mock-heroic act.

The modern mock-heroic, as illustrated in relatively simple form by
Horace's *Satires* 1.7 and as expanded in Pope's more sophisticated *Dunciad*,
gains scope and significance because its radical comparison of the lowly
modern to the elevated heroic unleashes related comparisons that are linguistic as well as literary and historical. The mock-heroic's ancient–modern
comparison is subsumed in a range of analogous contrasts. The humble
status of *Satires* 1.7 as the briefest of Horace's satires contrasts to the mon-
umentality of the epic, and the poem conjoins its trivial pun with historical, political, and literary significance, thus making the poem itself a
mock-heroic act that parallels its content. The mock-heroic, in its most
sophisticated form, involves far more than the confusion of the significant
past with the trivial present. *Satires* 1.7, like *Satires* 2.5, is marked by the
apparent absence of the poet. If the author of *Satires* 2.5 serves as the pro-
ducer of a latter-day satyr-play whose central characters come from the
Odyssey, the author of *Satires* 1.7 claims to tell a well-known anecdote from
which he dissociates himself. But it is the author who, in *Satires* 2.5, has
the bright idea of describing fortune-hunting in terms of Homeric heroism
and who, in *Satire* 1.7, transforms the simple anecdote with its simpler
pun into heroic language, allusion, and metaphor. The significance of the
mock-heroic depends in part on the reader's awareness of an authorial agent
who comprehends the multiple layers and diverse meanings of the poem.
This comprehension becomes more complex still in the case of Pope's
Dunciad.

One non-mock-heroic problem of the *Dunciad* cannot be neglected, for a contemporary reading of it would have been connected to the deliberate mysteries of its publication.[37] It was anonymously published in 1728 with a phony title page but without the apparatus it subsequently acquired. The guise of anonymity was further confused by the 1729 publication of the *Dunciad Variorum*, with multiple parodic notes and prefatory material, mostly written by Pope but partly by his friends. These notes were expanded and revised in further editions. Pope confirmed his authorship by including the poem in the 1735 edition of his works. In 1742 he published *The New Dunciad* as an independent poem, and in 1743 he added it as the fourth book to a revised version of the *Dunciad Variorum*, at the same time replacing the original hero Lewis Theobald (Tibbald in the poem) with Colley Cibber, the Poet Laureate, manager of the Drury-lane Theater, and author of the much-mocked *Apology*. One way of reading the *Dunciad* is as a palimpsest in which previous writings remain inscribed beneath the 1743 text and the textual changes themselves imply meaning.[38] Even beyond the problems of its multiple versions the *Dunciad* is, in several senses, a conscious impossibility. From the position of the reader, it moves in opposite directions simultaneously, and this diametric movement threatens to pull the poem apart at the same time as its energies generate meaning. The *Dunciad* simultaneously moves forward, backward, upward, and downward. Each direction needs to be identified individually, for each points to areas of significance in the poem, but both the energies of the poem and the problems it creates for readers lie in their interconnections. These movements and their attendant paradoxes derive from and define the poem's mock-heroic character.

The *Dunciad* moves forward to a conclusion, to the achievement of the rule of Dulness. Although John Dennis complained that the poem lacked action (and some critics complain that what action it has is not significant), Pope, in the guise of Martinus Scriblerus, claims that the action regarding Dulness is "the removal of her imperial seat from the City to the polite World; as the Action of the Aeneid is the restoration of the empire of *Troy*, and the removal of the race from thence to *Latium*" (p. 72). Scriblerus, as Aubrey Williams pointed out, establishes the *Aeneid* analogy, with Dulness as Venus and Tibbald/Cibber as Aeneas, and so defines an epic structure on which significant meaning will be built.[39] There is a great deal of forward movement in the poem, both geographical and temporal. It is perhaps missing the point to complain that Dulness never makes it to the polite world (though Book 4 does figuratively end at Westminster), that Cibber, the supposed hero, never actually does anything, and that the geographical movement (like the movement of the Lord Mayor's parade, on which it is based) ends up where it started.[40] For Dulness and for the dunces forward movement is inescapably circular, but the poem itself is linear.

That linear movement takes it through a series of tableaux that reveal the progressively effective reign of Dulness. In Book 1 Dulness and Cibber both contemplate the works of the dunces, who conclude the book by hailing Cibber as their king. In Book 2 the contemplation turns to frenetic action, as the dunces, imitating the Lord Mayor's parade, march through the streets, and, imitating the games of *Iliad* 23 and *Aeneid* 5, conduct their nasty allegorical contests, until the public reading of works (to test the endurance of critics) puts all to sleep. In Book 3 Cibber, in imitation of the journey of Aeneas in *Aeneid* 6, hears his predecessor Settle, echoing the prophecy of Anchises, celebrate the achievement of the empire of Dulness through her subversion of all forms of culture. Settle's vision is then brought to pass in Book 4. Cibber appropriately sleeps in the lap of Dulness, as she sits on her throne before the thronging dunces and acknowledges the contributions made to her power by education, collecting, science, politics, and religion. But her power is that of sleep, darkness, and confusion, and at her mighty yawn, all dunces sleep and all culture is perverted:

> Nor *public* Flame, nor *private*, dares to shine;
> Nor *human* Spark is left, nor Glimpse *divine!*
> Lo! Thy dread Empire, Chaos! is restor'd;
> Light dies before thy uncreating word:
> Thy hand, great Anarch! lets the curtain fall;
> And Universal Darkness buries All.
>
> (4.651–56)

The characteristic movement of Dulness and her dunces is circular, rising and falling, moving back and forth like the Lord Mayor's parade. The movement of Dulness is necessarily meaningless, and hence her hero is necessarily inactive. But the poem moves between the trivial and the sublime until the trivial becomes sublime.[41] The stasis that is the nature of Dulness becomes the powerful forward movement of the poem, and the stasis engulfs everything, even, in the final paradox, the poem itself – for the poet's record of the movement of Dulness has been unable to prevent her triumph, though it is ultimately the poet rather than Dulness who triumphs. Alvin Kernan articulates the paradoxical conclusion: "at the very moment that dullness becomes everything, everything becomes nothing, for dullness is finally nothingness, vacuity, matter without form or idea."[42]

The universality of Dulness derives from the arrogant assumption that she and her dunces speak for all and speak all-powerfully. The universal obliteration to which the poem moves is death – not that everyone must die but that all must die. The forward motion of the poem, the poet seems to warn, is irresistible.

The poem's mock-heroic is explicit in its backward movement. As readers follow the circular movement of Dulness and the linear progress of the poem, they repeatedly look back to the classical tradition reflected in its style and structure and in its swarm of allusions, which are sometimes identified in the notes. Pope had been engaged in translating Homer from 1713 to 1726, and the mock-heroic style of the *Dunciad* in general owes a great deal to that effort, but relatively few specific analogues to Homer have been found, compared to the many references to the *Aeneid* and *Paradise Lost*, which were traced in detail by Aubrey Williams.[43] Self-conscious analogy is crucial to the mock-heroic, which uses epic archetypes and refers to specific epics. But the poem's connections to earlier literary works and the frequent intrusions of the *Variorum* notes may stimulate readers to their own literary recollections, and these need not have been anticipated by the poet. The *Variorum* itself serves at a further mock-heroic level not merely by supplying information about epic analogues but by identifying present characters (who would not, presumably, be otherwise known) in much the same way as Pope's *Iliad* is jammed with notes explaining Homeric figures and glossing the Homeric text. The *Dunciad* thus includes what William Kinsley describes as both "useful real notes" and "ludicrously inept and overgrown mock-notes."[44] The mock-heroic becomes parody when it cites duncical books. These become actualized metaphors, as the words of the books are transformed into the actions of the dunces. This collapsing of writing and acting becomes another pointer to the cosmic confusion created by Dulness. The past creates the present meaning of the text but literally disrupts it by basing it on recollection. The reader discovers the meaning of the poem's forward movement by looking backward.

If looking backward reminds us of the past we have lost, the rich and witty profusion of epic conventions (especially epic metaphor) creates a further alternative. The most formal epic tableau of the poem is the description of heroic games in Book 2, and it is also the section that readers have found most offensive. But various critics, Emrys Jones in particular, have commented on the contrast between the childish and disgusting nature of Pope's material and the liveliness and artistry of his text, which suggests Pope's fascination with that which repels him.[45] The passage usually cited to illustrate this contrast is the emergence of Smedley "in majesty of Mud" from the slime of Fleet-ditch (2.325–46). But this coprological energy is a further manifestation of the mock-heroic force of the poem. For the poet's vitality flows out of the heroic, which is available to Pope not only as a reader of the past, the very past lost by his dunces, but as a writer of the present. As Thomas R. Edwards observes, "the contrast between the ugliness of Dulness and the beauty of moral intelligence may be taken as the main theme of the *Dunciad*."[46]

As the *Dunciad* moves forward and backward, it moves upward as well to elucidate the cultural problem it presents and to define the abstractions standing for that problem. The poem describes, in a series of epic tableaux, a mock-heroic scene and the moral and intellectual condition it represents. Action – the spread of the empire of Dulness and the activities of the dunces who are her agents – bridges those two descriptive levels. But the *Dunciad* needs to locate responsibility for the condition it describes. What is Dulness? Who is responsible? What is the real satiric target? As the poem moves forward the issue becomes not simply how it is going to end but the nature of Dulness. The dunces show both her nature and its effects. "In Pope's design the numerous votaries help to make Dulness visible, revealing the force and extent of her otherwise invisible 'sway,' much as smoke shows the direction of the wind."[47] But Dulness is a poetic abstraction, and a poem that locates moral responsibility in a poetic abstraction seems to follow the path of Dulness to obscurity and non-existence. The misty insubstantiality of Dulness, her apparent lack of referentiality, is useful in cloaking but gathering the variety of causes for moral and intellectual vacuity, as they are revealed by the forward motion of the poem. Though dunces (to paraphrase Yeats) are many, Dulness is one. The dunces reveal the presence of Dulness without revealing her essence. But this situation is only to be expected, because Dulness is non-being and by definition without essence.

Dunces and the consumers of duncedom are willingly but not knowingly responsible for the triumph of Dulness. Notwithstanding the traditional moral philosophy which sees knowledge as a condition of will, the paradox works out. Dunces know what they do. They see their actions as individualistic (self-centered, aggressive, acquisitive), and they will their actions. In a sense their flocking to the throne of Dulness to gain her blessing by narrating their contributions to her cause is itself a satiric fiction much like Pope's treatment of their writing as action: their self-centered activity is an aware participation in the cultural imperialism of Dulness. Darkness, after all, is a dominant image of the poem. The confusion of the duncical city derives from this essential blindness: the dunces know full well what they do but they do not know the significance of what they do. If they ceased to act (to write, to publish), Dulness would cease. The cloud of unknowing is perceived by the satirist but not by his morally responsible victims, and hence he creates the fictions that reveal their responsibility. But the mass and variety of duncical activity obscures the significance of their individual activity, and therefore one of the consequences of the abstraction and unknowability of Dulness is that the situation is beyond individual control. Pope's concern is with the cultural implications of individual activity. The upward movement of the poem towards the elaboration of Dulness, towards the moral relation between individual stupidity and the destruction of culture, supplies much of the major satiric meaning of the poem. The connection also gives particular significance to the poem's downward movement.

The poem moves downward to root its conflicting values and its conflicted abstractions in historical particularity. Gregory Colomb treats what I consider downward movement as upward movement in a poem that builds its general meaning out of the particularities of place and person.[48] I do not disagree, and the divergence in metaphorical directions does not reflect a difference in substance. From the position of the reader, the appearance of so many particulars distracts from the progress of the action and from the readers' analogous efforts to frame the issues of the poem, literally forcing their eyes down the page to the notes which identify the individuals who make their questionable appearance in the text. From the identification of these particulars, readers often (but not always) move up again to the delineation of Dulness. A conscious difficulty of the poem lies in the tension between these motions. In his Preface, Pope seems to treat names in a cavalier manner: "The *poem*," he says, "*was not made for these authors, but these authors for the poem*," and goes on, "I would not have the reader too much troubled or anxious, if he cannot decypher them; since when he shall have found them out, he will probably know no more of the persons than before" (p. 367). The comment probably ought not to be taken too seriously, given the number of notes devoted to precisely the anxieties Pope says the reader might avoid. But it does raise the problem, much discussed by critics, of the significance of names in the poem.[49] Does it make a difference whether Theobald or Cibber is the anointed of Dulness or whether Budgell or Moore Smythe is the plagiary? Does it make a difference that we even know these names? It does seem important that we know that they are real names belonging to historical authors. Their actuality pulls against the abstraction of Dulness. But Cibber and Theobald are interchangeable, and Pope suggests that knowing their names is unimportant since they are only ciphers, children of the literal non-entity Dulness. The record of non-being, the situation of existing only in Pope's text, is the ultimate satiric insult.

Dulness is an abstraction, a construct of the writer. But specific characters lose their identities not because they are treated abstractly but because they are easily replaced in different versions of the poem. For a poem that comes to such an apocalyptic conclusion, the *Dunciad* is particularly open, since each new edition changes the characters. If the 1743 version is the last, it is only because Pope died in 1744, and we are left to make the later substitutions ourselves. The dunces derive their nature – their non-being – from Dulness, but Dulness derives her nature from the activity of the dunces: we know (to paraphrase Ivan Karamazov) that Dulness exists because we know that there is a Cibber. This is only one of a series of paradoxes deriving from the ultimate mock-heroic paradox of the poem – that insignificant action can be represented significantly. What makes the dunces threatening is not the nature they derive from Dulness (non-being) but their number and the tendency of individuals to vanish into the aggregate. Here the exactness of Pope's imitation of Homeric practice seems underestimated. The Catalog of Ships, the massing of armies before battle, the rush and turmoil of battle itself, are all described with an epic force which identifies individuals and then subsumes them into larger actions over which they have no control. The heroes get more lines, but for the non-heroes we are forced to turn to Pope's notes, whether we are reading his *Iliad* translation or his *Dunciad*.

The enumeration of specific names and their disappearance into an anonymous collective, usually described figuratively, is thus another mock-heroic convention of the *Dunciad*. In addition to suggesting the qualities and effects of Dulness, names become the vehicles for the poem's more particular but not merely individual satire. The fall of Walpole, according to Maynard Mack, allowed the 1743 *Dunciad* to be recast so as to make Robert Walpole its real but hidden hero.[50] The pattern of Walpolism fits the pattern of overgenerality revealed by Pope's satiric attacks on the works of Dulness: the pretense to write for all parallels the pretense to govern for all. The fictionality of the *Dunciad*'s forward movement has to be in tension with the actuality of its downward movement in order for the poem to work as satire. But, as so often happens in the *Dunciad*, this tension becomes engaged with still further confusions in the triad of fiction, reality, and representation. The names refer to people who existed independently of Pope's poem; we can imagine them and their loved ones reading it. Descriptions of the people cannot make the same claim to actuality that the names do, and once the real people become names in a fiction, their fictional character becomes important not because it describes them accurately but because it points towards general ideas about the causes and nature of Dulness. The fact that those names refer to existing people indicates that the works of these people take their character by virtue of their association with patterns of culture in society.

Satire does not address its victims, whose identities here have become ontologically complex, but its audience. The real audience of *Dunciad* is not the dunces; its real purpose is not to change their behavior; and its real topic is not just bad art. Its real audience is its actual readers; the behavior to be changed is that of readers who at least ought to read more Pope and less Cibber. The real subject of the poem is the array of false values and devious practices that create false culture. (As with the array of dunces, the array of such values is open-ended because the possibilities of falsity are infinite.) The disunity of the poem created by its opposing directions of movement suggests three levels: the literature of the dunces falls apart because it describes nothingness; the *Dunciad* falls apart because its subject is the literature of the dunces and therefore the literature of nothingness; but literature, language, and culture fall apart because they are prone to the corruption identified as Dulness (non-being). The presence of Dulness does not end with the poem; the act of uncreation, like the act of creation, is perpetual, and the battle of the dunces is constantly being waged. The closing apocalypse is an unceasing moment. This is yet another manifestation of the mock-heroic paradox: the impossibility of the *Dunciad* lies in its representation of non-being.

This leaves us not with the paradoxical text but with the performing author. The presence of Pope as the hero of the *Dunciad* has been well described by Dustin Griffin, but his mock-heroic performance might be still more strongly underlined.[51] The role performed by the mock-heroic author is that of the bard, who stands in the same relation to the Muse as the dunces do to Dulness. The quasi-duncical presumption so often derided in Pope that, as poet, he is the self-proclaimed defender of civilization is the claim of those singers who celebrated Achaean glory, who memorialized the founding of Rome, or who justified the ways of God to men. But when the mock-heroic bard of the *Dunciad* writes, the horrors of the apocalypse turn out to be elegant, funny, witty, and redolent of meaning – precisely the way one would like the world to end. The poem is supercharged, flying off in all directions, and that extraordinary energy is its primary attraction. The energy supplied to the words dramatizes the inertia of Dulness. The mock-heroic bard comically and triumphantly embodies the ultimate act of creation by bringing life out of nothingness.

The hand of universal anarchy lets the curtain fall and the performance ends. The *Dunciad* is a mock-heroic poem by virtue of its epic energies. It engages directly with an epic tradition, claiming to be satiric epic in the tradition of the lost *Margites*, and, as Ricardus Aristarchus (Pope pretending to be Richard Bentley) points out, standing in the same relation to Homer, Virgil, and Milton as the satyr-play did to the tragic trilogy (77–78). Its epic pretensions govern its structure, its analogies and references (even its contemporary ones), its conventions, its figurative language, its heightened diction, and its heroic measure. It is unified by the imperialism of Dulness in the loose way that the *Iliad* is unified by the wrath of Achilles. But epics celebrate the triumph of a culture, and the mock-heroic's defining conflict between the heroic and the satiric ironizes its praise, transforms celebration to attack, generates the four-directional movement that here has served as a metaphor for the signifying tensions of the poem, and aligns the conflict between epic and satire with other conflicts and paradoxes. The mock-heroic, as exemplified by quasi-heroic satires of Horace and as perfected by the energies of the *Dunciad,* is not merely a formal genre but a satirist's way of performing.

THE SHIFTING SPEAKER

The shifting nature of Horace's satiric voice was described some years ago by C. O. Brink:

While his voice remains unmistakable, his person disappears behind his poetry, and changes from poem to poem. He knows how to make himself into a plurality of egos, a series of contrasting types, and he holds these contrasts in a humorous-ironic balance . . . He who seeks in poetry the force of *one* single attitude, *one* powerful emotion, will not find this poet his poet.[52]

Horace's shifting speaker is complex, giving rise to diverse interpretations of individual poems and to conflicting views of his satiric approaches. The situation is complicated by the difficulty of working out, at any moment in any poem, the precise relations among Horace's shifting speaker, his shifting audiences, and his shifting topic. Barbara K. Gold has described four audiences of *Satires* 1.1: the primary audience or dedicatee, the internal audience (the straight man to Horace's ironist), the authorial (historical) audience, and the actual audience, consisting of real readers at a given moment in time.[53] But multiple audiences thus described are present for virtually any ironic poem, and the shifting of emphasis among them depends largely on the shifting of speaker and subject. The shifting of subject is a crux

in interpreting Horace, and scholars such as Fraenkel and Rudd who seek
to account for the structures of the first three diatribes must explain the
disjunction between shifts in apparent subject and shifts in tone.

Horace announces at the outset the general subject not only for the first
satire but for the three diatribes that begin Book 1, and in doing so, he
raises central issues for satire itself.

> Qui fit, Maecenas, ut nemo, quam sibi sortem
> seu ratio dederit seu fors obiecerit, illa
> contentus vivat, laudet diversa sequentis?
>
> [How is it, Maecenas, that no one is content with his own lot –
> whether he has got it by an act of choice or taken it up
> by chance – but instead envies people in other occupations?]

The naming of Maecenas as the primary audience of the poem identifies
Horace the unknown poet as friend or conversational companion of the
well-known Maecenas. It is important for what it says about the speaker,
but it is also important for what it says about Maecenas, for the poem
argues that a major example of discontent is excessive (and universal) love
of wealth, and Maecenas is extremely rich. The relation of Maecenas to the
diatribist implies that, despite his wealth, he, like the speaker, understands
the limited role of wealth in happiness. (That understanding is consistent
with Horace's portrait of Maecenas in *Satires* 1.6 as a tolerant, generous
figure, concerned with human worth rather than superficial importance.)
The appearance of Maecenas in the first line as friend of the poet and sharer
of his inquiry into the perplexities of the human situation, may control how
the poem is read. However inconsistent the poem may be or however comic
the poses of its speaker, we need to see it as appropriate to be presented to
Maecenas. The historicity of the opening reference to Maecenas controls
and directs the fictionality of the speaker.[54]

Discontent, Horace's opening question implies, is universal regardless of
whether one has reached one's position as a result of rational choice (*ratio*)
or random chance (*fors*). Whether the major events of life are matters that
individuals can control seems a central issue of satire. If human beings
are merely the victims of circumstances they can neither understand nor
change, then the only possible satiric position would be to mock at the illusions of human volition (a position that Juvenal comes close to adopting
in *Satire* 10). But Horace's sentence structure sidesteps this issue: whether
chance or choice controls our fate, we will be dissatisfied. In a sense Horace's
concern is not about what people ought to do but about how they should
think about who they are. The subjective nature of this approach does not

eliminate moral concerns, since who people think they are is certainly connected to what they do. Horace proposes an equally subjective criterion for
evaluating self-awareness: happiness, or its pallid sibling content, becomes
the standard by which both thought and action are measured.[55]

The poem begins by asking why everyone is discontent, and exemplifies
the question by citing professional comparisons. By way of the example
of the hard-working ant, the poem shifts (line 41) to the topic of avarice,
which occupies the poet's attention until, in line 108, he returns to his initial
question. One of the disconcerting elements of this movement is that he
seems to have come to a conclusion about avarice: the proper course is a
middle one, avoiding both penury and waste: "est modus in rebus" ("things
have a certain proportion") (line 106). A proper satirist might carry this
conclusion with him when he returns to his larger question, but Horace
only exemplifies the question once more and leaves it unanswered. The
two subjects of the satire are avarice and discontent, but the question is
how they are related to one another. Are they directly related, so that,
for instance, avarice is a cause of discontent, though, as Fraenkel points
out, Horace never says so?[56] Are avarice and discontent related not directly
but to some third term that is the real but hidden satiric target, or are
they not really related at all? Is Horace's purpose to instruct his readers,
to establish a poetic identity, to parody moralists, or to use moral topics
as a frame for entertaining examples? These alternatives are not exclusive
or inconsistent, but various readers light on one or another to explain the
intellectual structure of the poem (or the lack thereof). Rudd argues that
discontent, for Horace, is based on the desire not for more money but for
an easier life; M. Dyson sees avarice and discontent both caused by envy.[57]
For John J. Bodoh the unity of its poem does not lie in its logical treatment
of a subject but in the general drift of its conversational style.[58] Thomas
K. Hubbard provides an elaborate schema showing ten sections moving
between theme, example, and transition and joined concentrically by the
thematic connections of dissatisfaction, change and moderation, security,
and excess.[59]

My own sense is that Horace writes, in 1.1 and its companion diatribes,
particularly open poems that emphasize not moral precepts but mental
attitudes. Avarice might be seen not as a cause of discontent (which has
other causes as well) but as an instance of it. His treatment of avarice does
lead to a moral conclusion in the Aristotelian mean, but he does not go
on to apply that principle to his general question for several reasons. He
wants to keep the question open because it underlies further satires. (Sexual
frustration, the topic of 1.2, is, like avarice, an example of discontent.) But he

also knows that a true generalization about one kind of discontent (avarice) may not be true of discontent in general, since reasonably if not perfectly moral people may be discontent as well. "Inde fit ut raro," he concludes, "qui se vixisse beatum dicat" ("So it is that we can rarely find a man who says he has lived a happy life") (lines 117–18). Horace needs to keep his negative conclusion open as well, for if no one claimed to have a happy life, the criterion of happiness would disappear as a subjective satiric norm. This insistence on openness means that while he may use moral precepts along the way, such as the Aristotelian golden mean, their function is local or temporary and their substance often banal. And he often avoids assertions altogether by arguing through metaphor and example. To fight the reader's (and scholar's) insistence on closure, he needs to adopt a shifting speaker.

The way in which the shifting speaker operates is apparent in *Satires* 1.3. The topic of 1.3, like that of 1.1, is unstable, not organizing the poem but emerging out of its movement between examples and generalizations, between divergent directions of logic and association, between negative vices and positive values, between the personal views or experience of the speaker and his appeals to public sentiments shared by his readers and verified by common sense. Topics, speakers, and audiences shift as the poem moves forward, and the changes in one may (or may not) concur with changes in the others. It makes some sense to think of the shifting speaker of the poem as progressing through a series of speech occasions or "utterances." The conversational nature of Horace's rhetoric controls his shifting material: the changes in topic and approach are indicated by shifts in the poet's manners of speaking.

There seem to me eight distinguishable conversational stances in *Satires* 1.3 (though other readers might distinguish more or fewer kinds of talk). (1.) *Satires* 1.3 opens with an impersonal (but negative) portrait of Tigellius, complaining particularly of his consistent inconsistency – his insistence on singing or not singing, depending on what his listener does not wish to hear. Both the subject of this brief satiric passage and its tone of impersonal attack are untypical of *Satires* 1.3, but at various points Horace moves from his personal tone of advice to impersonal descriptions of illustrative figures. At the opening of 1.3, the reader notes that the subject of Tigellius' inconsistency recollects the treatment of inconsistency in *Satires* 1.1 and that a portrait of Tigellius also began *Satires* 1.2. The opening figure attaches *Satires* 1.3 to previous satires without clearly establishing a subject or context for the present satire. (2.) Immediately after the opening sketch of Tigellius, an *adversarius*, identified only as *aliquis* (someone), addresses the speaker and asks if he is faultless himself. The *adversarius* thus puts the speaker on the defensive, while the audience becomes a witness to the debate (but not an impartial witness, for we too enjoyed the attack on Tigellius). With this shift of speakers, Tigellius ceases to become a subject, but his portrait does. The shift is crucial to the poem: if the portrait of Tigellius referred back to the satires of behavior in *Satires* 1.1 and 1.2, the attack of the *adversarius* on the speaker refers forward to the defense of satire itself in *Satires* 1.4. From this point onward, as the satiric topic of the evaluation of faults emerges, the poem retains as a secondary topic the justification of satire in attacking such faults.

(3.) The speaker defends himself by indulging in a variation on the first speech occasion (the negative but impersonal portrait). Here, instead of describing a character, he repeats a conversation analogous to the conversation in which he is engaged. The "brazen egotism" of Maenius attacking Novius is contrasted to the speaker's implicit humility. (4.) As the speaker moves away from the repeated conversation to generalize upon it and to explain why the egotism of Maenius is inappropriate, he adopts the common rhetorical position of the diatribe, addressing his audience as "you" and taking on himself the role of moral advisor. But the audience's earlier identification with the speaker, through the shared appreciation of the Tigellius portrait, remains important here, for the need to be aware of one's own faults that underlies the attack of the *adversarius* on the speaker is now the subject of the speaker's advice. Another shift must be noted as well. In his diatribe position, the speaker is now generally concerned with the audience's perception of the faults of friends. He develops his diatribe by moving between his position as moral advisor and his opening position as satiric describer.

(5.) But the problem of the diatribist's position is that it presupposes a moral distance between an authoritative speaker and an uninformed audience, and that distance is considerably shortened by the various invitations the audience has already received to identify with the speaker. Hence in the course of his discourse, Horace moves from the "I–you" distance of the diatribist to the "we" that includes both the flawed satiric poet and his imperfect audience: both the poet and his listeners should adopt the position of the lover or the parent not merely in neglecting the faults of others but in perceiving them as charming personal characteristics. (6.) This movement away from abstract moral problems leads to the most surprising of the speaker's rhetorical shifts: the list of faults that might be positively regarded includes the example of the uninhibited man who interrupts the conversation of others. Horace himself is such a person; the uninhibited interrupter is "qualem me saepe libenter / obtulerim tibi, Maecenas" ("like me eagerly bursting in on you, Maecenas,") lines 63–64 (my translation). The speaker's identification of himself as Horace only confirms an implicit connection, but the location of the audience with Maecenas reminds the general audience of the fact that the satire we are now perusing would have been read to Maecenas, so that the shift in tone presumably represents an actual occasion. What makes the shift surprising is the impossibility that Maecenas, if he is the audience at this point, could be the uninformed audience of the earlier diatribe section of the poem. But with this shift the poem takes on a still further topic; it becomes Horace's personal plea that Maecenas treat him with the indulgent toleration the poem argues should be universal.

By the time Horace has specifically incorporated Maecenas in the judging audience, he has revealed his subject and covered the major range of his rhetorical situations. Two other conversational positions can be seen as variations on the impersonal patterns of numbers 1 and 3. (7.) Horace's most general position, contrasting to his personal reference to Maecenas, is the stock moral pronouncement, succinctly reminding the reader of the points made indirectly by example: "Nam vitiis nemo sine nascitur: optimus ille est / qui minimis urgetur" ("no one is free from faults; the best is the man who is hampered by the smallest") (lines 68–69). Horace has still one further point to make, and it is a crucial one, for his plea for universal tolerance seems to render satire (and hence the opening portrait of Tigellius) inappropriate. Horace works his way out of this situation by attacking the Stoic position that all moral offences are the same, for if they are different, then one can attack the significant offenses of others. In making that point, Horace moves from examples (speech occasion 1) to moral generalizations (speech occasion 7), but he adds yet a further speech situation. (8.) He argues that the distinction of degrees of offence emerged historically as primitive people became civilized and framed laws to protect society from serious evils. Such historical generalizations differ from moral ones (position 7) because they do not imply any authority in the speaker other than the capacity to arrive at commonsense conclusions from familiar facts. After the historical argument on moral distinctions, the poem can conclude with its final portrait, returning to the opening speech occasion in the picture of the deluded Stoic who corresponds to the portrait of perverse Tigellius.

Horace's performance of shifting speech roles defines the nature of his diatribes, allowing him to look at social behavior simultaneously in various ways, achieving multiple perspectives, speaking in multiple voices, and arriving at conclusions that undermine the sureties of the traditional diatribist. Its shifting quality locates the central implications by eliminating alternatives. This closing off of alternatives resembles the answering of objections in dialogue, and thus, whether or not an explicit *adversarius* is present, the tone of Horace's performance is, as Brink and others have noted, significantly conversational. Its conversational quality also lies in the frequency with which it makes its points by metaphor and example, thus depending on unarticulated understandings among conversationalists. The conversational use of examples also allows Horace to transfer the attention of his reader from one aspect of the example to another, as in the initial case of the portrait of Tigellius. Such shifting insists on the openness of the poem and undermines the sense that life can be explained by moral maxims – though Horace uses such maxims along the way. As a result Horace's statements become complex because they account for the diversity and inconsistency of experience. Tigellius, the inconsistent performer of the opening, seems, by the end, an extreme instance of the inconsistency we all display, and the only consistent figure is the falsely wise Stoic who is mocked by the society of which he pretends to be the philosophical king. Faults should be tolerated but also condemned; universal absolutes are impossible, but moral distinctions must be made. Shifting performance becomes the appropriate mode of satiric statement for uncertain people in a changing world.

The shifting speaker is a performance that emerges only in certain sorts of poems – satiric or otherwise. The speaker's self-conscious awareness of his multiple roles in Horace's diatribes and his heightened responsibility to develop the substance of the poem from his talk throw further weight on his performances of identity. This shift of responsibility from the material to the speaker means that a number of elements that might otherwise seem predictable become undetermined, and that indeterminacy highlights the speaker's role in composing the poem. The speaker is caught by the audience's expectation that he is writing for a purpose and by his own desire to say whatever is on his mind, even when it diverges from such a purpose. The speaker must accommodate moral judgment with impersonal description, mental attitude with external behaviors, attacks on others with defense of himself, private audiences with public ones; he must give the audience the sense that the experience of interpreting the satire has been significant. In order to achieve that sense of significance in a sustained poem and amid responsibilities so intense and varied, the satirist needs to shift the nature and manner of his performance. The shifting speaker, then, is not merely a performance required by the personality of Horace. Its persistence in later poems can be verified by poems notable for their problematic and perhaps inconsistent speakers: Jonathan Swift's *Verses on the Death of Dr. Swift*, and that most Horatian of epics, Byron's *Don Juan*.

The speaker of *Verses on the Death of Dr. Swift, D.S.P.D.* shifts by conjuring up a sequence of ironic voices which, in turn, describe an inconsistent sequence of Jonathan Swifts. Much of the critical commentary on the poem concerns the last speaker's ironies and their implications. The poem's final speaker, described by the imagining poet as presenting "my character impartial" (line 306), praises Swift in terms so euphoric that Pope (himself no stranger to vanity) cut them when he was consulted on the London publication of the poem in 1739.[60] Moreover, the eulogist's assertions about Swift are partially untrue, and, therefore, Barry Slepian suggested, ironic, although James Woolley finds that Swift made similar statements about himself in his correspondence.[61] Marshall Waingrow, on the other hand, argues that "the poem is written in both serious and thoughtful praise of the satirist," and John Irwin Fischer insists that the poem is serious, moral, and Christian.[62] The problem of interpreting the poem's final eulogy of Swift is only the last of three vexations I find in this powerfully vexing poem. The first is Swift's use of the motto by La Rochefoucauld that the poem claims it is intended to illustrate. The second is that Swift exemplifies it by talking about his own death.

"Dans l'adversité de nos meilleurs amis nous trouvons quelque chose, qui ne nous deplaist pas." Swift translates Rochefoucauld's maxim as follows:

> In all distresses of our friends
> We first consult our private ends,
> While nature kindly bent to ease us,
> Points out some circumstance to please us.
> (lines 7–10)

Swift has added to the maxim the observations that self-interest is our first response to our friends' misfortunes and that the pleasure we find is supplied by the benevolence of nature. He has, in effect, darkened a maxim that is already dark by stressing the primacy of self-love as a driving force of human nature. The poem begins with the admission that the maxim "is thought too base for human breast," and in the face of resistance to this uncomfortable truth, he seeks to exemplify it. But when he does so, he reverses the maxim. He asserts not just that the pain of our friends causes us pleasure but that the pleasure of our friends causes us pain. In either case, friendship is corrupted by self-interest.

But as he proceeds in his exemplification, it is unclear whether he agrees with Rochefoucauld's unpopular observation (as he claims) or treats it

ironically. His complaints about Pope, Gay, and Arbuthnot illustrate the
interpretive difficulty:

> In Pope I cannot read a line,
> But with a sigh, I wish it mine:
> When he can in one couplet fix
> More sense than I can do in six:
> It gives me such a jealous fit,
> I cry, "Pox take him, and his wit."
> Why must I be outdone by Gay,
> In my own humorous biting way?
> Arbuthnot is no more my friend,
> Who dares to irony pretend;
> Which I was born to introduce,
> Refined it first, and showed its use.
>
> (lines 47–58)

Swift's claims as an ironist are surely verified by this passage. At the literal
level, Swift exemplifies the principle that self-love overrides friendship, for
he resents his friends, not merely for accomplishing more than he but for
doing so where he hoped to excel. But by showing that he too is guilty
of self-love, Swift reveals his humility rather than his pride. Moreover,
most readers note that these lines offer generous and graceful praise for
his friends; in so doing, Swift seems to contradict the notion that self-
love has a higher priority than friendship. But by publicly displaying his
generosity and his ability, through irony, to outmaneuver the universality
of La Rochefoucauld's maxim, Swift achieves his own end, at least insofar as he seeks to be well-regarded. Swift establishes an irony of infinite
regression in which affirmation of the positive side of the equation affirms what one would expect to be the negative side as well. But below
the surface of this mental game (and the poem is redolent of such mental
games) lies the possibility that generous behavior does not contradict the
maxim that self-love overrides friendship, as long as being well-regarded
is seen as serving self-love. (How he is regarded is one of Swift's major
topics in this poem.) If the maxim includes generosity as an attribute of
self-love, Swift has not denied its truth but minimized its baseness by setting out a continuum of self-interested and altruistic behavior. At one end
rests the good individual who wants to be perceived as good; at the other
the satanic figure whose self-assertion is not limited by moral or social
considerations.

Swift's self-regard and his interest in mental games lead him to the second
vexation of the poem. His consideration of his own death seems to present

disturbing alternatives, for either he looks at it directly and thus faces the meaning (or meaninglessness) of his own annihilation, or he looks at it ironically, thus dehumanizing himself and metaphorically practicing his own death. His choice of the second alternative gives a particular hardness of tone to the poem. He satirizes the selfishness of those who comment on his death, from the friend whose prediction will be happily fulfilled if Swift dies, to Bernard Lintot, whose economic interests will be served by consigning Swift's works to oblivion. If Swift's dehumanization of himself anticipates his actual death, the reactions of his friends and enemies share in the dehumanization that is death. At first glance, therefore, Swift's exploration of his postmortem insignificance seems far from the self-glorification ironically expressed in his reactions to his friends' accomplishments. But a similar irony is at work here. His account of the reactions of others implies that his life and reputation have been plagued by deceit, treachery, and willful misperception, an implication that is underlined by the direct, perhaps unironic (or differently ironic) voice of his notes. His willingness to contemplate the summation, after death, of the distortions of his life allows him to respond to them, while his imagined insignificance seems a humility that, like virtually everything else in the poem, is characterized by the initial paradox of regressive irony. (Humility is actually pride; but the recognition that humility is pride, as implied by La Rochefoucauld's maxim, is a manifestation of humility. Swift imagines reactions to his death, and we recognize the plausibility of what he imagines; but we recognize as well that he hopes that reality will be different from plausibility.)

Much the same pattern is then applied to the eulogist, whom Swift describes as "indifferent in the cause" and presenting "my character impartial." The occasion is a debate at the Rose Tavern about Swift himself; the eulogist (despite the title that critics have given him) is introduced as neutral. But there is a tension between his supposed neutrality and the fact that his subject (Swift) is imagining the speech. The negative distortions of the previous section give way to positive distortions, the claims that Slepian and others see as ironic. But since the mode of the poem is the suppositions of Swift, he is the author of the assertions, both as the person supposing that such a speech might take place and as the writer of the poem that records that supposition. In arguing for a modified ironic reading of the eulogy, Scouten and Hume admit that Swift himself was proud of some of the assertions it makes, and Woolley's finding that Swift, in his private correspondence, agreed with most of them extends the view that the eulogy and Swift himself exemplify the poem's initial claims about the prevalence of self-interest. If Swift did indeed share these views, that fact is not general knowledge, not broadly available to readers of the poem when Faulkner published the full version in 1739. But it may have been available to the friends among whom the poem circulated after 1731, when Swift wrote to Gay that he had written "near five hundred lines on a pleasant subject, only to tell what my friends and enemies will say on me after I am dead."[63] But for either set of readers the final eulogy represents the culmination of Swift's regressive irony: it enables Swift simultaneously to praise himself through the mouth of another, to undercut that praise as a collection of clichés and as inaccurate in its assertion that his satire "lashed the vice but spared the name" (line 464), and to admit that the praise is self-praise. If self-love is, as Swift's revision of La Rochefoucauld's maxim implies, a universal driving force, no one, not even Swift, can escape it. But if self-love drives the behavior of all humans, it does not drive all human behavior. The same person can be generous as well as selfish, humble as well as proud, honest in admitting self-love and at the same time in repeating the distortions that such self-love produces.

The speaker of *Verses* controls his shifts within a regressive irony where each term questions the other and affirmation affirms its opposite. The initial dreamer envisions the series of situations to which this irony applies: (1.) the maxim that we find good in the misfortunes of our friends; (2.) the reverse of that maxim which finds misfortunes in the accomplishments of our friends; (3.) the self-serving friends and enemies who consign the dead Swift to oblivion; (4.) the false eulogist who memorializes him. As Swift establishes each of these stages, a shift or reversal takes place, and by the end of the poem the shifting has shown that all people are guilty of self-love but that not all forms of self-love are equally noxious. This combination of universal and particular statements is a product of a shifting speaker who would have pleased Horace.

The speakers of these satires by Horace and Swift change their perspectives but not their identity. The same individual moves through a series of roles. Shifting of perspective parallels shifting topic, generating modifications that allow the poet to assert a strong but not universal moral position. *Verses on the Death of Dr. Swift* begins with a distinction between mind and nature. The problem, Swift claims, does not lie in the mind of La Rochefoucauld but in the nature of humanity. The poem goes on to play mental games that call the nature of nature into question: as long as he is living, Swift can assert a verifiable identity, but once he is dead, he becomes a construct in the minds of others. The mind–nature distinction is implicit as well in Horace's concerns for the subjective criterion of happiness and for the ways in which people conceive of themselves. It distinguishes between the selfishness of mental constructs and the naturalness of right opinion. It is central to the issue of whether behavior is corrigible because derived from ideas that are subject to change or incorrigible because rooted in the evil of human nature.

The exploration of the mind–nature continuum by the shifting satiric speaker implies that there is a stable human nature, that the difficulty of human nature lies in proper perception (hence the need for a shifting perspective), and that right perspective can channel natural selfishness in socially and individually useful ways. It is precisely this idea of an inherent stability perceptible by shifting perspective that Byron's *Don Juan* questions. The shifting perspective of the Byronic narrator has distinctly different implications from the shifting satiric speakers of Horace and Swift. It involves not only changes in narrative voice and role, but geographical movement (from Spain eastward to Russia and westward again to England), and shifts in genres, plots, subjects, and ideas. The poem is unstable in virtually every element, except its regular (but regularly unstable) stanzaic form.

On rare occasions Byron's narrator is presented as a fictional character. In the "Preface," the story-teller is "a Spanish Gentleman in a village in the Sierra Morena on the road between Monasterio and Seville," and both scene and time (during the Peninsular War) are described at length.[64] But Byron (or the preface-writer) admits that he has provided an impossible narrative situation in parody of Wordsworth, and the "Preface" was discarded. The narrator claims, when describing Don José's unhappy death in Canto 1, that he "knew him very well" (1.35.274). The word of the narrator implies the actuality of José's character, or the fictionality of José implies the narrator's fictionality. In either case, we know from early in the poem that the narrator is playing games and that the player of these games is Byron, who is in the anomalous situation of being the well-known author of an anonymous poem. He is the real figure behind the fictionalized narrator and often shares biographical details, such as his swim of the Hellespont (2.105.838–40). The poem thus shifts between a fictional narrator and the historical Byron, neither of whom is stable. (That is, having located Byron as a narrative voice, one has not pinned down the narrator's shifting nature.) A result of his paradoxical position as the well-known anonymous writer was his suppression of the "Dedication" against Southey because "I won't attack the dog in the dark."[65] Whether fictional or historical, the narrator presents himself as an experienced and cynical man-of-the-world in his thirties. Because of his pervasive double entendres and sexual innuendos (so pervasive that early reviewers could not find passages that they could decently quote), the narrator himself was regarded as a version of Don Juan: "an author with the reputation of a libertine writes a work about the infamous seducer Don Juan, indeed audaciously entitles that work, *Don Juan*, and composes it with a bravura display of 'smut,' insinuations, and obscenity," or so thought the early readers.[66] The title is doubly eponymous, identifying both the named hero and the unnamed narrator.

But the shifting narrator stands for other characters besides its author and its hero. He has appointed himself spokesman for a sophisticated readership that may or may not, at any given moment, include actual readers of the poem. That readership is invited to recognize and perhaps even translate the Latin phrases scattered throughout the poem, and it may identify the historical references and literary allusions with which the poem abounds. All actual readers are forced to recognize that other readers are more learned than they. But they share with the narrator the recognition that real life is quite different from the official illusions promulgated by moralists and politicians. The narrator thus becomes the spokesman for our unofficial selves, who know that the world is decidedly less stable than is usually (perhaps necessarily) assumed.

Some of the narrator's material, especially the shipwreck section of Canto 2 and the military description in the Ismail cantos, is not observed or imagined but derived from sources.[67] Byron expected readers to recognize at least some of these sources and to recollect the closeness of his raft scene to the alleged cannibalism on the raft of the Medusé (1816). In the "Preface to Cantos VI, VII, and VIII" he acknowledges his use of Castelnau. The material he narrates, though shocking, is verifiable. In presenting it, he literally represents his sources (though not uncritically in the case of Castelnau). More generally, the narrator seems prodigiously learned – citing a considerable range of analogues. He functions therefore not merely as a personal voice stating his own views and as a modern voice articulating opinions of a cadre in his audience but as the spokesman for a tradition of western knowledge. He is particularly concerned, at the beginning of Canto 7, to cite his many predecessors, in response to criticism of his "tendency to under-rate and scoff" (7.3.19). The shallowness of present ideas is revealed by the wisdom of the past. "Allusion," Peter J. Manning points out, "is only a special case of the way in which *Don Juan* continually unmasks the illusion of its own autonomy in order to reap the benefits of acknowledging all that lies outside it."[68] Byron's shifting narrator changes tone and discourse, moving from narrative to digression, but he shifts as well from fiction to figure to Byron himself, articulating the understandings shared with his audience, and tying such understandings to the sources, analogues, and authorities that support them.

The shifting of speakers is accompanied by an equally mysterious shifting of genres. The narrator announces, with some persistence, that his poem is epic, though its hero is not a civic example, its narrator's chatty voice is not Homeric, and its treatment of war is inglorious. The epic proclamations and analogies establish the mock-heroic and satiric nature of the poem. The poem seems satiric in several respects. Large sections are specifically satiric, attacking historical particulars with a vengeance – the political treatment of Castlereagh and Wellington, the literary demolition of Southey and Wordsworth, the war cantos. In other sections the satire is mixed or intermittent, modal rather than generic – as in the first canto and the English cantos. But one would expect that long satiric works would move between generic and modal satire and between satire and other genres. There are sections such as the shipwreck scene of Canto 2 that seem to defy generic classification. There are lyric passages both of natural description and of personal expression. But the lyricism of description (as in the case of Haidée's love) is undercut by the narrator's cynical comments on male–female relations, and indulgent personal expressions, such as the "no more" stanzas of Canto 1 (lines 214–16) dwindle from an unsustainable lyricism. Rather than expressing the heart's deepest feelings, lyricism is clearly labeled as performance, cynicism as sincerity. The mixture of lyricism with irony either of context or of language is a major generic dislocation in the poem.

Michael Cooke sees generic instability as one of the poem's unsettling effects, but the instability is not merely intellectual or even structural.[69] *Don Juan* develops an emotional irony in which the reader is invited, indeed forced, to feel a powerful sense of sympathy (with the text of Julia's letter, for example) or repulsion (at the cannibalism of Canto 2), which is then shifted by context or by the narrator's commentary or by the intrusion of inappropriate language. The reader, like Juan, is drawn to the enjoyment of the moment. We share, in effect, in the libertine's pleasure. But, like the libertine, we lose that moment in the movement of time. Like the hero and the narrator, the reader seems at times to be designated by the title of the poem. If the generic unpredictability of the poem implies the uncertainty of the world and our inability to know what we think about it, the emotional irony of the poem implies that we cannot know what to feel about it. Our feelings, however powerful, are not constant or permanent. Libertinism stands for the instability of all human feeling.

The generic uncertainty of the poem as a whole contrasts sharply with the rigidity of its stanzaic form. If the poem has achieved a kind of liberty by not binding itself to a defining and determining genre, it has paradoxically bound itself to an inflexible and limiting stanza. The lyrical possibilities of the opening quatrain are overextended to accommodate yet a third set of rhyme-words, and the pattern of alternative rhymes is rudely cut off by the concluding couplet. The poet struggles against line, stanza, and rhyme by enjambing, by running his sentences past the ends of stanzas, by preposterous rhyming. The narrator's fight for liberty or libertinism in a false and restrictive society is acted out by his effort to adopt his stanzaic form to a variety of feelings, ideas, and materials. But the rigidity of the form emphasizes the comic and even heroic efforts to escape it or transcend it. The Don Juan stanza defines the shifting nature of the poem.

In some dramatic versions of the Don Juan legend, the licentious character of the hero is paralleled by his movement from place to place, and Byron's largely unstructured poem is defined by spatial movement, beginning in Seville and moving to Cadiz, from which Atlantic port the vagaries of wind and wave take first the ship and then the raft to an Aegean Island. After the return of Lambro ends Juan's tryst with Haidée, the poem moves via slave ship to Constantinople. After Canto 6 there is a break, and the poem travels, without Juan, to Ismail, where he joins it in stanza 56 of Canto 7. Once Ismail is taken, Juan goes on to Russia, from where he is sent to England. There the poem visits London and, finally, Norman Abbey, the country house where it inconclusively ends. Byron exploits the exotic possibilities of his places. (Regency London seems exotic to a modern reader, but Byron's description would have been nostalgic to a reader of the 1820s.) These geographical shifts are arbitrary – sometimes unexplained and sometimes impossible (with the kind of impossibility one finds in the voyages of Odysseus, on which the movement of the poem is based). But the arbitrary nature of these shifts underscores their function as markers between separate plots, and it reveals that the poem has no *telos* or destination towards which it moves. That the poem was published as written, in units of several cantos, makes its random nature clearer. As the poem moves from west to east, Juan becomes more feminized, until he moves west again to England. From the outset he seems a passive partner, but his aggression towards the intrusive elderly husband (Alphonso in Canto 1) and the rival father (Lambro in Canto 4) proves his undoing in the Julia and Haidée plots. The sex roles shift literally in the harem plot, where Juan plays the virtuous woman to the libertine of Gulbeyaz. In Russia, Catherine, the female monarch, becomes sexual master, Juan the mistress.

The shifting of plots and sexual roles suggests the double image of the libertine. On one hand, libertinism is the illicit manifestation of masculine power that seeks to be universally attractive and to dominate women universally. For the libertine the world is the object of sexual desire and creativity, and this desire overrides the values by which sexual aggression should be controlled. For the aggressive libertine, power rather than sensuality seems the moving force, and he is akin to the military hero whom Byron rejects at the outset. On the other hand, the libertine is not aggressive but passive. Women, despite their claims to virtue, may be sexual aggressors, as are Julia, Haidée, Gulbeyaz, Catherine, and Fitz-Fulke. Men are dominated by sexual passion, so that the passive libertine becomes prey not only to female aggressors but to his sexuality. If Juan is a libertine, his passivity makes him one.

The image of the libertine seems a metonym for a broader human desire, for the regret that one is only an individual, for the wish to attain universal human experience. The libertine's desire to know every woman is akin to the desire to know everything, to exist as other people, to perceive the world from every vantage-point. The shifting of the speaker has its analogue in the shifting of the libertine hero who represents, without actually possessing, the desire to know all that can be known, despite the obstacles to that knowledge. The poem's rejection of a military hero and its adoption of a libertine instead marks, on one hand, its rejection of conventional values of patriotism and sexual morality and, on the other, its movement from the destruction represented by warfare to the creativity represented by libertinism. The problem of military heroes, as defined by the first two stanzas, is precisely the theme before us: heroes shift with each issue of the *Gazette*. The establishment of Juan as the poem's hero replaces mere change with transformation. Instead of the stable title of hero, as occupied by a weekly succession of individuals, the poem's hero is a single individual defined by shifts that have political as well as amorous implications.

Juan is one of several arguable heroes to participate in the siege of Ismail. His heroism seems a combination of sheer persistence with good luck, making him a naive hero, in contrast to the experienced or prudent heroism of Johnson. The ambiguous heroism of Suwarrow seems similarly based on persistence and calculation, in contrast to the desperate heroism of the old Khan, who dies with his sons, fighting in a cause already lost. Juan's heroism results in the rescue of Leila; his humanly significant act is politically insignificant. Although individuals may display personal heroism, Byron has no sympathy for the battle of imperial Russians and despotic Turks. War manifests the political subordination of human and individual aspirations to the abstractly defined interests of the state. But Byron does see battle against the tyrannical state as legitimate and appropriate – hence his celebration of Leonidas and Washington, "Whose every battle-field is holy ground, / Which breathes of nations saved, not worlds undone" (8.5.35–36). Such positive heroes contrast to Wellington and Castlereagh, who reign destruction to preserve the existing and unjust order.

For Malcom Kelsall, Byron's outbursts of radical politics and his skepticism "both come from being of 'no party' – using 'party' in its widest sense – and of belonging to a patrician caste which, traditionally antagonistic to the Crown, has lost its historic function of speaking on behalf of the people."[70] Andrew Rutherford sees Byron's political views as those of a Regency aristocrat, but for Michael Robertson they are those of an aristocratic Whig.[71] There is a high degree of reality, however, in Byron's political commitments. He lost his life as a result of his commitment to Greek independence, and, before writing the Ismail stanzas, was discouraged by the failures of the Italian independence movement with which he was associated.[72] The Ismail stanzas grow out of such political commitments. But on another level, the search to create Byron's specific politics from the text of *Don Juan* seems frustrated by the shifting nature both of his narrator and of politics itself. Byron feels that there is a kind of political shift – exemplified by Southey and Wordsworth – that represents the betrayal of principle by self-interest. But his own political inconsistencies manifest another problem of a stable position in contrast to the shifting position he takes in *Don Juan*.

An individual's broad political values are likely to be more idealistic and sweeping than political responses to specific situations. The political individual incessantly seeks to reconcile ideals with unsatisfactory practical alternatives, and sometimes the alternative paradoxically chosen is to withdraw from politics altogether. But even that alternative seems a temporary expedient, since it is no more satisfactory than the politics it rejects. In the siege of Ismail neither of the alternatives – the Russians or the Turks – is acceptable. There is, however, a further alternative. In the middle of the siege, Byron reflects on the growing strength of the common people (the mob).

> At first it grumbles, then it swears, and then,
> Like David, flings smooth pebbles 'gainst a giant;
> At last it takes to weapons such as men
> Snatch when despair makes human hearts less pliant.
> Then comes "the tug of war"; – 'twill come again,
> I rather doubt, and I would fain say "fie on't,"
> If I had not perceived that Revolution
> Alone can save the Earth from Hell's pollution. (8.51.401–08)

At this moment Byron's poem sounds like Shelley's *The Masque of Anarchy* ("Ye are many – they are few"), although Byron may not have shared Shelley's faith in a natural power that resists tyranny. Byron may have been a reluctant supporter of revolution, but he saw it as a likely consequence of present policies, defining a politics of the future. Specific politics responds to the harsh realities of the moment; political idealism can only be a commitment to the future. That political commitment constitutes the most positive implication of Byron's depiction of a world of instability and flux. This incessant shifting does not imply an inherently evil world (bad as that world may be) but rejects inherence itself. For Byron, flux implies the possibility of change. The Congress of Vienna will not stand in its effort to draw the map of Europe, once and for all, along the boundaries of outmoded dynasties. The effort to achieve political order by imposing national boundaries is, for Byron, another instance of false pretension. Despite the political rigidities of the present, the death of tyranny is a revolution for the future. In their openness to that future, Byron's uncertain politics and his unstable poem are positive and hopeful.

The crucial openness of the poem requires that it remain unfinished. Despite Byron's occasional suggestions of a final ending in which Juan is executed by the French Revolution – an ending that accords, as Jerome McGann has argued, with the time scheme of the later cantos – Byron himself never supplied even tentative endings when he thought he might abandon the poem. Despite the importance of openness and Byron's apparent efforts to assure it by leaving disjunctions between his structural units and the progress of the action, critics sometimes insist on writing endings. The favorite of such endings links Juan with Aurora Raby. She reflects, for Bernard Beatty, a religious mysticism that resolves the doubt and satire of the poem.[73] Caroline Franklin sees in her a feminism that has achieved financial, intellectual, and personal autonomy.[74] An open ending allows readers to complete the poem in terms of their own values. (One might imagine an ending in which Juan has an adulterous affair with Adeline Amundeville but breaks it off, leaving her, like Caroline Lamb, to write a grotesque and romantic novel. He might then marry the spiritual Aurora Raby, who, like Lady Byron, hearing of his scandalous early life and witnessing his erratic personality, insists on a separation. He would then, uniting Byron with Marcel Proust, go off to Italy to make the whole affair the subject of a long and digressive poem.)

Virtually any attempt to assign a final meaning to Byron's tentative and shifting poem is akin to creating the ending. It seems more fruitful to consider the significance of its intellectual and structural openness. The beginning of Canto 9 attacks the Duke of Wellington for what he has done and left undone: "Behold the World! and curse your victories!" (9.9.72). The attack leads Byron melodramatically to the mockery of death – the negative instance of change:

> Death laughs – Go ponder o'er the skeleton
>   With which men image out the unknown thing
> That hides the past world, like to a set sun
>   Which still elsewhere may rouse a brighter spring.
>   (9.11.81–84)

The question of life or death leads Byron to the prior question of the nature of being, and that question returns him to doubt and uncertainty:

> "Que sçais-je?" was the motto of Montaigne,
>   As also of the first Academicians:
> That all is dubious which Man may attain,
>   Was one of their most favourite positions.
> There's no such thing as certainty, that's plain
>   As any of Mortality's Conditions:
> So little do we know what we're about in
> This world, I doubt if doubt itself be doubting.
>   (9.17.129–36)

Byron's double dubiety here recalls his earlier defense of himself against the charge that he has "A tendency to under-rate and scoff / At human power and virtue, and all that" (7.3.19–20), a charge he answers by citing some dozen predecessors who "knew this life was not worth a potato" (7.4.28). (One suspects that "potato" was the vegetable chosen because it rhymes with Plato. Nonetheless, in some contexts potatoes are worth a great deal, and the statement that life is not worth one may rank with "truth lies at the bottom of a well," or "erst kommt das Fressen, dann kommt die Moral.") The idea is not that life is meaningless, but that we cannot know what its meaning is, or that, if we could, we would know it is not single and reductive but multiform – not incomprehensible in its vacuity but not comprehensible in its variety.[75] To know the meaning of life would be to close an intellectual journey whose interest lies in its lack of closure. In place of meaning Byron insists on maintaining a skeptical stance that is unwilling to accept artificial and conventional pretenses to meaning. He holds to ridicule the pursuit of power – sexual or political – that is based on what Engels would later call "false consciousness." Not all of Byron's characters are fully satiric targets, and the critique of ideologies represents no more a closure or complete description than other interpretive possibilities, but Byron's poem is strewn with the variously mangled satiric corpses of relatively benign victims of self-deception and of absolutely malignant perpetrators of false power. His critique of ideology as it pervades the power relations among individuals emerges as his satire of cant, whose duplicitous language is revealed by the mirror of irony.[76]

Byron is, I have suggested, Horatian,[77] but in most senses he seems quite unHoratian. He has a stronger narrative line, a more complex sense of character, a more pervasive irony, a more developed philosophical approach. Horace announces (sometimes misleadingly) a subject from which he wanders, to which he often returns, and which he sometimes transforms. The limited length of the Roman poetic diatribe defines the direction and extent of his wandering. For Byron particular topics emerge from the narrative or are significantly detached from it. In either case they reflect what he has on his mind. Frequently they represent the need to fill a stanza; Byron's imperative is to keep on writing. The view that Byron is Horatian is anachronistic, but there are two senses in which the comparison to Horace points to significant common aspects. The first is the comic, perceptive, sardonic, often self-deprecating, urbane, subtle, and sophisticated voice, speaking from experience and articulating a tradition of trenchant observation.[78] Secondly, the satiric voice in both poets shifts in tone, topic, and values from section to section and line to line, avoiding universal statements as a matter of principle, and condemning whoever, Stoic or Tory, uses universals as a source of unworthy power. The shifting satirist manifests the uncertainty that is a hallmark of the satiric frame of mind.

The uncertainty of the satirist requires not only his liberation from a fixed philosophical position but his liberation from a determining personal character. Real-life satirists may have such a character, but in functioning as satirists, they must adjust to the satiric situation revealed by their texts – they need, in short, to become performers, able to insult, exaggerate, and offend. As performers they are not protected from real consequences, as the beating of Dryden and the libeling of Pope indicate. But they undertake hypothetical roles and enter hypothetical situations. They address real conditions and distort actual events to reveal hidden meanings. Satiric texts identify performers who serve as guides – often ironic ones – for the reader. Such performers overlap with the author: Horace cannot deny that he is the friend and dependent who interrupts Maecenas and is grateful for his gift of a country estate; Swift admits that he is both the imagined corpse and the imaginer of its mourners; the multiple presences of Byron in *Don Juan* have just been explored. To describe these real presences as critical constructs seems an unneeded exercise in abstraction; to identify them with the biographies of their authors seems naive.

Satiric performance pervades the structure of satiric poems. Vertically the performances may shift between different kinds of presence, as the diatribist of Horace's *Satires* 1.3 and the narrator of *Don Juan* have revealed. Or the nature of the performance may reveal multiple levels of ironic play and significance, as in the case of *Verses on the Death of Dr. Swift*. Maneuvering these changes in direction may require some agility on the part of readers. The cumulative effect of such shifting may be to dislocate the reader, who may feel (as some readers of Horace feel) that the poem has lost coherence or that the reader has lost contact with a speaker who has fragmented into inconsistency. Whether such dislocation represents the absence of clear values outside the poem or merely indicates the difficulty of realizing those values in action or interpretation depends on the cultural assumptions which the satirist shares with readers. Shifting satiric performances allow meaning and openness to exist simultaneously.

CHAPTER 6

Satire and the novel

OVERLAPPING GENRES

In Horatian performances we recognize the presence of a satirist whose judgments on an unworthy world are implied by destabilizing but nonetheless entertaining performances. The performative nature of satiric drama produces, in turn, a performance by its characters that reveals the evil or silliness of society. Satire uses, even duplicates, the generic characteristics of poetry and drama to mount a critical attack. The same seems roughly true of the novel, but the situation here is complicated by the generic closeness of the forms. Elements that define the novel – its formal self-consciousness, its implicit criticism of its predecessors, its proclamations of originality (novelty), its incorporation or reflection of broad cultures, its consequent inclusion of various dialects and ideolects, its uncertain or ambiguous relationship both to its author and to its dominant ideology – are characteristics of satire as well. Satire and the novel are massively overlapping genres.

Satire, as everyone agrees, is a parasitic form, imitating other forms by way of parody or using such imitation as a way of fixing points of reference and judgment, but imitation is another characteristic that satire shares with the novel. Novels, Barbara Herrnstein Smith asserts, imitate other forms of written discourse – histories, biographies, memoirs, letters;[1] at a second level of imitation, they may imitate other novels as well. What makes the fit between novel and satire uncomfortable is that each tends to exploit other genres by transforming or undermining them. Bakhtin speaks of *Evgenij Onegin* as a novelized poem, indeed, as an example of how the novel operates.[2] Satire's need to distort its material in order to command attention resembles the alienation that Shklovsky found typical of the novel, and satire's defensiveness about the legitimacy of its attack and of its incursions on other genres makes it virtually as self-conscious as the novel.

Although novelistic characters are imaginary, the novel gives them importance as subjects in themselves; although satiric characters are actual, satire treats them as examples of broader problems. Satire and the novel have very different centers. Focus upon individual characters and individual consciousness sits uneasily with the satiric incitement to social judgment; personal sympathy for central characters is distinct from reflective judgment on a whole culture. These differences lead in differences in the instruments by which each produces its defining images. Stendhal, in a famous passage from *Le rouge et noir*, describes the novel as

un miroir qui se promène sur une grande route. Tantôt il réflète à vos yeux l'azur des cieux, tantôt la fange des bourbiers de la route. Et l'homme qui porte le miroir dans sa hotte sera par vous accusé d'être immoral! [a mirror carried on a great road. Sometimes it reflects to your eyes the azure of the sky, sometimes the mess of the quagmire. And you accuse the man who carries the mirror in his basket of being immoral.][3]

Novelists, according to Stendhal, record "les fanges des bourbiers" without being responsible for what they record – or even for the fact that they record it, since it merely appears in the mirrors they carry. In contrast to the mirror by which the realistic but fictitious images of the novel are presented to the reader, satire, as in Books I and II of *Gulliver's Travels*, looks through distorting lenses that reduce or magnify actualities, making human activity trivial and the human body grotesque. The actuality of satire and the imagination of the novel play against the exaggeration of the one and the realism of the other.

Novels are primarily concerned with individual consciousness, particularly the divided consciousness of characters in conflict. Characters are in conflict with other characters (so that differences of perception, interpretation, and communication are common features of plot), and individual characters have to work out conflicts within their own personalities. Clarissa is in conflict with Lovelace, but the uncertainties of that conflict are echoed by her inner uncertainties as well as his. Both characters are in conflict with larger social elements, most immediately their families. While novels such as *Clarissa* or *The Princess Casamassima* may attack society bitterly because of the harm it causes the aware and sensitive individual, this element of satiric attack is secondary to and contingent upon the intense depiction of consciousness. Consciousness in satire becomes instrumental to a broader attack. Thus the central consciousness of *A Tale of a Tub* ironically embodies the incoherent opportunism of modern writing and the fragmented culture it represents. But it further implies that coherent consciousness may itself be a myth, that the inconsistencies of the author are those of anyone who thinks within the constructs of that culture, and that the perhaps futile efforts of readers to interpret such a text reveal that they share that problem. The text of *Tale* creates the author in a sense that it does not create Swift, and the text is created by the expectations of a "modern" audience. Such satire uses fantastic structures to represent society and cultures and cannot be read in the same way as conventional novels. The consciousness of satiric characters may shift, but their shifts usually serve the satirist's need for multiple or different perspectives. Conventional novels operate by the rule that characters seem connected to themselves as they reappear in the text; satire need not be bound by that generic principle. When novels become satires, they usually do so because the centrality of consciousness dissipates, because sympathy wanes in the face of the games played between the author and the reader, or because the concern for social issues dwarfs the significance of individual dilemmas. When personal consciousness and the sympathy of readers are replaced by social awareness and by a mixture of analysis and anger, it becomes difficult to continue reading the work within the broad conventions of the novel. Novels are about time and therefore about a nexus of functions – sequences, coincidences, causes, motives, actions, and consequences – deriving from time. These functions are not absent from satire (as in Michael Seidel's argument that satire is about inheritance), but satire's concern with them is more analytic than narrative, more synchronic than diachronic.[4] Because of its actuality, satire despite its invocation of past and perhaps lost values, concentrates on the present of the satirist or the future of the audience, and seeks to produce a change in behavior or attitude. But here, as in other areas where satire and the novel overlap, narration and analysis are not exclusive, and individual works give them a particular balance.

The areas of overlapping and differentiation between satire and the novel inevitably raise the relationship between genre and mode. When prose fictions are perceived as satire, are they satiric novels or novelistic satires? If *Gulliver's Travels* is a fictional satire but *Handful of Dust* a satiric novel, is that difference determined by clear and even absolute criteria, or do readers see them as one or the other genre because they seem to resemble other works that are clearly labeled as satires or novels? Are works that straddle the genres placed in one category or the other by readers anxious to emphasize a particular interpretation, or does satire shift between generic and modal functions within a relatively lengthy novel? Despite areas of overlap and blurred lines of demarcation, the relationship of the satire to the novel can be mapped at least tentatively in terms of apparently contradictory assertions.

(1.) Novels and satires, one might say, are contrasting, inimical, or even exclusive forms. Novels, this contrastive argument would assert, are about individuals, satires about societies; novels narrate historical change, satires analyze the present; novels presuppose a unified consciousness, satires present shifting perspectives; novels are imaginative, satires are actual; novels are realistic, satires are distorted; novels entice sympathy, satires enforce judgment; novels are bourgeois, satires are aristocratic. Novels trace the impact of social problems on individuals; satires see individuals as representing social evils or contributing to social disorder.

(2.) But the same argument can be turned on its head to see novels as inherently satiric. The individual is set in an antagonistic relation to the surrounding society, and this antagonism defines the archetypal plot of fiction: the individual comes to terms with the social context and the novel ends in marriage, or the individual is destroyed by the social context and the novel ends in death. Novels are often about the education of satirists (Roderick Random, Julien Sorel, Stephen Dedalus) whose insights partially constitute the message of the novel. Or the problems encountered by the central character can be generalized in a way that makes the historical context problematic as well.

These assertions that satire and the novel are inconsistent and that novels are inherently satire are, of course, wildly overstated, though they make important points about both genres. Their overstatements push towards contradictions, but for actual readers the distinctions between satire and novel primarily serve to highlight significant elements of the text. What the assertions share are alternative readings of the relationship between individual consciousness and the surrounding context. Satire and the novel share this concern for the self and the others, for locating the self in relation to its social context, and for defining the nature of that context and the limitations it imposes on the possibilities of individual action. This central element becomes a fruitful subject in two notable satiric novels (or novelistic satires): Tobias Smollett's *Roderick Random* and Gustave Flaubert's *Bouvard et Pécuchet*.

Two other assertions about the relationship between satire and the novel are possible, and each deserves full development. (3.) While the second assertion proclaims that all novels are satires, the third, more modestly, states that some satires are novels – that there is a tradition of fiction, predating the emergence of the modern novel and extending to the present, that can be defined in terms of satire. This tradition is usually thought of as Menippean satire, but that phrase needs adjustment. The tradition can be exemplified by an important transitional nineteenth-century work, *Memórias Pósthumas de Brás Cubas* by Joaquim Maria Machado de Assis, a work that self-consciously recollects the novels of Sterne but also anticipates twentieth-century novels. (4.) The transitional position of *Memórias Pósthumas de Brás Cubas* suggests a historical reading of the relationship between satire and the novel. Rather than seeing them as contrasting or overlapping forms, one can look at them as paired forms that rotate around each other and present one or the other half to the observer, depending on the force of complex historical circumstances. Seen in this way, the novel seems to move to a forward position in the mid-eighteenth century, while satire becomes dominant in the later years of the twentieth. The third assertion implies that there have always been satires that take the form of fiction; the fourth implies a changing relationship between satire and the novel, whose relative positions shift in response to changing literary, social, and ideological circumstances. The first two assertions – that satire and the novel are exclusive forms and that novels are a kind of satire – yield a single topic for further discussion: satire and the individual consciousness. The second two – that satire established a Menippean form that became a distinct kind of novel, and that satire and the novel interchange their dominance at different historical periods – require distinct development.

SATIRE AND THE INDIVIDUAL CONSCIOUSNESS

A *locus classicus* for the overlapping of novels and satire is Smollett's *Roderick Random*.[5] Smollett himself presented his novel as a kind of satire:

> Of all kinds of satire, there is none so entertaining, and universally improving, as that which is introduced, as it were, occasionally, in the course of an interesting story, which brings every incident home to life; and by representing familiar scenes in an uncommon and amusing point of view, invests them with all the graces of novelty, while nature is appealed to in every particular.[6]

For Smollett the advantage of the novel as a form of satire lies in realism's capacity to become "universally improving" by combining the familiar and natural with the "uncommon and amusing." But such novelty is distinctly different from the imaginative workings of older fiction. Satiric realism rejects the fantasies of romance; satiric fictions seek to achieve a point of view that fictionalizes historical particulars to subject them to attack or new evaluation. Smollett announces his satiric theme as "modest merit struggling with every difficulty to which a friendless orphan is exposed" (xxxv), and he justifies the novel's descent into ordinary life on the grounds that the "humours and passions" of human nature can be seen there without the distortions imposed by the affectations of social position (xxxv).

For Paul-Gabriel Boucé "revenge" is a key word, not only for the first half of *Roderick Random* but for the whole novel and Smollett's other novels, except *Humphry Clinker*.[7] *Roderick Random* is identified by the sharp effectiveness of its anger. At the outset Roderick is cast out by his tyrannical grandfather, rejected by his relatives, and ill-treated by his schoolmaster; as a consequence he becomes the leader of a juvenile gang that seeks revenge on his family and, more generally, on adults. This revenge is reinforced by his uncle, Lieutenant Bowling, who joins Roderick, even leads him, in his pranks. When Roderick leaves to seek his fortune, the novel's thin plot seems less significant than the satiric incidents in which Roderick – at times naive and at times clever, at times satiric victim and at times manipulative satirist – struggles with a hostile, abusive world. After his expulsion from the family, he literally becomes a satirist, only to suffer the satirist's fate of fear and rejection. The strongest condemnation of Roderick's character is that he is "not a human personality but . . . an excuse, a simple formal strategem that permits the stringing together of certain episodes."[8]

Roderick Random is driven by conflicting impulses. At its beginning and end it follows a romantic formula. The orphan is rejected by his family, survives against impossible odds, and finally triumphs over those who rejected him; the lover overcomes severe obstacles to claim his somewhat pallid beloved at the end. But this conventional plot is set against the lack of direction that runs through most of the novel. Roderick is victim of a thousand fates; his feeble efforts at control may be temporarily successful but seem inevitably to end in failure until his final triumph (apparently as arbitrary as his defeats). He is blown by winds of self-interested power against which he cannot gain control, whatever his merits and efforts. This repeated pattern allows him to function as the agent of an angry satire against the absurdities that victimize him and, as he is careful to show, defeat others as deserving. The effect of these plots is to show "the rampant disorder of life, wrought into order by a benevolent authorial interposition," but with such energy that it "verges on a vision of existential absurdity."[9]

The early scene where Roderick organizes his schoolmates to humiliate their brutal master becomes a paradigm for the novel itself, but *Roderick Random* has other satiric characteristics than anger and attack. In sections, especially the story of Melopoyn (chs. LXII and LXIII), where Smollett mocks the theatrical managers who neglected his tragedy *The Regicide*, it becomes a *roman-à-clef*. The range of Roderick's adventures gives the novel broad social scope. Paulson asserts that the range derives from Roderick's love of adventure rather than his concern for survival.[10] But although he may be interested in adventure, he is also interested in paying back those who have done him wrong. More important, he wants to gain that position in society, the position of a gentleman, which he feels is his due by birth, education, and character. Until the end, his efforts, becoming more desperate and less legitimate, seem to take him further from that role. As he moves through the novel, diverse characters provide a cacophony of dialects and voices. Roderick is an attacking figure not only through language but through physical violence, which reproduces the satiric energy of the novel's style (so that satire's emblem seems the overturned chamber pot). The plot of the novel is the education of the satirist, on which has been imposed a romantic fantasy of the lost estate. At times Roderick seems less a satirist than an outraged victim. What he needs to become a satirist is to remove himself from the elemental struggle for survival, to achieve through the inheritance–marriage plot the independence that makes retrospective satire possible.

Paul-Gabriel Boucé argues that Smollett's "moral intentions" give the novel a unity that its plot does not; by fits and starts Roderick grows until he is "at last able to dominate the impulsiveness of his passions."[11] Critics such as Jerry Beasley and James T. Bunn, on the other hand, have seen *Roderick Random* as a celebration of essential randomness, and to this randomness is added the dominance of individual scenes over a linear plot, so that the novel seems a collage of discrete moments.[12] Beasley describes the novel as a series of social tableaux where it is more important to see the satiric patterns by which incidents operate than to see the connections among them (though Beasley does suggest broad causal connections). This pattern of analysis accounts for satiric techniques in the novel, but it does not propose a final target much more specific than the evils of human nature. The accumulation of scenes needs to be seen in the context of the novel's linear energies in order for an appropriate target to emerge.

The most apparent energy is that of style, especially style as a vehicle for the ludicrous and comic. Early in his London adventures (ch. XIII), Roderick and his sidekick Strap literally tumble into a cook's shop located in a cellar. The food is, to say the least, uninviting.

While I stood in amaze, undetermined whether to sit down or walk upwards again, Strap, in his descent missing one of the steps, tumbled headlong into this infernal ordinary, and overturned the cook as she was carrying the porringer of soup to one of the guests: In her fall, she dashed the whole mess against the legs of a drummer belonging to the foot guards, who happened to be in her way, and scalded him so miserably that he started up, and danced up and down, uttering a volley of execrations that made my hair stand on end. While he entertained the company in this manner, with an eloquence peculiar to himself, the cook got up, and after a hearty curse on the poor author of this mischance, who lay under the table scratching his rump with a woful countenance, emptied a salt-seller in her hand, and stripping down the patient's stocking which brought the skin along with it, applied the contents to the sore. – This poultice was scarce laid on, when the drummer, who had begun to abate of his exclamation, broke forth into such a hideous yell, as made the whole company tremble; then, seizing a pewter pint-pot that stood by him, squeezed the sides of it together, as if it had been made of pliant leather, grinding his teeth at the same time with a most horrible grin. Guessing the cause of this violent transport, I bid the woman wash off the salt, and bathe the part with oil, which she did, and procured him immediate ease. But here another difficulty occurred, which was no other than the landlady's insisting on his paying for the pot he had rendered useless; he swore he would pay for nothing but what he had eat, and bid her be thankful for his moderation, or else he would prosecute her for damages. – Strap, foreseeing it would all land at him, promised to satisfy the cook, and called for a dram of gin to treat the drummer with, which entirely appeased him, and composed all animosities. (65–66)

There is a rapid sequence of emblematic images in the comic confusion. The cook-shop is infernal; Strap's fall, though accidental, is typical of the falling action of the novel. It precipitates a series of causes and effects, until Roderick's intervention ends the pain of the drummer. The satire is heightened by the specificity of its detail. The soup lands not merely on a bystander but a "drummer belonging to the foot guards." The sentences gain force by a strong series of verbs and verbals which throw the motion of the scene forward. Once the pain has ended, the confusion has not, for it becomes a dispute over economic arrangements – the cook insisting on payment for the tankard, the drummer insisting on paying only for his actual food. The question of who should pay and for what becomes the satiric question of who is responsible. In a scene marked by so much verbal action, it appears that no one is really responsible, and Strap, who is no guiltier than any of the others, finally accepts responsibility. The demand for payment raises the absurd question of who is guilty in what is, after all, a series of accidents, and the causal absurdity seems to support a reading of the novel as a precursor of chaos theory. But the actions of the characters reveal their moral condition: we know that Strap is careless, the cook slovenly, and the soldier violent. Those predispositions are brought to catastrophic action by the disorder and crowding of the place, the poverty of the people who eat there, and the crass economic motives by which the eatery is operated.

The style of the scene – its succession of verbs and of details – keeps pushing us forward, and we know that the novel itself is constructed in the same rushing manner. The present incident is one of the first on Roderick's arrival in London, where his intention (frustrated, of course) is to make connections and gain a livelihood. The frustrations of his efforts to do so by fair means or, when fair means have failed, by foul, have the same qualities as the incident at the ordinary. Roderick is betrayed and stymied by characters who are stupid, self-centered, mean, and even evil, and the question is how they have the power to menace him as they do. The answer lies in the energies that structure society itself. As most critics have pointed out, *Roderick Random* is a particularly urban novel, and because London is the nexus of economic activity, outlanders of all sorts (Roderick, for example) come in search of opportunity, creating enormous competition. The system by which positions are gained in the competitive market operates through implicitly conflicting structures of an active bourgeoisie, where connections are based on money, and a residual aristocracy, where connections are based on association or patronage. Roderick offers merit and willingness, but both systems are based on artificialities, and it is in their interest not to advance him. Since money and association produce power, those with power are able to conceal their weaknesses, which the satiric force of the novel reveals. Roderick learns them from a series of outsiders who, poor or ignored, are unable to crack the system but know how it works. What is true of Roderick's efforts in the first half of the novel to gain security by working is, in the second half, true of his efforts to gain position through marriage, since the marriage market operates on the same principles as others.

The problem is that the individual cannot thrive when pitted against the system. But Roderick, who has maintained himself by a self-interest not unlike those of his oppressors, learns how to compromise effectively. He reaches his nadir in prison, where he is told the story of the poet Melopoyn's failure to have his play produced, despite repeated promises. The themes of Melopoyn's story, as Boucé has noted, parallel those of Roderick's. It demonstrates money and patronage operating through a social structure (in this case literary and theatrical). When Roderick's debts are paid by his nautical uncle, the two take to sea and ship slaves to the West Indies, where Roderick discovers his long-lost father, who has himself become rich. Roderick goes back to England and marries his beloved Narcissa, whose brother disinherits her – a futile gesture, since Roderick, with his father's backing, is now wealthy. They return to Scotland, where the heir to the family estate has ruined it, so that Roderick's father can easily buy it. The hero, somewhat uncomfortably, does not defeat the system of money and patronage that has frustrated him throughout the novel. Instead, he is fortuitously able to manipulate it successfully. The depressing nature of the satire seems confirmed rather than mitigated by the novel's happy ending. In the meantime, the novel itself has learned the lesson of the chaotic cook-shop and the problem of paying for the tankard. Many people are evil, some dangerously so, but the responsibility for chaos is distributed complexly throughout a society that is structured on the basis of self-interest. The task of uncovering the multiple sources of evil is therefore a complex one that the combination of satire and the novel is particularly effective in carrying out.

Roderick Random exemplifies the status of both the novel and satire as battles, pitting the major character against the encroachments of other people and of social institutions, and the force of its attack is largely located in the angry consciousness of the protagonist The typical subject of novels is the conflict between the consciousness of the central character and the impeding forces of society and culture, and that conflict defines the satiric perspective by which the beleaguered satiric hero strikes out against forces that threaten to make life unlivable. This battle generates the novel's satiric topics, and one criterion for distinguishing the novelistic satire from the satiric novel may be its prominence. But a text may move between satire and the novel, as characters become more complex or as the emergent topics yield to more compelling ideas. The process of shifting is particularly apparent in Flaubert's *Bouvard et Pécuchet*, where the characters begin as Daumier-like figures in a satire but become, in the course of their intellectual quest, more complicated and sympathetic, finally shifting, as the novel returns to satire, to their proper *métier* as satirists themselves. Harry Levin, in his notable essay on "Flaubert: Spleen and Ideal," quotes Flaubert's statement to George Sand's son Georges that "it is indignation alone that sustains me."[13] That anger sustains his text, but the text does not manifest it directly. More precisely, the text suggests anger but represents its contexts complexly. On the surface the target of Flaubert's satire is intellectual, but to separate thought from thinkers would be the kind of intellectual vacuity Flaubert abhorred. The core of the novel lies in the interaction among the ideas, the methods by which they are interpreted and applied, and the personalities who use them.

Bouvard et Pécuchet is commonly compared to encyclopedias. Like en-cyclopedias it reduces knowledge to comprehensive but fragmented fact.[14] Bouvard and Pécuchet are relentless in trying to coax classified fact into authoritative generalities and useful advice. Such advice is important to them because they are, despite their retirement from Paris to Normandy, active individuals seeking knowledge to plant their farm, to raise fruit trees, to decorate their house, to collect curious materials, to strengthen and heal the body, to take part in political life, and to educate children. There is hardly an area of activity, they find, without its accompanying body of often-contradictory theory, and they leave hardly an area of activity untried, accepting as an act of faith that knowing precedes doing. Although knowledge may appear in fragmented form in encyclopedias or in the texts which the heroes consume so ravenously, the problem for Bouvard and Pécuchet is that it is not fragmentary at all. Clear lines cannot be drawn between self-contained areas of study. What they discover is that knowledge in one area is incomplete or indecipherable without knowledge in others.

Le dilemme n'est point commode; si l'on part des faits, le plus simple exige des raisons trop compliquées, et en posant d'abord les principes, on commence par l'Absolu, la Foi. [The dilemma is a troublesome one. If you start from facts, the simplest fact requires reasons which are far too complicated, and if you first lay down principles, you begin with the absolute, faith.][15]

Ultimately, it seems, in order to know anything Bouvard and Pécuchet need to know everything. In order to preserve food or to make "Bouvarine," the healthful drink that Bouvard invents, they need to learn chemistry. Their own failures may be the result of ignorance, as they are willing to admit, but intellectual disciplines, they discover, are limited by the narrow bounds that define them. Archeology cannot be comprehended without knowing history. History is confounded not by the intractability of fact but the lack of it, covering ignorance with vague speculations and unable to reveal the origins of action, which lie in the secret nature of the personality. Hence fiction, unconfined to fact but open to imagination, is superior, but novelists turn out to be thoughtlessly anachronistic or carelessly inaccurate. The heroes' quests to heal their ignorance by pursuing knowledge and to correct the limits of one discipline by engrafting another create much of the plot of the novel. Archeology leads to history (chapter 4), disagreements over history to the need for truth:

Pour la juger impartialement, il faudrait avoir lu toutes les histoires, tous les mémoires, tous les journaux et toutes les pièces manuscrites, car de la moindre omission une erreur peut dépendre qui en amènera d'autres à l'infini. Ils y renoncèrent.

Mais le goût de l'Histoire leur était venu, le besoin de la vérité pour elle-même. (p. 188)

[To judge impartially they would have to read all the histories, all the memoirs, all the journals, and all the manuscript documents, for the slightest omission may cause an error which will lead to others ad infinitum. They gave up.

But they had acquired a taste for history, a need for truth in itself.] (p. 121)

At the same time as their quest becomes more personal, especially in their search for sexual happiness and in their quasi-parental education of Victor and Victorine, their "taste" for truth releases them from practicality and frees them, if that is the word, for abstract investigations unchecked by the criterion of utility. Hence the limitations of history yield to the imaginative possibilities of fiction, fiction to drama, and drama to aesthetics (chapter 5). But history also supplies the issues engaged by revolutionary politics and conservative reaction (chapter 6). The sensibilities awakened by the study of literature, combined with their loneliness, contribute to the sexual misadventures of chapter 7, and Pécuchet's consequent sexual disease leads to their study of medicine (chapter 8). But just as the failures of history lead to its imaginative alternative in fiction, so the failures of medicine lead to their experiments in spirituality, The weakness of spirituality produces despair and near suicide, from which they are rescued by the study of religion. Events outside this cycle are quickly drawn within it. Local and national reactions to the revolution of 1848 are characterized by ineffective and inconsistent political acts and indicate the poverty of political theory. Everything from God to husbandry has its body of scholarship. These bodies are joined by their mutual networks of arteries and nerves, and they are connected by experience to the outside world which they pretend to illuminate.

Bouvard and Pécuchet are also unlike encyclopedias in their dubiety. Encyclopedias resolve uncertainties because their fragmentary, compartmentalized nature allows specialists to write authoritatively about particular fields. Bouvard and Pécuchet lack this authority and come to the conclusion that it is impossible. In area after area they perceive intellectual certitude not as authoritative but pretentious, often the elevation of hypothesis to the level of fact. They are unable to reconcile practical advice to experience, theory to practice, faith to reason. As they give up search after search and field after field, readers may ultimately see them as peculiarly superior to their sources. The result is a paradox: the quest for certitude becomes satisfied in uncertainty, for all that they can know is that much is unknowable.

Bouvard and Pécuchet lack the experience by which they can test their reading, and hence they cannot make common-sense evaluations. They raise the paradox that in order to learn anything one must know it already. They fail to understand that advisory statements are normative rather than universal, subject to variation and exception. Hence their reading is over-literal and their expectations too high. The novel dramatizes a double shift in the objects of satiric attack: it moves from the personal and intellectual failures of the anti-heroes to the fallibility of their sources, from their own vanities and ignorant pretensions of authority (pretensions drawn in part from the texts they have studied) to the selfishness and ignorance of the villagers, as in the heroes' debates with the curé and the doctor. This shift from the central characters to the villagers is firmly established by chapter 6, with its disgust at both the false equality of democracy and the arbitrary cruelty of autocracy. Throughout, the abuse of knowledge is intertwined with the abuse of power, as when the curé humiliates the poor schoolmaster by bullying him into teachings that offend his radical conscience (244–48; 161–64).

The novel reaches a climax in the recognition by Bouvard and Pécuchet that things are stupid – or, more precisely, in their capacity to recognize stupidity: "Alors une faculté pitoyable se developpa dans leur esprit, celle de voir la bêtise et de ne plus la tolérer" (p. 319) ("Then a lamentable faculty developed in their minds, that of noticing stupidity and finding it intolerable") (p. 217). They recover from the thoughts of suicide to which this revelation leads them to go on to religion, but the transcendental is comprehensible only in fallible human terms. The capacity to see stupidity makes religion as inaccessible as their previous studies, and it separates them irrevocably from their fellow-villagers, whom they anger by their paradoxes. Recognizing stupidity is pitiable because it does not make life happy or successful. It is appropriate, therefore, that they return, with final satisfaction, to their original vocation as copyists. But what do they copy? Would the unwritten volume have contained the "Sottisiers," the silly statements that Flaubert collected from his wide reading for the novel? Or would it have consisted of the "Dictionnaire des idées reçues," the collection of bourgeois clichés defined largely by their misuse in conversation? In either case the copyists would, like Roderick Random, become satirists, and the novel would be about the making of the satirist. Satire, the exposure of vacuity, is, as the example of Lucian illustrates, the genre that doubters can write.

In his study of Flaubert's last novel, Lionel Trilling does not pull back from the pessimistic nature of its conclusion. *Bouvard et Pécuchet* goes beyond its mockery of bourgeois mentalities; it finds all culture inadequate.

The human mind experiences the massed accumulation of its own works, those that are traditionally held to be its greatest glories as well as those that are obviously of a contemptible sort, and arrives at the understanding that none will serve its purpose, that all are weariness and vanity, that the whole vast structure of human thought and creation are alien from the human person.[16]

The global nature of Trilling's formulation dwarfs the powerfully experienced specificities upon which the universal "nay" is based. The inner dynamics of the novel lie in the interaction between its specific satiric targets and the global condemnation towards which it points, and in the fact that this relationship is made possible through characters whose silliness we perceive but whose friendship and loyalty we respect. Because it is a novel, rooted in the deficiencies of character and in its rendition of social contexts, *Bouvard et Pécuchet* is genuinely satiric – a fictional diatribe on the problems of knowing and the pretensions of knowers. Its satiric nature unleashes and directs the force of Flaubert's anger.

Both the comedy and the anger of *Bouvard et Pécuchet* are never in doubt, and its satiric nature is quite clear, even though the particular nature of its satiric power is novelistic. It brings us to the troubling modern world where there may be no solution to the difficulty demonstrated by the satire. The novel's capacity to explore ambiguities and to complicate sympathies enables the shifting of satiric victims and the movement towards more sweeping condemnations that are the particular accomplishments of *Bouvard et Pécuchet*, where consciousness and its conflicts with the world's stupidity become vehicles for a broad and unsettling attack on human pretensions to knowledge. Novels are a kind of satire in which attack is manifested by the hostility between the motives and consciousness of the central figure and the external world with which he or she must battle. Its indirection lies in the dialogic discourse that opens a variety of satiric perspectives and, as in the case of *Bouvard et Pécuchet*, a significant shifting of satiric targets. The indirectness of narrative satire, as Frank Palmeri points out, generates openness.[17] But it generates as well a sustained sharpness of attack that can reach to a very general level.

THE MENIPPEAN NOVEL

Bakhtin, in a much-cited discussion of Menippean satire, links it with Socratic dialogue and sees it as the origin of carnevalesque literature and of the novel.[18] "Menippean satire became one of the main carriers and channels for the carnival sense of the world, and remains so to the present day."[19] Its origin is attributed to the philosopher Menippus, whose works have not survived. Its primary Roman embodiment was Varro, whose works exist in fragments. It is therefore represented by the plentiful works of Lucian, who occasionally used Menippus as a satiric spokesman. Bakhtin lists a series of characteristics of Menippean satire and stresses its comedy, its fantasy, its mixture of perspectives (especially "observation from some unusual point of view"), its use of various borrowed genres, its parody of these genres, its shifts of tone and style, its violation of conventions of behavior and language, its combination of bold invention with broad philosophical reflection, and its topicality.[20] These diverse characteristics unite to produce "the deep internal integrity of the genre," but Menippean satire also "possesses great external plasticity and a remarkable capacity to absorb into itself kindred small genres, and to penetrate as a component element into other large ones,"[21] including diatribe, soliloquy, symposium, and romance. Menippean satire is philosophical fantasy working through extreme manipulation of point-of-view and extremes of satiric material. Bakhtin is used, with some reservations, by Joel C. Relihan in his description of Menippean satire.[22] But Relihan's limitation of the genre to satires actually containing both verse and prose seems narrow. As Relihan points out, "Menippean satire" is not an ancient generic term and may not have been a consciously defined form.[23] Writers of Menippean satire, even Varro, who called his satires "Menippean," did not think of their texts as part of a rule-driven genre; they thought of themselves as writing works that resembled those of earlier authors. Menippus serves Lucian as a collection of signs about interpretation, just as Lucian in turn becomes a model for More, Erasmus, Rabelais, and Swift. Menippean satire is recognizable through the signs and characteristics associated with a long-lost predecessor, Menippus himself, rather than through a predetermined form. Menippean satire might appropriately be seen as a tradition of satire rather than as a particular genre.

Interesting as it is, Bakhtin's account of Menippean satire is open to some skepticism and elaboration. It seems a synthetic form created by Bakhtin by assembling various features, but its basis is the satire of Lucian which, does, at one point or another, contain most of the features Bakhtin lists. These Menippean elements coalesce into contrasting pairs. Familiar and even "low" material becomes unfamiliar by virtue of its fantastic treatment. Philosophical disputes are treated imaginatively. The expectations created by familiarity with prior models are repeatedly violated. The Menippean text is a parody of previous texts or genres, even when they are not its primary satiric target. It creates disparities between the object observed and the point of view from which it is perceived, thus seeing the familiar in disconcertingly new ways. Most significantly, it is anti-traditional and anti-conventional, initiating its readers into attitudes that renounce the official accounts of life that most have accepted as useful (if not true). The claim that official culture has things all wrong is its most threatening but most liberating element.

Menippean satire might be seen as a node at the junction of narrative, drama, poetry, and expository prose. Menippean narrative, as I have argued elsewhere in the case of the *Satyricon* of Petronius, owes much of its character to the oral, spoken occasion of its performance.[24] The satires of Lucian were essentially public performances. Bakhtin neglects the impact of Old Comedy on Menippean satires and on some of the satires of Lucian in particular.[25] A primary feature of Menippean satire in its Varronian (but not Lucianic) form is its prosimetric movement between prose and verse; Menippean satire, as described by Bakhtin, could as easily be in verse as in prose, and many of its characteristics can be found in the satires of Horace. Menippean satire often imitates rhetorical occasions, as in *The Praise of Folly*, that are fictitious but not narrative. More significantly, the intersection of Menippean narrative and exposition interrupts the linear movement of the story with patterns of analysis. Menippean satire is poised between narration and performance. The diversity of Menippean satire and its capacity to shift among competing genres identifies it with the pre-generic nature of the satiric frame of mind. Menippean satire extends beyond fiction, but some novels are clearly Menippean, although their number and nature seems more limited than Bakhtin claims. Given variables contributing to a description of the Menippean, it is unclear where the demarcation between Menippean novels and other novels can be made. Nonetheless, one can identify two distinct traditions of narrative satire – one Lucianic, the other Quixotic. The first tradition is distinctly generic – decidedly satiric but different from satire in verse. The second seems modal, reflecting the combination, even battle, of sharply identifiable satiric and novelistic elements, but consisting ultimately of satiric novels. Both embody the Menippean quality of generic mockery, and in both cases, the resultant discord disrupts the parodied form.

Lucian's *Bis Accusatus* ("The Double Indictment") provides a self-conscious explanation that points to central aspects of his satire. *Bis Accusatus* begins with the unhappy Zeus complaining of the work the gods must do and of the lack of appreciation shown by humans, as illustrated by their complaints that their petitions for justice have gone unanswered. But if Zeus has been tardy in dispute resolution, it is, he claims, because of overwork. He sends Justice to earth to clear things up, but she is hesitant to face yet again the snarls of Injustice. She is assured that philosophers have made justice respected. The issue becomes whether philosophy has actually succeeded, and, indeed, the first cases seem to suggest that philosophy ought properly to combine a concern for moral behavior with common sense about human nature. The final case is that of a Syrian (Lucian himself) who is accused both by his wife Rhetoric and his companion Dialogue. Rhetoric, appropriately filling her speech with borrowings from Demosthenes, claims to have taken up the untutored Syrian, hellenized him, made him adept at language, and accompanied him throughout the world as he displayed his rhetorical skills, only to be deserted when he took up with Dialogue. The Syrian, in defense, admits that Rhetoric educated him but charges that she rather than he has been unfaithful, that Rhetoric's willingness to serve any cause makes her hardly better than a whore. The jury finds in his favor. Dialogue, echoing Plato, claims that he was given to contemplating the eternal verities only to be degraded by the Syrian. His tale of woe is almost a Bakhtinian description of Menippean satire.

Whisking off the seemingly tragic mask I then wore, he clapped on in its place a comic one that was little short of ludicrous: his next step was to huddle me into a corner with Jest, Lampoon, Cynicism, and the comedians Eupolis and Aristophanes, persons with a horrible knack of making light of sacred things, and girding at all that is as it should be. But the climax was reached when he unearthed a barking, snarling old Cynic, Menippus by name, and thrust *his* company upon me; a grim bulldog, if ever there was one; a treacherous brute that will snap at you while his tail is yet wagging. Could any man be more abominably misused? Stripped of my proper attire, I am made to play the buffoon, and to give expression to every whimsical absurdity that his caprice dictates. And, as if that were not preposterous enough, he has forbidden me either to walk on my feet or to rise on the wings of poesy: I am a ridiculous cross between prose and verse; a monster of incongruity, a literary Centaur.[26]

The Syrian responds that he has made Dialogue accessible and kept him from his own abstractions. Again, he wins the verdict.

Bis Accusatus illustrates key elements of Lucian's method. In the first place, the subject is elusive. It is usually treated as Lucian's self-explanation because it ends with the Syrian's defense. But it begins with the familiar Lucianic question of whether the gods, if they exist at all, actually do anything useful. It then seems to shift, by the reappearance of Justice on earth, to the equally familiar question of whether philosophy fulfills its function. The answer to both questions is negative, leaving the satiric Lucian to use and pervert both Rhetoric and Dialogue. The monstrous combinations to which, Dialogue claims, Lucian has reduced him seem echoed in the fact that Lucian must respond to the combined complaints of Rhetoric and Dialogue, and therein lies a key to Menippean satire – the metonymic extension of prosimetric form. Lucian's position is that a single point of view is never satisfactory, and he manipulates perspective, especially (as here) through parody, to create a conflicted or disoriented view that reveals matters clearly. This manipulated perspective distinguishes Lucianic satire from other kinds of fiction, for Lucian and his followers fight the illusions of ordinary narrative. Lucianic satire is inherently anti-fictional, and Menippean novels tend to distinguish themselves from conventional ones.

The Lucianic tradition includes, among others, Erasmus, More, Rabelais, Swift, Sterne, Diderot, Peacock, Jean Paul Richter, Machado de Assis, and such postmodern figures as Borges, Rushdie, and Kundera.[27] What makes the traditional nature of this eccentric sequence clear is the self-consciousness with which authors connect themselves to their predecessors. Erasmus and More were translators and adapters as well as imitators of Lucian; Rabelais continues the tradition with such conspicuous Lucianic imitations as Panurge's mock-encomium in praise of debt (*Tiers Livre*) and the fantastic quest of the *Quart Livre*. But a more narrative quality, concentrating on a group of characters, and exploring, if oddly and intermittently, motivation and causality, appears in later members of the tradition: in Sterne, Diderot, Machado de Assis, and the postmoderns (where the attribution of causality often becomes a central object of mockery). But even here the novel's difficulty in detaching itself from the essay parallels its difficulty in maintaining a straightforward narrative chronology.

A primary Menippean pattern mixes philosophical topics with discordant familiarity and vulgarity, and the resultant compound is subjected to the catalyst of fantasy. Often this concatenation of elements unites in the figure of a massively solipsistic individual, who may be a figure of irony, as is Folly in the *Moriae Encomium* of Erasmus, or who may be treated with sympathetic ridicule (Panurge in *Tiers Livre*). Other instances of this solipsistic center include the "author" of *A Tale of a Tub*, Tristram Shandy, Jacques in *Jacques le fataliste*, and Braz Cubas in *Memórias póstumas de Brás Cubas*. Readers (and authors) may regard such characters with uncomfortable sympathy: their massive self-assertion, moderated by a comic ineptitude, reflects human traits which bring them disconcertingly close to the readers who condemn them. In this way, they echo the generic self-mockery of the Lucianic tradition, and they share the ambivalence of the novel. But they also embody the dialogic nature of the tradition. The mockery of Panurge requires him to play roles in two kinds of conversation – as the ironic and unreliable speaker talking to the reliable and ideal

Pantagruel and as the unreliable listener (often in company with a reliable one) to statements of false wisdom (sometimes metaphorically true but literally false).

A figure of Panurgic self-centeredness is Braz Cubas, the narrator of *Memórias póstumas de Brás Cubas* by Joaquim Maria Machado de Assis.[28] He is dead when he writes his autobiography, and apart from authorial complications his death may cause, it severely changes his opportunity for personal self-display. He had caught a chill while contemplating the glory to be gained by his anti-melancholy plaster, "The Braz Cubas Plaster," and the chill led to pneumonia and death. His book, though in some senses starkly pessimistic, is itself rather an antidote to melancholy.[29] For all his isolating egoism, Braz Cubas has a quizzical charm in his attitudes towards his life, his friends, and even the reader. But part of that charm derives from the negative nature of his message. Before he dies (but after he narrates his death) he suffers a delirium in which he meets "Nature or Pandora," who describes herself as "your mother and your enemy": "Do not be afraid," she said, "my enmity does not kill; it is through life that it affirms itself. You are alive: I wish you no other calamity" (chapter 7). Her prime law is egoism, acted out in history. She shows Braz the cyclical movement of history, in which people struggle to escape their loneliness and end each age "as miserable as the others." History is revealed as an illusion, prompted by the false assignment of purpose to the random movement of time. But there is no purpose, only repetitions with meaningless variations. Braz's comprehension of his own insignificance and the insignificance of human activity marks the transition between the self-assertion of life and the self-mockery of death.[30] His role as posthumous author is like the medieval role of Death: he mocks at all human affairs and reveals the seven deadly sins.[31] He is a fitting character to perceive Nature's vision. Coddled from infancy, he remains caught between his love of fame and his inability to value anything, between active assertion and desperate inactivity. He has no great adventures and commits no monumental depravity, and he encounters characters who are presented with the same flat derision with which, as deceased author, he presents himself. Egoism, Nature's only law, is faithfully rendered by an egoistic fool. But Machado's narrative method separates egoism from the recognition of folly; Braz the character is egoistic; Braz the narrator becomes a satiric spokesman by recognizing his folly.[32]

Critics differ on the relationship of Braz Cubas to Machado de Assis. Maia Neto argues that Braz is a reliable narrator, but such critics as Caldwell, Callen, Cypess, and Nunes see both the foolish character and the mocking narrator as flawed in their incapacity to love in any committed way.[33] But personal love does not resolve the problems raised by the novel. Setting aside the question of whether such love also rests on illusion, it is not represented in this novel; it is a relatively rare exception to Nature's law of egoism. But it may be distracting to seek for Machado's personal attitude towards his creations. His novel tells a sad but comic truth, and it seems to explore its paradoxical consequences (not to know the futility of human existence is to be a fool, but to know it is foolishly to lose the capacity to act) without coming to final conclusions. Indeed, even the statement of Nature's final law takes place in a "delusion." The death of Braz transforms narrative into essay, for its appearance at the outset makes the novel, episodic as it is, less an account of his life than a rumination about it.

Critics such as Mac Adam, Maia Neto, and Nunes who see the work as a satire approach it as a treatment of ideas to which is added the Lucianic fantasy of a dead author. Its narrative vision repeats that of Lucian's Charon, who, with the guidance of Hermes surveys from a mountaintop the fruitlessness of human activity: "Yes! I see it all; and I ask myself, what is the satisfaction in life? What is it that men bewail the loss of? . . . There you have human life. All men are bubbles, great or small, inflated with the breath of life. Some are destined to last for a brief space, others perish in the very moment of birth: but all must inevitably burst" (*Works*, vol. I, 179–80). Beyond its Lucianic view from the grave, *Memórias póstumas de Brás Cubas* also shows the Menippean qualities of generic parody and literary self-consciousness. Braz's preface consciously places the book in the tradition of the satiric Sterne and the non-satiric Xavier de Maistre.[34] Critics have pointed out significant allusions and comparisons not only to Sterne but Erasmus's *Praise of Folly*, Le Sage's *Gil Blas* (noting that, for Machado, Blas and Braz are equivalent), Shakespeare's *As You Like It*, and Virgil's *Aeneid*, as well as *The Divine Comedy*, *Don Quixote* (where Fierebras's balm resembles Braz's plaster), and *Gulliver's Travels*.[35] Braz makes further connections between literature and life. His love of fame haltingly persists in anticipation of "the four or five readers of the novel" (chapter 34) and the joy of a "bibliomaniac" who secures an only copy (chapter 72), among many Shandean references to the reader. One of his whimsical theories is his "Theory of Human Editions": "Each period of life is a new edition that corrects the preceding one and that in turn will be corrected by the next, until publication of the definitive edition, which the publisher donates to the worms" (chapter 27).

At the end Braz tries to balance the positive and negative trivia that have been his life:

Adding up and balancing all these items, a person will conclude that my accounts showed neither a surplus nor a deficit and consequently that I died quits with life. And he will conclude falsely; for, upon arriving on the other side of the mystery, I found that I had a small surplus, which provides the final negative of this chapter of negatives: I had no progeny, I transmitted to no one the legacy of our misery. (chapter 160)

His final balance sheet is as much of a conundrum as the rest of the novel: he comes out on the positive side because of a negative, the failure to pass on the legacy of misery, but otherwise his life was neutral rather than miserable. The combination of cosmic gloom with personal comedy is a recurrent motif of Menippean satire. By seeing life through the lens of death, Braz can reveal the inner secrets that the conformity of ordinary social life struggles to conceal. The mockery and self-mockery of his posthumous memoirs initiate us into the silent circle of comic unbelievers. His literary elusiveness and his playful metaphors are the deceased manifestation of the self-assertion and melancholy that characterize his life and that make him, as character and author, distant from the reader but, at the same time, charming. His egocentricity encapsulates the mockery, fantasy, and intellectuality that place him strongly in the Lucianic tradition.

The Quixotic tradition includes novels by Fielding, Smollett, Thackeray, Dickens, and Meredith. The temporal structure of fiction characteristically emphasizes the relations of imagined events in time, and the novel explores other relations within and through the framework of this temporal one. Hence fiction is interested in causality and motive and, especially, in the temporal development of character, and it assumes that actions may be given significant cohesion. By replacing plot by the imitation of speech events, satiric narrative, in the novels of Evelyn Waugh for example, undermines that assumption – as does, in quite different ways, Cervantes himself.[36] While the Lucianic tradition is dominated by highly selfish figures, the Quixotic takes up failures. Most novels that are organized around an uncomprehending central figure (such as Tony Last in Waugh's *Handful of Dust*) or around a confusing and meaningless quest (a recurrent pattern in the novels of Thomas Pynchon) are inherently Quixotic, even if they lack a conspicuous narrator.

The novels of Muriel Spark exemplify the force of satiric disruptions in the flow of realistic narrative. Written in an economical style, they include disconcertingly unrealistic elements that call appearances of reality into question. In *Memento Mori* elderly people, mostly associated with the literary world, get anonymous phone calls telling them to remember they must die, and the novel traces the effects of these calls (apparently from death himself or herself) on each of these characters. In *The Ballad of Peckham Rye* a satanic figure acts as satiric performer to make significant mischief in a London suburb. In *The Comforters* a central character cannot escape the sense that she is a character in a novel, which turns out to be the novel we are reading and she has written. The connection between the contrivances of authorship and of character are explored in other novels as well (*Loitering with Intent* and *A Far Cry from Kensington*). In *The Only Problem* the central character, who is occupied in writing a commentary on the book of *Job*, becomes himself involved in a disturbingly Job-like plot. *The Abbess of Crewe* (perhaps the most overly satiric of her novels) transposes the Watergate scandal to an election in a convent, won by a charming but conniving Abbess. In other novels (*The Prime of Miss Jean Brodie* being a significant and complex example) discordant elements undermine the surety of readers and characters that what is apparent is actually there. Spark concentrates on exposing the complexities and ambiguities of evil. Satire introduces fantasic elements that jar the narrative pattern and render causality inexplicable.

Lucianic or Menippean satire constitutes a distinct strain, blurred at the edges, of both satire and the novel. It is a tradition within both. Many Menippean satires are novels; some (such as *The Praise of Folly* and *A Tale of a Tub*) are not. Many novels contain significant satiric elements without being satires, and in such cases their satire is modal rather than generic. The distinctions work out in different ways for individual readers interpreting particular novels. In exploring the complex overlap between satire and the novel, I am arguing here that some satires take the form of novels and that these fictional satires occur when a dislocating shift, usually but not always of narrative perspective, drives readers' attention away from character and towards ideas or towards a broad analysis of society. Such novelistic satires do not appear to be a distinct form as much as a literary tradition, traceable to Lucian. Menippean satire occupies a distinct position in the area where narrative, drama, poetry, philosophical prose overlap. Especially in the works of Lucian, it is an embodiment of satire's pre-generic nature.

SHIFTING PHASES

Genres, of course, change over time, differing in given periods; different, as well, are the positions they occupy in particular cultures. The classical generic hierarchy, with the epic at the top, now seems a historical curiosity, as does the understanding of genres governed by such a hierarchy. But the fact that genres are specific to cultures and thus temporal in nature does not prevent generalizations about them, such as the assertion that satires are about the ideas that govern behavior. Partly such generalizations are possible because some elements of shifting genres persist; partly they are possible because genres are intellectual constructs that have genuine but tentative force. Satire and the novel, as we have seen, are overlapping genres, and their position relative to each other has changed over time. This generic shifting is prominent at two historical moments: in the mid-eighteenth century the functions of satire were subsumed and transformed by the emergence of the novel; although important satiric works continued to be written, traditional forms, especially formal verse satire, become marginal; in the late twentieth century satire emerged as a dominant characteristic of postmodern novels, replacing formal features (causal plot, focus on individual consciousness) that had been primary expectations signaled by the novel, although such satiric fictions continue to be called "novels." In each change the newly prominent genre transforms the functions taken over from the old. The shifting dominance of satire and the novel overlaps with the rise of the novel itself, but the issues need to be distinguished. The multiplication of variables contributing to the emergence of the novel in the eighteenth century has spawned a variety of accounts largely derived from Ian Watt's claim that the novel's formal realism is shaped by the values of an emergent Protestant bourgeoisie. My contention in looking at the shift between satire and the novel in the eighteenth century is more modest: although I agree that satire, like such other genres as spiritual biography, prepared the way for the novel, my argument is that the overlap of satire and novel allowed the novel successfully to fulfill major functions formerly carried out by satire.

The emergence of a bourgeois consciousness that privileges individual success through personal values and effort rather than through hierarchical status in a social order is reflected in the emergence of a genre whose salient characteristic is heightened individual consciousness, especially, as the argument that novels are satiric emphasizes, individual consciousness in battle with the restraints of social convention. This emphasis on consciousness is supported by the economic individualism of Lockean political philosophy and the subjectivity of Lockean psychology. The result of this dual emergence may by paradoxical, as in Richardson's *Clarissa*. *Clarissa* attacks the consequences of unrestrained bourgeois acquisitiveness, as caricatured by the Harlowe family, but its celebration of the virtuous individual consciousness of its heroine promulgates the location of goodness in individual conscience. Success, whether defined as wealth or salvation, is achieved by individuals in conflict with the corrupt ethos in which they live, but whether that success is defined in spiritual or economic terms is a central conflict in *Clarissa*. Because the ethos is concerned with wealth as the consequence of individual activity, it in turn validates the individuals who engage in conflict with it. Although Clarissa is well aware of the wrongness of her family's values and of the degree to which she has been victimized by them, she seeks to return despite their rejection. The paradox of the alienated individual whose rebellion is implicitly endorsed by the alienating society may explain the ambiguities of *Moll Flanders* as well as *Clarissa*. The conflict rests on central inconsistencies of early bourgeois capitalism and is an essential subject of the early novel.

The shift from the satire to the novel as a dominant genre in the eighteenth century was political as well as literary. Traditionally, satire derived from a concern for the well-being of the *polis*, for the retention of social order threatened by the emergence of self-interest, translated as individual wealth or even individual aggression. This concern prompts Swift's attacks on the corrupting function of self-interest as a driving principle of human behavior. In broad terms, then, satire was a weapon of Tory efforts to retain the hierarchies of the past;[37] the novel was a Whig exploration of a liberating individual consciousness that destabilized old hierarchies, reaching and giving voice to people excluded by previous literature. But what allowed satire to survive the collapse of the orders it sought to preserve was its concern to define evil in terms of its dangers to the community, so that satire became available, for rather different reasons, to writers on the relative left as well as on the relative right. (One might plausibly argue that satire is not so much inherently liberal or conservative as concerned for the welfare of the community rather than the well-being of the individual. Hence verse satire, which to some degree is subsumed into the novel of the 1740s, emerges as a critical social force during the Regency.)

Such cultural and political shifting emphasizes differences between the genres. But in other senses the literary power of the novel derived from its capacity to perform certain functions more effectively than satire. Satire characteristically attacks historical individuals and institutions, and through these particular attacks it implies a general criticism of human nature. But the characters of novels are usually fictitious – non-existent. Thus a claim for the early novel is that it shifts its mockery from individuals to general human nature, as Fielding asserted in his "Preface" to *Joseph Andrews*, but such a claim may be illusory, as I have argued in the case of Fielding.[38] Of course, Fielding uses and attacks historical characters, and satire is ultimately concerned with the corruptions of general human nature. But the claim seeks to avoid the politeness problem associated with the centrality of attack in satire. If the victim of attack is merely a fictitious example of fallible humanity, the attacker hardly commits an impropriety by making the attack. Defenders of Salman Rushdie's *The Satanic Verses* assert that Mahound is not, in the context of the novel, an image of the historic Muhammad but a figure in the mad dreams of a fictitious character.

The most significant factor marking the shift from satire to the novel is the novel's superiority as an instrument for representing and evaluating the world around it. Such compendious works as *Tom Jones* and *Roderick Random* involve an enlargement over most satire both in the range of material included and the scales used to measure it. Satiric forms are usually brief and focused; their frequent parody links them to the circumscribed forms they imitate. When their length is extended, as in Rabelais, for example, or even in *Gulliver's Travels*, they accumulate a sequence of distinct units. *Gargantua* in effect rewrites *Pantagruel*; *Le tiers livre* is organized by the dual structures of quest and disputation; *Le quart livre* is a voyage in the manner of Lucian. Books I and II of *Gulliver's Travels* are a contrastive unit driven by relative size and shifts in perception and judgment. Book III explores knowledge by a systematic fantasy of philosophy and history, to conclude that philosophy is delusive and history degenerative. Book IV separates the affective and rational capacities of human beings, assigning the first to humanoid Yahoos and the second to equine Houyhnhnms, and presents that disjunction through Gulliver's identification of himself and the rest of us with Yahoos. In both works characters, themes, and an authorial identity run through the sequence of different structures. An alternative mode for organizing long satires is illustrated by Robert Burton's classification of the varieties of melancholy and his epidemiological analysis of causes, symptoms, and cures. The narrative form of the novel places particular weight on change in plot and on the development of character within a structure that often invites predictions as to its outcome. This form allows novels to hold together considerably more material than the usual satiric structure, while remaining, if anything, still more open in its interpretive possibilities. The length of novels allows them to frame broader representations of society than fit within satire. In relatively closed societies the personal perspective and conversational medium of Horace are satisfactory vehicles of complex attack. The theatrical representation of the community in Old Comedy corresponds closely to the community of the audience. An alternative to these direct representations is analytical distance and the higher level of abstraction characteristic of Lucian. But that distance and abstraction come at the relative loss of historicity and immediacy in attack. Novels operate in a printed medium and are read individually or in small groups, rather than

being witnessed by a community, as in performed (theatrical or oral) satire.
Satire seems elite in comparison to the more accessible and comprehensible
novel. Genres, like cities, are dangerously strained when their infrastructure
is inadequate to the increase in demand.

What the novel supplies in place of the historicity or abstraction of satire
is a method for using thematic structures to manipulate a number of disparate strands. Such structures might be called heuristic; they may organize
large bodies of material and open them to satiric scrutiny. They are large
motifs that are central – often defining – subjects in themselves, but they are
also a nexus of subsidiary themes that are relevant to that subject in a variety
of ways, and they point to independent themes connected to the central
subject by the activities of major characters. These themes are often articulated by characters who become satirists themselves or who function in that
role by informing naive heroes about the strange worlds they encounter.[39]
Such heuristic structures also organize the somewhat disparate treatment
of satiric themes. Thus the journey that organizes *Humphry Clinker* proposes a series of more-or-less defined goals: Matthew Bramble's recovery of
health, the resolution of Lydia Melford's romance, the maturation of Jery
Melford, the recovery of Baynard's estate, the marriage of Tabitha Bramble,
the identification of Humphry himself, and the bonding of the family.
But the journey moves them through a variety of locations (Bath, London,
Yorkshire, Scotland) that are variously connected to its goals but in turn become centers of satiric exploration. Hence Smollett is able to incorporate
satire on medical practice, Whig politics, criminal justice, colonial nou-
veaux riches, London food, Grub-Street writers, Methodism, economic
waste, and other targets. The nexus is extended further through the interaction of major characters with subsidiary figures (Martin, Lismahago,
Baynard, Dennison) who are beset by socially significant problems. The
extensions of a simple journey structure present a large but not necessarily
consistent interpretation of society and thereby serve the satiric function of
literary commentary on society and politics. Jery Melford concludes that
"the greatest advantage acquired in travelling and perusing mankind in the
original, is that of dispelling those shameful clouds that darken the faculties
of the mind, preventing it from judging with candour and precision."[40]
But beyond this conclusion, the journey is not a prominent subject of the
novel so much as it is the device that reveals major themes.

Examples of such heuristic structures can easily be multiplied: patterns
of sexuality, courtship, and marriage; crime, its consequences, and its pun-
ishments; education and the development of the hero; the first emergence of the central character (often an ingénue heroine, as in *Evelina*)

into conventional society; the heroine's flight from aggressive masculinity; the recurrent dualogue of dissimilar characters (Pantagruel and Panurge, Quixote and Sancho, Walter and Toby Shandy, Jacques and his master). Such heuristic structures have a double function: they are themselves central and defining subjects of novels, and, at the same time, they provide connections that address various issues simultaneously and can speak of them significantly if not conclusively. By providing these connections, heuristic structures undertake a concerted analysis of society that remains open, imaginative, and often ambivalent.

The emergence of the novel as a dominant genre that subsumes, with new and enlarged resources, many of the functions of traditional satire, is not the only explanation for the retreat of that genre into marginal status. The function of satire as a medium for reporting and commenting on current events, as in *Poems on Affairs of State* in the late seventeenth century, was subsumed by the development of the periodical press as a means of political hostility. The emergence of graphic satire of events in Hogarth, Gillray, Rowlandson, and Cruikshank, among many others, provided an immediate perception on the part of the viewer as well as an immediate response on the part of the artist. Nonetheless, the focus on individual consciousness, the replacement of a narrowly individual perspective by a cultural openness, and the novel's capacity to supply heuristic structures, enabled the novel to subsume and transform satire. Satiric verse declamation may have reached its apogee in Pope, whose proclamations, in the *Dunciad* and *Epilogue to the Satires*, of its feeble decline may have been historical observation. For verse satire proved to be too narrow a form to engage regularly and effectively in satiric commentary for a wider audience in a more complicated society.

We are presently undergoing another cultural and generic change, an element of which may be seen as the partial replacement of the novel by satire. The satire that replaces the novel is not a nostalgic recreation of the time before the Enlightenment; the Enlightenment too is questioned by this change. Nor can it be a return to the universal and absolute values that once may have served as a norm for judgment. Satire, particularly historic in its determination, is summoned from the margins to the center in order to pose a new set of questions. To do so, it uses the husk of the novel, in its usual parasitic fashion, much as the novel, in the eighteenth century, took upon itself many of the functions of satire.

Postmodern literary reactions to the limitations of modernism can be revealed in a variety of ingredients, any significant combination of which can identify a work as a postmodern one. A heightened and self-conscious complexity is characteristic of high modernism but is extended to the point of playful and regressive distortion in such novels as Italo Calvino's *If on a winter's night a traveler*. Philosophical and scientific ideas are extracted from the implicit depths of fiction and displayed on the surface, where they are fragmented and manipulated. The language of scientific theory hovers, like a quantum wave-particle, between the literal and the figurative, and the postmodern novel literalizes the figurative or figures the literal, as in the physics, metaphysics, and metaphors of rocketry in Thomas Pynchon's *Gravity's Rainbow*. Such fiction mixes physical and psychological realism with fantasy, and it destabilizes ideas of character as it does ideas of truth. Attitudes towards dominant ideologies shift from the modern to the post-modern. Instead of Enlightenment hostility to repressive systems of belief ("écrasez l'infame"), a hostility continued by much modernist writing, the postmodern envisions old beliefs much as St. George must have regarded the slain dragon, for, intellectually at least, they can never come to life again. But if such beliefs now seem untenable, the effect of believing them was incalculable, and the postmodern mourns the loss of past, irrecoverable faith. Changes in technology and in its functions give the media a primary rather than ancillary role in ordinary life; they ensure individuals consid-erable choice but trivialize much of what may be chosen. Information is distributed before its accuracy can be tested or its significance scrutinized, and the rate at which new knowledge replaces old intensifies the instabil-ity of the knowers. Literary forms are no longer securely seated in a given culture but subsume simultaneous possibilities of a variety of cultures. The problem of those who move from one culture to another (as in the case of satiric exile) becomes a metaphor for the loss of communal values and the lack of integral personal identity. Values, the definition of culture, and even a sense of reality are personal, subjective, and fragmentary, but con-sciousness itself seems the product of cultures whose terms dictate what is perceived and judged. Change and its anxieties emerge as driving subjects of most intellectual disciplines. Despite its fascination with popular culture, postmodernism must confront the power of the entertainment business to transform art into profit, and that vortex is resisted by making it an object of attack and by parodying its forms. The Menippean element of fantasy dislodges fiction from the peg of realism. The novelistic narrator disappears (as in the later novels of William Gaddis), becomes significantly unstable (Kinbote in *Pale Fire*), or is replaced by an essayistic author such as Kundera and Rushdie. The text becomes labyrinthine or mirror-like, sometimes playfully indeterminate in its order (as in Cortázar's *Hopscotch*). History like culture becomes an explicit topic. Difficult to define as the postmodern may be as a period, postmodern novels are sharply aware of their own periodicity.

These postmodern developments shift satire to a position of literary dominance. Postmodernism's attention to the exchange of signs and its tendency to stress the analogies among sign-systems (language, artistic forms, media, currency) lead to a heightened linguistic consciousness – sometimes expressed in parody, sometimes in self-deprecating irony, sometimes in intertextuality, and sometimes in distortions of conventional language and forms. At the root of this semiotic concern is the failure of signifiers to refer to external reality. Meanings can no longer be seen as referring to the external universe or as shared by subjective understanding (the modernist position) but become, like words themselves, the products of particular cultures. Satire, with its skepticism of appearances and its self-consciousness about language, moves from the margins of literature to the center. Irony becomes a key vehicle for exploiting the relations of ideas. Satire (especially Menippean satire) uses fantasy, the magic realism of the postmodern novel, to discover and represent the ideas and ideologies beneath political appearances. Satiric fantasy addresses the fragmentation of character, the replacement of causality with absurdity, and the irrelevance of reason that are elements of the postmodern novel. In wake of the loss of grand narratives, the collapse of totalizing meaning, fantasy becomes a source of local meaning. The formal equivalent to the analytic dislocation of magic realism is a satiric distortion of generic conventions. Satire, as the imitator and violator of familiar genres, is ideally located to use formal distortions as meaningful signs. The effect of such distortion is not only to question the nature and location of meaning but to show the failure and irrelevance of previous forms.

The shift from the novel back to satire (or the development of a new, more insistently satiric novel) encompasses these diverse factors: the importance of culture in contrast to the individual consciousness; the general, political, and theoretical nature of the author's concerns; the loss of a strong sense of the integrally developed individual; the paradox posed by the need to reject the trivializing elements of late capitalist culture but the failure to find universal values that authorize the rejection. In this situation the novel's capacity to enlist sympathy takes on particular force. In cases where readers come to care about characters (and such caring is often not the case in postmodern novels), sympathy itself becomes a satiric tool, generating anger or distress at the chaotic universe that threatens the sympathetic figure. The postmodern, J. P. Lyotard contends, privileges message over aesthetics as a renunciation of formal solace. That rejection of aesthetic pleasure becomes in itself an aesthetic statement that governs not only the postmodern but satire, the unpleasant genre that undertakes personal attack or demonstrates corruption. In rejecting aesthetic consolation, postmodern satire renounces closure in order to uncover the universality of the negative (moral wrong, personal loss, systemic degeneration). In William Gaddis's unnarrated novel *J R*, life seems more complicated than the stereotypical dichotomy of satire and the novel, where satire's attack on systems seems to imply that individual victims are helpless but where the novel's charting of responsibility treats characters as determining moral agents. The absence of an author who assigns responsibility leaves open both the responsibility of the system for its destruction of individuals and the responsibilities of individuals for the consequences of their weakness. The combination of satire and novel frees both genres from the conceivable limitations of each, enabling both the novel's compassionate understanding and the systemic anger expressed by satire. The intermingling of distinct elements of the novel (sympathy) and of satire (sharp or widespread attack) emerges as a final form of their relationship. Satire, in exploiting the novel as its host form, uses the novel's capacity for sympathy to attack both the heartlessness of the oppressor and the victim's complicity in the oppression. These elements of sympathy and condemnation become so interwoven that the merging of satire and novel seems complete.

CHAPTER 7

Satire and the press: the Battle of Dunkirk

The study of satire as a genre has little to say about it as an expository – especially journalistic – form. The problem is to define the literary character of journalistic satire, to delineate the characteristics that distinguish it from ordinary reportage and from essays of opinion. What distinguishes satire in a journalistic medium that, like satire, is historical and frequently dialectical? Once these questions have been addressed, a more basic question – how satire operates within the variety of discourses that make up journalism – can then be answered. Journalistic satire is characteristically a journalism of attack, but it shares that characteristic with much non-satiric journalism. Its satiric character becomes more apparent in the indirections, concealments, and strategies by which it attacks. Its nature is revealed when it becomes less concerned with the accuracy of facts or the validity of arguments than with the nature of political discourse itself. My contention in this chapter is that the primary function of journalistic satire is not to disprove or outargue an opponent but to assert that the opponent lacks the capacity to communicate. Satire's concern is secondarily with the intricacies of the opponent's argument but primarily with the act of communication itself. Two examples, considered in some detail, stand imperfectly for a range of satiric journalism, but they provide a model of satire's contention that its opponent supplies at best an illusion of communication. A 1713–14 debate regarding the unfulfilled French promise to demolish the harbor and fortifications of Dunkirk engages not only a squadron of leading Whig and Tory writers but an arsenal of satiric weapons. In contrast to this global attack, which seeks to destroy every source of communicative authority, the satire of Karl Kraus, the subject of the next chapter, both uses and targets language as the point where communication fails. As a dominant satirist – perhaps the dominant satirist of the twentieth century – Kraus exemplifies a number of the concerns not only of this chapter but of this book.

One factor distinguishing satire prose from journalism is pointed by Michael Seidel's argument that satire represents an "unresolved state of crisis" rooted not only in events but in "absurd, skeptical, despairing, or even subversive assessments of human capacity where the powers necessary to resolve life's crises are absent or concealed."[1] Seidel's claim that crisis is a distinguishing mark of satire seems appropriate to a propaganda debate whose central document is Steele's *The Crisis*. Journalistic argument, such as Steele's pamphlet, frames ordinary events by a text whose very existence raises them to crisis, thus justifying recurrent complaints about the sensationalism of journalism (as in Tory assertions that Steele's pamphlet, rather than naming the crisis, was the crisis). Such crises often pass without resolution because they have been replaced by subsequent events, and hence journalism often seems unconcerned with the outcome of the problems it reports. The cosmic crisis of despair, which Seidel sees as characteristic of satire, is comically enacted in the diurnal crises of the press. Like the journalist, the satirist makes the chronic disorder of history urgent by writing it down. But what often distinguishes the satirist is his self-consciousness about the cosmic implications of the present scene, while the journalist marks each crisis as abnormal. Such awareness defines Swift as a satirist and occasional journalist, Steele as a journalist and occasional satirist. That self-consciousness leads the satirist to blame the messenger as well as the message, for cosmic disorder eliminates all journalistic pretense of innocent and disinterested observation.

For Seidel the situation of crisis intensifies this tendency to blame the messenger, for "the power relations supposedly sanctioned by political rhetoric are precisely what are at issue. Crisis makes words *actionable*, even if the result is an ill fit between circumstances that manifest power and the language employed to forestall events or benefit from them."[2] Satire's distortions and fictions point to the disparity between language and action: the French have said they will demolish the port of Dunkirk, but they have not done so. Or satire identifies the threat that the language of satiric exaggeration may well become real: James III may, like Charles II, pretend to Protestantism in order to assume the throne, bringing with him an absolutist state that would destroy the settlements reached after 1688. The only defense against such attacks is to claim that the disjunction between language and action is only apparent, that the port of Dunkirk is not dangerous because it is in British hands, and that the Protestant succession is protected by parliamentary acts and political will.

A major political issue of the autumn of 1713 concerned the port of Dunkirk, whose fortifications and harbor the French had promised, in the Treaty of Utrecht, to demolish. But by the summer of 1713 no progress had been made, prompting Whig complaints that the Tory Ministry tolerated inaction out of deference to French interests and in deliberate hostility to British trade and military security. (In fact, the demolition of Dunkirk continued to be a British demand until 1783, when the issue was abandoned in the peace of Versailles.)[3] Whigs suggested that French failure to fulfill its treaty obligation foreboded French support for a Jacobite invasion, and that Dunkirk was an ideal port from which it might be launched. The issue marked the emergence of Steele as the major Whig propagandist and developed into a series of pamphlet disputes that included most of the political writers on both sides: Steele, Swift, Defoe, John Toland, William Oldisworth, William Wagstaff, Delarivière Manley, Benjamin Hoadley, Samuel Croxall, George Sewell, Francis Hoffman, John Lacy, and Leonard Welsted, as well as anonymous writers. The debate resulted in the expulsion of Steele from Parliament and the offer of a reward for identifying the author of *The Publick Spirit of the Whigs* (Swift), but its present interest lies in its implicit issues, in its satiric techniques, and in what that they imply about journalistic satire as a form of political debate. One might look at the Dunkirk debate as a battle about the terms and territories of political discourse.

The controversy included a variety of literary forms – the poems of Swift, Croxall, and Welsted (among others), political allegories, classical and historical comparisons, ghostly visitations, narratives, dialogues, biography and mock-biography, literary criticism, parody, the analysis or the mockery of texts, and direct argument. Thus a central problem for distinguishing the satiric nature of the discourse lies in identifying the common features running through so many genres. But I will argue that once such commonality is identified it requires the multiplicity of forms through which it is realized. I will try to arrive at that commonality by looking briefly at the range of audiences and subjects, at the profusion of attacks on authors and their personae, at the satiric possibilities of political allegory, at the interpretive practices of Swift, and at the interpretive theories of Steele.

Satiric attacks on the press during the Dunkirk campaign were addressed to various segments of the reading audiences and served various propagandistic purposes.[4] There was, after all, an election in 1713, and propaganda was directed at specific constituencies. Thus *The Englishman* argued that London, as a trading city, should be represented by traders, who, not coincidentally, were Whigs (no. 3, October 10, 1713); the *Examiner* tells its country readers that the next Parliament should look like the present one (4, no. 31, August 21–September 4, 1713).[5] But if political propaganda were driven by electoral zeal, one would expect it to be bunched more tightly around elections than appears to be the case.[6] The flurry of pamphlets that

included and surrounded Steele's *The Crisis* in early 1714 appeared well after the Tory victory. Pamphlet wars, though surely attempts to gain power,
purported a concern for issues on which members of Parliament occasionally voted in opposition to their own parties. Thus the Tories, with help
of the twelve new Lords created for the purpose, gained approval for the
Treaty of Utrecht from both Houses but, despite the support of the Crown,
were unable to win approval of the commercial treaty because a significant
number of them voted with the Whigs. One direction of political satire
was towards possible deviants from the other party, whose votes might be
gained on particular measures. The ambivalence of propagandists about a
system of political parties supported the possibility that such shifts might
occur. Hence there were two separate and basically inconsistent lines of political argument. One argued that factional rivalry is itself unworthy of the
national interest and of the moral interests of citizens. Here Steele, in his
Whig propaganda of 1713–14, is hoist on the petard of his assertions in the
Tatler and *Spectator* that interest in political news is a frivolous curiosity.[7]
The other line of attack was against the opposing party. This line usually sought to identify the writer's party as representating legitimate public
concerns and the other party as a narrow, self-interested faction. The distinction between misguided adherents of the opposing party and extremist
fanatics who dominated the press was addressed to possible moderate converts or occasional supporters. While moderate Whigs (according to the
Tories) properly supported the settlement of 1688, extremists sought to insinuate the Commonwealth principles of 1641; sincere Tories who feared for
the welfare of the Anglican Church, Whigs claimed, should fear the dangers of Jacobitism, a return to Catholicism, and ministerial tyranny (e.g.,
Examiner, 5, no. 50; *The Englishman*, No. 5). *Examiner* 4, no. 23 (July 31–
August 3, 1713) seeks to separate Old Whigs from new by showing how
responsibly the Ministry has acted in the interests of trade; *Examiner* 4,
no. 42 (October 26–30, 1713) complains of false efforts to identify such
supposed factions as Jacobite Tories and Hanover Tories. But whatever
the propagandistic intention, Members of Parliament rarely shifted from
their party's position.[8] The exploration of points of attack that might split
interest-groups within the opposing party is one function served by shifts
of topic both in periodicals and in the exchange of pamphlets.

Subjects shifted repeatedly because of the strategies of propaganda or
because new events prompted new responses. French delay at the demolition of Dunkirk (at least the Tories argued) reflected a reaction to the
failure of Parliament to pass the commercial Treaty of Utrecht, a failure
that derived in part from a Whig sense that the Treaty of Utrecht did not

reflect the military successes of the allies. Whigs claimed not only that the failure to demolish Dunkirk threatened to increase commercial competition with France but that it showed the Ministry's willingness to condone privateering from Dunkirk's commanding position at the east end of the Channel. Whigs asserted (especially in Steele's *The Crisis*) that one failure to observe the treaty suggested the possibility of further violations, and that the Ministry was subverting the established succession to the crown, an argument prompted in part by the serious illness of Queen Anne in the winter of 1713–14. This argument engaged the usual attacks on Roman Catholicism and celebrations of the "revolution" of 1688. Tories, in turn, accused the Whigs of positive rejoicing at the illness of the Queen and prospects of her death.[9] The Tory side of the argument (beyond denials of any threat to the succession) was further served by the introduction of a bill to prevent "the growth of schism" (that is, to prevent Dissenters from educating their children in their own faith), a step which pleased Bolingbroke because it placed his Tory rival Robert Harley, Earl of Oxford in the position of acting against his own background. The bill placed similar burdens on Defoe, who temporarily left the Tories to support Steele's contention that repressing education by Dissenters violated an understanding about mutual rights and served the interests neither of the Queen nor of the Church.[10] There were, of course, a number of subsidiary and contributing disputes, some of them economic, as in the debates of Defoe's *Mercator* and the Whig *British Merchant*, others religious, such as the High-church claim that lay baptism, and hence baptism by Dissenting ministers, is invalid (to which White Kennett responded that "it now remained to make the Bosom of the Church no wider than just to hold the *Tory Party*").[11] The fact of debate itself became a serious issue, so that the propaganda of these months is distinctly self-consciousness not only about the substance of the argument but about the fact that it is being made at all. Steele's expulsion from Parliament for his authorship of *The Crisis* and *The Englishman* was only the legislative manifestation of incessant authorial attacks that had plagued him. These raise questions about the authority of authors, the credibility of their arguments, the propriety or even legality of their language, and what should be done about them. The dangers of attack, counter-attack, mining, spying, and enfilade gave pamphlet battles a metaphorically military appearance.

The military metaphor becomes explicit in *An Invitation to Peace: Or, Toby's Preliminaries to Nestor Ironsides, Set forth in a Dialogue between Toby and his Kinsman* (London: Mr. Lawrence [1714]), in which the Treaty of Utrecht has its counterpart in negotiations to end the pamphlet war.

"Toby" was a prominent Tory persona, while Ironside (as an obvious play on "Steele") was the putative editor of the *Guardian* and, after Steele's initial Dunkirk sally in early August, a figure of much vituperation by the Tories, when they wanted a change from attacking Steele directly by name. Although Toby's negotiations are not as witty as one might hope, flat writing may have been a tactic, for one purpose of the tract is to reduce Steele's grandiose political concerns to party bickering and profitable bookselling. Toby's interlocutor accuses Steele of beginning "the Paper-War with no other View but supporting the Ballance of Pamphleteering" (3). Toby sets forth a series of peace proposals, including the surrender of Button's Coffee-house, the assignment of rights to the "Province of Scandal," the assurance of publication rights for Jacob Tonson, and various other measures. He is most concerned for the absent role of the Dunkirk-like Addison: "Sir, you may talk till Doomsday if you please; but I shall make you no other Reply than Fort Ad—son, Fort Ad—son" (4). Toby's hopes for a settlement may be frustrated by the ineptitude of Ironside himself: "one who vainly imagines to become, from a Bankrupt in Poetry, a Haberdasher in Politicks" (10). Ironside's lack of talent, he suggests, is the real crisis, whatever Steele might intend in his forthcoming tract. (From the Tory point of view, *The Crisis* aptly advertises a Whig disaster in pamphlet warfare rather than a Tory crisis in affairs of state.) *An Invitation to Peace* is doubly or triply metaphorical: the image of warfare stands for writing, and here, as in so much else of the debate, writing itself becomes an image of the real issues. The Battle of Dunkirk itself, so soon to become subsumed in the War of Hanoverian Succession, stands for the financial, civil, and religious interests of factions and reflects personal enmity and loyalty. This variety of factors makes political associations unstable, as in the cases of Nottingham, Swift, and even Oxford, and it makes political argument unstable as well. The Whigs, Tories repeatedly remind them in 1713, thought Dunkirk insignificant when Britain won it in the Treaty of Utrecht.

The displacement of political issues onto writing itself is particularly notable in Swift's *The Importance of the Guardian Considered*, which appeared in late October 1713.[12] Swift had been in Ireland when Steele's *Guardian*, no. 128 first raised the Dunkirk issue (August 7) and when Defoe's *The Honour and Prerogative of the Queen's Majesty Vindicated* (London: John Morphew, 1713) made the first substantial response a week later. After his arrival in London in early September, further pamphlets appeared on both sides – *Reasons Concerning the Immediate Demolishing of Dunkirk* (probably by Defoe) in September (London: John Morphew, 1713), John Toland's alarmist *Dunkirk or Dover; or, The Queen's Honour, The Nation's Safety, The*

Liberties of Europe, and The Peace of the World, All at Stake till that Fort and Port be totally demolish'd by the French (London: A. Baldwin, 1713), and Steele's *The Importance of Dunkirk Consider'd* (London: A. Baldwin, 1713 [September 22]). The major issues had been joined, and Swift could attack Steele personally, both in order to undermine his effectiveness as a political opponent and to settle old scores from the previous spring, when Steele had alluded to him as a fallen-away friend (perhaps no great insult) and, more seriously, as a faithless priest.[13] Swift thus took obvious pleasure in recounting an insulting version of Steele's life, in pointing out the crudities of his style, and in suggesting that where it is not crude it is vacuous. "If I have ill interpreted him, it is his own Fault, for studying Cadence instead of Propriety, and filling up Niches with Words before he has adjusted his Conceptions to them" (*Prose Works*, vol. VIII, 22).

Beyond this ingenuity, however, Swift strikingly if not originally raises two important issues: the nature of the Queen's prerogative, and Steele's lack of authority as a private citizen to meddle in state affairs. None of the writers on either side doubted that the monarch had a special prerogative, but they were uncertain as to how far it extended. Did the Queen have the authority to abrogate provisions of a treaty approved by Parliament? Did prerogative extend to the Ministry acting in the name of the Queen? Since questioning the royal prerogative seemed tantamount to treason, the issue had sharp implications for the freedom of writers to criticize national policy. Swift, writing for the Ministry, wants to extend the royal prerogative to include actions that the opposition saw as unprotected. Steele's contention is that his authority as an author derives from his rights as an informed citizen concerned about an issue of national importance. The force of that contention is modified but not denied by the fact that he was also a member of a political faction seeking to return to power. By attacking Steele as a "Brother-Scribler," Swift adopts Steele's language in order to diminish his authority. Later, of course, Swift took Steele's position on these issues (the prerogative and the citizen-writer's authority) in *The Drapier's Letters*, when he wrote in opposition to the Ministry rather than in its support.[14] Swift's shift to occupy in 1724 the position he had attacked in 1713 suggests that political arguments may be generated by the place the arguer occupies in the structure of the political debate, so that writers for the Ministry seek a broad definition of prerogative and writers for the opposition insist on a narrow one.

Steele sought to redefine the role of the opposition in political propaganda, and in the summer of 1713, the Whigs needed such redefinition. Their efforts to block the Treaty of Utrecht in 1712 had been frustrated by

Swift's adroit propaganda and the Ministry's constitutional maneuvering. Arthur Mainwaring, the director of Whig propaganda, had died in 1712. Whigs were unlikely to improve their parliamentary status in the elections of 1713. In June of 1713, Steele gave up his position with the Stamp Office to campaign for Parliament from the borough of Stockbridge. His parliamentary interests may have been partly personal, since Parliament provided a haven from creditors, Steele's constant companions. (Steele's need for economic protection was a favorite theme of the Tories.) Running for Parliament had propaganda purposes as well. The idea was for Steele to make speeches in the House (whether his own or those written for him by Addison, Walpole, and others) and then to reprint them for mass distribution, in this way uniting Parliamentary deliberations with general propaganda and violating the understanding that Parliamentary debates were private matters, not properly subject to public scrutiny.[15] Both inside and outside the House, Steele sought to test the Ministry's toleration for political debate and to explore its legal limits. At the opening of Parliament on February 16, 1714, he spoke briefly in praise of Sir Thomas Hanmer, who had been nominated as Speaker of the House; his speech was only four short paragraphs long, but was duly published. (The Tories published a parody of an imagined speech, *A Speech Suppos'd to be Spoke by R———St———l, Esq; At the Opening this Present Parliament* [London: John Morphew, 1714], which rambles through a series of Steelian or quasi-Steelian topics.) On February 19, Defoe wrote to the Earl of Oxford that "Mr. Steele, is now to try an experiment upon the Ministry, and shall set up to make speeches in the House and print them, that the malice of the party may be gratified and the Ministry be bullied in as public a manner as possible."[16] But as early as the previous August, the Tories were apparently resolved not to allow him to sit in Parliament. In its issue of August 14–21 (4, no. 27) the *Examiner* had warned Steele that if he is elected and continues to insult the Queen (as he allegedly did by asserting that the nation expects the demolition of Dunkirk), he will "obtain the *Honour,* as another of their haughty Leaders [Walpole] has already done, *of being Expelled the House.*" On August 31 Alexander Pope wrote to John Caryll that a petition was likely to be lodged against Steele and that Steele probably knew it.[17] From the outset, then, both sides seemed aware that Steele sought to combine parliamentary and propaganda roles, and both sides knew that he would not be allowed to do so for long. During the Battle of Dunkirk and the other propaganda campaigns between August 7, 1713, when the *Guardian* published Steele's first attack, and March 18, 1714, when Steele was expelled from Parliament for alleged sedition in *The Crisis* and *The Englishman*, Steele sought to exploit every advantage that he could from the Parliament–propaganda combination. Writing political tracts as a sitting Member of Parliament challenged the Tory contention that as a mere author Steele had no authority for discussing complex affairs of state. Tory rebuttals hinted that Steele would discover, on the contrary, that the outrageous contentions he made as a pamphleteer would be out of order or worse in a Parliamentary debate: "What think you, Mr. *Steele, Would* the people resent the treatment of that Sovereign, and think those Men unworthy ever to represent a Loyal, Dutiful Nation any more, *Or would they not?*"[18]

In order to solidify the Parliamentary connection, Steele took the unusual step of publishing under his own name, a practice he had begun in May 1713, by signing his letter to the *Guardian*, no. 53, which asserted that the *Examiner* was written by his exasperated former mistress (Delarivière Manley) or by his estranged friend (Swift). (The origin of the dispute was the *Examiner*'s attack on Lady Charlotte, daughter of the Earl of Nottingham, for "*Knotting*" in Church "in the immediate Presence of both *God* and *Her Majesty*," *Examiner*, 3, no. 44 [April 20–24, 1713]); the Tories responded that Steele's jibe at Mrs. Manley was more scandalous than theirs at Lady Charlotte (*Examiner*, 4, no. 2 [May 18–22, 1713]). Steele continued to sign his name to his letter to *Guardian*, no. 128 (August 7, 1713), to *The Importance of Dunkirk Consider'd* (September 22, 1713), to *The Crisis* (January 19, 1714), and to the last number of *The Englishman* (February 15, 1714). Idealists would argue that Steele's identification of his authorship meant that he took responsibility for his views, that he sought to speak with continuity and authority, and that integrity emerged as a central characteristic (or pretense) of the political voice. Cynics assert that Steele's identification was an appeal for patronage, probably from the Earl of Nottingham.[19] Steele may have sought Nottingham's support in May, when he wrote in defense of Lady Charlotte, but probably acted from other motives in August. His opponents saw Steele as shifting the rules of discourse, as making personal (and hence self-interested) the political discourse that ought to be directed to issues, and as trying to gain credit for a moral integrity he did not deserve. That judgment may have led to their ample demonstrations of his lack of desert; at any rate, Steele's use of his name made him the target of extended personal attack.[20] Steele is willing, he tells the electors of Stockbridge in *The Importance of Dunkirk Consider'd*, to "give up my self to all nameless Authors, to be treated just as their Mirth or their Malice directs them" (122). The invitation could hardly be resisted. Swift, in *The Importance of the Guardian Consider'd*, gratefully accepts Steele's call "to treat him only as my Brother-Scribler" (*Prose Works*, vol. VIII, 4) and suggests that "the Letter called, *The Importance of Dunkirk*, is chiefly taken up in showing you the *Importance* of Mr. *Steele*" (*Prose Works*, vol. VIII, 5).

Steele's invitation was answered by many more than Swift.[21] Such attacks stressed what they saw as the arrogance implicit in his use of his personal name in political discourse. *The Character of Richard St——le, Esq.: with some Remarks* (London: J. Morphew, [November 12] 1713), probably by William Wagstaff, takes what became the standard line: Steele was excellent as Bickerstaff or Mr. Spectator, but was foolishly persuaded by his friends at Button's, who played on his vanity and his fear of arrest for debt, to go into Parliament and to take up as a political writer, a role for which he is unqualified: "Mr. *St——le*, in short, has neither an Head, nor a Style, for Politics; there is no one Political *Englishman* but contains either some notorious Blunder in his Notions or his Language" (18). In the madness which inflicted Steele after the election, according to an anonymous Tory, the ghost of John Tutchin appeared (probably in December 1713) to tell Steele in Miltonic verse that he has inherited his political mantle.[22] Steele's institution of *The Englishman* on October 6 led his opponents to observe that Steele was born in Ireland and was not an Englishman at all. *The Life of Cato the Censor* (London: J. Woodward and J. Baker, 1714) takes advantage of Steele's use of "Delenda est Cathago" as the motto for various Dunkirk papers to attack Steele in the guise of Cato the Censor. Both Steele and Cato, the poem suggests, were braggarts whose propensity for trouble-making unsuccessfully concealed their personal immorality. The attacks on Steele continued after his expulsion from Parliament. John Lacy's *Ecclesiastical and Political History of Whig-land* (London: J. Morphew, [July] 1714) begins with four abusive and fictional chapters on Steele, before turning to an allegorical treatment of Whigs in general.

Lacy is also the putative author of an allegorical mock-heroic poem that represents yet another mode of personal attack.[23] Here the satire celebrates the *Examiner* as "*England*'s Guardian ORATOR," who defends the country against the Whigs' foul misrepresentations of it to Hanover. But, in the dialectic that transfers political discourse to the discussion of writing, the *Examiner*'s quest leads him to Mount Parnassus (here a Whig anti-Parnassus, where terms like "loyalty" and "patriotism" reverse their meaning) and on to the Poet's Paradise, where the great British poets of the past adjudicate the claims of political truth and literary merit. They admit the *Examiner* to Paradise, but send Steele back to the pamphleteers. The comic exaggerations of the poem redirect the personal vituperation of Lacy's *Political History* towards the broader generalities of allegory. One important Whig allegory was an imitation Spenserian canto, *An Original Canto of Spencer: Design'd as Part of his Fairy Queen, but never Printed. Now made Publick, by Nestor Ironside, Esq*, written by Samuel Croxall and published (A. Baldwin) in November or December 1713. It and its sequel (*Another Original Canto of Spencer*) allegorically attack Harley in the form of the evil Archimago who enchanted Britomart (Queen Anne). Croxall's poems were answered in the *Examiner* (which thought them written by Steele), to which Croxall weakly responded by questioning the *Examiner*'s comprehension of history and of Horace. The *Examiner* further responded with an attack on Marlborough, which Steele answered in *The Englishman*. Steele's response in turn prompted Swift's *The First Ode of the Second Book of Horace Paraphras'd: And Addressed to Richard St—— le, Esq*, which predicted that Steele would trot out familiar arguments, false alarms, and overworked themes. Croxall's elaborate allegory on Oxford spurred personal attack, defamation, and defense of Marlborough, literary and historical criticism, and Swift's lively poem.

Despite the unanticipated troubles they could bring, political allegory and literary imitation were important weapons in the skirmishing over Dunkirk. The essential battle of political discourse concerns the validity of its truth claims, and these claims become the target of debate. The Tory or insider position is that such claims cannot be evaluated without access to privileged information. Since ordinary readers cannot verify the truth, the best they can do is accept its probable representation. Therefore the literary appearance of truth becomes important, and such literary appearance derives from style, motive, and character. But it also derives from abstract principles whose truth is tested not by verifiable knowledge but by emotional force and general agreement. The political allegories of 1713–14 sought to connect partisan squabbles to such general truths. The reader's recognition of the particularity of the abstract figures verifies and reinforces the insulting identification and implicates the reader in creating subversive meanings, for the missing term that makes the allegory significant lies in the political understanding that readers share with the author. The implicit claim is that the missing term refers to the actual political world, whose shape and nature replicate the archetype set out by allegory.[24] The literary force of Lacy's allegory lies in its depiction of the distortion of language wrought by political misapplication; Archimago and Harley both, Croxall implies, enact an archetype of self-interested treachery.

A further indirect attack on personality was the defamation not of the author but of his fictional persona. *An Invitation to Peace* manages to include particularly nasty comments about "Ironsides" (as Toby, its persona, calls the *Guardian*'s Nestor Ironside), and these are made more telling by their

resemblances to Steele himself. The attack upon Ironside is continued in
the same vein in *The Crisis upon Crisis. A Poem. Being an Advertisement
Stuck in the Lion's Mouth at Button's: and Addressed to Doctor S———t*
(London: J. Morphew, 1714), a long poem in bad verse couplets which
picks up the Hudibrastic possibilities of the Ironside-armor equation but
is more elaborate than witty or subversive. Swift is compared to Quixote
and Hudibras in *The Publick Spirit of the Tories, Manifested in the Case of
the Irish Dean and his Man Timothy* (London: J. Roberts, 1714), and the
nature of political quixotism is in turn defined by the *Examiner*: "The true
Spirit of *Quixotism*, or *Martial Lunacy*, consists in forming strong Ideas
of imaginary Dangers and Adventures, and in violent Fits of a Romantick
Rage or Impulse, worked up to such a Height, that every thing, which
comes in the way, is taken for an Enemy, and represented to the Mind as a
proper Object of Valour and Prowess" (5, no. 43 [April 23–26]).

Attacks on personae afford a variety of minor tactical advantages. They
aim at loopholes in the fictional defenses that the enemy has erected and
make fun of a weakness in the enemy's self-representation. Points where
the fictional persona corresponds closely to characteristics of its author
are often the most effective targets. Despite such minor gains, attacks on
personae lack the personal force of attacking actual authors, and they lack
allegory's drive towards generality. Emphasizing the fictionality of the target
persona undermines his claim to political authority. Political authors in the
Dunkirk–Hanover campaign are caught in a persona trap. If they write as a
fictional persona, they seem to imply that what they are saying is fictional;
if they boldly write in their own person, as Steele did, they become open
to personal counter-attacks, the most persistent of which is that as private
citizens they have no authority to claim privileged political wisdom. (The
Examiner's anonymity implied its status as representing the Ministry.) Swift
avoided the persona trap in two ways: he used an ironic persona, such as the
arguer for preserving Christianity, whose eccentricities represented not his
own characteristics but those he wished to attack, or, as in *The Conduct of the
Allies* and in the two tracts against Steele, he adopted a weakly characterized
persona and allowed his witty attacks to develop from his mockery of the
position taken by the enemy.[25] Part of the wit (such as it was) of attacks on
personae depended on the sharp-edged or strongly determined character
of these figures. But there was fun to be had from exploiting the softer,
undetermined end of the rhetorical relationship by assuming the position
of a reader. The trick here was to pose as a member of the opponent's
target audience, and to answer the opponent's argument as if sharing the
same position. (The *Examiner* describes this as a "worn and antiquated"

stratagem [4, no. 22 (July 27–31, 1713)].) Defoe was particularly adept in reading works as if he were part of their audience, and in *The Honour and Prerogative of the Queen's Majesty Vindicated* he reads Steele's *Guardian*, no. 128, as if he were a country squire who is aghast that Steele seems to confirm the Tory claim that Whigs were capable only of mindless objection to the government's actions. He asks if Steele is a secret Tory satirizing the Whigs (11), an odd question given Defoe's position as a secret Whig acting as a Tory propagandist by pretending to be a Whig.

Jonathan Swift by far is the most effective and interesting reader – or misreader – of Steele. While *The Importance of the Guardian Considered* is primarily devoted to the dismemberment of Steele himself, *The Publick Spirit of the Whigs* analyzes the text of *The Crisis*. Swift's attention to Steele's solecisms lead him to assert that the author's text would not be a bad one, "provided he would a little regard the Propriety and Disposition of his Words, consult the Grammatical Part, and get some Information in the Subject he intends to handle" (*Prose Works*, vol. VIII, 32). Swift's treatment runs through a seriatim analysis or mock-analysis of Steele's tract, beginning with the title page – or, more specifically, with the hawker offering it to the prospective buyer. Swift's primary objection to the title page is Steele's use of the word "discourse" to describe a concatenation of parliamentary acts. Swift proceeds in this analytical manner through Steele's tract, stymied, he asserts, by the paradoxical nature of his task: "What shall I say to a Pamphlet, where the Malice and Falshood of every Line would require an Answer, and where the Dulness and Absurdities will not deserve one" (*Prose Works*, vol. VIII, 36)? The issue is joined with the equation of religion and politics. Catholicism stands for Toryism; Protestantism stands for Whiggery. The Anglican *via media* becomes a political battleground, assaulted by the excesses of both sides. Steele's fear is that the possible future conversion of the Pretender would allow him not only to inherit the throne but to establish absolute monarchy in England, undoing the settlement of 1688. Swift does not see the conversion of James III as a problem, despite Steele's apprehensions to the contrary: "I can assure him, that no good Subject of the QUEEN is under the least Concern whether the *Pretender* be converted or no, farther than their Wishes that all Men would embrace the true Religion" (*Prose Works*, vol. VIII, 65). But some of Swift's Tory colleagues were interested in the Pretender's conversion, and it is difficult to believe that Swift was unaware of this interest, even though, as Ehrenpreis contends, he may not have known about specific contacts between Tories and the Jacobite court.[26] Indeed, it is unlikely that Oxford and Bolingbroke were fully aware of each other's manipulations regarding James.[27]

(The conclusion of the pamphlet War of Hanoverian Succession may have less to do with Steele's expulsion from Parliament than with the announcement of James's refusal to convert to Anglicanism, which brought an end to Tory hopes for a succession that was both Protestant and Stuart.) Swift finds a weakness in Steele's argument: precisely because Britain is protected by the parliamentary Acts that Steele cites, there can be no real crisis of succession. The limited but real success of *The Publick Spirit of the Whigs* is essentially one of tone. By adopting the position of a bemused reader who is required by the obligations of debate to respond to Steele's assertions, Swift's persona is able to pour scorn and mockery on Steele at the same time that he can display real concern for what he claims are the dangerous implications of his argument.

Steele in turn is readerly in defense. *Mr. Steele's Apology for Himself and his Writings* supplies further variations on authorship and interpretation.[28] The pamphlet describes Steele's expulsion from Parliament; most of it consists of the speech he purportedly gave in his defense. But it was not published until October 1714, seven months after the expulsion took place and one month after George I had arrived in England. Its ostensible purpose was to vindicate Steele's reputation from the charge of sedition and to show the injustice that can be done by an arbitrary majority. But one suspects that it was also intended to remind the King and his advisors that the topic causing such trouble for Steele was the King's title to the throne. (Steele's efforts on behalf of the Hanovers were well rewarded thereafter: in January 1715 he received a gift of £500 from King George and was made one of the managers of Drury-lane Theater; in February he was returned as a Member of Parliament; in April he was knighted.)

The *Apology* reveals a series of Richard Steeles. A grateful Steele thanks Robert Walpole for his support and dedicates the pamphlet to him. Steele the publisher of the pamphlet explains its purposes and the circumstances that delayed its appearance. Steele begins to narrate in a personal tone the events of the expulsion and the debate surrounding it but switches to the third person, as if distancing his narrative self from his parliamentary self. This Parliamentary self delivers the speech that defends himself from the charges brought against him – denying, in effect, that he is the false self created by Tory propagandists, and especially by Swift. He claims that this "great Affair" is only "a Paper War between two private Persons" (301), in which Parliament ought not to be involved. In order to counteract the Tory image of Steele, he quotes extensively from his own writings, proclaiming thereby an integrity that seems at odds with the multiple self-images in the pamphlet. When he finishes his speech, returning to his narrative self from his Parliamentary one, he disingenuously admits that "most of what I said was put into my Mouth by my Friends" (337). By the time he finishes, it seems that the character of Richard Steele is as contrived and composite as those of Mr. Spectator and Nestor Ironside. Nonetheless, the image of the integral self is important to the idea of interpretation that he needs to advance; integrity amid shifting personae is required by the shifting contexts for interpretation. Parliament is not a court of law, and the occasion is not the ordinary reading of a political pamphlet. The procedure was to identify the allegedly seditious passages and lay them before the House, which would then (by majority vote) agree that they were seditious and determine a penalty. The proceedings were different from legal action; the concern was to interpret a particular passage of the text rather than the text as a whole, and the function of interpretation was to reach a conclusion about sedition.

Both *The Crisis* and *The Englishman*, no. 57, the two allegedly seditious texts, were signed, and Steele had no alternative but to admit that he wrote them. His major line of defense, therefore, was to question the process of interpretation and to insist on careful critical judgment. His method was less rigorous than the argument itself: he took up the contested passages in order and explained why the charge of sedition depended on misreading. But making this defense he implicitly developed a series of positions we would now identify as theoretical. (1.) The essential unit of language, he implies, consists of full utterances rather than groups of words or even sentences. Therefore passages should not be abstracted from their contexts so that they express a meaning quite different from, or even opposite to, the meaning of the full utterance. "It would be very unfair to separate my Words, and to pronounce a Meaning in them, which I have not expressed, when that which I have expressed is a positive Denial of having entertained any such Meaning" (307). (2.) Passages whose meaning is doubtful should be elucidated by passages where the meaning is clear. (3.) An obvious and innocent interpretation must be preferred to a strained and guilty one: "if an Author's Words, in the obvious and natural Interpretation of them, have a Meaning which is Innocent, they cannot without great Injustice be condemned of another Meaning which is Criminal" (317). (4.) Statements of fact are matters of history, and authors cannot be found seditious for recording historical events. (5.) Questionable passages should be read and interpreted in terms of the consistent positions of the writer, as found in other works.

These critical statements are not original to Steele. They were echoed by other authors, including Swift, who sought to control interpretations of what they had written. Steele's position rests on the writer's intentions and asserts that these can be measured by the bulk of public statements that constitute his authorial identity. But Steele's position is false, as the rhetoric and circumstances of his *Apology* indicate. He presents multiple images of himself as author and politician. The significance of his tract has been changed by the death of Queen Anne and by his interest in presenting himself as a martyr seeking his reward from his King and party. Even beyond the *Apology* and the tracts it discusses, the authorship of political pamphlets is hidden by a variety of concealments, and their texts are produced in part by their structural place within a political argument, in part by the statements to which they respond, and in part by the political exigencies of a given moment. Insofar as meaning is the product of its contexts, the integrity of the author seems irrelevant. Political writers often hide their real meanings under deceptively innocuous surfaces, making it difficult to determine where intention ends and misinterpretation begins. But although Steele's argument is false, it seems allowably false as a response to the threat of Parliamentary expulsion, for the Tories, in seeking to hold him personally responsible for his political writings, assume the same fallacious position.

The Battle of Dunkirk and the War of Hanoverian Succession raise issues of continuing importance in propaganda disputes. Who has the right to discuss public affairs, and what qualifies a writer to speak with authority? What is the relationship between Parliamentary deliberation and the discussion of issues by the press? What is the public nature of what we now call "public issues," and to what degree were they then protected by the privilege that interdicted publication of Parliamentary debates? Does the Ministry speak and act for the monarch, or are the Crown and its ministers separate actors? Therefore, is an attack on public policy an attack on the Queen? Are speakers individually responsible for their political statements, or does the identification of authorial identity falsely shift the debate from politics to personalities? Can individual writers be guilty of sedition when they articulate the well-known positions of a faction? What responsibility must political writers take for their particular language, and what offenses against linguistic propriety become offenses against political correctness as well? Are political writers at the legal mercies of political deconstructionists, who can bring charges against any possible meaning, or are writers responsible only for the most obvious interpretations of what they have written (Derrida for the Tories; Hirsh for the Whigs)?

Logicians, of course, argue that attacks on the person of the arguer, such as those waged by Swift, Lacy, and Wagstaff on the person of Richard Steele, are merely fallacies. But in the discourse of political satire, *ad hominem* arguments are not fallacious; they are central to the nature of political debate, which often has little to do with substantial issues. The rhetoric of political debate is the familiar one where a speaker (a historical figure or a created persona) addresses actual and implied audiences, within a historical context, about issues affecting that context, drawing on general principles about which the speaker hopes the audience will agree, and using a code that may include both the ordinary language of direct reference and the privileged or semi-private discourse of shared political knowledge or assumptions.[29] Satire of such political discourse renders every part of this model of communication unstable. It attacks the identity and authority of the opposing speaker. It asserts that the text's contentions lack real substance but are reducible to personal animosity or to the quest for power. It claims that the discourse falls outside definable areas of appropriate political concern and therefore outside the appropriate interests of its audience. It insists that the actors in the affair, as distinct from those who merely write about it, have an irreproachable authority or are privy to knowledge not available to the writer or to the audience. It asserts that the general principles assumed by the opposing argument are wrong, dangerous, or simply inappropriate to the argument that has been made. It identifies inconsistencies in the argument or between the argument and the actual behavior of the faction the argument seeks to advance. It points out that the language of the argument is solecistic, too vague to mean anything, or a systematic distortion of reality effected by faction.[30] The argument itself could be true if all of these assertions of incompetence were correct, but the purpose of political discourse is not to establish or deny the truth of the opponent's argument (a truth which few if any members of the audience could be in a position to verify). The purpose of political satire is to disrupt every element of the communication model in order to show that credible communication has not taken place.

The range of satiric forms utilized in the Dunkirk debate, from personal attack, through direct and serious analysis, to literary parody, criticism of parody, and parody of criticism, places each of the elements of communications – speakers, audiences, messages, contexts, and codes – under assault, though it is rarely capable of assaulting all of them simultaneously. The shifting of political topics and literary genres not only allows propagandists to destabilize the enemy's defenses by attacking at multiple points, it allows them to abandon positions that have been undermined by hostile operations. The need to attack the enemy's lines of communication at so many different points and with so many different weapons implies that the pamphlet wars should be seen as extended campaigns requiring a series of maneuvers rather than as a random collection of discrete texts. Propaganda war becomes satiric, then, when, by making debate itself the center of concern, it directs its attack at the rhetorical processes by which the war is conducted in order to show that real communication is no longer possible because the connections necessary to convey meaning no longer work.

CHAPTER 8

White snow and black magic: Karl Kraus and the press

KRAUS AS SATIRIST

It is anachronistic to speak of the "press" in the early eighteenth century, for the medley of pamphlets, tracts, poems, broadsides, and periodicals involved in the debates over Dunkirk hardly has the generic and institutional shape and predictability that we understand by the press since the late nineteenth century. The press did not exist as a distinct kind of business organization. It did not report facts but factional opinion regarding events and rumors, and the public's interest in such events often outran the press's capacity to verify them. But the uncertainty and openness of such discourse allowed the range of its satiric attack, as I have suggested, to be directed at all elements of communication and to imply that they had failed to communicate. For the modern press, with its more positive sense of actuality and its tighter organizational definition, the satiric strategy had to be narrower and deeper. Perhaps the most important enemy of the press in the twentieth century and the most important satirist is the Viennese writer Karl Kraus. Among the elements in Roman Jakobson's communications model, Kraus's satire focuses most significantly almost exclusively on code, for his concern throughout his active satiric life was language, its nature, and its abuses.

Attacking the press provides the opportunity of decrying the material it presents as a sign of the sorry state of contemporary life, but, at the same time, it allows comment on the press itself as a creature of bourgeois capitalism that selects, suppresses, arranges, and presents its material in order to make money and to shape (or misshape) the culture of its readers in its own interests. The medium of the press's influence is language, and language is the cultural product it influences. Kraus's characteristic method is to concentrate on journalistic solecisms, especially on revealing the trivial. The self-evident demonstration of triviality may be amusing but hardly rises to the level of serious satire. Kraus rises very high indeed by asserting that the trivial contains apocalyptic implications. When a newspaper in 1912 announced a forthcoming performance of "King Lehar," Kraus saw the fortuitous substitution of operetta for tragedy as "the measure of our time."[1] Kraus later described World War I as those years "da Operettenfiguren dies Tragödie der Menschheit spielen" ("those years in which operetta figures enacted the tragedy of mankind").[2] Alternatively, Kraus worries the trivial at length until he can expose (or indicate without exposing directly) its terrible consequences. "Untergang der Welt durch schwarze Magie" ("Destruction of the World by Black Magic") grows organically out of an advertisement for a coffee-brewer that is cast in heroic terms.[3] Kraus uses his own complex and carefully wrought language as the device that disassembles and examines the language of others. His concern is for code.

It is this concern that distances Kraus from English and American readers of satire. He is not merely concerned with language but with the German language, to which he attaches deep significance. And his own language combines an exactness of expression with elaborate and incessant wordplay, with sharp aphoristic turns, with grand rhetorical gestures, sometimes sustained for many sentences, with surprising and revealing introductions of jargon or dialect. Translating him is at times like riding a roller coaster, where sudden linguistic dips and turns keeping throwing readers off balance and threatening to toss them into the void. Not only is his German demanding, his Viennese is daunting as well. His attention to the cosmic significance of detail requires his readers to map some of the territory between trivia and the universe. Readers need to be aware of the context to identify the details, and they need to understand the cultural and historical significance of that context in order to perceive the urgency of the satire. It would be an overstatement to assert that Kraus is comprehensible only by people who spoke German with an Austrian accent and lived within the Ringstrasse between 1890 and 1936. It would be a doubly ironic overstatement, because Kraus insisted that his works be reprinted without annotation, which he believed unnecessary, because Kraus saw his ultimate audience as posterity (and reprinted his own *Fackel* essays in volume form several years after they first appeared), and because Kraus denounced the narrow pretensions of nationality in the face of what he saw as universally human.[4] We are left, then, with the problematic paradox of a Viennese satirist in and of German who claimed for his work a timeless significance that transcends place – the cosmic significance of detail.

Virtually every translator of Kraus describes as well-worn the truism that he is untranslatable but repeats it to apologize that only a few of his many plays on language have been preserved and that the few works translated are the more accessible but not necessarily the most important. The situation is thus particularly difficult for English readers with no or little German who seek to approach his significance in a responsible way. Fortunately, the scholarship on Kraus in English, although dwarfed by the scholarship in German, is particularly useful. Harry Zohn's Kraus volume for the Twayne series is judicious and informative, and he has recently given an account of scholarship on Kraus.[5] Edward Timms's study of Kraus's work through World War I and *Die letzten Tage*, though not a full biography, is particularly strong on the connections between Kraus's life and his work, on literary connections, on Kraus as a satirist, and on shifts and developments in Kraus's writing and thought through the first twenty years of *Die Fackel*.[6] Frank Field supplies little new information about Kraus's works but substantial material on their social and, especially, political contexts.[7] Wilma Abeles Iggers provides a topical treatment that lacks depth but allows access to Krausian statements and ideas.[8] Particular note should be made of translations of the important German essays by Walter Benjamin and Erich Heller and of the chapter on Kraus in *Wittgenstein's Vienna* by Allan Janik and Stephen Toulmin.[9] Despite this help, the reader of English is left at some distance from Kraus's texts and from his concern for the German language, and there is no strategy to close the gap successfully.

Since I am basically a reader of English myself (that is, my German is roughly comparable to Kraus's English), I need, I think, to be forthright about my own encounter with Kraus, about what I can consequently say, and why it seems important to say it. I have read everything by Kraus that has been translated into English, and some of what I have read (but certainly not all) I have compared to the German texts. In addition I have read in German (slowly and perhaps inaccurately) a half-dozen particularly relevant essays by Kraus that have not been translated. I have read everything written about Kraus in English that I could find, some of what has been written in French, and a very small amount of what has been written in German. On the basis of this imperfect acquaintance, I can hardly pretend to speak authoritatively about him or to add significantly to what has already been said. The virtual silence about Kraus among English and American writers on satire is quite understandable. But he is as close as one can find in the twentieth century to a defining figure of satire. I propose to read Kraus not to see what new information I can contribute about him but to discover what he can tell me about satire. Fortunately, he can tell a great deal, even to struggling readers, and he is too important and too valuable an informant to be dismissed as inaccessible.

Erich Heller asserts that Kraus is "the first European satirist since Swift."[10] Without argument about the satiric claims of intervening writers, the assertion seems true if, by "first European satirist," one understands that Kraus is the most important embodiment of the satirist. Like Swift (but unlike Byron or Flaubert) he can be defined almost exclusively in terms of his satire. And, like Swift, he was a public figure as a satirist – in a sense a professional writer of satire. Unlike Swift, who often wrote double-edged satires in the guise of a satiric victim, Kraus wrote in his own voice (although his satiric voice was not his only voice). He was (because of his position as writer, editor, and publisher of *Die Fackel* he had to be) a satirist in real life as well as a satirist in print. His character as a human being was not, of course, limited to his public role as a satirist. But in his self-descriptions (for example, in "Lob der verkehrten Lebensweise," "Praise of a Topsy-Turvy Life-Style," 1908) Kraus presents himself as an isolated man, proudly sleeping through the morning and working through the night so as to avoid the ordinary world.[11] His letters and personal recollections of him, however, reveal him as a charming man with many friends, and his long, complex relationship to Sidonie Nádherný is documented by two volumes of correspondence. Descriptions of his public readings attest to the force of his personality. Elias Canetti recounts the effect of a 1924 reading: "These sentences, built like cyclopean fortresses and always carefully dovetailing, shot out sudden flashes of lightning, not harmless, not illuminating, not even theatrical flashes, but deadly lightning. And this process of annihilatory punishment, occurring in public and in all ears at once, was so fearful and dreadful that no one could resist it."[12] His position in the center of this satiric vortex made him particularly aware of his responsibilities as a satirist. Unlike Swift, he rejected fiction, and his satire was not sustained by large structural devices that embody and enable its force and direction. Therefore the emphasis is thrown on language, and the "plots" of Kraus's satires lie in the unfolding of their sentences and in their often subtle movements from one sentence to the next.

Karl Kraus is known primarily for *Die Fackel* (The Torch), a journal that he published between 1899 and 1936, and for *Die letzten Tage der Menschheit* (The Last Days of Mankind), which might be described as a satire in the form of a play. *Die Fackel* was founded quite consciously as a journal whose purposes were destruction and clearance. He sought to purge public discourse of its distorting linguistic affectations, to provide drainage for the vast swamp of phrases, as he put it ("Trockenlegung des weiten Phrasensumpfes").[13] The swamp in particular need of drainage was the *Neue Freie Presse*, the leading liberal newspaper, whose editor, Moriz

Benedikt, was Kraus's particular *bête noire*. In its early years *Die Fackel* in-cluded a number of distinguished contributors, but Kraus gradually stopped publishing contributions and, in 1911, announced that he would do with-out them entirely, on the grounds that "they repel those readers whom I want to lose myself."[14] The journal might be thought of as a kind of grid whose horizontal dimension is made up of on-going events and occasions, as these are supplied by and filtered through the press, and whose vertical dimension consists of themes and concerns that characteristically set Kraus off: the dangerous foolishness of the press, the vapid artificiality of literature and the theater, hypocritical social attitudes and practices regarding sexual-ity, the self-fulfilling and reductive nature of psychoanalysis, the disjunction between justice and the legal system, the corruption of language in all forms of public discourse, the replacement of imagination and intrinsic purpose by technology and profit. Kraus conjoins these concerns with emergent oc-casions by commentary, aphorism, quotation, parallel contrasting columns, personal polemic, literary and cultural analysis, and occasional poems.

The occasion which produced *Die letzten Tage der Menschheit* was, of course, World War I. The war engaged many issues that Kraus had already articulated in the pre-war numbers of *Die Fackel*, and it supplied a wider and more horrendous range of examples. Kraus composed much of the play in the early years of the war, but continued to add material even after its initial publication in *Die Fackel* (1919). The result was a powerful master-piece and perhaps the most sustained satire ever written, but as a dramatic work it is literally unperformable. It is nearly eight hundred pages long, with over two hundred scenes, and some five hundred characters. Various critics have argued that the play, or at least an arrangement of scenes from it, is stageworthy, despite Kraus's claims to the contrary and his own re-fusal to allow the performance of any part of it except the Epilogue and the excerpts he gave at public readings.[15] Although I find the argument for staging versions of the play convincing, it also seems to me in some respects beside the point. It seems reasonable to think of *Die letzten Tage* as a satire in which drama becomes the host form for the satiric parasite. Although the artistic structures traced by Mary Snell and Franz H. Mautner are im-portant (and difficult to retain in abridgment), what satire here represents is actuality.[16] The stage on which, as Kraus maintains in his foreword, tragic parts are played by operetta figures, is not theatrical but real life, the war itself. Virtually one-third of the play is drawn from documentary sources, and, except for the expressionistic final scenes, the invented material is highly realistic. Perhaps the crucial sense that readers have about the play is that they are perceiving the actual war, not the war as misrepresented by the illusions and contradictions also represented in the play. (The central series of conversations between the satiric Grumbler, more-or-less representing Kraus himself, and the reasonable but deluded Optimist is paralleled by discussion between a Subscriber and a Patriot; the first pair seeks to understand the war, while the second seeks, in the face of absurd contradictions, to maintain the illusions promulgated by the press.) Kraus's crucial concern is that a war of almost unimaginable horror has been made possible and sustained by the deluding force of public discourse and by the lack of common skepticism that allows those delusions to flourish. The interplay between horror and delusion parallels the interplay between historicity (the truth of war as represented by satire) and theatricality. Kraus's assertion that the play is unactable has deep levels of meaning.

Although the themes developed in Kraus's pre-war satire had prepared him to make strong assertions about the First World War, he was not similarly prepared for the advent of Nazism. After the establishment of the Austrian Republic he supported the Social Democrats, but he continued to criticize the party, its policies, and its press. He transformed his public recitations into a "Theater der Dichtung," where he read the works of Shakespeare, Nestroy, Offenbach, and others whom he admired, in contrast to the commercial theater, which he accused of artifice and empty spectacle.[17] He conducted acerbic polemics against the journalist Imre Békassy and against the Viennese police chief Johannes Schober, whose police rioted against a demonstration and killed ninety people. Angered at the belated, lukewarm support by the Social Democrats for these campaigns, Kraus left the party, declaring himself independent of political connections.[18] He later supported Engelbert Dollfuss, despite the repressions of his regime, as the only viable alternative to the Nazis, but Dollfuss was assassinated in 1934. Kraus was horrified by the Nazis, but he lacked the satiric tools to oppose them effectively. His satire had always been directed against the center and the left, especially the liberal press, because the excesses of the right seemed to him too self-evident to require his analysis. World War I was conducted on the basis of deceit and illusions, and Kraus's satire contrasted those untruths to reality. Despite the Nazis' well-known distortion of language, the direct relationship between Nazi ideology and Nazi atrocities allowed little scope for satire. One response to the Nazis, therefore, was a silence whose significance was proclaimed in his much-quoted ten-line poem in *Fackel* no. 888, which concludes "Das Wort entschlief, als jene Welt erwachte" ("the word died when that world awoke"). Kraus's other two responses were wordy rather than silent – his 315-page *Fackel* (nos. 890–905) of 1934 and *Die*

Dritte Walpurgisnacht, which he had prepared for publication in 1933 but withheld, in fear, he told his friends, of reprisals against Austria and against Jews. (It was published in 1952.) Harry Zohn describes it as "the rambling monologue of a worried man who talks incessantly in an effort to keep the demons at bay."[19] Kraus felt that the evils of the times had finally exceeded the capacity of satire to attack them effectively. He died in 1936.

Kraus's religious and political positions are not easy to determine. Caroline Kohn sees Kraus as sympathetic to socialism and consistently libertarian.[20] Wilma Iggers sees him as conservative and argues that Nazi polemics and irrationalism were not far from those of Kraus himself.[21] Edward Timms traces a shift in Kraus's position during the war: before the war Kraus had been essentially a conservative critic of modern society, its dehumanizing technology, and the profit motive of bourgeois capitalism; after the war, which was supported by the conservative forces with which Kraus had sympathized, his critical position allowed him to embrace, however warily, socialism and democracy.[22] Kraus's religious shifts are similar, though not exactly parallel. His family was Jewish, but he became quickly assimilated and formally renounced his Judaism in 1899. In 1911, for what he claimed were private reasons, he was baptized in the Catholic Church, but he did not reveal his religious position to his readers until, in 1923, he broke publicly with the church on aesthetic rather than theological issues. Some of his principal targets – the liberal press, the profit motive, and psychoanalysis – were publicly identified with Judaism, and Kraus thus identified with them as well. The resulting anti-Semitism scattered through *Die Fackel* remains one of its most discomforting elements. John Theobald, in a full account of Kraus's Jewish anti-Semitism, argues that it was in large part motivated by an effort to prevent Jewish behavior that might verify the more dangerous anti-Semitism of non-Jews.[23] I suspect that for Kraus religious and political affiliations, and such labels as revolutionary and reactionary, were external tokens and institutional manifestations of spiritual and moral commitments, and that shifts in his religious and political identification were efforts on his part to express those commitments in particular historical exigencies.

Central to Kraus's thought are the meanings he attaches to the terms *Ursprung* (source or origin) and *Ziel* (aim, goal, limit).[24] It is possible to see *Ursprung* as an inner, conceptual parallel of religion and *Ziel* as an inner equivalent of politics. In his much-discussed poem "Zwei Laufer" ("Two Runners"), Kraus privileges *Ursprung* over *Ziel*, but both must remain separable from their religious and political manifestations. Indeed, Kraus's sense of an inner self that remained independent of such identification was crucial to his position as a satirist, and writing *Die Fackel* allowed him to express that spiritual commitment in ways that were not circumvented by the compromises that seemed inescapable in religious and political affiliations. For Kraus that spiritual commitment is closely tied to his moral sense of language and his satiric attacks on the language of the press.

KRAUS AND CODE

Kraus's obsession with language as the primary element of his satire and its moral judgments raises philosophical issues that are crucial to satire. What is the relationship between language and reality, between language and thought, between language and action? Since satire often occupies a medial, paradoxical position that insists on the difference of imagination from other ways of thinking and yet insists with equal vigor that its primary object is the immediate world of historical experience, the role of language as the mediator of imagination and experience needs explanation. It is precisely in search of such an explanation that, despite my own linguistic problems in doing so, I have turned to Kraus both as a theorist of language and as a practitioner of satire.

Help in mapping the conceptual territory where Kraus's language is spoken might be supplied by the classic formulation suggested by the semanticist Alfred Tarski: "'Snow is white' is true if, and only if, snow is white."[25] Tarski distinguishes between the first (quoted) appearance of the phrase and the second in order to define the difference between object language and metalanguage. As a guide to Kraus, the formulation can be used more modestly. The whole assertion appears at first to be unacceptably tautological and positivist. But Tarski asserts that his principle is neutral regarding epistemologies, that it will work regardless of how the whiteness of snow is perceived or postulated. Tarski further admits that his statement is language specific but true in any language that has words equivalent to "snow" and "white." Since language is a cultural creation, meaning (statements about truth) must be a cultural creation as well. Kraus's concern for language is thus in itself a concern about the nature of his culture: the empty phrase shows the vacuity of that culture. The printer's error of Lehar for Lear manifests the culture's incapacity to appreciate the heights and depths of human tragedy because of its shallow self-absorption in the trivial. Kraus's perception of the error shows his awareness of that superficiality.

If I look out of the window and observe that the snow piling up outside my office is white, and if you look out and agree, I may have made a true statement because the words refer (positively) to observed facts or because you and I have agreed (conventionally) that the terms describe a perception that we share. But if I say the snow is white after it has been on the ground for ten days, I may be imperceptive, or I may be making a generalization that I know is untrue in order to deceive, or, if I know that you know the snow's real color, to be ironic. In addition to the problems of ignorance, deception, and irony, the statement "snow is white," when I look out of my office window, is a specific description, but as a scientific statement about snow, made without reference to particular observations, it becomes a normative assertion to which we understand there will be many exceptions. The fact that most generalizations are normative statements in this way (generalizations are rarely universals) shows the approximate character of ordinary language – subject to exception, inaccuracy, error, lying, and deception. Kraus saw the work of the satirist as preserving language against such corruptions and, at the same time, as exploiting its ambiguities. But the satirist's concern for language goes beyond the task of preservation. His obligations grow particularly urgent when the object language and the metalanguage no longer agree. One cannot reveal that last week's snow is no longer white by appealing to common observation when a shift has taken place in the meaning of language itself so that one's fellow-speakers define white as whatever color snow happens to be. Rather than shouting that it is not so, the satirist needs to attend to the language that now controls not only how thought is expressed but how reality is perceived. The satiric problem is one of code.

Kraus seeks to wrest language back to its previous (its original, *ursprunglich*) formulation. Hence he provides glosses that reveal the solecisms of the press, and he devotes many pages (mostly collected in *Die Sprache*) to moralistic discourses on minute matters of grammar and syntax.[26] A Krausian paradox is that language, carefully crafted, becomes the standard by which language, sloppily used, may be judged, but not even the careful craftsman – and Kraus himself devoted great care to his prose – can entirely escape the inherent instability of his medium. Kraus opened this paradox so that it became a satiric tool: he insisted that writers ought to be aware of the ambiguities inherent in their language and hence that they can be held responsible for them. To return language to its origins, Kraus develops a style of writing that itself moves towards the metalanguage that Tarski advocates as the basis of semantics. Merely by quoting, Kraus changes the context of the quotation and renders it satiric. As Walter Benjamin observed, "in the quotation that both saves and chastises, language proves the matrix of justice. It summons the word by its name, wrenches it destructively from its context, but precisely thereby calls it back to its origin ... In quotation the two realms – of origin and destruction – justify themselves before language."[27]

A second means of retrieving language is to develop a style that is itself more truly and correctly German, more original in every sense of the word, than the loose and easy phrases of the press. Kraus's satire emerges out of his style, a situation that parallels his dicta about the primacy of language over thought.[28] His style is praised as being quintessentially German, but it seems German turned in upon itself – highly metaphorical, sometimes aphoristic or hyperbolic, shifting in meaning and direction, playing with clichés by interchanging them or, more fatally, by perversely reading them in literal terms. The much-analyzed opening sentence of "In dieser grossen Zeit" ("In These Great Times"), which Kraus initially delivered as a speech in November 1914, shifts sharply among its structural devices, forcing the auditor quickly and successively off balance. Kraus was a master of the subordinate clause, through which he builds overarching and governing structures of thought that sometimes are perpetuated through successive sentences. In addition to these figural and structural elements, Kraus includes a sometimes complex, even bewildering, cross-hatching of allusion, self-reference, and quotation. J. P. Stern's description verifies the English reader's discomforts with Kraus's German:

This means that the functions of certain words in his sentences are unusually complex; verbal and nominal inflections are preferred to prepositions, conjunctions are omitted whenever possible; the links between nouns and pronouns are left for the reader to establish, a single finite verb is made to do duty in several phrases, there is an abundance of ellipses – it all comes to an intensity of verbal means which is, for Kraus, the hallmark of poetry.[29]

These devices are, of course, demanding, and Kraus insisted that his works ought to be read several times: "Lieber aber ist mir, man liest sie überhaupt nicht, als bloss einmal. Die Kongestionem eines Dummkopfs, der keine Zeit hat, möchte ich nicht verantworten" ("However, I prefer their not being read at all to their being read only once. I would not want to be responsible for the congestions of a blockhead who has no time").[30] The appearance Kraus sometimes gives to the superficial reader (the "Dummkopf" of his aphorism) is of mere linguistic eccentricity or even crankiness. But even superficial readers sometimes find themselves arrested by possibilities of meaning that they did not see at first, and such discoveries may eventuate in their taking a place among the knowledgeable. Ascending to the ranks of knowledge, however, does not save Kraus's readers, for he was well aware of disciples who, rejecting newspapers that did not let them think for themselves, now let Kraus do their thinking for them. "After you heard ten or twelve lectures by Karl Kraus," Elias Canetti reported, "after you read his journal *Die Fackel* for a year or two, the first thing to happen was a general shrinkage of the desire to do your own judging."[31] But this usurpation of judgment is an unintended consequence of Kraus's efforts to return language to its essential nature.

For Erich Heller the problem behind the problem of translating Kraus is his elusive ambiguity:

With only a few exceptions, his work must remain untranslated; and it is untranslatable because he did not write "in a language," but through him the German language seemed to assume personal shape in order to become the crucial witness in the case this great prosecutor brought against his time . . . The work of Karl Kraus is rich in words; and every single word is of the greatest possible precision. It is precise through its infinite ambiguity. He intended it to be like that, in protest against the rationalist superstition that a word could ever create or convey a clear-cut concept, and fix a definite object in the void of the universe.[32]

This precision in ambiguity, however, raises questions about the nature and meaning of Kraus's equation of language and morality. If the ambiguity of Kraus's language, as Heller contends, reveals the illusion that the universe is fixed and definite, how can Kraus also contend that language in and of itself supplies the basis for moral judgment, that incorrect language reveals faulty values or bad behavior? But Kraus saw the indeterminate nature of language as one of its prime riches: "Die Sprache ist die einige Chimäre, deren Trugkraft ohne Ende ist, die Unerschöpflichkeit, an der das Leben nicht verarmt" ("Language is the only chimera whose power to deceive is unending, the inexhaustible by which life does not become poorer").[33] In his 1966 essay on Kraus, J. P. Stern attacks what he sees as Kraus's naive equation of language and morality and his consequent belief that knowledge implies goodness; for Stern that connection excludes the will to act exemplified by Nazism.[34] Kraus's vision of language may, after all, reflect just another version of Viennese passivity.[35] In an introductory essay for *Encounter* in 1975, and again in 1986, Stern argues that Kraus's effort to use language as the criterion for moral judgment might best be viewed as a fiction.[36] But if it is fiction, it is in the sense that myth is fiction: it is a fiction that serves truth.

The language–morality equation might be seen as normative rather than universal. While it is most unreliably true that good language implies moral goodness, it may more often be the case that bad language, when it is not merely ignorant or illiterate, implies questionable morality. At least bad language acts as a signal to the possibilities of illusion, deception, or confusion (from which bad acts flow), and these states can be revealed by an analysis of language as it shows its own weakness – precisely the kind of analysis that Kraus characteristically undertakes. He saw doubt as the great but scorned gift for which humankind is indebted to language ("Der Zweifel als die grosse moralische Gabe, die der Mensch der Sprache verdanken könnte und bis heute verschmäht hat"; "Die Sprache," 382). Language correlates with morality because language depends on choices that in turn depend on values. Thus language and morality share the idea of responsibility. Kraus insisted that writers take responsibility for their language and its ambiguities and that individuals take responsibility for their actions. Just as the poor writer thoughtlessly uses comfortable phrases, the individual behaves according to thoughtless or hypocritically conventional values. But although aesthetics and morality share these qualities, the distinction between the two is in other senses essential, for language should not substitute emotional (aesthetic) effect for information. Moral action requires knowledge, but bad language replaces knowledge with phrases of enticing artificiality. Kraus's lifelong interest in advertisements exemplifies his scorn for this artificiality, which he saw as threatening to replace reality altogether.[37] He identified the emergence of the enticing phrase with Heine's introduction of the French feuilleton into the German press.[38] Kraus's campaign against the artificiality of language paralleled the campaign by his friend Adolf Loos against the artificiality of architecture. He and Loos, Kraus asserted, showed the difference between an urn and a chamber pot, the difference that allowed space for culture.[39] Language not only reflects personal values by which the responsibilities of individual writers will be judged but also cultural values embedded in its history. Hence language is the product both of individual choices and the cultural history that shapes the conventional meanings of words. The gap between *langue* and *parole* is one of several that Kraus exploits and manipulates to satiric effect, for it parallels the gap between subjective values and values sanctioned by tradition. Either side of the gap can be played both ways: the individual user becomes the new liberal capitalist whose language, motivated by profit, deceives by replacing old words with new meanings, or the traditional language loses meaning precisely because it is not rethought and its meaning rediscovered by new users. The flexibility that allows Kraus to use language both as relative (subject to corruption) and quasi-absolute (the source of moral judgments embedded in culture) is one of the main values of Kraus's identification of language with morality.

The distinction between language as used by individual speakers and language as the product of culture parallels the distinction between language as the vessel of knowledge and language as a spur to action. However ephemeral or "fictional" the connection between language and morality may be, language, as we have seen, is characteristically used to produce effects on its readers and hence to lead its audience to act in certain ways. Such a function seems to define public language or the language of the press. Language is thus moral both in the values from which it derives and in the personal, social, economic, and political actions it is intended to produce. When one uses language publicly, one can hardly avoid using it to produce an effect, and Kraus's powerful public readings of his own works were surely examples of such persuasion. The important distinction concerns the purpose of persuasion. Kraus's readings do not result in profit or entertainment or even, perhaps, in self-advertisement but in the heightened skeptical capacity of his audience to evaluate the truth-claims of language. But the power to distinguish between self-serving and educational purposes derives from the language itself. In his own writing and in his criticism of others, Kraus remains concerned with how the relationship between the thing said and the mode of saying reveals assumptions about value that might otherwise remain hidden.

Kraus's assertion of the authority of language seems at first glance to place him among the Houyhnhnms, who tell Gulliver "That the Use of Speech was to make us understand one another, and to receive Information of Facts; now if any one *said the Thing which was not*, these Ends were defeated; because I cannot properly be said to understand him, and am so far from receiving Information, that he leaves me worse than in Ignorance" (*Gulliver's Travels*, Book IV, chapter IV). But this reduction of language to reporting information makes it difficult for the Houyhnhnms to understand Gulliver's account of Europe, and it might rob lesser beasts of the means of critical interpretation (*Sprachkritik*), precisely the capacity that Kraus insists upon. Although Kraus berates the press because it has abandoned its simple obligation to use language to report facts, he does not equate the reporting of facts with the telling of truth. Kraus is concerned with language as the expression of *Geist* and *Ursprung*, the underlying sources and mental capacities from which language emerges, which it represents but cannot fully describe.

Walter Benjamin describes Kraus as "Cosmic Man" (*Allmensch*), as "Demon" (*Dämon*), and as "Monster" (*Unmensch*), and these terms organize his essay on Kraus.[40] Kraus the monster is Kraus the satirist, the cannibal admitted into civilized society, the misanthropic Timon, the assaulter of reputations, and the disembodier of quotations. But the monstrous nature of his satire leads to its linguistic refinement.

His work is innocent and pure, consuming and purifying masterliness. And therefore the monster stands among us as the messenger of a more real humanism. He is the conqueror of the empty phrase. He feels solidarity not with the slender pine but with the plane that devours it, not with the precious ore but with the blast furnace that purifies it.[41]

In a desperate and anomic age satire succeeds by negation in preserving what is most human. Kraus's language–morality equation allows internal and self-validating criteria for satiric judgment. If traditional morality turns out to be hypocrisy, if philosophical efforts to find ethical roots succeed only in digging holes, the use of language as a basis for condemning behavior (and not only linguistic behavior) allows the satirist to attack without claiming to have located ultimate moral truth. Kraus's big philosophical terms – *Ursprung* in particular – point to locations where the substance is imperceptible and undescribable by words but whose presence can be indicated by the negative operations of language. If the language–morality equation is a fiction, it is, like the claim that God delivered the moral law to Moses, a fiction that enables truth.

But the introduction of another term makes its status seem less fictitious. Because morality is the criterion for evaluating actual behavior, the language–morality equation may actually yield a triad of the world, ideas about the world, and language. Thus language may purport to describe the world but characteristically describe ideas about the world. The notion of such a triad may save Kraus from critics who associate him with a naive word–world dualism. These argue that Kraus's project, though interesting and perhaps even noble, is doomed to fail in its historical circumstances because his exclusive focus on language cuts him off from the real world of action. A sign of such exclusion is his identification of real social and cultural ills but his failure to trace them to their social, economic, and political causes, his failure, in short, to discover the real enemy.[42] It is no anomaly, the antagonists go on, that Nazism should rise despite Kraus's years of satire against the elements that make it up, and if Kraus laments and warns against the rise of Nazism, his words are not only ponderous but irrelevant, for Nazism is the triumph of will over intellect. But Nazism is an idea about the world, even if it is an idea that will overcomes intellectual and moral scruples, and it is precisely such ideas that produce the evils and dangers that Kraus also describes. The position of ideas about the world as mediators between language and the world restores relevance to Kraus's satire. Words refer to ideas, which in turn determine behavior. The wrongness of the word reveals the wrongness of the idea to which it refers and the behavior it produces. Seen in this light, the language–morality equation is an abbreviation which, taken literally, may be misleading. But it is not a fiction.

KRAUS AND THE PRESS

Die Mission der Presse ist, Geist zu verbreiten und zugleich die Aufnahmsfähigkeit zu zerstören. (*Aphorismen* 76)[43]

Kraus's essential quarrel with the press concerned the idea of the world that it presented, and language became both the object and the means of his attack. In considering in more detail the relationship between Kraus's satiric uses of language and his attacks on the press, one might usefully distinguish between the press as an ultimate object of Kraus's judgment and the press as as a means of making that culture accessible to Kraus's satiric scrutiny. The press has both functions for Kraus, and Kraus tends to shift between the two in order to use the press as a metaphor for culture in general. He satirizes a number of political and social attitudes as these are revealed by the reports of the press. Therefore, much as Kraus disliked the press, it became useful to him in providing the occasion for satiric attacks against targets separable from the press itself. Such reports in the press make them available not only to Kraus but to his readers as well. His comments on significant trials, for example, provide him with three targets – the events that constitute the material of the trial, the court system that replaces justice with legality, and the press that reports the trial. In many cases these trials concerned sexual matters that Kraus believed should not be the business of the state at all. The press justified the official insistence on strict sexual morality (a morality Kraus saw as unnatural), but it contained personal advertisements with thinly veiled offers of sexual services of all sorts. This condemnation on the front page of what was offered in the back made the press the prime exemplar of the sexual hypocrisy of turn-of-the-century Vienna. "Das Ehrenkreuz" ("The Good Conduct Medal") reports the fining of a prostitute for wearing, in a brothel, a good-conduct medal that a customer had given her in lieu of more usual payment. The medal, which irritated the other customers, is comically compared to the license she was granted to practice her trade, and Kraus goes on to distinguish among women who practice sex without being licensed to do so, women who do not practice it although licensed, and the woman who practiced the supposed immorality for which she had been licensed but got into trouble for wearing a good-conduct medal that aroused unlicensed emotions.[44] The whore whose wages were the medal is compared to the court whose wages were the fine she was forced to pay. For Kraus, prostitution is a natural and unpreventable practice, and attempts to impose legal control are inherently hypocritical.

Prostitution and the advertisement of sexual services were only manifestations of Kraus's larger concern with advertising as a characteristic – perhaps primary – function of the press. *Die Fackel* appeared with no advertising whatsoever, and Kraus condemned the Social-Democrat *Arbeiter-Zeitung* because its advertisements conflicted with, and therefore tended to restrain, positions taken by the paper itself. Advertising, of course, typified the use of laudatory and even heroic language to describe mundane and trivial items, a situation that stimulated Kraus's exercises in the mock-heroic. The false claims of advertising contributed to the general tendency of the press to corrupt the consciousness of its readers. They also tended to corrupt the nature of personal relations, as exemplified by Kraus's sardonic comments on sexual and marital advertisements.[45] The corruption inherent in advertising, where the press becomes the servant of its advertisers rather than its readers, is paralleled in the cultural sphere by the corruption inherent in its treatment of the theater. Kraus naturally objects to the bad taste reflected in reviews of performances, but areas of direct corruption included the tendency to base favorable treatment of actors on their cooperation with the press (for example by attending the Concordia, a gala ball sponsored by the press) and the writing of reviews by dramatists whose plays were performed by the theaters (principally the Burgtheater) being reviewed. The primary offender in this last case, as in many others, was Hermann Bahr.[46]

Notable among the various corruptions presented to Kraus and his viewers by the press is the reporting of news that does not exist, the assertion of manifest falsehoods. These became particularly evident in the Friedjung trial, in which Kraus took great interest.[47] The discovery of forged documents revealed the crimes of a triple alliance of politics, press, and science ("der schliessige Dreibund von Politik, Presse, und Wissenschaft").[48] Elements of the Austrian government, anxious to find an excuse for war against Serbia, passed forged papers, alleging a treasonous conspiracy among members of the Croatian Parliament, to Heinrich Friedjung, a professor of history, who used them in a warmongering article published in the *Neue Freie Presse* without bothering to check the facts. But a trial for libel brought against Friedjung surprisingly revealed discrepancies that proved the documents false, thereby calling into question the officials who forged them, the scientific credentials of the professor who published them without verification, the integrity of the newspaper that distributed them, and the credulity of an Austrian public willing to believe all this. Not only can the press, the great practitioner of delusion, be deluded itself, it can make news by reporting it. One of Kraus's favorite targets was Siegmund Münz, who specialized in vacuous interviews with the royalty of various countries, especially the Balkans.[49] When the King of Greece made some undiplomatic remarks about Crete that were carelessly reported by Münz in the *Neue Freie Presse*, war between Greece and Turkey was only narrowly averted. "Das ganze was ein Missverständnis. Alles bleibt aufrecht, nur habe es sich nicht um die kretanische Frage gehandelt, sondern um die Frage, ob der Kretinismus heilbar ist" ("The whole thing was a misunderstanding. Everything was reliably reported except that it did not have anything to do with the Cretan question but with the question of whether or not cretinism is curable").[50]

Münz's chatty and pretentious feuilletons regarding the private character of royal families become, as Kraus treats them, parodies of Schiller's *Don Carlos*, in which the stupidity of royalty is stupidly reported by the idiot-reporter. His reports show once again the confusion of public and private life by the press. But the intrusion of the press on the private has sadder examples than those of royalty. In "Interview mit einem sterbenden Kind" ("Interview with a Dying Child") Kraus gives in full the brief newspaper account of a nine-year-old boy who leapt from the window of a fourth-floor apartment following his mother and three-year-old brother. He had tried to persuade his mother not to commit suicide, but she jumped, holding her younger son. The older unthinkingly jumped after her and remained conscious long enough to give the story to the press. Kraus's comment could hardly be more biting: "Der Presse ringt mit dem Tode, um früher als er am Sterbebett eines bludenden Kindes zur Information zu kommen. Vor diesem Schauspiel verstummt aller Hass und alle Verachtung der Presse" ("The press struggled with death in order to beat it to the deathbed of a bleeding child for the sake of getting information. Before this spectacle all hatred and contempt for the press fall silent").[51] Readers whose interest may have been engaged by the sad complexities of the suicide story itself find themselves betrayed into a dreadful voyeurism by the intrusive press. Kraus's quotation of such press stories and his citation of significant news events as reported by the press – the discovery of the North Pole, the sinking of the Titanic (which he sees as the manifest failure of arrogant technology), or the murder of a white missionary in New York by her Chinese lover – made them cultural symbols that re-echoed in successive works.

The confusion of, in, and between public and private spheres that runs through many of the issues presented by the press points to Kraus's concern for the press's power to select and to suppress the news, an example of which is the silence of the *Neue Freie Presse* about Kraus himself. Since it could not respond to Kraus's rapid-fire attacks on it and on its editor Moriz Benedikt, it pretended Kraus did not exist. The press's complete control over the news is for Kraus a paradoxical result of the freedom of the press. The press's freedom from the monitoring of the state enables it not only to publish but to repress news. This repressive freedom becomes an image of liberal capitalism, where freedom empowers financial and social exploitation.[52] The press distributes its misinformation to a mass audience for commercial purposes, and the size of its audience and its financial interests are major reasons why the *Neue Freie Presse* has a power that *Die Fackel* does not. But *Die Fackel* repeatedly testifies that the press's ostensible position as observer and reporter of society is false, for the press is as active an agent as any other. The press is both cause and effect of the destruction of human will and natural order itself by the process of mechanization. The last Grumbler scene of *Die letzten Tage* (v, 54) begins with the reading of a *Fackel* essay describing the transformation of trees into newsprint, and Kraus often reminds his readers that the word for leaf (*Blatt*) is the same as the word for newspaper.[53] The confusion of public and private spheres in the pages of the press is echoed by an equally sinister confusion of literary discourse and the transmission of information, and it is here that Kraus performs the Cerberean function of satire by seeking to protect the imagination from rival and encroaching forms of discourse. Pretentious phrases and stale clichés substitute for facts and reflective responses, and Kraus responds in turn by a pseudo-naive overliteralization of dead metaphors that restores them to their native inanity.

The function of the press ought to be to provide information to readers who can then use their own imaginative and analytic abilities to understand its significance. For Kraus the encroachment of technology, commercialism, and false literature on this function leads to the disappearance of the critical faculty to evaluate information. Indeed, the whole point of the commercialization of the press – most evident in advertising – is to forestall such analysis. Thus a consequence of the press is the loss of *Geist*, the intellectual, analytic, and imaginative power that allows the observer to move from facts as perceived to the inner and underlying origin (*Ursprung*) that gives them their ultimate meaning. The press threatens to destroy an essential human capacity. In 1908, when he wrote "Apokalypse," this loss of individual and social capacity was the apocalyptic event that Kraus feared, though he was well aware of the threat to peace posed by the Austrian annexation of Bosnia. It was Kraus's tragedy and the tragedy of Europe that his metaphorical apocalypse became literal. As it did so, he explored the connection between the loss of *Geist* and the coming of war – the symbol and result of that loss. The press proclaims its inherent evil in its own corrupted language, it represents the full range of societal evils in its pages, and it serves as the target of a variety of satiric maneuvers. The apocalyptic character of Kraus's satire, most powerfully represented by the final scene and Epilogue of *Die letzten Tage*, may be the most illusory element of his own thought. Lucien Goldmann observed that Kraus, unable to recognize positive values in the present, saw in the last convulsions of an epoch the last days of mankind.[54] But the presence of hope may be a product of history: Kraus died in 1936; Goldmann wrote of him in 1945.

Kraus's satiric art is often and rightly described as contrastive.[55] He might be thought of as prying at gaps, especially the linguistic gaps between what is said and what is intended, between what the speaker means and what the language means, between the primary meanings of words and all the secondary meanings that provide a linguistic commentary. As he widens these gaps, he makes them more apparent, and he lengthens them as well, so that they connect with others, developing a cross-hatching of gaps that in turn reveals larger patterns implying the unstable and crumbling nature of the whole structure in which they appear. Readers eventually become familiar with the characteristic gaps from which Krausian topics flow, and hence the merest allusion to them may signal their relevance to the issue at hand and their place in the wider pattern. Kraus's chiseling analysis picks apart the unconscious polysemy of fraudulent language and analyzes it in language that is consciously polysemous. Thus code becomes both the object and the means of attack. Object language is quoted and glossed by metalanguage. The black magic of printer's ink is demystified by the cold reality of white snow. Because his attacks on the press and the world represented by the press have their origin in the philosophical implications of language itself, Kraus becomes a powerful modern exemplar of the satiric frame of mind.

Conclusion

Karl Kraus brings us to the center of the satiric enterprise, where the triad of words, ideas, and actuality operates as both object and vehicle of scrutiny. Gaps in the relationships within the triad reveal the meaninglessness of language or the evil of the culture that uses it. Disjunctions created by the satirist's manipulation of the triad force the audience to look at the world and ideas about it from a new perspective. Kraus's location of this center enables, by way of conclusion, a look back at the depiction of satire here and outward from the center to the concentric frames that satire incorporates. Kraus's interest in language, specifically with public language, and more specifically still with the language of the press, is a manifestation of the satiric press's concern with whether communication has properly taken place at all. As I argued in chapter 7, the debates over French failure to disarm Dunkirk following the War of Spanish Succession suggest a concerted (although probably not organized) attack on each element of the communications model set out by Roman Jakobson. The author is incompetent; the message is mistaken; the audience is deluded; the context is irrelevant; the code is solecistic or tautological; the satiric warning is itself a danger.

Satire manipulates this communications model through its characteristic adoption, parody, and transformation of pre-existent genres. Its independence of the genres that it uses proclaims its pre-generic nature. In using such genres to attack and in using attack to imply meaning, it exploits particular characteristics of the host form. At times it contests these characteristics, so that the text becomes a battle for generic dominance. This is particularly the case of the novel, whose primary features overlap considerably with those of satire itself. The forward movement of narrative is forced to carry emblematic meanings along with it. Narrative itself must fend off the intrusions of essays, and at times those intrusions transform the nature of the narrative itself, as they do in the case of *The Book of Laughter and Forgetting*, where Tamina's story shifts from the realism of her experience in France to the fantasy of her imprisonment on the Children's Island. The plot of the novel, as in the cases of *Roderick Random* and *Bouvard et Pécuchet*, may trace the education of the satirist. The novel's concentration on a central consciousness may, as it does with Panurge and Braz Cubas, present a self-conscious egoist whose narrative both embodies and observes the foolishness or futility of the world. Where the emphasis on consciousness produces sympathy, it may pull against satire's interest in judgment or it may enlist concern or even anger at the systemic forces that render the sympathetic individual helpless. The novelist pushes the narrative towards resolution; the satirist remains mired in doubt, and hence novels such as *Pale Fire* end inconclusively or, like *The Posthumous Memoirs of Brás Cubas*, finish where they begin. The generic conflicts and confusions create problems for critics like myself who seek to make formal distinctions, but they become an enabling force for the satiric novel.

The novel's realism makes the presence of a self-conscious and dramatized author intrusive, and hence the emergence of such authors marks a significant dislocation of the form. But in the case of satiric poems, such performing authors are the rule rather than the exception. For purposes of economy I have confined my treatment of such performances to those modeled by Horace (and not even all of those). Such performances differ from common imitation (as in Pope's Horatian imitations) where the language, structure, and statements of the imitated poem are transposed by the imitator to contemporary topics and settings. Once a performance has taken place, its gestures and character become available to other satirists, and kinds of performances become, in effect, sub-genres of satire. But satire on the stage generates still further layers of performance. Beyond the performative nature of language itself, it casts characters in social roles that, distinct from the personality of the character who plays them, become performative and, when the discrepancy between personality and role is pronounced, satiric. Still more significantly, it may include characters who, whether satirists themselves or not, manipulate performances within the play that reveal the performing or hypocritical nature of the other characters. The interplay of these levels questions the falsity of the world and may, as in the cases of Molière's *Le Misanthrope* and Ostrovsky's *Even a Wise Man Stumbles*, question the truth of the questioner.

Beyond the frame of form lies the frame of context, which may, as in the case of the relative dominance of satire and the novel at various cultural moments, determine the nature of the form. Satire is insistently historical in nature, and in discussing the formal features of satire I have often (particularly in considering satire and the press) had to consider historical context as well. But the meaning of satire is not limited to the product of its historical sources and references, and hence I have considered satire's historical context under the semi-metaphorical headings of satiric nationalism and satiric exile. What the satiric exile and the satiric nationalist share are the drawing, penetrating, erasing, and wishing away of boundaries. The satiric nationalist may draw boundaries by attacking the stereotyped others who live outside them, or may undermine them by imagining an observer for whom the satirist's nation becomes the other, or may hope for a world of higher values where such boundaries become unnecessary. The excluded exile comes to recognize that the boundaries of nations stand for personal and social boundaries of all sorts, and that the crossing of boundaries is fraught with danger. Satiric boundaries raise the central issue of the relation of satirists to the cultures surrounding them that may constitute communities, imagined or otherwise, or may seem prisons from which satire is the only escape.

This series of frames might be judiciously rearranged: the play of borrowed forms becomes a frame within which the historical context and the triad of language, idea, and actuality serve as the picture framed. But even this rearrangement runs afoul of the interchangeability of objects and vehicles of judgment. That interchangeability modifies much of what can be said in a grandiose way about satire. Morality certainly may function as a source of judgment, but it may also be a subject of judgment. The satiric frame of mind may not be rooted in a disposition as definite as doubt. It may lie in a discomfort at the perception that something is wrong in the world of discourse, that the connections between words and ideas and between ideas and appearance have been broken. At the outside of the frame stand the observers of the satire, who experience the life to which it refers. The interchangeability extends even here. The picture framed may be glassed as well, so that in looking at its image we faintly see ourselves. Or, like the Democritus of Velásquez, the satirist may point to the world he finds so foolish but laugh directly at us, the final figures in the satiric frame of mind.

Notes

INTRODUCTION: THE SATIRIC FRAME OF MIND

1. José Gudiol reports the consensus that it was painted during Velásquez's early Madrid period and dates it between 1624 and 1628; *The Complete Paintings of Velásquez 1599–1660*, Kenneth Lyons (trs.) (New York: Greenwich House, 1983), pp. 87, 328.
2. M. M. Bakhtin, *Speech Genres and Other Late Essays*, Caryl Emerson and Michael Holquist (eds.), Vern W. McGee (trs.) (Austin: University of Texas Press, 1986), pp. 60–102; Bakhtin's distinction between "primary" and "secondary" speech genres (61–62) particularly differentiates between the traditional genres and the conventional, often unwritten, speech occasions that satire imitates.
3. The skeptical basis of Augustan satire is developed by James Noggle, *The Skeptical Sublime: Aesthetic Ideology in Pope and the Tory Satirists* (Oxford: Oxford University Press, 2001), which traces a combination of philosophical skepticism with the Longinian tradition of the sublime as an intellectual basis for satires by Rochester, Dryden, Swift, and (especially) Pope.
4. John Dryden, "Discourse concerning the Original and Progress of Satire," *The Works of John Dryden*, A. B. Chambers, William Frost, and Vinton Dearing (eds.), 20 vols. (Berkeley: University of California Press, 1974), vol. IV, p. 55.
5. Edward A. Bloom and Lillian D. Bloom, *Satire's Persuasive Voice* (Ithaca and London: Cornell University Press, 1979), pp. 16–17.
6. Wyndham Lewis, *Men Without Art* (London: Cassell, 1934); rpt. Ronald Paulson (ed.), *Satire: Modern Essays in Criticism* (Englewood Cliffs, NJ: Prentice-Hall, 1971), p. 70.
7. Dustin Griffin, *Satire: A Critical Reintroduction* (Lexington: University Press of Kentucky, 1994), pp. 35–70.
8. Felicity A. Nussbaum, *The Brink of All We Hate: English Satires on Women 1660–1750* (Lexington: University Press of Kentucky, 1984).

I IMAGINATION'S CERBERUS

1. Edward W. Rosenheim, Jr., *Swift and the Satirist's Art* (Chicago: University of Chicago Press, 1963), pp. 31–34.

2. Dustin Griffin, *Satire: A Critical Reintroduction* (Lexington: University Press of Kentucky, 1994), pp. 39–52.
3. Northrop Frye, *Anatomy of Criticism: Four Essays* (Princeton: Princeton University Press, 1957), pp. 223–39.
4. Milan Kundera and Philip Roth, "Afterword: A Talk with the Author," Peter Kussi (trs.), in *The Book of Laughter and Forgetting*, Michael Henry Heim (trs.) (Harmondsworth: Penguin, 1981), p. 231.
5. Gian Baggio Conte sees genre as a mediator between empirical and theoretical worlds, providing models of the world that allow reality (itself a cultural construct) to be represented; *Genres and Readers* (Baltimore: Johns Hopkins University Press, 1994), pp. 105–28.
6. The text of Diomedes on satire is presented, translated, and discussed in C. A. Van Rooy, *Studies in Classical Satire and Related Literary Theory* (Leiden: E. J. Brill, 1966) pp. xii–xiii, 1–29, whose text and translation I quote below; the full Latin text is available in H. Keil (ed.), *Grammatici Latini*, 6 vols. (1855–1880; rpt. Hildesheim: Georg Olms, 1961), vol. 1, pp. 297–529.
7. References to Plato use the standard Stephanos numbers.
8. John Sallis, *Being and Logos*, second edition (Atlantic Highlands, NJ: Humanities Press, 1986), p. 262; Sallis patiently explores the multiple implications, pp. 215–65, especially pp. 232–35.
9. Varro, *De Lingua Latina*, Roland G. Kent (trs.) (1938; rpt. London: Heinemann; Cambridge, MA: Harvard University Press, 1958); Quintilian, *Institutio Oratoria*, H. E. Butler (trs.) (1920; rpt. London: Heinemann; Cambridge, MA: Harvard University Press, 1969).
10. F. Leo, "Varro und die Satire," *Hermes* 24 (1889), 67–84; Van Rooy adopts this view, with modifications in light of subsequent criticism, *Studies in Classical Satire*, pp. 2–4.
11. Henry Osborn Taylor, *The Mediaeval Mind*, 4th edn., 2 vols. (Cambridge, MA: Harvard University Press, 1951), vol. 1, p. 107.
12. Alvin B. Kernan, *The Cankered Muse: Satire of the English Renaissance* (New Haven: Yale University Press, 1959), pp. 54–63.
13. The formal characteristics of the epigram, particularly its "maximal closure" and "hyperdetermination," are discussed by Barbara Herrnstein Smith, *Poetic Closure: A Study of How Poems End* (Chicago: University of Chicago Press, 1968), pp. 196–210.
14. R. R. Nauta, "Seneca's *Apocolocyntosis* as Saturnalian Literature," *Mnemosyne*, 4th ser., 40 (1987), 69–96.
15. In chapter 5 below I return to Saturnalian satire to discuss Horace and Burns (and the problems of Bakhtin).
16. For Christian and Roman views of Juvenal, see Michael Coffey, *Roman Satire* (London: Methuen; New York: Barnes and Noble, 1976), pp. 144–46.
17. Milan Kundera, *The Book of Laughter and Forgetting*, Aaron Asher (trs.) (New York: Perennial, 1996), pp. 85–87; the equivalent pages in the Heim translation (Harmondsworth: Penguin, 1981) are 61–62; see also the "Afterword" in the Heim translation, pp. 232–33.

18. See, for example, the rhetorical analysis appended to the translation of Hoyt Hopewell Hudson (Princeton: Princeton University Press, 1941), pp. 129–42.
19. Desiderius Erasmus, *The Praise of Folly*, Clarence H. Miller (trs.) (New Haven: Yale University Press, 1979), further references will be parenthetical, by page.
20. Wayne A. Rebhorn, "The Metamorphosis of Moria: Structure and Meaning in *The Praise of Folly*," *PMLA* 89 (1974), 472.
21. W. David Kay, "Erasmus' Learned Joking: The Ironic Use of Classical Wisdom in *The Praise of Folly*," *Texas Studies in Literature and Language* 19 (1977), 262; Richard Sylvester, "The Problem of Unity in *The Praise of Folly*," *English Literary Renaissance* 6 (1976), 133.
22. For a discussion of whether "farcimen" in Diomedes refers to stuffing or sausage, see Van Rooy, *Studies in Classical Satire*, 13–14; for metaphorical purposes I will regard it as sausage.
23. Griffin, *Satire*, 191–92.
24. Charles A. Knight, "Listening to Encolpius: Modes of Confusion in the *Satyricon*," *University of Toronto Quarterly* 58 (1989), 340–43.
25. L. R. Shero, "The Cena in Roman Satire," *Classical Philology* 18 (1923), 126–43.
26. François Rabelais, *The Histories of Gargantua and Pantagruel*, J. M. Cohen (trs.) (Harmondsworth: Penguin, 1955), pp. 38, 284–87.
27. See Leon Guilhamet, *Satire and the Transformation of Genre* (Philadelphia: University of Pennsylvania Press, 1987), pp. 55–67.
28. William S. Anderson sees Juvenal as abandoning and condemning his former moral indignation for Democritean laughter, *Essays on Roman Satire* (Princeton: Princeton University Press, 1982), pp. 350–56; for Gilbert Highet the "vindictive and hateful" elements of Juvenal's character prevent him from abandoning the possibilities of revenge, *Juvenal the Satirist* (Oxford: Clarendon Press, 1954), pp. 140–44; E. Courtney finds "a tone of weary acceptance of contemporary dishonesty, which should be countered by a measure of impassivity," *A Commentary on the Satires of Juvenal* (London: Athlone Press, 1980), p. 534.
29. Juvenal, Satire 13, lines 159–60; Juvenal, *The Sixteen Satires*, Peter Green (trs.) revised edn. (Harmondsworth: Penguin, 1974), p. 254.
30. P. K. Elkin, *The Augustan Defence of Satire* (London: Clarendon Press, 1973), pp. 75–77 gives examples of satire defended as a supplement to the law.
31. Wittgenstein's approach in *Philosophical Investigations* has been applied to satire by Robert C. Elliott, "The Definition of Satire," *Yearbook of Comparative and General Literature* 11 (1962), 19–23.
32. In preparing the various references to Lucian in the paragraphs that follow, I have used the translation of H. W. and F. G. Fowler, 4 vols. (Oxford: Clarendon Press, 1905), but in some instances, where works or passages oddly seemed too naughty for Edwardian eyes (e.g., *Eunuchus*), I have used the Loeb translation of A. M. Harmon, K. Kilburn, and M. D. Macleod, 8 vols. (London: Heinemann; New York: Macmillan, 1913–67).
33. Graham Anderson, *Lucian: Theme and Variation in the Second Sophistic* (Leiden: E.J. Brill, 1976), pp. 175–76; Christopher Robinson, *Lucian and his Influence in Europe* (London: Duckworth, 1979), pp. 237–38.

34. R. Bracht Branham, *Unruly Eloquence: Lucian and the Comedy of Traditions* (Cambridge, MA: Harvard University Press, 1989), sees Lucian as manipulating, combining, parodying, and disturbing various literary and rhetorical traditions, an approach that parallels my argument that his targets are intellectual discourses.

35. See, for example, David Worcester, *The Art of Satire* (1940; rpt. New York: Russell and Russell, 1960), pp. 3–10.

36. Frederick Stopp, *Evelyn Waugh: Portrait of the Artist* (London: Chapman and Hall, 1958), p. 201.

37. James W. Nichols, *Insinuation: The Tactics of English Satire* (The Hague: Mouton, 1971), pp. 54, 59.

38. Guilhamet, *Satire and the Transformation of Genre*, pp. 11–13.

39. Tzvetan Todorov, "The Origin of Genres," *New Literary History* 8 (1976), 162; see also 164–65.

40. M. M. Bakhtin, *The Dialogic Imagination*, Caryl Emerson and Michael Holquist (trs.) (Austin: University of Texas Press, 1981), pp. 16–17.

41. William S. Anderson, *Essays on Roman Satire*, 3–11; see also the discussion of satiric performance in chapter 5 below.

42. P. Rau, *Paratragodia: Untersuchung einer komishen Form des Aristophanes*, Zetemata, no. 45 (Munich: Beck, 1967).

43. Cedric H. Whitman, *Aristophanes and the Comic Hero* (Cambridge, MA: Harvard University Press, 1964), pp. 21–58.

44. K. J. Dover, *Aristophanic Comedy* (Berkeley and Los Angeles: University of California Press, 1972), pp. 59–65.

45. Robert C. Elliott, *The Power of Satire: Magic, Ritual, Art* (Princeton: Princeton University Press, 1960), pp. 162–67.

46. Kernan, *The Cankered Muse*, p. 194.

47. John Peter, *Complaint and Satire in Early English Literature* (Oxford: Clarendon Press, 1956), pp. 255–68.

48. Anne Barton, *Ben Jonson, Dramatist* (Cambridge: Cambridge University Press, 1984), pp. 113–14.

49. Barbara Herrnstein Smith, *On the Margins of Discourse: The Relation of Literature to Language* (Chicago: University of Chicago Press, 1978), pp. 14–40.

50. *Ibid.*, p. 28.

51. R. Bracht Branham, *Unruly Eloquence*, pp. 32–34, treats *Piscator* ("The Fisherman") as essentially an Aristophanic satire.

52. Roman Jakobson, "Linguistics and Poetics," in *Selected Writings*, Stephen Rudy (ed.), 8 vols. (The Hague: Mouton, 1981), vol. III, pp. 27–29.

53. Paul Grice, *Studies in the Way of Words* (Cambridge, MA: Harvard University Press, 1989), pp. 22–40; I discuss the utility of Grice's maxims for the interpretation of satire in "Satire and Conversation: The Logic of Interpretation," *The Eighteenth Century: Theory and Interpretation* 26 (1985), 239–61, from which I derive the material in this paragraph.

54. Alastair Fowler, *Kinds of Literature: An Introduction to the Theory of Genres and Modes* (Cambridge, MA: Harvard University Press, 1982), pp. 110–11.

55. Fredric V. Bogel, *The Difference Satire Makes: Rhetoric and Reading from Jonson to Byron* (Ithaca and London: Cornell University Press, 2001), pp. 41–83, takes a different view of the rhetorical triad from the one I do here. He attacks rigid and moralistic views of the satirist and the reader but sees them abstractly in terms of shifting patterns of identification and difference. He limits the rhetoric of satire to the relations among satirist, satiric victim, and reader, while I, following Jakobson, want rhetoric to include such elements as context, referentiality, language, and discourse. I have discussed Bogel's argument at length in "Identifying Satire," *Review* 24 (2002), 1–21.

56. Jonathan Swift, *Prose Works*, Herbert Davis et al. (eds.), 14 vols. (Oxford: Basil Blackwell, 1957), vol. I, p. 31.

57. Robert Scholes, *Structuralism in Literature* (New Haven: Yale University Press, 1974), pp. 27–28.

58. Irvin Ehrenpreis, *Swift: The Man, his Works, and the Age*, 3 vols. (Cambridge, MA: Harvard University Press, 1967), vol. II, pp. 282–84.

59. *Ibid.*, vol. III, p. 35.

60. Phillip Harth, "The Problem of Political Allegory in *Gulliver's Travels*," *Modern Philology* 73 (1976), S40–47; F. P. Lock, *The Politics of Gulliver's Travels* (Oxford: Clarendon Press, 1980), pp. 89–122; J. A. Downie, "The Political Significance of *Gulliver's Travels*," in *Swift and his Contexts*, John Irwin Fischer, Hermann J. Real, and James Woolley (eds.) (New York: AMS, 1989), pp. 1–19.

61. George Orwell, *The Collected Essays, Journalism and Letters of George Orwell*, Sonia Orwell and Ian Angus (eds.), 4 vols. (New York: Harcourt Brace Jovanovich, 1968), vol. IV, p. 75.

62. Andrej Kodjak, *Alexander Solzhenitsyn* (Boston: Twayne, 1978), pp. 69–70.

63. Ellendea Proffer, *Bulgakov: Life and Work* (Ann Arbor, MI: Ardis, 1984), p. 647.

64. Michael McKeon, "Cultural Crisis and Dialectical Method: Destabilizing Augustan Literature," in *The Profession of Eighteenth-Century Literature* (Madison: University of Wisconsin Press, 1992), pp. 42–61.

65. Jakobson, *Selected Writings*, vol. III, p. 26.

66. Bakhtin, *The Dialogic Imagination*, p. 5.

67. Jacques Derrida, "La Loi du Genre / The Law of Genre," *Glyph* 7 (1980), 202.

2 SATIRIC NATIONALISM

1. George A. Test, *Satire: Spirit and Art* (Tampa: University of South Florida Press, 1991), pp. 67–84.

2. Lloyd Kramer, "Historical Narratives and the Meaning of Nationalism," *Journal of the History of Ideas* 58 (1997), 525–45, stresses the inability of nationalist theory to reach intellectual closure, in part because the conditions described by that theory continue to change.

3. Ernest Renan, "What is a Nation?" Martin Thom (trs.), in *Nation and Narration*, Homi K. Bhabha (ed.) (London and New York: Routledge, 1990), p. 19.

4. E. J. Hobsbawm, *Nations and Nationalism since 1780: Programme, Myth, Reality* (Cambridge: Cambridge University Press, 1992), pp. 5–9.

5. Ernest Gellner, *Nations and Nationalism* (Ithaca and London: Cornell University Press, 1983), p. 1.

6. Ernest Gellner, *Nationalism* (New York: New York University Press, 1997), p. 3.

7. Anthony D. Smith, *Theories of Nationalism* (New York: Harper and Row, 1971), p. 171.

8. Benedict Anderson, *Imagined Communities: Reflections on the Origin and Spread of Nationalism*, revised edn. (London and New York: Verso, 1991), pp. 6–7.

9. Louis Althusser, "Ideology and Ideological State Apparatuses (Notes Towards an Investigation)," in *Lenin and Philosophy and Other Essays*, Ben Brewster (trs.) (London: NLB, 1971), pp. 123–73.

10. *Ibid.*, p. 169, Althusser's emphasis; p. 145.

11. Anderson, *Imagined Communities*, pp. 37–46.

12. "Il n'y a point de patrie dans le despotique," La Bruyère, *Les Caractères*, "Du Souverain ou de la république" (Paris: Garnier, 1962), p. 276; see Hans Kohn, *The Idea of Nationalism* (New York: Macmillan, 1961), pp. 199–204, on the distinctions between nationalism and the divinely ordained economic as well as political power of the monarch.

13. See, for example, the discussion of Herder, *Ideen zur Philosophie der Geschichte der Menschheit* (1784), in Carleton J. H. Hayes, *The Historical Evolution of Modern Nationalism* (New York: Macmillan, 1931), pp. 27–33.

14. "Il est triste que souvent, pour être bon patriote, on soit l'ennemi du reste des hommes," Voltaire, *Dictionnaire philosophique*, "Patrie" (Paris: Garnier, 1961), p. 336; K. P. Minogue (whose view seems even more hostile than Voltaire's) calls nationalism, among other things, "a political movement depending on a feeling of collective grievance against foreigners," in *Nationalism* (New York: Basic Books, 1967), p. 25.

15. Liah Greenfeld, *Nationalism: Five Roads to Modernity* (Cambridge, MA: Harvard University Press, 1992), p. 47.

16. *The Tenure of Kings and Magistrates* (1649), in *John Milton: Selected Prose*, C. A. Patrides (ed.), revised edn. (Columbia: University of Missouri Press, 1985), p. 257.

17. Linda Colley, *Britons: Forging the Nation 1707–1837* (New Haven and London: Yale University Press, 1992), p. 369; Gerald Newman, *The Rise of English Nationalism: A Cultural History 1740–1830*, revised edn. (New York: St. Martin's, 1997).

18. Howard D. Weinbrot, *Britannia's Issue: The Rise of British Literature from Dryden to Ossian* (Cambridge: Cambridge University Press, 1993).

19. Josep R. Llobera, *The God of Modernity: The Development of Nationalism in Western Europe* (Oxford and Providence, RI: Berg, 1994), p. 112.

20. Anderson, *Imagined Communities*, pp. 37–46.

21. Juvenal, *Satire* 3, lines 58–125.

22. Johnson, *London*, lines 113–16, in *The Poems of Samuel Johnson*, David Nichol Smith and Edward L. McAdam (eds.), 2nd edn. (Oxford: Clarendon Press, 1974).

23. Johnson, *Journey to the Western Islands of Scotland*, Mary Lascelles (ed.) (New Haven: Yale University Press, 1971), p. 164.

24. "Longum usque adeo tardumque putavit / expectare focos, contenta cadavere crudo" (lines 82–83); Peter Green translates, "Building an proper fire-pit / Was a bore, and took time – so they scoffed the poor devil raw," *Juvenal: The Sixteen Satires* (Harmondsworth: Penguin, 1974), p. 284.

25. These images are illustrated graphically and discussed from a psychological point of view in Sam Keen, *Faces of the Enemy: Reflections of the Hostile Imagination* (San Francisco: Harper and Row, 1985).

26. Chester Noyes Greenough, "Characters of Nations," in *Collected Studies* (Cambridge, MA: Harvard Cooperative Society, 1940), pp. 224–45.

27. Michael Duffy, *The Englishman and the Foreigner, The English Satiric Print 1600–1832* (Cambridge: Chadwyck-Healey, 1986), p. 19.

28. *Ibid.*, pp. 23–27.

29. *Ibid.*, pp. 27–31.

30. John Tutchin, *The Foreigners* (1701) directs its anti-Dutch satire at such transplanted Hollanders as Bentinck and Keppel rather than at William; Defoe's *The True-Born Englishman*, in response, has little to say against the Dutch.

31. For general and specific anti-Dutch attitudes and their effect on Swift, see Ellen Douglas Leyburn, "Swift's View of the Dutch," *PMLA* 66 (1951), 734–45; Anne Barbeau Gardiner, "Swift on the Dutch East India Company: A Context of 1672–73 War Literature," *Huntington Library Quarterly* 54 (1991), 235–52 traces the source of Swift's images of Holland in the anti-Dutch propaganda of 1672–73.

32. Duffy, *The Englishman and the Foreigner*, pp. 31–39; images of the French are discussed by Edward A. and Lillian D. Bloom, *Satire's Persuasive Voice* (Ithaca and London: Cornell University Press, 1979), pp. 265–69.

33. Ronald Paulson, *Hogarth: His Life, Art, and Times*, 2 vols. (New Haven: Yale University Press, 1971), vol. II, pp. 75–78.

34. Annabel M. Patterson, *Marvell and the Civic Crown* (Princeton: Princeton University Press, 1978), p. 120.

35. Warren Chernaik, *The Poet's Time: Politics and Religion in the Work of Andrew Marvell* (Cambridge: Cambridge University Press, 1983), p. 163.

36. Suvir Kaul, *Poems of Nation, Anthems of Empire: English Verse in the Long Eighteenth Century* (Charlottesville: University of Virginia Press, 2000), p. 56.

37. *Ibid.*, p. 88.

38. John Arbuthnot, *The History of John Bull*, Alan W. Bower and Robert A. Erickson (eds.) (Oxford: Clarendon Press, 1976); see especially their discussion of "national characters," pp. lvii–lxviii.

39. Donna Isaacs Dalnikoff discusses the foreign observer model in "A Familiar Stranger: The Outsider of Eighteenth-Century Satire," *Neophilologus* 57 (1973), 121–34; Frederick M. Keener, *The Chain of Becoming* (New York: Columbia

University Press, 1983) discusses several philosophical tales using foreign observers – *Gulliver's Travels* (pp. 89–126), *Lettres persanes* (pp. 127–93), and *Candide* (pp. 194–216).

40. Montesquieu, *Lettres persanes*, ed. Paul Vernière (Paris: Garnier, 1960), p. 4; the English translation is that of C. J. Betts (Harmondsworth: Penguin, 1973), p. 284; further citations of these editions will be parenthetical, usually by letter.

41. *Collected Works of Oliver Goldsmith*, Arthur Friedman (ed.), 5 vols. (Oxford: Clarendon Press, 1966), vol. II; further citations of this edition will be parenthetical, by letter.

42. Goldsmith notably takes up issues of nationalism in "The Traveler," and less notably in "A Comparative View of Races and Nations," a series of essays contributed to *Royal Magazine* during the run of "The Chinese Letters" (Summer, 1760), reprinted in *Collected Works*, vol. III, pp. 66–86; John McVeagh stresses both the range and Irishness of Goldsmith's views of nationalism, in "Goldsmith and Nationality," in *All Before Them. Vol. I: 1660–1780* (London: Ashfield, 1990), pp. 217–31.

43. On Voltaire and the Quaker, Jean Sareil, "Les Quatre Premières *Lettres philosophiques* ou les complications du jeu satirique," *Romanic Review* 76 (1985), 277–86, also Edith Philips, *The Good Quaker in French Legend* (Philadelphia: University of Pennsylvania Press, 1932), pp. 43–67; Voltaire's attitudinizing in the opening letters is noted by S. S. B. Taylor, "Voltaire's Humour," *Studies on Voltaire* 179 (1979), 114; a more general study is A. M. Rousseau, *L'Angleterre et Voltaire*, Studies on Voltaire 145–47 (Banbury: The Voltaire Foundation, 1976).

44. Donna Isaacs Dalnikoff, "The Meaning of Eldorado: Utopia and Satire in *Candide*," *Studies on Voltaire and the Eighteenth Century* 127 (1974), 41–59.

45. Voltaire's general views on nationalism are discussed in Merle L. Perkins, *Voltaire's Concept of International Order*, Studies on Voltaire 36 (Geneva: Institut et Musée Voltaire, 1965), esp. 141–58; my view of the nations of *Candide* corresponds roughly to the gardens described by William F. Bottiglia, Jr., *Voltaire's "Candide": Analysis of a Classic*, 2nd edn., Studies on Voltaire 7A (Geneva: Institut et Musée Voltaire, 1964), 101–18, but seeing them as nations emphasizes the fact that the scenes of cruelty are historically real, not fictional or utopian.

46. Charles H. Hinnant, *Purity and Defilement in "Gulliver's Travels"* (London: Macmillan, 1987), pp. 3–14, discusses Swift's use of boundaries in the countries Gulliver visits, with particular reference to the distinctions that are made within each culture.

47. Quotations, cited parenthetically by book and chapter, use *The Prose Works of Jonathan Swift*, Herbert Davis (ed.), vol. XI (Oxford: Basil Blackwell, 1965).

48. The seminal study of science in Book III is Marjorie Hope Nicolson and Nora M. Mohler, "The Scientific Background of Swift's *Voyage to Laputa*," *Annals of Science* 2 (1937), 299–334; see also (among others) Frederik N. Smith, "Scientific Discourse: *Gulliver's Travels* and *The Philosophical Transactions*," in *The Genres of "Gulliver's Travels,"* Frederik N. Smith (ed.) (Newark: University of Delaware Press, 1990), pp. 139–62; Douglas Lane Patey points out that Swift

and other eighteenth-century writers used the term "science" in the broad sense of knowledge in general; "Swift's Satire on 'Science' and the Structure of *Gulliver's Travels*," *ELH* 58 (1991), 811.

49. Renan, "What is a Nation?" pp. 19, 11.

50. Anderson, *Imagined Communities*, p. 26.

51. William Freedman sees the Struldbruggs as the personification of history and hence the emblem of Swift's attack on progress, "Swift's Struldbruggs, Progress, and the Analogy of History," *Studies in English Literature 1500–1900* 35 (1995), 457–72.

52. *The Correspondence of Jonathan Swift*, Harold Williams (ed.), 5 vols. (Oxford: Clarendon Press, 1962–65), vol. III, p. 103.

53. The complexities of perspective are traced in Robert Benet, "Du regard de l'Autre dans les *Lettres persanes*: investigation, voilement, dévoilement," *L'Information littéraire* 44.3 (May–June 1992), 6–13.

54. Mark Hulliung, *Montesquieu and the Old Regime* (Berkeley: University of California Press, 1976), p. 135; Suzanne Gearhart, *The Open Boundary of History and Fiction: A Critical Approach to the French Enlightenment* (Princeton: Princeton University Press, 1984), pp. 95–128, sees Usbek as a less sympathetic character than Rica: "It would seem that Rica's Paris provides the ultimate alternative to the despotic social forces constructed by Usbek's egocentric desire. It would seem too that the contradictions in Usbek's seraglio have been liquidated in Rica's Paris" (p. 121).

55. A. M. Boase, for example, sees *Lettres persanes* primarily as a prelude to *L'Esprit des lois*, and he finds the harem story merely tedious; "The Interpretation of the *Lettres Persanes*," in *The French Mind: Studies Presented to Gustave Rudler*, Will Moore et al. (eds.) (Oxford: Clarendon Press, 1952), pp. 152–69.

56. A number of studies look at the harem sequence with scant attention to Usbek as a philosopher; for example, Josué V. Harari, "The Eunuch's Tale: Montesquieu's Imaginary of Despotism," in *Scenarios of the Imaginary: Theorizing the French Enlightenment* (Ithaca: Cornell University Press, 1987), pp. 67–101.

57. For an account of Usbek's vacillation between the rationality of Descartes and the empiricism of Locke, see Robert Shackleton, *Montesquieu: A Critical Biography* (London: Oxford University Press, 1961), pp. 41–42; Ronald Grimsley sees reason in *Lettres persanes* as the means by which humans can recognize their relative place in the world, avoid illusion, and "provide a sounder basis for happiness," *From Montesquieu to Laclos* (Geneva: Droz, 1974), p. 10.

58. The complex effects of chronology in *Lettres persanes* have been discussed by a number of scholars, especially by Robert Shackleton, "The Moslem Chronology of the *Lettres persanes*," *French Studies* 8 (1954), 17–27; see also Philip Stewart, "Toujours Usbek," *Eighteenth-Century Fiction* 11 (1999), 141–50.

59. Diana J. Schaub, *Erotic Liberalism: Women and Revolution in Montesquieu's "Persian Letters"* (London: Rowman and Littlefield, 1995), pp. 79–86.

60. A now-classic study of the Persian–Parisian connections is Aram Vartanian, "Eroticism and Politics in the *Lettres persanes*," *Romanic Review* 60 (1969), 23–33, but they have been taken up by a number of subsequent critics, for

example, Alain Grosrichard, *The Sultan's Court: European Fantasies of the East*, Liz Heron (trs.) (London and New York: Verso, 1998).

61. David B. Young, "Libertarian Demography: Montesquieu's Essay on Depopulation in the *Lettres persanes*," *Journal of the History of Ideas* 36 (1975), 669–82, points out that Montesquieu's investigations implicitly criticize a variety of despotisms and advance the responding principle of liberty.

62. Frederick M. Keener sees Usbek as arriving at "a less rigorous and abstract view of human motivation and ethics, based not upon comparatively selfless virtue but upon a practical, naturalistic attempt to reconcile virtue, self-love, and the individual's perspective on them," *The Chain of Becoming*, p. 183.

63. See Theodore Braun, "'La Chaîne secrète: A Decade of Interpretations," *French Studies* 42 (1988), 278–91. The temptation is for interpreters to assert that a central point of their own interpretation constitutes that chain, a temptation to which I succumb here.

64. John Breuilly, *Nationalism and the State* (New York: St. Martin's, 1982), p. 62: "co-ordination is the part ideology plays in bringing together a set of diverse political interests into a single movement by providing them with a unity of values and purpose."

65. See, for example, the discussion of "Jacobin Nationalism" by Hayes, *The Historical Evolution of Modern Nationalism*, pp. 43–83.

3 SATIRIC EXILE

1. Brecht and Ovid, as exiles, are contrasted by Tom Kuhn, "Ovid and Brecht: Topoi of Poetic Banishment," *Brecht Yearbook / Brecht-Jahrbuch* 24 (1999), 163–75.

2. Edward Said, "Reflections on Exile," *Granta* 13 (Autumn 1984), 163.

3. Emil Draitser, "Fighting the Shadows: Four Crises of a Russian Satirist in Exile," *Studies in Contemporary Satire* 17 (1990), 15–30.

4. Speculation as to the cause of Ovid's exile – including the possibility that he himself did not know its true cause – has been inconclusive; see John C. Thibault, *The Mystery of Ovid's Exile* (Berkeley: University of California Press, 1964).

5. A. D. Fitton Brown, "The Unreality of Ovid's Tomitian Exile," *Liverpool Classical Monthly* 10.2 (February 1985), 18–22.

6. Jo-Marie Claassen, "Ovid's Poetic Pontus," *Papers of the Leeds International Latin Symposium* 6 (1990), 65–94; see also Gareth D. Williams, *Banished Voices: Readings in Ovid's Exile Poetry* (Cambridge: Cambridge University Press, 1994), pp. 3–49.

7. Joseph Brodsky, "The Condition We Call 'Exile,'" in *Literature in Exile*, John Glad (ed.), (Durham, NC: Duke University Press, 1990), p. 106.

8. Michael Seidel, *Exile and the Narrative Imagination* (New Haven: Yale University Press, 1986), p. 8.

9. Barbara Herrnstein Smith, *On the Margins of Discourse: The Relation of Literature to Language* (Chicago: University of Chicago Press, 1978), pp. 14–40.

10. Vladimir Nabokov, *Pale Fire* (1962; rpt. New York: Vintage, 1989), pp. 300–01; parenthetical citations will use line numbers for references to Shade's poem but page numbers for other references.

11. Brian Boyd, *Vladimir Nabokov: The American Years* (Princeton: Princeton University Press, 1991), p. 709; see also D. Barton Johnson, *Worlds in Regression: Some Novels of Vladimir Nabokov* (Ann Arbor, MI: Ardis, 1985), pp. 60–73.

12. Page Stegner, *Escape into Aesthetics: The Art of Vladimir Nabokov* (New York: Dial, 1966), pp. 129–30.

13. Boyd, *Vladimir Nabokov: The American Years*, pp. 443–56; Boyd's later retraction of this reading and advancement of another will be discussed below.

14. Martine Hennard, "Playing a Game of Words in Nabokov's *Pale Fire*," *Modern Fiction Studies* 40 (1994), 306; Hennard's essay (299–317) uses "exile" as the central concept of her deconstructive reading.

15. Milan Kundera, *The Book of Laughter and Forgetting*, trs. Aaron Asher (1996; rpt. New York: Perennial, 1999), pp. 91–92; further references, unless otherwise indicated, will use this edition.

16. Maria Němcová Banerjee, *Terminal Paradox: The Novels of Milan Kundera* (New York: Grove Weidenfeld, 1990), p. 143.

17. Salman Rushdie, *Shame* (1983; rpt. London: Picador, 1984), p. 38; further references will use this edition.

18. In sorting through the versions of *Book*, I have triangulated among Heim's English translation of the Czech text (Harmondsworth: Penguin, 1981), Asher's English translation of the French text (1996), which Kundera has in effect authorized, and the 1985 French text translated from the Czech by François Kérel and revised by Kundera (Paris: Gallimard, 1985). The details of Kundera's responses to translations are rather unsympathetically described in Caleb Crain, "Infidelity: Milan Kundera is On the Outs with his Translators. But Who's Betraying Whom," *Lingua Franca* 9.7 (October 1999), 38–50.

19. Banerjee, *Terminal Paradox*, p. 149.

20. One senses the influence of Günter Grass in the case of Shakil, and elsewhere in the novel; for the influence of Grass on *Midnight's Children*, see Rudolf Bader, "Indian *Tin Drum*," *International Fiction Review* 11 (1984), 75–83.

21. Victoria Glendinning, "A Novelist in the Country of the Mind," *Sunday Times* (October 25, 1981), 38; cited in Timothy Brennan, *Salman Rushdie and the Third World: Myths of the Nation* (New York: St. Martin's; London: Macmillan, 1989), p. 118.

22. Rufus Cook, "Place and Displacement in Salman Rushdie's Work," *World Literature Today* 68 (1994), 24.

23. Samir Dayal, "The Liminalities of Nation and Gender: Salman Rushdie's *Shame*," *Journal of the Midwest Modern Language Association* 31.2 (1998), 40.

24. Seidel, *Exile and the Narrative Imagination*, pp. 193–94.

25. The resemblance of Hazel and Kinbote is discussed by James F. English, "Modernist Joke-Work: *Pale Fire* and the Mock Transcendence of Mockery," *Contemporary Literature* 33 (1992), 83–85, and by David Galef, "The Self-Annihilating Artists of *Pale Fire*," *Twentieth Century Literature* 31 (1985), 421–37;

Brian Boyd, in *Nabokov's "Pale Fire"; The Magic of Artistic Discovery* (Princeton: Princeton University Press, 1999), argues that Hazel is the unsung heroine of *Pale Fire*, an emanation from the spirit world who manipulates the central events of the novel so that her loving father can rejoin her in the world of death. Although this reading explains some mysteries of the novel, I am unconvinced. It shifts the center of attention away from Kinbote and from this life to the next, but it certainly emphasizes the land of death or the realm of the spirit as another country of exile.

26. See, for example, Seidel, *Exile and the Narrative Imagination*, pp. 183–87, on the rich mirror images of Kinbote, whose name means regicide, and the would-be assassin Gradus.

27. Brennan, *Salman Rushdie*, p. 124.

28. M. D. Fletcher, "Rushdie's *Shame* as Apologue," *Journal of Commonwealth Literature* 21 (1986), 120–32, describes *Shame* as a parody of revenge tragedy, among other models.

29. *Ibid.*, p. 130.

30. Feroza Jussawalla, "Rushdie's *Shame*: Problems in Communication," in *Studies in Indian Fiction in English*, G. S. Balarama Gupta (ed.), (Gulbarga, India: JIWE Publications, 1987), p. 7.

31. Stephanie Moss, "The Cream of the Crop: Female Characters in Salman Rushdie's *Shame*," *International Fiction Review* 19 (1992), 28–30.

32. Inderpal Grewal, "Salman Rushdie: Marginality, Women, and *Shame*," *Genders* 3 (Fall 1988), 24–42.

33. Anuradha Dingwaney Needham links the repression of women with the situation of the exiled narrator: "The Politics of Post-Cultural Identity in Salman Rushdie," *Massachusetts Review* 29 (1988–89), 609–24; rpt. in M. D. Fletcher (ed.), *Reading Rushdie: Perspectives on the Fiction of Salman Rushdie* (Amsterdam; Atlanta, GA: Rodopi, 1994), especially pp. 153–57.

34. Aijaz Ahmad, *In Theory: Classes, Nations, Literatures* (London: Verso, 1992), pp. 123–58.

35. Margareta Petersson, *Unending Metamorphoses: Myth, Satire and Religion in Salman Rushdie's Novels* (Lund: Lund University Press, 1996), p. 193.

36. Kathryn Hume, "Taking a Stand while Lacking a Center: Rushdie's Postmodern Politics," *Philological Quarterly* 74 (1995), 223.

37. Tariq Rahman, "Politics in the Novels of Salman Rushdie," *Commonwealth Novel in English* 4 (1991), 33.

38. Ellen Pifer, "*The Book of Laughter and Forgetting*: Kundera's Narration against Narration," *Journal of Narrative Technique* 22 (1992), 89.

39. Herbert Eagle, "Genre and Paradigm in Milan Kundera's *Book of Laughter and Forgetting*," in *Language and Language Theory: In Honour of Ladislav Matejka*, B. Stolz, I. R. Titunik, L. Dolezel (eds.) (Ann Arbor: University of Michigan Press, 1984), pp. 251–84; rpt. in Peter Petro (ed.), *Critical Essays on Milan Kundera* (New York: G. K. Hall, 1999), pp. 152, 155.

40. Lars Kleberg, "On the Border: Milan Kundera's *The Book of Laughter and Forgetting*," *Scando-Slavica* 30 (1984), 66.

41. Ann Stewart Caldwell, "The Intrusive Narrative Voice of Milan Kundera," *Review of Contemporary Fiction* 9 (1989), 46.
42. Ann Jefferson, "Counterpoint and Forked Tongues: Milan Kundera and the Art of Exile," *Renaissance and Modern Studies* 34 (1991), 117.
43. Jussawalla, "Rushdie's *Shame*," pp. 1–13.
44. Salman Rushdie, "*Midnight's Children* and *Shame* (Interview at the University of Aarhus, October 7, 1983)," *Kunapipi* 7 (1985), 16.
45. Peter Brigg, "Salman Rushdie's Novels: The Disorder in Fantastic Order," *World Literature Written in English* 27 (1987), 130.

4 SATIRE AS PERFORMANCE

1. Aliki Lafkidou Dick, *Paedeia through Laughter: Jonson's Aristophanic Appeal to Human Intelligence* (The Hague: Mouton, 1974), pp. 57–88, compares *The Alchemist* to *The Clouds* of Aristophanes, particularly in terms of their comic inversions.
2. Coburn Gum provides general characterizations of Aristophanes and Jonson, as well as comparisons of plots, characters, inversions, obscenities and indecencies, personal satire, self-conscious critical commentary (parabasis), and parallel passages, in *The Aristophanic Comedies of Ben Jonson: A Comparative Study of Jonson and Aristophanes* (The Hague: Mouton, 1969).
3. The dating is worked out by Ian Donaldson from detailed references in the text, and he reports the time-scheme developed in the Herford–Simpson edition; *Jonson's Magic Houses: Essays in Interpretation* (Oxford: Clarendon Press, 1997), pp. 92–105.
4. *Ibid.*, p. 77.
5. Quotations use the edition of Alvin Kernan (New Haven: Yale University Press, 1974).
6. Thomas M. Greene, "Ben Jonson and the Centred Self," *Studies in English Literature* 10 (1970), 345.
7. R. L. Smallwood, "'Here in the Friars': Immediacy and Theatricality in *The Alchemist*," *Review of English Studies* n.s. 32, 126 (1981), 148.
8. Alvin Kernan, *The Cankered Muse: Satire of the English Renaissance* (New Haven: Yale University Press, 1959), p. 173.
9. *Ibid.*, p. 180.
10. *Ibid.*, p. 174.
11. Paul Goodman, "Comic Plots: *The Alchemist*," in *Ben Jonson: A Collection of Critical Essays*, Jonas A. Barish (ed.) (Englewood Cliffs, NJ: Prentice-Hall, 1963), p. 119.
12. Alan C. Dessen, *Jonson's Moral Comedy* (Evanston, IL: Northwestern University Press, 1971), pp. 105–37, describes *The Alchemist* as a play about the failures of Renaissance "estates," especially as exemplified by Mammon (the secular order) and the Puritans (the religious order).
13. Peter Womack, *Ben Jonson* (Oxford: Basil Blackwell, 1986), p. 117.
14. *Ibid.*, p. 31.

15. The first version of the play, *Tartuffe, ou l'Hypocrite*, was performed at Versailles in May 1664, but the King advised against its public performance. In August 1667, when the King was away on a military expedition, a second version, *Panulphe, ou l'Imposteur*, was staged at the Palais Royal, but Molière's significant changes were not sufficient to avert its interdiction. The final version, *Le Tartuffe, ou l'Imposteur*, was performed, to great acclaim, in February 1669.

16. Michael Spingler, "The King's Play: Censorship and the Politics of Performance in Molière's *Tartuffe*," *Comparative Drama* 19 (1985), 240; an earlier view of the sequence of performances in *Tartuffe* is J. D. Hubert, *Molière and the Comedy of Intellect* (Berkeley and Los Angeles: University of California Press, 1962), pp. 91–102.

17. Lionel Gossman, *Men and Masks: A Study of Molière* (Baltimore: Johns Hopkins University Press, 1963), pp. 100–44.

18. French quotations of Molière are from *Oeuvres complètes*, Georges Couton (ed.), 2 vols. (Paris: Gallimard, 1971); *Tartuffe* in vol. I, pp. 895–984, *Le Misanthrope* in vol. II, pp. 141–218. English translations are those of Richard Wilbur, *The Misanthrope and Tartuffe* (New York: Harvest, 1965). References for the French texts are to act, scene, and line; Wilbur's translations retain the acts and scenes but not the lines of the original.

19. James F. Gaines, *Social Structures in Molière's Theater* (Columbus: Ohio State University Press, 1984), p. 199; on the Jesuits, see Andrew Calder, *Molière: The Theory and Practice of Comedy* (London: Athlone, 1973), pp. 153–79; on *La Compagnie*, see Emanuel S. Chill, "*Tartuffe*, Religion, and Courtly Culture," *French Historical Studies* 3 (1963), 151–83.

20. Jules Brody, "*Dom Juan* and *Le Misanthrope*, or the Esthetics of Individualism in Molière," *PMLA* 84 (1969), 569.

21. Nathan Gross, *From Gesture to Idea: Esthetics and Ethics in Molière's Comedy* (New York: Columbia University Press, 1982), p. 120.

22. Richard E. Goodkin, "Between Genders, Between Genres: Célimène's Letter to Alceste in Molière's *Le Misanthrope*," *Romanic Review* 85 (1994), 553–72.

23. "Voilà, Monsieur, ce que je pense de la comédie du Misanthrope amoureux, que je trouve d'autant plus admirable, que le héros en est le plaisant sans être trop ridicule," Donneau de Visé, "Lettre écrite sur la comédie du 'Misanthrope,'" in *Oeuvres complètes*, Couton (ed.), vol. II, p. 139.

24. George Meredith, "An Essay on Comedy," in *Comedy*, Wylie Sypher (ed.) (New York: Doubleday, 1956), p. 44.

25. Jacques Guicharnaud, *Molière: une aventure théâtrale* (Paris: Gallimard, 1963), pp. 22–31.

26. I am indebted in this paragraph to the biographical treatments in Margaret Wettlin, "Alexander Ostrovsky and the Russian Theater before Stanislavsky," in *Alexander Ostrovsky: Plays* (Moscow: Progress, 1974), pp. 7–79, and in Marjorie L. Hoover, *Alexander Ostrovsky* (Boston: Twayne, 1981), pp. 15–32.

27. David Magarshack, "Introduction," in Ostrovsky, *Easy Money and Two Other Plays* (1944; rpt. Westport, CT: Greenwood, 1970), p. 6; Ostrovsky, *A Domestic Picture; A Scene from Moscow Life*, E. L. Voynich (trs.), in *The Humour of Russia*

(London: Walter Scott, 1985), pp. 142–66; Ostrovsky, *It's a Family Affair – We'll Settle It Ourselves*, in *Five Plays of Alexander Ostrovsky*, Eugene K. Bristow (trs.) (New York: Pegasus, 1969), pp. 37–108.

28. Robert Whittaker, "The Ostrovskii–Grigor'ev Circle Alias the 'Young Editors' of the *Moskvitianin*," *Canadian–American Slavic Studies* 24 (1990), 385–412.

29. *Five Plays of Alexander Ostrovsky*, Bristow (trs.), pp. 211–76.

30. For folkloristic elements see, for example, Irene Esam, "Folkloric Elements as Communication Devices – Ostrovsky's Plays," *New Zealand Slavonic Journal* 2 (1968), 67–88; Esam compares the alienating effect of Ostrovsky's proverbs and songs to that of Brecht's slogans (83).

31. For Ostrovsky's direct involvement in the development of the theater and the popularity of his plays in Russia, see Wettlin, "Alexander Ostrovsky," pp. 7–79; *Five Plays of Alexander Ostrovsky*, Bristow (trs.), pp. 15–24; and Hoover, *Alexander Ostrovsky*, pp. 29–32.

32. My treatment of Ostrovsky was written before I had the chance to read Kate Sealey Rahman, *Ostrovsky: Reality and Illusion*, Birmingham Slavonic Monographs 30 (1999). Rahman argues that Ostrovsky's plays transcend the Russian nineteenth century because they explore elements of the relationship between reality and illusion: "realism and idealism, the web of deception, a concern with the superficiality of outward appearance, blindness to reality, the psychological and philosophical elements, the mirror and picture symbolism" (pp. 188–89).

33. John Laurence Seymour (trs.), in *Plays by Alexander Ostrovsky*, George Rapall Noyes (ed.) (1917; rpt. New York: AMS Press, 1969), pp. 11–63.

34. *Five Plays of Alexander Ostrovsky*, Bristow (trs.), pp. 363–459.

35. *Ibid.*, pp. 116–202.

36. Ostrovsky, *Without a Dowry and Other Plays*, Norman Henley (trs.) (Dana Point, CA: Ardis, 1997), pp. 147–204.

37. Hoover, *Alexander Ostrovsky*, pp. 22–23, 57; Wettlin, "Alexander Ostrovsky," pp. 45–49.

38. *Wolves and Sheep*, Act I, David Magarshack (trs.), in *Easy Money*, p. 212.

39. I have used the translation of Magarshack in *Easy Money and Two Other Plays*, pp. 14–93. The play is variously translated; its alternative titles include *Even the Wise Can Err*, *The Scoundrel*, *The Diary of a Scoundrel*, and *Too Clever by Half*.

40. Constantin Stanislavsky describes his creation of this role in *My Life in Art*, J. J. Robbins (trs.), (1924; rpt. Boston: Little, Brown, 1938), p. 405.

41. *Easy Money*, Magarshack (trs.), pp. 95–186.

42. Peter Brooker, "Key Words in Brecht's Theory and Practice of Theatre," in *The Cambridge Companion to Brecht*, Peter Thomson and Glendyr Sacks (eds.) (Cambridge: Cambridge University Press, 1994), p. 187.

43. Bertolt Brecht, *Brecht on Theatre: The Development of an Aesthetic*, John Willett (ed. and trs.), (New York: Hill and Wang, 1964), p. 23.

44. "A Short Organum for the Theatre," paragraph 64, in *ibid.*, p. 200.

45. *Ibid.*, pp. 276, 281.

46. "Short Organum," paragraph 42, in *ibid.*, p. 192.
47. "Theatre for Pleasure or Theatre for Instruction," in *ibid.*, p. 71.
48. Quoted in Margaret Eddershaw, "Actors on Brecht," in *The Cambridge Companion to Brecht*, p. 261.
49. In an interesting treatment of dramaturgy and individualism, Darko Suvin contrasts Brecht to Ibsen: *To Brecht and Beyond: Soundings in Modern Dramaturgy* (Brighton, Sussex: Harvester; New Jersey: Barnes and Noble, 1984), pp. 56–74.
50. One would not think the title difficult to translate. I use the translation included in *Bertolt Brecht Collected Plays*, John Willett and Ralph Manheim (eds.) (London: Eyre Methuen, 1979), vol. II, part I. The editors find "A Man's a Man" too Burnsian and "Man is Man" too Germanic, and translate the title as "Man Equals Man," which I find too mathematical. Therefore I use the German title. There are three published versions of the play: the first appeared in 1926, the second, much revised, in 1938, but Brecht produced a conflated version of the two for the Suhrkamp collected edition of 1954, and this is the version translated by Willett and Manheim. But the Suhrkamp edition of 1988 includes the 1926 and 1938 versions rather than the 1954 conflation. I use the 1938 German text.
51. Brecht's specific borrowings, general inspirations, and reminiscences from Kipling's works are traced by James K. Lyons, "Kipling's 'Soldiers Three' and Brecht's *A Man's a Man*," in *Essays on Brecht: Theater and Politics*, Siegfried Mews and Herbert Knust (eds.), (Chapel Hill: University of North Carolina Press, 1974), pp. 99–113.
52. Jan Needle and Peter Thomson note that Gay and Bloody Five are split characters representing "the opposite faces of man" and anticipating *The Good Person of Setzuan*, in *Brecht* (Oxford: Basil Blackwell, 1981), p. 39.
53. Brecht, *Collected Plays*, vol. II, part I, p. 103.
54. Brecht commented with typical irony on this reading in a 1927 radio broadcast; see *Collected Plays*, vol. II, part I, p. 100.
55. Again I use the Willett–Manheim edition of the *Collected Plays* (vol. VI, part I) and the 1989 Suhrkamp edition (vol. VI) for the German text. The frequent mistranslation of the title as "The Good Woman of Setzuan" eliminates the androgeny possible in the German *Mensch*.
56. Brecht, *Collected Plays*, vol. VI, part I, p. 107.
57. Alternatively, John Fuegi sees the truly good person emerging in the perplexed combination of male and female who asks vainly for the gods' help at the end; "The Alienated Woman: Brecht's *The Good Person of Setzuan*, in *Essays on Brecht*, Mews and Knust (eds.), p. 196.

5 HORATIAN PERFORMANCES

1. Robert Elliott, *The Literary Persona* (Chicago: University of Chicago Press, 1982), pp. 19–32.
2. William S. Anderson, *Essays on Roman Satire* (Princeton: Princeton University Press, 1982), pp. 297–314.

3. Elliott, *The Literary Persona*, p. 68.
4. Roland Barthes, "The Death of the Author," in *Image, Music Text*, Stephen Heath (trs.) (London: Fontana, 1977), p. 145.
5. Michel Foucault, "What is an Author?" in *The Foucault Reader*, Paul Rabinow (ed.) (New York: Pantheon, 1984), pp. 102–03.
6. William S. Anderson, "Roman Satirists and Literary Criticism," *Bucknell Review* 12 (1964), 106–13; "Anger in Juvenal and Seneca," *California Publications in Classical Philology* 19 (1964), 127–96; rpt. in *Essays on Roman Satire*, pp. 3–10, 293–361.
7. Gilbert Highet, "Masks and Faces in Satire," *Hermes: Zeitschrift für klassische Philologie* 102 (1974), 321–37; the quotation is on 331.
8. Kirk Freudenburg, *The Walking Muse: Horace on the Theory of Satire* (Princeton: Princeton University Press, 1993), p. 17.
9. David Armstrong, *Horace* (New Haven: Yale University Press, 1989), p. 41.
10. Ellen Oliensis, *Horace and the Rhetoric of Authority* (Cambridge: Cambridge University Press, 1998), pp. 1–16; the quotation is on p. 18.
11. Randall L. B. McNeill, *Horace: Image, Identity, and Audience* (Baltimore: Johns Hopkins University Press, 2001) appeared after this chapter was written. It takes the approach to Horace's deployment of self-images that I call for here, although its emphasis is different from my own. I will note those areas where our topics overlap.
12. Charles Martindale and David Hopkins (eds.), *Horace Made New: Horatian Influences on British Writing from the Renaissance to the Twentieth Century*, (Cambridge: Cambridge University Press, 1993), especially David Hopkins on Cowley (pp. 103–26), Robin Sowerby on Pope (pp. 159–83) and Felicity Rosslyn on Pope and Gray (pp. 184–98); see also William Kupersmith, *Roman Satirists in Seventeenth-Century England* (Lincoln: University of Nebraska Press, 1985); treatments of Pope's Horatian imitations include Frank Stack, *Pope and Horace: Studies in Imitation* (Cambridge: Cambridge University Press, 1985), and Jacob Fuchs, *Reading Pope's Imitations of Horace* (Lewisburg, PA: Bucknell University Press, 1989).
13. Marianne Thormählen points out that the poem "imparts Horatian grace to Juvenalian subject matter," *Rochester: The Poems in Context* (Cambridge: Cambridge University Press, 1993), p. 140.
14. Howard D. Weinbrot, "The Swelling Volume: The Apocalyptic Satire of Rochester's *Letter from Artemisia In The Town To Chloe In The Country*," *Studies in the Literary Imagination* 5 (1972), 34; David M. Vieth also finds her "little more than a scandal-monger," "Toward an Anti-Aristotelian Poetic: Rochester's *Satyr against Mankind* and *Artemisia to Chloe*, with Notes on Swift's *Tale of a Tub* and *Gulliver's Travels*," *Language and Style* 5 (1972), 123–45, rpt. in *John Wilmot, Earl of Rochester: Critical Essays*, David M. Vieth (ed.) (New York: Garland, 1988), p. 271.
15. Carole Fabricant, "The Writer as Hero and Whore: Rochester's *Letter from Artemisia to Chloe*," *Essays in Literature* 3 (1976), 155; David Farley-Hills, *Rochester's Poetry* (Totowa, NJ: Rowman and Littlefield; London: Bell and Hyman, 1978), p. 212; Thormählen, *Rochester*, pp. 104–18.

16. I use *The Works of John Wilmot, Earl of Rochester*, Harold Love (ed.) (Oxford: Oxford University Press, 1999), pp. 63–70.

17. M. M. Bakhtin famously uses the Saturnalia as the archetype of Rabelaisian carnival, especially in *Rabelais and His World*, Helene Iswolsky (trs.) (Bloomington: Indiana University Press, 1984), pp. 5–8; the *locus classicus* for the feast is Macrobius, *Saturnalia*.

18. Throughout, the Latin texts are those edited by P. Michael Brown for Book I and Frances Muecke for Book II (Warminster: Aris and Phillips, 1993); the English translations (with a very few exceptions, parenthetically noted) are those of Niall Rudd (Harmondsworth: Penguin, 1973). Here Rudd's translation substitutes an English cliché for a Latin one: the person who insults Damasippus will be told what hangs from his back, where he cannot look.

19. Burns's poem is also familiar as "The Jolly Beggars"; I use *Robert Burns: Selected Poems*, Carol McGuirk (ed.) (Harmondsworth: Penguin, 1993), pp. 69–85.

20. Allan H. MacLaine, "Radicalism and Conservatism in Burns's *The Jolly Beggars*," *Studies in Scottish Literature* 13 (1978), 125–43, emphasizes the contrast between the anarchic beggars and the conservative, orthodox narrator; but the conservatism of the narrator seems to lie only in his record of the facts of their situation rather than in overt judgments.

21. Michael André Bernstein, "O Totiens Servus: Saturnalia and Servitude in Augustan Rome," *Critical Inquiry* 13 (1987), 450–74.

22. A Lucilian parallel to Horace's wet dream is recorded in *Remains of Old Latin*, E. H. Warmington (ed. and trs.), 4 vols. (Cambridge, MA: Harvard University Press, 1961), vol. III, fragment 1193; see pp. 94–118 for fragments of the equivalent travel poem of Lucilius.

23. Niall Rudd, *The Satires of Horace: A Study* (London: Cambridge University Press, 1966), pp. 54–64.

24. Emily Gowers, "Horace's *Satires* 1.5: An Inconsequential Journey," *Proceedings of the Cambridge Philological Society* n.s. 39 (1993), 61.

25. P. M. W. Tennant, "Political or Personal Propaganda: Horace, *Sermones* 1.5 in Perspective," *Acta Classica* 34 (1991), 51–64.

26. *The Second Advice* and *The Third Advice* were plausibly but not conclusively attributed to Marvell by George de F. Lord, "Two New Poems by Marvell?" *Bulletin of the New York Public Library* 62 (1958), 551–70, but the attribution has remained controversial. Clearly, however, Marvell was aware of the previous poems, even if he did not write them.

27. See Michael Gearin-Tosh, "The Structure of Marvell's 'Last Instructions to a Painter,'" *Essays in Criticism* 22 (1972), 48–57 on the "graphic enterprise" as the organizing element of the poem; Annabel Patterson discusses the *ut pictura poesis* tradition, *Marvell and the Civic Crown* (Princeton: Princeton University Press, 1978), pp. 117–38.

28. Warren Chernaik finds it "a fruitless endeavor to seek for a structural pattern," *The Poet's Time: Politics and Religion in the Work of Andrew Marvell* (Cambridge: Cambridge University Press, 1983), p. 198; David Farley-Hills, among others,

suggests an elaborate but unified structure, in *The Benevolence of Laughter: Comic Poetry of the Commonwealth and Restoration* (London: Macmillan, 1974), pp. 72–98.

29. The sexual imagery of the poem has been analyzed by Steven N. Zwicker, "Virgins and Whores: the Politics of Sexual Misconduct in the 1660s," in *The Political Identity of Andrew Marvell*, Conal Condren and A. D. Cousins (eds.) (Aldershot: Scolar Press, 1990), pp. 85–110; and Barbara Riebling, "England Deflowered and Unmanned: The Sexual Image of Politics in Marvell's 'Last Instructions,'" *SEL* 35 (1995), 137–57; James Grantham Turner argues that "*The Last Instructions* in fact draw together a whole network of sexual–political tropes from the clandestine subculture of libels and whispers," as well as from a royalist culture of visual display, "The Libertine Abject: The 'Postures' of *Last Instructions to a Painter*," in *Marvell and Liberty*, Warren Cherniak and Martin Dzelzainis (eds.) (London: Macmillan; New York: St. Martin's, 1999), pp. 217–48 (the quotation is on p. 227).

30. The text is that of *The Poems and Letters of Andrew Marvell*, 3rd edn., H. M. Margoliouth (ed.), Pierre Legouis, with E. E. Duncan-Jones (rev.), (Oxford: Clarendon Press, 1971), vol. I, pp. 147–72, 346–74.

31. John M. Wallace, *Destiny His Choice: The Loyalism of Andrew Marvell* (Cambridge: Cambridge University Press, 1968), p. 179.

32. The mock-heroic mingles with a variety of other terms: comic-epic, mock-epic, travesty, burlesque, parody, hudibrastic poem, and Menippean satire. Ulrich Broich is useful in sorting out these terms in *The Eighteenth Century Mock Heroic Poem*, David Henry Wilson (trs.), (Cambridge: Cambridge University Press, 1990), pp. 1–26. Gregory G. Colomb, *Designs for Truth: The Poetics of the Augustan Mock-Epic* (University Park: Pennsylvania State University Press, 1992), uses the term "mock-epic" to designate a few works (Dryden's *Mac-Flecknoe*, Garth's *Dispensary*, Swift's *Battle of the Books*, Pope's *Rape of the Lock* and *Dunciad*) which constitute, as he sees them, a well-defined genre. I retain my sense that what Colomb calls "mock-epic" is a particular kind of mock-heroic, but his comments on the mock-epic's representation of reality are stimulating. George de Forest Lord, *Heroic Mockery: Variations on Epic Themes from Homer to Joyce* (Newark: University of Delaware Press, 1977) distinguishes heroic mockery from the mock-heroic on the grounds that it may include non-satiric works, especially festive ones.

33. Claude Rawson, *Satire and Sentiment 1660–1830* (Cambridge: Cambridge University Press, 1994), pp. 29–97; the quoted passage is from p. 89.

34. The satiric characteristics of the advice itself are discussed by Michael Roberts, "Horace *Satires* 2.5: Restrained Indignation," *American Journal of Philology* 105 (1984), 426–33; Niall Rudd, *Satires of Horace*, p. 232, sees the poem as "firmly rooted in the social life of Rome."

35. Rudd, *Satires of Horace*, p. 67; Eduard Fraenkel, *Horace* (Oxford: Clarendon Press, 1957), p. 121.

36. "Horace's jolly tale incisively juggles its own (Brutus') voice away, severs its Brutus from language: in the process, it courts re-activation of the founding

principle of the assortment of meanings heaped together under the figure 'Brutus'"; John Henderson, *Fighting for Rome: Poets and Caesars, History and the Civil War* (Cambridge: Cambridge University Press, 1998), p. 82.

37. Shef Rogers investigates the mysteries of publication, in "Pope, Publishing, and Popular Interpretation of the *Dunciad Variorum*," *Philological Quarterly* 74 (1995), 279–95.

38. I will use the 1743 version, *The Dunciad in Four Books*, Valerie Rumbold (ed.), (Harlow, Essex: Longman, 1999); parenthetical references are to this edition.

39. Aubrey L. Williams, *Pope's "Dunciad": A Study of its Meaning* (Baton Rouge: Louisiana State University Press, 1955), p. 16–26.

40. *Ibid.*, pp. 34–35, provides a map of the movement of the dunces through the City and back.

41. James Noggle sees the satirical sublime of Book IV as deriving from the overlapping of the poet's skepticism with that of the dunces, in *The Skeptical Sublime* (Oxford: Oxford University Press, 2001), pp. 181–207; he concludes that "the final *Dunciad* testifies to the compulsive power of cultural representations infused with the divisive, ambiguous energy of epistemology, creating doubt with claim to certainty, reversing every rapturous effort to ascend to higher truth, alienating every intention in the sublime, impersonal, inertia of the subject's 'own' thought" (p. 207).

42. Alvin B. Kernan, *The Plot of Satire* (New Haven: Yale University Press, 1965), p. 115.

43. Williams, *Pope's "Dunciad"*, pp. 16–25 for Virgil (especially in Book I), and pp. 131–41 for Milton (especially in Book IV).

44. William Kinsley, "The *Dunciad* as Mock-Book," *Huntington Library Quarterly* 35 (1971–72), 38.

45. Emrys Jones, "Pope and Dulness," *Proceedings of the British Academy* 54 (1968), 252–57. See also Rawson, *Satire and Sentiment*, pp. 89–94.

46. Thomas R. Edwards, Jr., *This Dark Estate: A Reading of Pope* (Berkeley: University of California Press, 1963), p. 116.

47. John E. Sitter, *The Poetry of Pope's "Dunciad"* (Minneapolis: University of Minnesota Press, 1971), p. 92.

48. Colomb, *Designs for Truth*, especially pp. 41–42.

49. In addition to Colomb, *Designs for Truth*, pp. 35–58, the issue of names has been considered literarily by Pat Rogers, "The Name and Nature of Dulness: Proper Names in *The Dunciad*," *Anglia* 92 (1974), 79–112; and philosophically by Blakey Vermeule, "Abstraction, Reference, and the Dualism of Pope's *Dunciad*," *Modern Philology* 96 (1998), 16–41.

50. Maynard Mack, *The Garden and the City: Retirement and Politics in the Later Poetry of Pope* (Toronto: University of Toronto Press, 1969), pp. 150–62.

51. Dustin H. Griffin, *Alexander Pope: The Poet in the Poems* (Princeton: Princeton University Press, 1978), pp. 217–77.

52. C. O. Brink, *On Reading a Horatian Satire: An Interpretation of "Sermones"* II 6, sixth Todd memorial lecture (Sydney: Sydney University Press, 1965), p. 12; although Brink speaks generally here, he is particularly concerned to trace Horace's shifts in *Satires* 2.6.

53. Barbara K. Gold, "Openings in Horace's Satires and Odes: Poet, Patron, and Audience," *Yale Classical Studies* 29 (1992), 162–63; other treatments of audience include McNeill, *Horace*, pp. 35–60, Oliensis, *Horace*, pp. 6–14, and Frances Muecke, "The Audience of/in Horace's *Satires*," *AUMLA* 74 (1990), 34–47.

54. McNeill, *Horace*, pp. 10–34, analyzes Horace's exploitation of his relations to Maecenas as patron and friend.

55. C. A. van Rooy sees *Satires* 1.1 as the appropriate introduction to Book 1 because it proposes content as the central idea; "Horace's Sat. 1.1 as Prooemium and its Relation to Satires 2 to 10," *Latinität und alte Kirche*, Wiener Studien Beiheft 8 (1977), 263–74.

56. Fraenkel, *Horace*, p. 94.

57. Rudd, *Satires of Horace*, p. 13; M. Dyson, "Avarice and Discontent in Horace's First Satire," *Classical Quarterly* n.s. 30.1 (1980), 133–39.

58. John J. Bodoh, "Unity in Horace 'Sermo' 1.1," *L'Antiquité classique* 39.1 (1970), 164–67.

59. Thomas K. Hubbard, "The Structure and Programmatic Intent of Horace's First Satire," *Latomus* 40 (1981), 305–21.

60. The poem's vexatious publication history, paralleling its unstable structure, is discussed in detail in Arthur H. Scouten and Robert D. Hume, "Pope and Swift: Text and Interpretation of Swift's Verses on His Death," *Philological Quarterly* 52 (1973), 205–31; for the text of the poem I use Jonathan Swift, *The Complete Poems*, Pat Rogers (ed.) (New Haven: Yale University Press, 1983), pp. 485–98.

61. Barry Slepian, "The Ironic Intention of Swift's Verses on His Own Death," *Review of English Studies* n.s. 14 (1963), 249–56; James Woolley, "Autobiography in Swift's Verses on his Death," in *Contemporary Studies of Swift's Poetry*, John Irwin Fischer and Donald C. Mell, Jr, with David M. Vieth (eds.), (Newark: University of Delaware Press, 1981), pp. 112–22.

62. Marshall Waingrow, "Verses on the Death of Dr. Swift," *Studies in English Literature* 5 (1965), 513–18; John Irwin Fischer, "How to Die: Verses on the Death of Dr. Swift," *Review of English Studies* n.s. 21 (1970), 422–41.

63. Jonathan Swift, *Correspondence*, Harold Williams (ed.), 5 vols. (Oxford: Clarendon Press, 1962–65), vol. III, p. 506; quoted in *Poems*, Rogers (ed.), p. 848.

64. Byron, *The Complete Poetic Works*, Jerome J. McGann (ed.), 7 vols. (Oxford: Clarendon Press, 1980–93), vol. V, p. 82; further references to *Don Juan*, usually parenthetical by canto and stanza, will use this edition.

65. *Don Juan*, McGann (ed.), pp. 670–71.

66. Moyra Haslett, *Byron's "Don Juan" and the Don Juan Legend* (Oxford: Clarendon Press, 1997), p. 119.

67. For the shipwreck, Byron used J. G. Dalyell (ed.), *Shipwrecks and Disasters at Sea* (Edinburgh, 1812) and *A Narrative of the Honourable John Byron* (London, 1768), among others; for Ismail he used Marquis Gabriel de Castelnau, *Essai sur l'Histoire ancienne et moderne de la Nouvelle Russie*, 3 vols. (Paris, 1820).

68. Peter J. Manning, "*Don Juan* and Byron's Imperceptiveness to the English Word," *Studies in Romanticism* 18 (1979), 228.

69. Michael G. Cooke, "Byron's *Don Juan*: The Obsession and Self-Discipline of Spontaneity," *Studies in Romanticism* 14 (1975), 285–302, especially 285–90; Cooke goes on to elaborate a relatively abstract and systematic pattern to account for the movement of the poem.

70. Malcolm Kelsall, *Byron's Politics* (Brighton, Sussex: Harvester; New Jersey: Barnes and Noble, 1987), p. 168.

71. Andrew Rutherford, *Byron: A Critical Study* (Palo Alto, CA: Stanford University Press, 1961), 13–14; Michael Robertson, "The Byron of *Don Juan* as a Whig Aristocrat," *Texas Studies in Language and Literature* 17 (1976), 709–24.

72. *Don Juan*, McGann (ed.), p. 718.

73. Bernard Beatty, *Byron's Don Juan* (London: Croom Helm, 1985), pp. 137–219.

74. Caroline Franklin, *Byron's Heroines* (Oxford: Clarendon Press, 1992), pp. 156–60.

75. "The true significance of sequential events is not that they confirm a wonderful, harmonious order in the world but that they reveal the equally wonderful, apparently endless, and yet finite possibilities of order and disorder"; Jerome McGann, *Don Juan in Context* (Chicago: University of Chicago Press, 1976), p. 102.

76. Frederick Garber, *Self, Text, and Romantic Irony: The Example of Byron* (Princeton: Princeton University Press, 1988), pp. 269–90.

77. Jerome McGann argues that *Don Juan* represents a deliberate assertion of Horatian aesthetics, in contradistinction to that of the Lake poets; *Don Juan in Context*, pp. 68–79.

78. Anne Barton, *Byron, Don Juan* (Cambridge: Cambridge University Press, 1992), p. 21.

6 SATIRE AND THE NOVEL

1. Barbara Herrnstein Smith, *On the Margins of Discourse: The Relation of Literature to Language* (Chicago: University of Chicago Press, 1978), pp. 14–40.

2. M. M. Bakhtin, *The Dialogic Imagination*, Caryl Emerson and Michael Holquist (trs.) (Austin: University of Texas Press, 1981), pp. 43–49.

3. Stendhal, *Le rouge et noir*, 2 vols. (Paris: Bibliothèque Lattès, 1988), vol. II, p. 208.

4. Michael Seidel, *The Satiric Inheritance: Rabelais to Sterne* (Princeton: Princeton University Press, 1979).

5. Ronald Paulson sees *Roderick Random* as a novel with an approximate picaresque form whose hero is sharply distinct from the picaro, functioning instead as a Juvenalian satirist; *Satire and the Novel in Eighteenth-Century England* (New Haven: Yale University Press, 1967), pp. 167–86.

6. Tobias Smollett, *Roderick Random*, Paul-Gabriel Boucé (ed.), (Oxford: Oxford University Press, 1979), p. xxxiii; further references to this edition will be parenthetical.

7. Paul-Gabriel Boucé, *The Novels of Tobias Smollett*, Antonia White (trs.) (London: Longman, 1976), p. 106.

8. Damian Grant, *Tobias Smollett: A Study in Style* (Manchester: Manchester University Press; Totowa, NJ: Rowman and Littlefield, 1977), p. 46.

9. Jerry C. Beasley, "Smollett's Art: The Novel as Picture," in *The First English Novelists: Essays in Understanding*, J. M. Armistead (ed.), *Tennessee Studies in Literature* 29 (1985), 158.

10. Paulson, *Satire and the Novel*, p. 168.

11. Boucé, *Novels of Tobias Smollett*, p. 124.

12. Jerry C. Beasley, *Tobias Smollett Novelist* (Athens: University of Georgia Press, 1998), pp. 35–74, especially pp. 72–74; James T. Bunn, "Signs of Randomness in *Roderick Random*," *Eighteenth-Century Studies* 14 (1981), 452–69.

13. Harry Levin, *The Gates of Horn* (New York: Oxford University Press, 1963); rpt. in *Flaubert: A Collection of Critical Essays*, Raymond Giraud (ed.) (Englewood Cliffs, NJ: Prentice Hall, 1964), p. 61.

14. Hugh Kenner, *Flaubert, Joyce, and Becket: The Stoic Comedians* (Boston: Beacon, 1962), pp. 1–4.

15. Gustave Flaubert, *Bouvard et Pécuchet*, Claudine Gothot-Mersch (ed.), (Paris: Gallimard, 1979), p. 383; A. J. Krailsheimer (trs.), (Harmondsworth: Penguin, 1976), p. 265; parenthetical references will be to this edition and translation.

16. Lionel Trilling, *The Opposing Self* (New York: Viking, 1955), p. 195.

17. Frank Palmeri, *Satire in Narrative: Petronius, Swift, Gibbon, Melville, and Pynchon* (Austin: University of Texas Press, 1990), pp. 4–5.

18. M. M. Bakhtin, *Problems of Dostoevski's Poetics*, Caryl Emerson (trs.) (Minneapolis: University of Minnesota Press, 1984), pp. 112–21.

19. *Ibid.*, p. 113.

20. *Ibid.*, pp. 114–19.

21. *Ibid.*, p. 119.

22. Joel C. Relihan, *Ancient Menippean Satire* (Baltimore: Johns Hopkins University Press, 1993), pp. 4–9.

23. *Ibid.*, p. 9.

24. Charles A. Knight, "Listening to Encolpius: Modes of Confusion in the *Satyricon*," *University of Toronto Quarterly* 58 (1989), 335–54.

25. See, for example, R. Bracht Branham, *Unruly Eloquence: Lucian and the Comedy of Traditions* (Cambridge, MA: Harvard University Press, 1989), pp. 32–34.

26. *The Works of Lucian of Samosota*, H. W. Fowler and F. G. Fowler (trs.), 4 vols. (Oxford: Clarendon Press, 1905), vol. III, p. 165.

27. Christopher Robinson, *Lucian and his Influence in Europe* (London: Duckworth, 1979); David Marsh, *Lucian and the Latins* (Ann Arbor: University of Michigan Press, 1998); for Peacock, see Linda M. Brooks, "Lucian and Peacock: Peacock's Menippean Romanticism," *Revue belge de philologie et d'histoire* 66 (1988), 590–601; I discuss Machado de Assis and postmodern novels below.

28. *Memórias póstumas de Brás Cubas* was translated by William L. Grossman as *Epitaph of a Small Winner* (New York: Noonday, 1952), and I use this translation, which has now been reissued (1990); it has also been translated by Gregory Rabassa as *The Posthumous Memoirs of Brás Cubas* (New York: Oxford

University Press, 1997), and for the convenience of readers using either translation, I refer parenthetically to chapters, which are quite short.

29. See Helen Caldwell, *Machado de Assis: The Brazilian Master and his Novels* (Berkeley: University of California Press, 1970), pp. 96–97.

30. See José Raimundo Maia Neto, *Machado de Assis: The Brazilian Pyrrhonian* (West Lafayette, IN: Purdue University Press, 1994), pp. 88–94.

31. Richard J. Callan, "Notes on 'Braz Cubas,' " *Hispania* 47 (1964), 531.

32. Alfred J. Mac Adam, "Machado de Assis: Satire and Madness," in *Modern Latin American Narratives: The Dreams of Reason* (Chicago: University of Chicago Press, 1977), p. 19.

33. Maia Neto, *Machado de Assis*, p. 88; Caldwell, *Machado de Assis*, pp. 100–101; Sandra Messinger Cypess, "Machado de Assis vs. Brás Cubas: The Narrative Structure of *Memórias póstumas de Brás Cubas*," *Kentucky Romance Quarterly* 25 (1980), 355–70; Maria Luisa Nunes, *The Craft of an Absolute Winner: Characterization and Narratology in the Novels of Machado de Assis*, Contributions in Afro-American and African Studies 71 (Westport, CT: Greenwood Press, 1983), pp. 74–75.

34. Maria José Somerlate Barbosa sees Sterne and Machado as postmodernist, deconstructive writers, "Sterne and Machado: Parodic and Intertextual Play in *Tristram Shandy* and *Memórias*," *Comparatist* 16 (1993), 24–48.

35. For Sterne, see, in addition to Caldwell, *Machado de Assis*, pp. 96, 99–101; Christopher Eustis, "Time and Narrative Structure in *Memórias Póstumas de Brás Cubas*," *Luso-Brazilian Review* 16 (1970), 18–28; for Erasmus, see Clothilde Wilson, "Machado de Assis: Encomiast of Lunacy," *Hispania* 32 (1949), 198–201; for Le Sage, Shakespeare, and Virgil, see Caldwell, *Machado de Assis*, pp. 94–103, 105–10; for Cervantes, see Caldwell, *Machado de Assis*, pp. 105–10; for Dante and Swift, see Mac Adam, *Modern Latin American Narratives*, pp. 15–17.

36. Frederick J. Stopp, *Evelyn Waugh: Portrait of the Artist* (London: Chapman and Hall, 1958), p. 201.

37. Louis I. Bredvold, "The Gloom of the Tory Satirists," in *Pope and His Contemporaries: Essays Presented to George Sherburn*, James L. Clifford and Louis A. Landa (eds.) (Oxford: Clarendon Press, 1949), pp. 1–19.

38. Charles A. Knight, "*Joseph Andrews* and the Failure of Authority," *Eighteenth-Century Fiction* 4 (1992), 111–12.

39. Paulson's treatment of Smollett's satire often discusses these heroic or secondary satirists, *Satire and the Novel*, pp. 165–208.

40. Tobias Smollett, *The Expedition of Humphry Clinker*, Thomas R. Preston and O. M. Brack, Jr. (eds.) (Athens: University of Georgia Press, 1990), p. 318.

7 SATIRE AND THE PRESS: THE BATTLE OF DUNKIRK

1. Michael Seidel, "Crisis Rhetoric and Satiric Power," *New Literary History* 20 (1988), 165, 167.

2. *Ibid.*, 169.

3. John Robert Moore, "Defoe, Steele, and the Demolition of Dunkirk," *Huntington Library Quarterly* 13 (1950), 279–302.
4. Richard I. Cook discusses Swift's particular concern for a country audience in *Jonathan Swift as Tory Pamphleteer* (Seattle: University of Washington Press, 1967), pp. 19–30.
5. For *The Englishman* (first series) I use the text edited by Rae Blanchard (Oxford: Clarendon Press, 1955); for the *Examiner* I use the folio half-sheets (London: J. Morphew, 1712–14). The *Examiner* was separately numbered by volume.
6. James O. Richards summarizes the 1713 electoral debates, especially those regarding succession and the commerce bill, in *Party Propaganda Under Queen Anne: The General Elections of 1702–1713* (Athens: University of Georgia Press, 1972), pp. 129–53.
7. *Tatler*, No. 232; cf. *Examiner*, 4, no. 40; for an argument regarding the indirect political tactics of the *Spectator*, see Charles A. Knight, "*The Spectator's* Generalizing Discourse," in *Telling People What to Think: Early Eighteenth-Century Periodicals from "The Review" to "The Rambler,"* J. A. Downie and Thomas N. Corns (eds.), (London: Frank Cass, 1993), pp. 44–57.
8. Geoffrey Holmes, *British Politics in the Age of Anne*, revised edn. (London: Hambledon Press, 1987), pp. 33–36; for the emergence of the Hanover Tories, see pp. 280–84.
9. Delarivière Manley, *A Modest Inquiry into the Reasons of the Joy Expressed by a Certain Sett of People, upon the Spreading of a Report of Her Majesty's Death* (London: John Morphew, 1714).
10. Steele, *A Letter to a Member of Parliament Concerning the Bill for Preventing the Growth of Schism* (London: Ferd. Burleigh, 1714), rpt. in *Tracts and Pamphlets by Richard Steele*, Rae Blanchard (ed.) (Baltimore: Johns Hopkins Press, 1944), pp. 241–54; Defoe, *A Letter to Mr. Steele, Occasioned by his Letter to a Member of Parliament, Concerning the Bill for Preventing the Growth of Schism. By a Member of Parliament* (London: J. Baker, 1714).
11. The quotation from Kennett, *The Wisdom of Looking Backward* (1715) and a description of the debate regarding baptism can be found in Rae Blanchard's note to *The Englishman* (first series), no. 39, p. 433.
12. London: John Morphew, 1713; rpt. Jonathan Swift, *Prose Works*, Herbert Davis, et al. (eds.), 14 vols. (London: Basil Blackwell, 1964), vol. VIII, pp. 3–25; further quotations from this edition are referred to parenthetically by volume and page.
13. See the *Guardian*, no. 53; the dispute is summarized in Bertrand A. Goldgar, *The Curse of Party: Swift's Relations with Addison and Steele* (Lincoln: University of Nebraska Press, 1961), pp. 112–19.
14. See, for example, *A Letter to the Lord Chancellor Middleton*, in *Prose Writings*, vol. X, pp. 108–10.
15. Frederick Seaton Siebert, *Freedom of the Press in England 1476–1776: The Rise and Decline of Government Control* (1952; rpt. Urbana: University of Illinois Press, 1965), pp. 288, 346–47.

16. Quoted in Calhoun Winton, *Captain Steele: The Early Career of Richard Steele* (Baltimore: Johns Hopkins University Press, 1964), p. 200.

17. *The Correspondence of Alexander Pope*, George Sherburn (ed.), 5 vols. (Oxford: Clarendon Press, 1956), vol. I, p. 189.

18. Daniel Defoe, *The Honour and Prerogative of the Queen's Majesty Vindicated* (London: John Morphew, 1713), p. 16.

19. Robert H. Hopkins, "The Issue of Anonymity and the Beginning of the Steele–Swift Controversy of 1713–14: A New Interpretation," *English Language Notes* 2 (1964), 15–21; Hopkins suggests that Swift's efforts to trivialize Steele in *The Importance of the Guardian Consider'd* may have sought to undercut his appeal for patronage.

20. The contrast between Steele and Swift on the issue of naming themselves as authors is discussed in Paul Hyland, "Naming Names: Steele and Swift," in *Irish Writing: Exile and Submission*, Paul Hyland and Neil Sammells (eds.), (London: Macmillan, 1991), pp. 13–31; Hyland suggests that by "naming" Swift as author of the *Examiner* (though Steele does not quite do this), Steele asserts his role as leader of Whig propaganda, and he notes that, as a result of anonymity, neither could be certain of the responsibility of the other for personal attacks.

21. A description of attacks on Steele is provided by Edward A. and Lillian D. Bloom, "Steele and his Answerers: May 1709–February 1714," in *The Dress of Words: Essays on Restoration and Eighteenth Century Literature in Honor of Richmond P. Bond*, Robert B. White, Jr. (ed.) (Lawrence: University of Kansas Libraries, 1978), pp. 167–97.

22. *John Tutchin's Ghost to Richard St———le, Esq.* (London: J, Morphew, 1714 [1713]). John Tutchin, who died in 1709, was a Whig party writer and scandalmonger, often, as in *Dunciad* II, 146, linked with Defoe. His mantle may suggest a double inheritance, as he was tried for seditious libel in 1704.

23. John Lacy, *The Steeleids, or, the Tryal of Wit. A Poem, in Three Cantos* (London: J. Morphew, 1714).

24. See Ellen Douglass Leyburn, *Satiric Allegory: Mirror for Man* (New Haven: Yale University Press, 1956), pp. 10–14.

25. Bertrand A. Goldgar notes Swift's effective shifting between ironic commentary and direct criticism in *The Importance of the Guardian Consider'd*; see *The Curse of Party*, p. 129.

26. Irvin Ehrenpreis, *Swift: The Man, his Works, and the Age*, 3 vols. (Cambridge, MA: Harvard University Press, 1967), vol. II, p. 708.

27. Edward Gregg, *The Protestant Succession in International Politics, 1710–1716* (New York: Garland, 1986), pp. 184–85.

28. Quotations refer to Blanchard (ed.), *Tracts and Pamphlets*, pp. 277–346, which uses the text of *The Political Writings of Richard Steele* (1715).

29. For the general satiric utility of this model of communication, drawn from Roman Jakobson, see chapter 2, above.

30. For Swift's view of language and faction see Daniel Eilon, *Faction's Fictions: Ideological Closure in Swift's Satire* (Newark: University of Delaware Press, 1991).

8 WHITE SNOW AND BLACK MAGIC: KARL KRAUS AND THE PRESS

1. "Ich glaube an den Druckfehlerteufel" ("I believe in the Printer's Gremlin," 1912); in *In These Great Times: A Karl Kraus Reader*, Harry Zohn (ed. and trs.) (1976; rpt. Chicago: University of Chicago Press, 1990) p. 69; hereafter cited as *Reader*.

2. Karl Kraus, "Vorwort" to *Die letzten Tage der Menschheit* (Frankfurt: Suhrkamp, 1986) p. 9; *The Last Days of Mankind*, Frederick Ungar (ed.), Alexander Gode and Sue Ellen Wright (trs.) (New York: Ungar, 1974), p. 3. The German text uses the edition of 1926. *Die letzten Tage*, like other works of Kraus, appeared in various versions – first in *Die Fackel* (1919) and then, with considerable revisions, in book form in 1922. The Ungar version presents about one-third of the full play.

3. *Fackel* 363–65 (1912), 1–28; *Untergang der Welt durch schwarze Magie* (1922; rpt. Frankfurt: Suhrkamp, 1989), pp. 424–54.

4. Kraus's reprinting of *Fackel* essays mostly written between 1908 and 1914 as *Untergang der Welt durch schwarze Magie* in 1922, the same year as the volume publication of *Die letzten Tage*, is particularly telling, for the essays document both the cultural attitudes that led to the war and Kraus's prediction that they would do so.

5. Harry Zohn, *Karl Kraus* (New York: Twayne, 1971); *Karl Kraus and the Critics* (Columbia, SC: Camden House, 1997).

6. Edward Timms, *Karl Kraus Apocalyptic Satirist: Culture and Catastrophe in Hapsburg Vienna* (New Haven and London: Yale University Press: 1986).

7. Frank Field, *The Last Days of Mankind: Karl Kraus and his Vienna* (London: Macmillan; New York: St. Martin's, 1967).

8. Wilma Abeles Iggers, *Karl Kraus: A Viennese Critic of the Twentieth Century* (The Hague: Martinus Nijhoff, 1967).

9. Walter Benjamin, "Karl Kraus," in *One-Way Street and Other Writings*, Edward Street and Kingsley Shorter (trs.), (London: NLB, 1979), pp. 258–90; Erich Heller, "Karl Kraus: Satirist in the Modern World," in *The Disinherited Mind: Essays in Modern German Literature and Thought* (London: Bowes and Bowes, 1975), pp. 235–60; Allan Janik and Stephen Toulmin, "Language and Society: Karl Kraus and the Last Days of Vienna," in *Wittgenstein's Vienna* (New York: Simon and Schuster, 1973), pp. 67–91.

10. Heller, "Karl Kraus," p. 252.

11. *Reader*, pp. 35–38.

12. Elias Canetti, "Karl Kraus: The School of Resistance," in *The Conscience of Words*, Joachim Neugroschel (trs.) (New York: Continuum-Seabury, 1979), p. 31.

13. *Fackel* 1, 2, quoted in Timms, *Karl Kraus*, p. 41.

14. *Fackel* 338; quoted in *Reader*, p. 5.

15. See especially Timms, *Karl Kraus*, pp. 380–87.

16. Mary Snell, "Karl Kraus's *Die Letzten Tage der Menschheit*: An Analysis," *Forum for Modern Language Studies* 4 (1968), 324–47; Franz H. Mautner, "Die letzten

Tage der Menschheit," in *Das Deutsche Drama*, vol. ii, pp. 357–82; abr. and trs. in *The Last Days of Mankind*, Ungar (ed.), pp. 239–63.

17. Kraus's critical pronouncements on the theater, which appeared throughout his life as a writer, have been analyzed in detail by Kari Grimstad, *Masks of the Prophet: The Theatrical World of Karl Kraus* (Toronto: University of Toronto Press, 1982).

18. The politics of Kraus's later years, especially his unsuccessful campaign against Schober and his self-identification with the satiric and misanthropic figure of Shakespeare's Timon, are clearly explained in Edward Timms, "Kraus's Shakespearian Politics," in *Austria in the Thirties: Culture and Politics*, Kenneth Segar and John Warren (eds.) (Riverside, CA: Ariadne Press, 1991), pp. 345–58.

19. Zohn, *Karl Kraus*, p. 130.

20. Caroline Kohn, *Karl Kraus: le polémiste et l'écrivain, défenseur des droits de l'individu* (Paris: Didier, 1962), e.g. pp. 395–400.

21. Iggers, *Karl Kraus*, pp. 150–51.

22. Timms, *Karl Kraus*, pp. 352–68; see also C. E. Williams, "Karl Kraus: the Absolute Satirist," in *The Broken Eagle: The Politics of Austrian Literature from the Empire to Anschluss* (London: Paul Elek, 1974), pp. 187–235.

23. John Theobald, *The Paper Ghetto: Karl Kraus and Anti-Semitism* (Frankfurt: Peter Lang, 1996); see also Zohn, *Karl Kraus and the Critics*, pp. 19–26.

24. A philosophical treatment of Kraus's terminology is Jay F. Bodine, "Karl Kraus's Conception of Language," *Modern Austrian Literature* 8, (1975), 268–314; see also John Pizer, "'Ursprung is das Ziel': Karl Kraus's Concept of Origin," *Modern Austrian Literature* 27 (1994), 1–21.

25. Alfred Tarski, "The Semantic Conception of Truth and the Foundations of Semantics," *Philosophy and Phenomenological Research* 4 (1941), 341–75.

26. Zohn, *Karl Kraus*, p. 133.

27. Benjamin, "Karl Kraus," p. 286.

28. E.g., "Die Sprache ist die Mutter, nicht die Magd des Gedankens" ("Language is the mother, not the maid, of thought"); Kraus, *Aphorismen* (Frankfurt: Suhrkamp, 1986), p. 235.

29. J. P. Stern, "Karl Kraus's Vision of Language," *Modern Language Review* 61 (1966), 75.

30. Kraus, *Aphorismen*, p. 116; Zohn, *Karl Kraus*, p. 157.

31. Canetti, "Karl Kraus," p. 31.

32. Heller, "Karl Kraus," pp. 237, 239.

33. "Die Sprache," *Fackel*, 885–87; rpt. in *Karl-Kraus-Lesebuch*, Hans Wollschläger (ed.) (Frankfurt: Suhrkamp, 1987), p. 383.

34. Stern, "Karl Kraus's Vision of Language," pp. 79–84.

35. *Ibid.*, p. 83.

36. J. P. Stern, "Karl Kraus and the Idea of Literature," *Encounter* 45.2 (August 1975), 44; "Karl Kraus: Language and Experience," in *Karl Kraus in neuer Sicht: Karl Kraus in a New Perspective*, Sigurd Paul Scheichl and Edward Timms (eds.) (Munich: text + kritic, 1986), pp. 21–31; Stern's *Encounter* essay, in addition to providing very useful remarks on Kraus's style, is more appreciative of his

achievement in *Die Dritte Walpurgisnacht* than other critics such as Zohn and Iggers.

37. See, for example, "Die Welt der Plakate" ("The World of Posters"), *Reader*, pp. 42–47.

38. Kraus's 1910 essay "Heine und die Folgen" (rpt. in *Untergang*, pp. 185–210) is described by Zohn, *Karl Kraus*, pp. 54–55.

39. "Adolf Loos und ich, er wörtlich, ich sprachlich, haben nichts weiter getan als gezeigt, dass zwischen einer Urne und einem Nachttopf ein Unterschied ist und dass in diesem Unterschied erst die Kultur Spielraum hat"; Kraus, *Aphorismen*, p. 341.

40. The terms are discussed in detail in C. J. Thornhill, *Walter Benjamin and Karl Kraus: Problems of a "Wahlverwandtschaft,"* Stuttgarter Arbeiten zur Germanistik 319 (Stuttgart: Heinz, 1996), especially pp. 18–63.

41. Benjamin, "Karl Kraus," p. 289.

42. See Alfred Pfabigan, *Karl Kraus und der Sozialismus: Eine politische Biographie* (Vienna: Euroverlag, 1976); Pfabigan's views are summarized, with some hostility, in Zohn, *Karl Kraus and the Critics*, pp. 39–45.

43. "The mission of the press is to spread culture while destroying the attention span"; Karl Kraus, *Dicta and Contradicta*, Jonathan McVity (trs.) (Urbana: University of Illinois Press, 2001), p. 50.

44. *Fackel* 272–73 (1909), 2–5; rpt. Kraus, *Lesebuch*, pp. 109–11; *Reader*, pp. 39–41.

45. E.g., "Ich habe nie ein Hehl daraus gemacht" ("I have never denied the fact," 1911); *Reader*, pp. 64–65; "Die Nebensache" ("A Minor Detail," 1915), *Reader*, 84–85.

46. Timms, *Karl Kraus*, pp. 51–53; Grimstad, *Masks of the Prophet*, pp. 21–30.

47. Timms, *Karl Kraus*, pp. 151–53.

48. "Prozess Friedjung" (December 1909), in Kraus, *Untergang*, p. 27.

49. Four of the Münz satires from 1910–11 are translated by Harold B. Segel in *The Vienna Coffeehouse Wits 1890–1930* (West Lafayette, IN: Purdue University Press, 1993), pp. 86–103.

50. *Fackel* 305–06 (1910); rpt. Kraus, *Lesebuch*, p. 153; Segel (ed.), *Vienna Coffeehouse Wits*, p. 100.

51. *Fackel* 347–48 (1912): 55–56; rpt. Kraus, *Lesebuch*, pp. 179–80; *Reader*, pp. 66–68.

52. The issues of choice, silence, and press freedom are of concern to Helmut Arntzen, *Karl Kraus und die Presse* (Munich: Wilhelm Fink, 1975), especially pp. 25–36.

53. E.g., "Apokalypse," *Fackel* 261–62 (1908); rpt. Kraus, *Untergang*, pp. 10–11.

54. "Aussi, n'ayant pu reconnaître de valeurs positives que dans le passé, a-t-il pris les dernières convulsions d'une époque pour les derniers jours d'humanité"; Lucien Goldmann, "Un grand polémiste: Karl Kraus," in *Recherches dialectiques* (Paris: Gallimard, 1959), p. 234.

55. E.g., Timms, *Karl Kraus*, pp. 41–46.

Bibliography

PRIMARY SOURCES

Arbuthnot, John, *The History of John Bull*, Alan W. Bower and Robert A. Erickson (eds.), Oxford: Clarendon Press, 1976.

Brecht, Bertolt, *Brecht on Theatre: The Development of an Aesthetic*, John Willett (ed. and trs.), New York: Hill and Wang, 1964.

Collected Plays, John Willett and Ralph Manheim (eds.), vol. II, part 1 and vol. VI, London: Eyre Methuen, 1979.

Werke, Werner Hecht, et al. (eds.), 30 vols., Frankfurt: Suhrkamp, 1988–2000.

Burns, Robert, *Selected Poems*, Carol McGuirk (ed.), Harmondsworth: Penguin, 1993.

Byron, George Gordon, Lord, *Don Juan*, vol. V of *The Complete Poetic Works*, Jerome J. McGann (ed.), Oxford: Clarendon Press, 1986.

Defoe, Daniel, *The Honour and Prerogative of the Queen's Majesty Vindicated*, London: John Morphew, 1713.

A Letter to Mr. Steele, Occasioned by his Letter to a Member of Parliament, Concerning the Bill for Preventing the Growth of Schism. By a Member of Parliament, London: J. Baker, 1714.

Dryden, John, "Discourse concerning the Original and Progress of Satire," in *The Works of John Dryden*, 20 vols., A. B. Chambers, William Frost, and Vinton Dearing (eds.), vol. IV, Berkeley: University of California Press, 1974.

Erasmus, Desiderius, *The Praise of Folly*, Hoyt Hopewell Hudson (trs.), Princeton: Princeton University Press, 1941.

The Praise of Folly, Clarence H. Miller (trs.), New Haven: Yale University Press, 1979.

Flaubert, Gustave, *Bouvard et Pécuchet*, Claudine Gothot-Mersch (ed.), Paris: Gallimard, 1979.

Bouvard et Pécuchet, A. J. Krailsheimer (trs.), Harmondsworth: Penguin, 1976.

Goldsmith, Oliver, *Collected Works*, Arthur Friedman (ed.), 5 vols, Oxford: Clarendon Press, 1966.

Horace, *Satires*, 2 vols. P. Michael Brown and Frances Muecke (eds. and trs.), Warminster: Aris and Phillips, 1993.

Satires and Epistles, Niall Rudd (trs.), Harmondsworth: Penguin, 1973.

John Tutchin's *Ghost to Richard St—le, Esq.*, London: J. Morphew, 1714 (1713).

Johnson, Samuel, *Journey to the Western Islands of Scotland*, Mary Lascelles (ed.), New Haven: Yale University Press, 1971.
The Poems of Samuel Johnson, David Nichol Smith and Edward L. McAdam (eds.), second edn., Oxford: Clarendon Press, 1974.
Jonson, Ben, *The Alchemist*, Alvin Kernan (ed.), New Haven: Yale University Press, 1974.
Juvenal, *The Sixteen Satires*, Peter Green (trs.), revised edn., Harmondsworth: Penguin, 1974.
Keil, H. (ed.), *Grammatici Latini*, 1857; rpt. Hildesheim: Georg Olms, 1961.
Kraus, Karl, *Aphorismen*, Frankfurt: Suhrkamp, 1986.
Dicta and Contradicta, Jonathan McVity (trs.), Urbana: University of Illinois Press, 2001.
In These Great Times: A Karl Kraus Reader, Harry Zohn (ed. and trs.), 1976; rpt. Chicago: University of Chicago Press, 1990.
Karl-Kraus-Lesebuch, Hans Wollschläger (ed.), Frankfurt: Suhrkamp, 1987.
The Last Days of Mankind, Frederick Ungar (ed. and abbr.), Alexander Gode and Sue Ellen Wright (trs.), New York: Ungar, 1974.
Die letzten Tage der Menschheit, Frankfurt: Suhrkamp, 1986.
Untergang der Welt durch schwarze Magie, Frankfurt: Suhrkamp, 1989.
Kundera, Milan, *The Book of Laughter and Forgetting*, Aaron Asher (trs.), 1996; rpt. New York: Perennial, 1999.
The Book of Laughter and Forgetting, Michael Henry Heim (trs.). Harmondsworth: Penguin, 1981.
Le livre du rire et de l'oubli, François Kérel (trs.), new edn., revised by the author, Paris: Gallimard, 1985.
Lacy, John. *The Steeleids, or, the Tryal of Wit. A Poem, in Three Cantos*, London: J. Morphew, 1714.
Lucian of Samosata, *Works*, H. W. and F. G. Fowler (trs.), 4 vols., Oxford: Clarendon Press, 1905.
Works, A. M. Harmon, K. Kilburn, and M. D. Macleod (trs.), 8 vols. London: Heinemann; New York: Macmillan, 1913–67.
Lucillius, *Remains of Old Latin*, 4 vols., E. H. Warmington (ed. and trs.), vol. III. Cambridge, MA: Harvard University Press, 1961.
Machado de Assis, Joaquim Maria, *Epitaph of a Small Winner*, William L. Grossman (trs.), New York: Noonday, 1952.
The Posthumous Memoirs of Brás Cubas, Gregory Rabassa (trs.), New York: Oxford University Press, 1997.
Manley, Delarivière, *A Modest Inquiry into the Reasons of the Joy Expressed by a Certain Sett of People, upon the Spreading of a Report of Her Majesty's Death*, London: John Morphew, 1714.
Marvell, Andrew, *The Poems and Letters of Andrew Marvell*, 2 vols., 3rd edn., H. M. Margoliouth (ed.), Pierre Legouis, with E. E. Duncan-Jones (rev.), Oxford: Clarendon Press, 1971.
Milton, John, *Selected Prose*, C. A. Patrides (ed.), revised edn., Columbia: University of Missouri Press, 1985.

Molière, Jean-Baptiste Poquelin, *The Misanthrope and Tartuffe*, Richard Wilbur (trs.), New York: Harvest, 1965.

Oeuvres complètes, Georges Couton (ed.), 2 vols., Paris: Gallimard, 1971.

Montesquieu, Baron Charles Louis de Secondat de, *Lettres persanes*, Paul Vernière (ed.), Paris: Garnier, 1960.

Persian Letters, C. J. Betts (trs.), Harmondsworth: Penguin, 1973.

Nabokov, Vladimir, *Pale Fire*, 1962; rpt. New York: Vintage, 1989.

Ostrovsky, Alexander Nikolayevich, *A Domestic Picture; A Scene from Moscow Life*, E. L. Voynich (trs.), in *The Humour of Russia*, London: Walter Scott, 1985, 142–66.

Easy Money and Two Other Plays, David Magarshack (trs.), 1944; rpt. Westport, CT: Greenwood, 1970.

Five Plays of Alexander Ostrovsky, Eugene K. Bristow (trs.), New York: Pegasus, 1969.

Plays by Alexander Ostrovsky, George Rapall Noyes (ed.), 1917; rpt. New York: AMS Press, 1969.

Without a Dowry and Other Plays, Norman Henley (trs.), Dana Point, CA: Ardis, 1997.

Pope, Alexander, *The Correspondence of Alexander Pope*, George Sherburn (ed.), 5 vols., Oxford: Clarendon Press, 1956.

The Dunciad in Four Books, Valerie Rumbold (ed.), Harlow, Essex: Longman, 1999.

The Poems of Alexander Pope, The Twickenham Edition, 11 vols., London: Methuen; New Haven: Yale University Press, 1951–69.

Quintilian, *Institutio Oratoria*, H. E. Butler (trs.), 1920; rpt. London: Heinemann; Cambridge, MA: Harvard University Press, 1969.

Rabelais, François, *The Histories of Gargantua and Pantagruel*, J. M. Cohen (trs.), Harmondsworth: Penguin, 1955.

Rochester, John Wilmot, Earl of, *The Works of John Wilmot, Earl of Rochester*, Harold Love (ed.), Oxford: Oxford University Press, 1999.

Rushdie, Salman, *Shame*, 1983; rpt. London: Picador, 1984.

Segel, Harold B. (ed.), *The Vienna Coffeehouse Wits 1890–1930*, West Lafayette, IN: Purdue University Press, 1993.

Smollett, Tobias, *The Expedition of Humphry Clinker*, Thomas R. Preston and O. M. Brack, Jr. (eds.), Athens: University of Georgia Press, 1990.

Roderick Random, Paul-Gabriel Boucé (ed.), Oxford: Oxford University Press, 1979.

Steele, Richard, *The Englishman*, Rae Blanchard (ed.), Oxford: Clarendon Press, 1955.

The Guardian, John Calhoun Stephens (ed.), Lexington: University Press of Kentucky, 1982.

Tracts and Pamphlets by Richard Steele, Rae Blanchard (ed.), Baltimore: Johns Hopkins University Press, 1944.

Stendhal, Henri Beyle, *The Red and the Black*, C. K. Scott Moncrieff (trs.), New York: Modern Library, 1926.

Le rouge et noir, 2 vols., Paris: Bibliothèque Lattès, 1988.

Swift, Jonathan, *The Complete Poems*, Pat Rogers (ed.), New Haven: Yale University Press, 1983.

Correspondence, Harold Williams (ed.), 5 vols., Oxford: Clarendon Press, 1962–65.

The Examiner, London: J. Morphew, 1712–14.

Prose Works, Herbert Davis et al. (eds.), 14 vols., Oxford: Basil Blackwell, 1957–74.

Varro, *De Lingua Latina*, Roland G. Kent (ed.and trs.), 1938; rpt. London: Heinemann; Cambridge, MA: Harvard University Press, 1958.

Voltaire, François Marie Arouet, *Candide, ou, l'optimisme*, Lester G. Crocker (ed.), London: University of London Press, 1958.

Dictionnaire philosophique, Paris: Garnier, 1961.

Lettres philosophiques, René Pomeau (ed.), Paris: Garnier-Flammarion, 1964.

SECONDARY SOURCES

Ahmad, Aijaz, *In Theory: Classes, Nations, Literatures*, London: Verso, 1992.

Althusser, Louis, "Ideology and Ideological State Apparatuses (Notes Towards an Investigation)," in *Lenin and Philosophy and Other Essays*, Ben Brewster (trs.), London: NLB, 1971, 123–73.

Anderson, Benedict, *Imagined Communities: Reflections on the Origin and Spread of Nationalism*, revised edn., London and New York: Verso, 1991.

Anderson, Graham, *Lucian: Theme and Variation in the Second Sophistic*, Leiden: E. J. Brill, 1976.

Anderson, William S., *Essays on Roman Satire*, Princeton: Princeton University Press, 1982.

Arntzen, Helmut, *Karl Kraus und die Presse*, Munich: Wilhelm Fink, 1975.

Armstrong, David, *Horace*, New Haven: Yale University Press, 1989.

Bader, Rudolf, "Indian *Tin Drum*," *International Fiction Review* 11 (1984), 75–83.

Bakhtin, M. M., *The Dialogic Imagination*, Caryl Emerson and Michael Holquist (trs.), Austin: University of Texas Press, 1981.

Problems of Dostoevski's Poetics, Caryl Emerson (trs.), Minneapolis: University of Minnesota Press, 1984.

Rabelais and His World, Helene Iswolsky (trs.), Bloomington: Indiana University Press, 1984.

Speech Genres and Other Late Essays, Caryl Emerson and Michael Holquist (eds.), Vern W. McGee (trs.), Austin: University of Texas Press, 1986.

Banerjee, Maria Němcová, *Terminal Paradox: The Novels of Milan Kundera*, New York: Grove Weidenfeld, 1990.

Barbosa, Maria José Somerlate, "Sterne and Machado: Parodic and Intertextual Play in *Tristram Shandy* and *Memórias*," *Comparatist* 16 (1993), 24–48.

Barthes, Roland, "The Death of the Author," in *Image, Music Text*, Stephen Heath (trs.), London: Fontana, 1977.

Barton, Anne, *Ben Jonson, Dramatist*, Cambridge: Cambridge University Press, 1984.

Byron, Don Juan, Cambridge: Cambridge University Press, 1992.

Beasley, Jerry C., "Smollett's Art: The Novel as Picture," in *The First English Novelists: Essays in Understanding*, J. M. Armistead (ed.), *Tennessee Studies in Literature* 29 (1985), 143–83.

Tobias Smollett Novelist, Athens: University of Georgia Press, 1998.

Beatty, Bernard, *Byron's Don Juan*, London: Croom Helm, 1985.

Benet, Robert, "Du regard de l'Autre dans les *Lettres persanes*: investigation, voilement, dévoilement," *L'Information littéraire* 44 (May–June 1992), 6–13.

Benjamin, Walter, "Karl Kraus," in *One-Way Street and Other Writings*, Edward Jephcott and Kingsley Shorter (trs.), London: NLB, 1979, 258–90.

Bernstein, Michael André, "O Totiens Servus: Saturnalia and Servitude in Augustan Rome," *Critical Inquiry* 13 (1987), 450–74.

Bloom, Edward A. and Bloom, Lillian D., *Satire's Persuasive Voice*, Ithaca, NY and London: Cornell University Press, 1979.

"Steele and his Answerers: May 1709–February 1714," in *The Dress of Words: Essays on Restoration and Eighteenth Century Literature in Honor of Richmond P. Bond*, Robert B. White, Jr. (ed.), Lawrence: University of Kansas Libraries, 1978, 167–97.

Boase, A. M., "The Interpretation of the *Lettres Persanes*," in *The French Mind: Studies Presented to Gustave Rudler*, Will Moore, et al. (eds.), Oxford: Clarendon Press, 1952, 152–69.

Bodine, Jay F., "Karl Kraus's Conception of Language," *Modern Austrian Literature* 8, (1975), 268–314.

Bodoh, John J., "Unity in Horace 'Sermo' 1.1," *L'Antiquité classique* 39.1 (1970), 164–67.

Bogel, Fredric V., *The Difference Satire Makes: Rhetoric and Reading from Jonson to Byron*, Ithaca, NY and London: Cornell University Press, 2001.

Bottiglia, William F., Jr., *Voltaire's "Candide": Analysis of a Classic*, second edn., Studies on Voltaire 7A, Geneva: Institut et Musée Voltaire, 1964.

Boucé, Paul-Gabriel, *The Novels of Tobias Smollett*, Antonia White (trs.), London: Longman, 1976.

Boyd, Brian, *Nabokov's "Pale Fire": The Magic of Artistic Discovery*, Princeton: Princeton University Press, 1999.

Vladimir Nabokov: The American Years, Princeton: Princeton University Press, 1991.

Branham, R. Bracht, *Unruly Eloquence: Lucian and the Comedy of Traditions*, Cambridge, MA: Harvard University Press, 1989.

Braun, Theodore, "'La Chaîne secrète': A Decade of Interpretations," *French Studies* 42 (1988), 278–91.

Bredvold, Louis I., "The Gloom of the Tory Satirists," in *Pope and His Contemporaries: Essays Presented to George Sherburn*, James L. Clifford and Louis A. Landa (eds.), Oxford: Clarendon Press, 1949, 1–19.

Brennan, Timothy, *Salman Rushdie and the Third World: Myths of the Nation*, New York: St. Martin's; London: Macmillan, 1989.

Breuilly, John, *Nationalism and the State*, New York: St. Martin's, 1982.

Brigg, Peter, "Salman Rushdie's Novels: The Disorder in Fantastic Order," *World Literature Written in English* 27 (1987), 119–30.

Brink, C. O., *On Reading a Horatian Satire: An Interpretation of "Sermones" 11, 6*, sixth Todd Memorial Lecture, Sydney: Sydney University Press, 1965.

Brodsky, Joseph, "The Condition We Call 'Exile,'" in *Literature in Exile*, John Glad (ed.), Durham, NC: Duke University Press, 1990, 100–30.

Brody, Jules, "*Don Juan* and *Le Misanthrope*, or the Esthetics of Individualism in Molière," *PMLA* 84 (1969), 559–76.

Broich, Ulrich, *The Eighteenth Century Mock Heroic Poem*, David Henry Wilson (trs.), Cambridge: Cambridge University Press, 1990.

Bunn, James T., "Signs of Randomness in *Roderick Random*," *Eighteenth-Century Studies* 14 (1981), 452–69.

Calder, Andrew, *Molière: The Theory and Practice of Comedy*, London: Athlone, 1973.

Caldwell, Ann Stewart, "The Intrusive Narrative Voice of Milan Kundera," *Review of Contemporary Fiction* 9 (1989), 46–52.

Caldwell, Helen, *Machado de Assis: The Brazilian Master and his Novels*, Berkeley: University of California Press, 1970.

Callan, Richard J., "Notes on 'Braz Cubas,'" *Hispania* 47 (1964), 530–33.

Canetti, Elias, *The Conscience of Words*, Joachim Neugroschel (trs.), New York: Continuum-Seabury, 1979.

Chernaik, Warren, *The Poet's Time: Politics and Religion in the Work of Andrew Marvell*, Cambridge: Cambridge University Press, 1983.

Chill, Emanuel S. "*Tartuffe*, Religion, and Courtly Culture," *French Historical Studies* 3 (1963), 151–83.

Claassen, Jo-Marie, "Ovid's Poetic Pontus," *Papers of the Leeds International Latin Symposium* 6 (1990), 65–94.

Coffey, Michael, *Roman Satire*, London: Methuen; New York: Barnes and Noble, 1976.

Colley, Linda, *Britons: Forging the Nation 1707–1837*, New Haven and London: Yale University Press, 1992.

Colomb, Gregory C., *Designs for Truth: The Poetics of the Augustan Mock-Epic*, University Park: Pennsylvania State University Press, 1992.

Connery, Brian A. and Kirk Combe (eds.), *Theorizing Satire: Essays in Literary Criticism*, New York: St. Martin's, 1995.

Conte, Gian Baggio, *Genres and Readers*, Baltimore: Johns Hopkins University Press, 1994.

Cook, Richard I., *Jonathan Swift as Tory Pamphleteer*, Seattle: University of Washington Press, 1967.

Cook, Rufus, "Place and Displacement in Salman Rushdie's Work," *World Literature Today* 68 (1994), 24.

Cooke, Michael G., "Byron's *Don Juan*: The Obsession and Self-Discipline of Spontaneity," *Studies in Romanticism* 14 (1975), 285–302.

Courtney, E., *A Commentary on the Satires of Juvenal*, London: Athlone Press, 1980.

Crain, Caleb, "Infidelity: Milan Kundera is On the Outs with his Translators. But Who's Betraying Whom," *Lingua Franca* 9.7 (October 1999), 38–50.

Cypess, Sandra Messinger, "Machado de Assis vs. Brás Cubas: The Narrative Structure of *Memórias póstumas de Brás Cubas*," *Kentucky Romance Quarterly* 25 (1980), 355–70.

Dalnikoff, Donna Isaacs, "A Familiar Stranger: The Outsider of Eighteenth-Century Satire," *Neophilologus* 57 (1973), 121–34.

"The Meaning of Eldorado: Utopia and Satire in *Candide*," *Studies on Voltaire and the Eighteenth Century* 127 (1974), 41–59.

Dayal, Samir, "The Liminalities of Nation and Gender: Salman Rushdie's *Shame*," *Journal of the Midwest Modern Language Association* 31.2 (1998), 39–62.

Derrida, Jacques, "La Loi du Genre/The Law of Genre," *Glyph* 7 (1980), 176–229.

Dessen, Alan C., *Jonson's Moral Comedy*, Evanston, IL: Northwestern University Press, 1971.

Dick, Aliki Lafkidou, *Paedeia through Laughter: Jonson's Aristophanic Appeal to Human Intelligence*, The Hague: Mouton, 1974.

Donaldson, Ian, *Jonson's Magic Houses: Essays in Interpretation*, Oxford: Clarendon Press, 1997.

Dover, K. J., *Aristophanic Comedy*, Berkeley and Los Angeles: University of California Press, 1972.

Downie, J. A., "The Political Significance of *Gulliver's Travels*," in *Swift and his Contexts*, John Irwin Fischer, Hermann J. Real, and James Woolley (eds.), New York: AMS, 1989, 1–19.

Draitser, Emil, "Fighting the Shadows: Four Crises of a Russian Satirist in Exile," *Studies in Contemporary Satire* 17 (1990), 15–30.

Duffy, Michael, *The Englishman and the Foreigner*, *The English Satiric Print 1600–1832*, Cambridge: Chadwyck-Healey, 1986.

Dyson, M., "Avarice and Discontent in Horace's First Satire," *Classical Quarterly* n.s. 30.1 (1980), 133–39.

Eagle, Herbert, "Genre and Paradigm in Milan Kundera's *Book of Laughter and Forgetting*," in *Language and Language Theory: In Honour of Ladislav Matejka*, B. Stolz, I. R. Titunik, L. Dolezel (eds.), Ann Arbor: University of Michigan Press, 1984, 251–84.

Edwards, Thomas R. Jr., *This Dark Estate: A Reading of Pope*, Berkeley: University of California Press, 1963.

Ehrenpreis, Irvin, *Swift: the Man, his Works, and the Age*, 3 vols., Cambridge, MA: Harvard University Press, 192–83.

Eilon, Daniel, *Faction's Fictions: Ideological Closure in Swift's Satire*, Newark: University of Delaware Press, 1991.

Elkin, P. K., *The Augustan Defence of Satire*, London: Clarendon Press, 1973.

Elliott, Robert C., "The Definition of Satire," *Yearbook of Comparative and General Literature* 11 (1962), 19–23.

The Literary Persona, Chicago: University of Chicago Press, 1982.

The Power of Satire: Magic, Ritual, Art, Princeton: Princeton University Press, 1960.

English, James F., "Modernist Joke-Work: *Pale Fire* and the Mock Transcendence of Mockery," *Contemporary Literature* 33 (1992), 74–90.

Esam, Irene, "Folkloric Elements as Communication Devices – Ostrovsky's Plays," *New Zealand Slavonic Journal* 2 (1968), 67–88.

Eustis, Christopher, "Time and Narrative Structure in *Memórias Póstumas de Brás Cubas*," *Luso-Brazilian Review* 16 (1970), 18–28.

Fabricant, Carole, "The Writer as Hero and Whore: Rochester's *Letter from Artemisia to Chloe*," *Essays in Literature* 3 (1976), 152–66.

Farley-Hills, David, *The Benevolence of Laughter: Comic Poetry of the Commonwealth and Restoration*, London: Macmillan, 1974.

Rochester's Poetry, Totowa, NJ: Rowman and Littlefield; London: Bell and Hyman, 1978.

Field, Frank, *The Last Days of Mankind: Karl Kraus and his Vienna*, London: Macmillan; New York: St. Martin's, 1967.

Feinberg, Leonard, *Introduction to Satire*, Ames: Iowa State University Press, 1967.

The Satirist: His Temperament, Motivation, and Influence, Ames: Iowa State University Press, 1963.

Fischer, John Irwin, "How to Die: *Verses on the Death of Dr. Swift*," *Review of English Studies* n.s. 21 (1970), 422–41.

Fitton Brown, A. D., "The Unreality of Ovid's Tomitian Exile," *Liverpool Classical Monthly* 10.2 (February 1985), 18–22.

Fletcher, M. D. (ed.), *Reading Rushdie: Perspectives on the Fiction of Salman Rushdie*, Amsterdam; Atlanta, GA: Rodopi, 1994.

"Rushdie's Shame as Apologue," *Journal of Commonwealth Literature* 21 (1986), 120–32.

Foucault, Michel, "What is an Author?" in *The Foucault Reader*, Paul Rabinow (ed.), New York: Pantheon, 1984.

Fowler, Alastair, *Kinds of Literature: An Introduction to the Theory of Genres and Modes*, Cambridge, MA: Harvard University Press, 1982.

Fraenkel, Eduard, *Horace*, Oxford: Clarendon Press, 1957.

Franklin, Caroline, *Byron's Heroines*, Oxford: Clarendon Press, 1992.

Frautschi, R. L., "The Would-Be-Invisible Chain in *Les Lettres persanes*," *French Review* 40 (1967), 604–612.

Freedman, William, "Swift's Struldbruggs, Progress, and the Analogy of History," *Studies in English Literature 1500–1900* 35 (1995), 457–72.

Freudenburg, Kirk, *The Walking Muse: Horace on the Theory of Satire*, Princeton: Princeton University Press, 1993.

Frye, Northrop, *Anatomy of Criticism: Four Essays*, Princeton: Princeton University Press, 1957.

Fuchs, Jacob, *Reading Pope's Imitations of Horace*, Lewisburg, PA: Bucknell University Press, 1989.

Fuegi, John, "The Alienated Woman: Brecht's *The Good Person of Setzuan*," in *Essays on Brecht: Theater and Politics*, Siegfried Mews and Herbert Knust (eds.), Chapel Hill: University of North Carolina Press, 1974, 190–96.

Gaines, James F., *Social Structures in Molière's Theater*, Columbus: Ohio State University Press, 1984.

Galef, David, "The Self-Annihilating Artists of *Pale Fire*," *Twentieth Century Literature* 31 (1985), 421–37.

Garber, Frederick, *Self, Text, and Romantic Irony: The Example of Byron*, Princeton: Princeton University Press, 1988.

Gardiner, Anne Barbeau, "Swift on the Dutch East India Company: A Context of 1672–73 War Literature," *Huntington Library Quarterly* 54 (1991), 235–52.

Gearhart, Suzanne, *The Open Boundary of History and Fiction: A Critical Approach to the French Enlightenment*, Princeton: Princeton University Press, 1984.

Gearin-Tosh, Michael, "The Structure of Marvell's 'Last Instructions to a Painter,'" *Essays in Criticism* 22 (1972), 48–57.

Gellner, Ernest, *Nationalism*, New York: New York University Press, 1997.

Nations and Nationalism, Ithaca, NY and London: Cornell University Press, 1983.

Gill, James F. (ed.), *Cutting Edges: Postmodern Critical Essays on Eighteenth-Century Satire*, Knoxville: University of Tennessee Press, 1995.

Gold, Barbara K., "Openings in Horace's Satires and Odes: Poet, Patron, and Audience," *Yale Classical Studies* 29 (1992), 162–63.

Goldgar, Bertrand A., *The Curse of Party: Swift's Relations with Addison and Steele*, Lincoln: University of Nebraska Press, 1961.

Goldmann, Lucien, *Recherches dialectiques*, Paris: Gallimard, 1959.

Goodkin, Richard E., "Between Genders, Between Genres: Célimène's Letter to Alceste in Molière's *Le Misanthrope*," *Romanic Review* 85 (1994), 553–72.

Goodman, Paul, "Comic Plots: *The Alchemist*," in *Ben Jonson: A Collection of Critical Essays*, Jonas A. Barish (ed.), Englewood Cliffs, NJ: Prentice-Hall, 1963, 106–20.

Gossman, Lionel, *Men and Masks: A Study of Molière*, Baltimore: Johns Hopkins University Press, 1963.

Gowers, Emily, "Horace's *Satires* 1.5: An Inconsequential Journey," *Proceedings of the Cambridge Philological Society* n.s. 39 (1993), 48–66.

Grant, Damian, *Tobias Smollett: A Study in Style*, Manchester: Manchester University Press; Totowa, NJ: Rowman and Littlefield, 1977.

Greene, Thomas M., "Ben Jonson and the Centred Self," *Studies in English Literature* 10 (1970), 325–48.

Greenfeld, Liah, *Nationalism: Five Roads to Modernity*, Cambridge, MA: Harvard University Press, 1992.

Greenough, Chester Noyes, "Characters of Nations," in *Collected Studies*, Cambridge, MA: Harvard Cooperative Society, 1940, 224–45.

Gregg, Edward, *The Protestant Succession in International Politics, 1710–1716*, New York: Garland, 1986.

Grewal, Inderpal, "Salman Rushdie: Marginality, Women, and *Shame*," *Genders* 3 (Fall 1988), 24–42.

Grice, Paul, *Studies in the Way of Words*, Cambridge, MA: Harvard University Press, 1989.

Griffin, Dustin H., *Alexander Pope: The Poet in the Poems*, Princeton: Princeton University Press, 1978.
Satire: A Critical Reintroduction, Lexington: University Press of Kentucky, 1994.
Grimsley, Ronald, *From Montesquieu to Laclos*, Geneva: Droz, 1974.
Grimstad, Kari, *Masks of the Prophet: The Theatrical World of Karl Kraus*, Toronto: University of Toronto Press, 1982.
Grosrichard, Alain, *The Sultan's Court: European Fantasies of the East*, Liz Heron (trs.), London and New York: Verso, 1998.
Gross, Nathan, *From Gesture to Idea: Esthetics and Ethics in Molière's Comedy*, New York: Columbia University Press, 1982.
Gudiol, José, *The Complete Paintings of Velásquez 1599–1660*, Kenneth Lyons (trs.), New York: Greenwich House, 1983.
Guicharnaud, Jacques, *Molière: une aventure théâtrale*, Paris: Gallimard, 1963.
Guilhamet, Leon, *Satire and the Transformation of Genre*, Philadelphia: University of Pennsylvania Press, 1987.
Gum, Coburn, *The Aristophanic Comedies of Ben Jonson: A Comparative Study of Jonson and Aristophanes*, The Hague: Mouton, 1969.
Harari, Josué V., "The Eunuch's Tale: Montesquieu's Imaginary of Despotism," in *Scenarios of the Imaginary: Theorizing the French Enlightenment*, Ithaca, NY: Cornell University Press, 1987, 67–101.
Harth, Phillip, "The Problem of Political Allegory in *Gulliver's Travels*," *Modern Philology* 73 (1976), S40–47.
Haslett, Moyra, *Byron's "Don Juan" and the Don Juan Legend*, Oxford: Clarendon Press, 1997.
Hayes, Carleton J. H., *The Historical Evolution of Modern Nationalism*, New York: Macmillan, 1931.
Heller, Erich, "Karl Kraus: Satirist in the Modern World," in *The Disinherited Mind: Essays in Modern German Literature and Thought*, London: Bowes and Bowes, 1975, 235–60.
Henderson, John, *Fighting for Rome: Poets and Caesars, History and the Civil War*, Cambridge: Cambridge University Press, 1998.
Hennard, Martine, "Playing a Game of Words in Nabokov's *Pale Fire*," *Modern Fiction Studies* 40 (1994), 299–317.
Highet, Gilbert, *The Anatomy of Satire*, Princeton: Princeton University Press, 1962.
Juvenal the Satirist, Oxford: Clarendon Press, 1954.
"Masks and Faces in Satire," *Hermes: Zeitschrift für klassische Philologie* 102 (1974), 321–37.
Hinnant, Charles H., *Purity and Defilement in "Gulliver's Travels"*, London: Macmillan, 1987.
Hobsbawm, E. J., *Nations and Nationalism since 1780: Programme, Myth, Reality*, Cambridge: Cambridge University Press, 1992.
Hodgart, Matthew, *Satire*, New York: McGraw-Hill, 1969.
Holmes, Geoffrey, *British Politics in the Age of Anne*, revised edn., London: Hambledon Press, 1987.
Hoover, Marjorie L., *Alexander Ostrovsky*, Boston: Twayne, 1981.

Hopkins, Robert H., "The Issue of Anonymity and the Beginning of the Steele–Swift Controversy of 1713–14: A New Interpretation," *English Language Notes* 2 (1964), 15–21.

Hubbard, Thomas K., "The Structure and Programmatic Intent of Horace's First Satire," *Latomus* 40 (1981), 305–21.

Hubert, J. D., *Molière and the Comedy of Intellect*, Berkeley and Los Angeles: University of California Press, 1962.

Hulliung, Mark, *Montesquieu and the Old Regime*, Berkeley: University of California Press, 1976.

Hume, Kathryn, "Taking a Stand while Lacking a Center: Rushdie's Postmodern Politics," *Philological Quarterly* 74 (1995), 209–30.

Hyland, Paul, "Naming Names: Steele and Swift," in *Irish Writing: Exile and Submission*, Paul Hyland and Neil Sammells (eds.), London: Macmillan, 1991, 13–31.

Iggers, Wilma Abeles, *Karl Kraus: A Viennese Critic of the Twentieth Century*, The Hague: Martinus Nijhoff, 1967.

Jakobson, Roman, *Selected Writings*, Stephen Rudy (ed.), 8 vols., The Hague: Mouton, 1981.

Janik, Allan and Toulmin, Stephen, "Language and Society: Karl Kraus and the Last Days of Vienna," in *Wittgenstein's Vienna*, New York: Simon and Schuster, 1973, 67–91.

Jefferson, Ann, "Counterpoint and Forked Tongues: Milan Kundera and the Art of Exile," *Renaissance and Modern Studies* 34 (1991), 115–36.

Johnson, D. Barton, *Worlds in Regression: Some Novels of Vladimir Nabokov*, Ann Arbor, MI: Ardis, 1985.

Jones, Emrys, "Pope and Dulness," *Proceedings of the British Academy* 54 (1968), 231–63.

Jussawalla, Feroza, "Rushdie's *Shame*: Problems in Communication," in *Studies in Indian Fiction in English*, G. S. Balarama Gupta (ed.), Gulbarga, India: JIWE Publications, 1987, 1–13.

Kaul, Suvir, *Poems of Nation, Anthems of Empire: English Verse in the Long Eighteenth Century*, Charlottesville: University of Virginia Press, 2000.

Kay, W. David, "Erasmus' Learned Joking: The Ironic Use of Classical Wisdom in *The Praise of Folly*," *Texas Studies in Literature and Language* 19 (1977), 247–67.

Keen, Sam, *Faces of the Enemy: Reflections of the Hostile Imagination*, San Francisco: Harper and Row, 1985.

Keener, Frederick M., *The Chain of Becoming*, New York: Columbia University Press, 1983.

Kelsall, Malcolm, *Byron's Politics*, Brighton, Sussex: Harvester; New Jersey: Barnes and Noble, 1987.

Kenner, Hugh, *Flaubert, Joyce, and Becket: The Stoic Comedians*, Boston: Beacon, 1962.

Kernan, Alvin P., *The Cankered Muse: Satire of the English Renaissance*, New Haven: Yale University Press, 1959.

The Plot of Satire, New Haven: Yale University Press, 1965.

Kinsley, William, "The *Dunciad* as Mock-Book," *Huntington Library Quarterly* 35 (1971–72), 29–47.

Kleberg, Lars, "On the Border: Milan Kundera's *The Book of Laughter and Forgetting*," *Scando-Slavica* 30 (1984): 57–72.

Knight, Charles A. "Identifying Satire," *Review* 24 (2002), 1–21.

"*Joseph Andrews* and the Failure of Authority," *Eighteenth-Century Fiction* 4 (1992), 109–24.

"Listening to Encolpius: Modes of Confusion in the *Satyricon*," *University of Toronto Quarterly* 58 (1989), 340–43.

"Satire and Conversation: The Logic of Interpretation," *The Eighteenth Century: Theory and Interpretation* 26 (1985), 239–61.

"The Spectator's Generalizing Discourse," in *Telling People What to Think: Early Eighteenth-Century Periodicals from "The Review" to "The Rambler*," J. A. Downie and Thomas N. Corns (eds.), London: Frank Cass, 1993, 44–57.

Kodjak, Andrej, *Alexander Solzhenitsyn*, Boston: Twayne, 1978.

Kohn, Caroline, *Karl Kraus: le polémiste et l'écrivain, défenseur des droits de l'individu*, Paris: Didier, 1962.

Kohn, Hans, *The Idea of Nationalism*, New York: Macmillan, 1961.

Kramer, Lloyd, "Historical Narratives and the Meaning of Nationalism," *Journal of the History of Ideas* 58 (1997), 525–45.

Kuhn, Tom, "Ovid and Brecht: Topoi of Poetic Banishment," *Brecht Yearbook/ Brecht-Jahrbuch* 24 (1999), 163–75.

Kupersmith, William, *Roman Satirists in Seventeenth-Century England*, Lincoln: University of Nebraska Press, 1985.

Leo, F., "Varro und die Satire," *Hermes* 24 (1889), 67–84.

Levin, Harry, *The Gates of Horn*, New York: Oxford University Press, 1963.

Lewis, Wyndham, *Men Without Art*, London: Cassell, 1934.

Leyburn, Ellen Douglas, *Satiric Allegory: Mirror for Man*, New Haven: Yale University Press, 1956.

"Swift's View of the Dutch," *PMLA* 66 (1951), 734–45.

Llobera, Josep R., *The God of Modernity: The Development of Nationalism in Western Europe*, Oxford and Providence, RI: Berg, 1994.

Lock, F. P., *The Politics of Gulliver's Travels*, Oxford: Clarendon Press, 1980.

Lord, George de Forest, *Heroic Mockery: Variations on Epic Themes from Homer to Joyce*, Newark: University of Delaware Press, 1977.

"Two New Poems by Marvell?" *Bulletin of the New York Public Library* 62 (1958), 551–70.

Lyons, James K., "Kipling's 'Soldiers Three' and Brecht's *A Man's a Man*," in *Essays on Brecht: Theater and Politics*, Siegfried Mews and Herbert Knust (eds.), Chapel Hill: University of North Carolina Press, 1974, 99–113.

Mac Adam, Alfred J., *Modern Latin American Narratives: The Dreams of Reason*, Chicago: University of Chicago Press, 1977.

McGann, Jerome, *Don Juan in Context*, Chicago: University of Chicago Press, 1976.

Mack, Maynard, *The Garden and the City: Retirement and Politics in the Later Poetry of Pope*, Toronto: University of Toronto Press, 1969.

McKeon, Michael, "Cultural Crisis and Dialectical Method: Destabilizing Augustan Literature," in *The Profession of Eighteenth-Century Literature*, Madison: University of Wisconsin Press, 1992, 42–61.

MacLaine, Allan H., "Radicalism and Conservatism in Burns's *The Jolly Beggars*," *Studies in Scottish Literature* 13 (1978), 125–43.

McNeill, Randall L. B., *Horace: Image, Identity, and Audience*, Baltimore: Johns Hopkins University Press, 2001.

McVeagh, John, "Goldsmith and Nationality," in *All Before Them. Vol. 1: 1660–1780*, London: Ashfield, 1990, 217–31.

Maia Neto, José Raimundo, *Machado de Assis: The Brazilian Pyrrhonian*, West Lafayette, IN: Purdue University Press, 1994.

Manning, Peter J., "*Don Juan* and Byron's Imperceptiveness to the English Word," *Studies in Romanticism* 18 (1979), 207–33.

Martindale, Charles and Hopkins, David (eds.), *Horace Made New: Horatian Influences on British Writing from the Renaissance to the Twentieth Century*, Cambridge: Cambridge University Press, 1993.

Meredith, George, "An Essay on Comedy," in *Comedy*, Wylie Sypher (ed.), New York: Doubleday, 1956, 3–57.

Minogue, K. P., *Nationalism*, New York: Basic Books, 1967.

Moore, John Robert, "Defoe, Steele, and the Demolition of Dunkirk," *Huntington Library Quarterly* 13 (1950), 279–302.

Moss, Stephanie, "The Cream of the Crop: Female Characters in Salman Rushdie's *Shame*," *International Fictional Review* 19 (1992), 28–30.

Muecke, Frances, "The Audience of/in Horace's *Satires*," *AUMLA* 74 (1990), 34–47.

Nauta, R. R., "Seneca's *Apocolocyntosis* as Saturnalian Literature," *Mnemosyne*, 4th ser., 40 (1987), 69–96.

Needham, Anuradha Dingwaney, "The Politics of Post-Cultural Identity in Salman Rushdie," *Massachusetts Review* 29 (1988–89), 609–24.

Needle, Jan and Thomson, Peter, *Brecht*, Oxford: Basil Blackwell, 1981.

Newman, Gerald, *The Rise of English Nationalism: A Cultural History 1740–1830*, revised edn., New York: St. Martin's, 1997.

Nichols, James W., *Insinuation: The Tactics of English Satire*, The Hague: Mouton, 1971.

Nicolson, Marjorie Hope and Mohler, Nora M., "The Scientific Background of Swift's *Voyage to Laputa*," *Annals of Science* 2 (1937), 299–334.

Noggle, James, *The Skeptical Sublime: Aesthetic Ideology in Pope and the Tory Satirists*, Oxford: Oxford University Press, 2001.

Nunes, Maria Luisa, *The Craft of an Absolute Winner: Characterization and Narratology in the Novels of Machado de Assis*, Contributions in Afro-American and African Studies 71, Westport, CT: Greenwood Press, 1983.

Nussbaum, Felicity A., *The Brink of All We Hate: English Satires on Women 1660–1750*, Lexington: University Press of Kentucky, 1984.

Oliensis, Ellen, *Horace and the Rhetoric of Authority*, Cambridge: Cambridge University Press, 1998.

Orwell, George, *The Collected Essays, Journalism and Letters of George Orwell*, Sonia Orwell and Ian Angus (eds.), 4 vols., New York: Harcourt Brace Jovanovich, 1968.

Palmeri, Frank, *Satire in Narrative: Petronius, Swift, Gibbon, Melville, and Pynchon*, Austin: University of Texas Press, 1990.

Patey, Douglas Lane, "Swift's Satire on 'Science' and the Structure of *Gulliver's Travels*," *ELH* 58 (1991), 809–31.

Patterson, Annabel M., *Marvell and the Civic Crown*, Princeton: Princeton University Press, 1978.

Paulson, Ronald, *Satire and the Novel in Eighteenth-Century England*, New Haven: Yale University Press, 1967.

Paulson, Ronald (ed.), *Satire: Modern Essays in Criticism*, Englewood Cliffs, NJ: Prentice-Hall, 1971.

Perkins, Merle L., *Voltaire's Concept of International Order*, Studies on Voltaire 36, Geneva: Institut et Musée Voltaire, 1965.

Peter, John, *Complaint and Satire in Early English Literature*, Oxford: Clarendon Press, 1956.

Petersson, Margareta, *Unending Metamorphoses: Myth, Satire and Religion in Salman Rushdie's Novels*, Lund: Lund University Press, 1996.

Petro, Peter (ed.), *Critical Essays on Milan Kundera*, New York: G. K. Hall, 1999.

Pfabigan, Alfred, *Karl Kraus und der Sozialismus: Eine politische Biographie*, Vienna: Euroverlag, 1976.

Philips, Edith, *The Good Quaker in French Legend*, Philadelphia: University of Pennsylvania Press, 1932.

Pifer, Ellen, "The *Book of Laughter and Forgetting*: Kundera's Narration against Narration," *Journal of Narrative Technique* 22 (1992), 84–96.

Pizer, John, "'Ursprung is das Ziel': Karl Kraus's Concept of Origin," *Modern Austrian Literature* 27 (1994), 1–21.

Proffer, Ellendea, *Bulgakov: Life and Work*, Ann Arbor, MI: Ardis, 1984.

Rahman, Kate Sealey, *Ostrovsky: Reality and Illusion*, Birmingham Slavonic Monographs 30, University of Birmingham, 1999.

Rahman, Tariq, "Politics in the Novels of Salman Rushdie," *Commonwealth Novel in English* 4 (1991), 24–37.

Rau, P., *Paratragodia: Untersuchung einer komishen Form des Aristophanes, Zetemata*, no. 45, Munich: Beck, 1967.

Rawson, Claude (ed.), *English Satire and the Satiric Tradition*, Oxford: Basil Blackwell, 1984.

   Satire and Sentiment 1660–1830, Cambridge: Cambridge University Press, 1994.

Rebhorn, Wayne A., "The Metamorphoses of Moria: Structure and Meaning in *The Praise of Folly*," *PMLA* 89 (1974), 463–76.

Relihan, Joel C., *Ancient Menippean Satire*, Baltimore: Johns Hopkins University Press, 1993.

Renan, Ernest, "What is a Nation?" Martin Thom (trs.) in *Nation and Narration*, Homi K. Bhabha (ed.), London and New York: Routledge, 1990, 8–22.

Richards, James O., *Party Propaganda Under Queen Anne: The General Elections of 1702–1713*, Athens: University of Georgia Press, 1972.

Riebling, Barbara, "England Deflowered and Unmanned: The Sexual Image of Politics in Marvell's 'Last Instructions,'" *SEL* 35 (1995), 137–57.

Roberts, Michael, "Horace *Satires* 2.5: Restrained Indignation," *American Journal of Philology* 105 (1984), 426–33.

Robertson, Michael, "The Byron of *Don Juan* as a Whig Aristocrat," *Texas Studies in Language and Literature* 17 (1976), 709–24.

Robinson, Christopher, *Lucian and his Influence in Europe*, London: Duckworth, 1979.

Rogers, Pat, "The Name and Nature of Dulness: Proper Names in *The Dunciad*," *Anglia* 92 (1974), 79–112.

Rogers, Shef, "Pope, Publishing, and Popular Interpretation of the *Dunciad Variorum*," *Philological Quarterly* 74 (1995), 279–95.

Rosenheim, Edward W. Jr., *Swift and the Satirist's Art*, Chicago: University of Chicago Press, 1963.

Rudd, Niall, *The Satires of Horace: A Study*, London: Cambridge University Press, 1966.

Rushdie, Salman, "*Midnight's Children* and *Shame* (Interview at the University of Aarhus, October 7, 1983)," *Kunapipi* 7 (1985), 1–19.

Rutherford, Andrew, *Byron: A Critical Study*, Palo Alto, CA: Stanford University Press, 1961.

Said, Edward, "Reflections on Exile," *Granta* 13 (Autumn 1984), 159–72.

Sallis, John, *Being and Logos*, second edn., Atlantic Highlands, NJ: Humanities Press, 1986.

Sareil, Jean, "Les Quatre premières *Lettres philosophiques* ou les complications du jeu satirique," *Romanic Review* 76 (1985), 277–86.

Schaub, Diana J., *Erotic Liberalism: Women and Revolution in Montesquieu's "Persian Letters,"* London: Rowman and Littlefield, 1995.

Scholes, Robert, *Structuralism in Literature*, Hew Haven: Yale University Press, 1974.

Scouten, Arthur H. and Hume, Robert D., "Pope and Swift: Text and Interpretation of Swift's Verses on His Death," *Philological Quarterly* 52 (1973), 205–31.

Seidel, Michael, "Crisis Rhetoric and Satiric Power," *New Literary History* 20 (1988), 165–86.

   Exile and the Narrative Imagination, New Haven: Yale University Press, 1986.

   Satiric Inheritance: Rabelais to Sterne, Princeton: Princeton University Press, 1979.

Shackleton, Robert, *Montesquieu: A Critical Biography*, London: Oxford University Press, 1961.

   "The Moslem Chronology of the *Lettres persanes*," *French Studies* 8 (1954), 17–27.

Shero, L. R., "The Cena in Roman Satire," *Classical Philology* 18 (1923), 126–43.

Shklovsky, Victor, "Sterne's *Tristram Shandy*: Stylistic Commentary," in *Russian Formalist Criticism: Four Essays*, Lee T. Lemon and Marion J. Reis (trs.), Lincoln: University of Nebraska Press, 1965.

Siebert, Frederick Seaton, *Freedom of the Press in England 1476–1776: The Rise and Decline of Government Control*, 1952; rpt. Urbana: University of Illinois Press, 1965.

Sitter, John E., *The Poetry of Pope's "Dunciad,"* Minneapolis: University of Minnesota Press, 1971.

Slepian, Barry, "The Ironic Intention of Swift's Verses on His Own Death," *Review of English Studies* n.s. 14 (1963), 249–56.

Smallwood, R. L., "'Here in the Friars': Immediacy and Theatricality in *The Alchemist*," *Review of English Studies* n.s. 32.126 (1981), 142–60.

Smith, Anthony D., *Theories of Nationalism*, New York: Harper and Row, 1971.

Smith, Barbara Herrnstein, *On the Margins of Discourse: The Relation of Literature to Language*, Chicago: University of Chicago Press, 1978.

Poetic Closure: A Study of How Poems End, Chicago: University of Chicago Press, 1968.

Smith, Frederik N., "Scientific Discourse: *Gulliver's Travels* and *The Philosophical Transactions*," in *The Genres of "Gulliver's Travels,"* Frederik N. Smith (ed.), Newark: University of Delaware Press, 1990, 139–62.

Snell, Mary, "Karl Kraus's *Die Letzten Tage der Menschheit*: An Analysis," *Forum for Modern Language Studies* 4 (1968), 324–47.

Snyder, John, *Prospects of Power: Tragedy, Satire, the Essay, and the Theory of Genre*, Lexington: The University Press of Kentucky, 1991.

Spingler, Michael, "The King's Play: Censorship and the Politics of Performance in Molière's *Tartuffe*," *Comparative Drama* 19 (1985), 240–57.

Stack, Frank, *Pope and Horace: Studies in Imitation*, Cambridge: Cambridge University Press, 1985.

Stanislavsky, Constantin, *My Life in Art*, J. J. Robbins (trs.), 1924; rpt. Boston: Little, Brown, 1938.

Stegner, Page, *Escape into Aesthetics: The Art of Vladimir Nabokov*, New York: Dial, 1966.

Stern, J. P., "Karl Kraus and the Idea of Literature," *Encounter* 45.2 (August 1975), 37–48.

"Karl Kraus: Language and Experience," in *Karl Kraus in neuer Sicht: Karl Kraus in a New Perspective*, Sigurd Paul Scheichl and Edward Timms (eds.), Munich: text + kritic, 1986, 21–31.

"Karl Kraus's Vision of Language," *Modern Language Review* 61 (1966), 71–84.

Stewart, Philip, "Toujours Usbek," *Eighteenth-Century Fiction* 11 (1999), 141–50.

Stopp, Frederick, *Evelyn Waugh: Portrait of the Artist*, London: Chapman and Hall, 1958.

Suvin, Darko, *To Brecht and Beyond: Soundings in Modern Dramaturgy*, Sussex: Harvester; New Jersey: Barnes and Noble, 1984.

Sylvester, Richard, "The Problem of Unity in *The Praise of Folly*," *English Literary Renaissance* 6 (1976), 125–39.

Tarski, Alfred, "The Semantic Conception of Truth and the Foundations of Semantics," *Philosophy and Phenomenological Research* 4 (1941), 341–75.

Taylor, Henry Osborn, *The Mediaeval Mind*, fourth edn., Cambridge, MA: Harvard University Press, 1951.

Tennant, P. M. W., "Political or Personal Propaganda: Horace, *Sermones* 1.5 in Perspective," *Acta Classica* 34 (1991), 51–64.

Test, George A., *Satire: Spirit and Art*, Tampa: University of South Florida Press, 1991.

Theobald, John, *The Paper Ghetto: Karl Kraus and Anti-Semitism*, Frankfurt: Peter Lang, 1996.

Thibault, John C., *The Mystery of Ovid's Exile*, Berkeley: University of California Press, 1964.

Thomson, Peter and Sacks, Glendyr (eds.), *The Cambridge Companion to Brecht*, Cambridge: Cambridge University Press, 1994.

Thormählen, Marianne, *Rochester: The Poems in Context*, Cambridge: Cambridge University Press, 1993.

Thornhill, C. J., *Walter Benjamin and Karl Kraus: Problems of a "Wahlverwandtschaft,"* Stuttgarter Arbeiten zur Germanistik 319, Stuttgart: Heinz, 1966.

Timms, Edward, *Karl Kraus, Apocalyptic Satirist: Culture and Catastrophe in Hapsburg Vienna*, New Haven and London: Yale University Press, 1986.

"Kraus's Shakespearian Politics," in *Austria in the Thirties: Culture and Politics*, Kenneth Segar and John Warren (eds.), Riverside, CA: Ariadne Press, 1991, 345–58.

Todorov, Tzvetan, "The Origin of Genres," *New Literary History* 8 (1976), 159–70.

Trilling, Lionel, *The Opposing Self*, New York: Viking, 1955.

Turner, James Grantham, "The Libertine Abject: The 'Postures' of *Last Instructions to a Painter*," in *Marvell and Liberty*, Warren Cherniak and Martin Dzelzainis (eds.), London: Macmillan; New York: St. Martin's, 1999, 217–48.

Van Rooy, C. A., "Horace's Sat. 1.1 as Prooemium and its Relation to Satires 2 to 10," *Latinität und alte Kirche*, Wiener Studien Beiheft 8 (1977), 263–74.

Studies in Classical Satire and Related Literary Theory, Leiden: E.J. Brill, 1966.

Vartanian, Aram, "Eroticism and Politics in the *Lettres persanes*," *Romanic Review* 60 (1969), 23–33.

Vermeule, Blakey, "Abstraction, Reference, and the Dualism of Pope's *Dunciad*," *Modern Philology* 96 (1998), 16–41.

Vieth, David M., "Toward an Anti-Aristotelian Poetic: Rochester's *Satyr against Mankind* and *Artemisia to Chloe*, with Notes on Swift's *Tale of a Tub* and *Gulliver's Travels*," *Language and Style* 5 (1972), 123–45.

Waingrow, Marshall, "Verses on the Death of Dr. Swift," *Studies in English Literature* 5 (1965), 513–18.

Wallace, John M., *Destiny His Choice: The Loyalism of Andrew Marvell*, Cambridge: Cambridge University Press, 1968.

Weinbrot, Howard D., *Britannia's Issue: The Rise of British Literature from Dryden to Ossian*, Cambridge: Cambridge University Press, 1993.

Eighteenth-Century Satire: Essays on Text and Context from Dryden to Peter Pindar, Cambridge: Cambridge University Press, 1988.

The Formal Strain: Studies in Augustan Imitation and Satire, Chicago: University of Chicago Press, 1969.

"The Swelling Volume: The Apocalyptic Satire of Rochester's *Letter from Artemisia In The Town To Chloe In The Country*," *Studies in the Literary Imagination* 5 (1972), 19–37.

Wettlin, Margaret, "Alexander Ostrovsky and the Russian Theater before Stanislavsky," in *Alexander Ostrovsky: Plays*, Moscow: Progress, 1974, 7–79.

Whitman, Cedric H., *Aristophanes and the Comic Hero*, Cambridge, MA: Harvard University Press, 1964.

Whittaker, Robert, "The Ostrovskii–Grigor'ev Circle, Alias the 'Young Editors' of the *Moskvitianin*," *Canadian–American Slavic Studies* 24 (1990), 385–412.

Williams, Aubrey L., *Pope's "Dunciad": A Study of its Meaning*, Baton Rouge: Louisiana State University Press, 1955.

Williams, C. E., *The Broken Eagle: The Politics of Austrian Literature from the Empire to Anschluss*, London: Paul Elek, 1974.

Williams, Gareth D., *Banished Voices: Readings in Ovid's Exile Poetry*, Cambridge: Cambridge University Press, 1994, 3–49.

Wilson, Clothilde, "Machado de Assis: Encomiast of Lunacy," *Hispania* 32 (1949), 198–201.

Winton, Calhoun, *Captain Steele: The Early Career of Richard Steele*, Baltimore: Johns Hopkins University Press, 1964.

Wittgenstein, Ludwig, *Philosophical Investigations*, G. E. M. Anscombe (trs.), third edn., New York: Macmillan, 1958.

Womack, Peter, *Ben Jonson*, Oxford: Basil Blackwell, 1986.

Woolley, James, "Autobiography in Swift's Verses on his Death," in *Contemporary Studies of Swift's Poetry*, John Irwin Fischer and Donald C. Mell, Jr, with David M. Vieth (eds.), Newark: University of Delaware Press, 1981, 112–22.

Worcester, David, *The Art of Satire*, 1940; rpt. New York: Russell and Russell, 1960.

Young, David B., "Libertarian Demography: Montesquieu's Essay on Depopulation in the *Lettres persanes*," *Journal of the History of Ideas* 36 (1975), 669–82.

Zohn, Harry, *Karl Kraus*, New York: Twayne, 1971.

Karl Kraus and the Critics, Columbia, SC: Camden House, 1997.

Zwicker, Steven N. "Virgins and Whores: the Politics of Sexual Misconduct in the 1660s," in *The Political Identity of Andrew Marvell*, Conal Condren and A. D. Cousins (eds.), Aldershot: Scolar Press, 1990, 85–110.

Index